First Workshop on Evaluation and Comparison of NLP Systems (Eval4NLP 2020)

Online
20 November 2020

ISBN: 978-1-7138-1985-1

EMNLP 2020

Evaluation and Comparison of NLP Systems

Proceedings of the First Workshop

November 20, 2020

The Eval4NLP organizers gratefully acknowledge the support from the following sponsors.

Introduction

Welcome to the First Workshop on Evaluation and Comparison of NLP Systems (Eval4NLP).

Fair evaluations and comparisons are of fundamental importance in tracking the development of NLP. This is particularly challenging within the current deep learning revolution, as many techniques are black-box and new state-of-the-art results are reported in ever shorter intervals. On the other hand, the rapid evolution of NLP methods endows the community with ever more tools for evaluating and understanding existing NLP systems. With both these challenges and opportunities in mind, we organize this workshop, aiming at providing a platform to present and discuss the latest advances in NLP evaluation methods and resources.

The workshop has attracted considerable attention from the community, with 38 research papers finally submitted. After double-blind reviewing by two reviewers each, 19 papers were selected to be presented in the workshop, consisting of 15 long papers, two short papers and two non-archival papers. The accepted papers cover a wide range of topics in NLP evaluation and comparison, including novel evaluation metrics for multiple NLG systems (summarization, translation, image captioning, and dialogue generation), word embeddings, OpenIE systems, and language grammaticality; discussions about how to properly report the evaluation results; and a survey on using Textual Entailment for generic NLP evaluation.

We wish to thank all of the authors for their contributions, the members of the Program Committee for their thoughtful reviews, the invited speakers for sharing their vision and outlook, the sponsors (Google and Amazon) for their generous support, and all the attendees of their participation. We believe all these will contribute to a successful workshop. Looking forward to meeting you all (virtually) at Eval4NLP!

Eval4NLP Organization Team,
Steffen Eger, Yang Gao, Maxime Peyrard, Wei Zhao, Eduard Hovy

Organizers:

    Steffen Eger, Technische Universität Darmstadt, Germany
    Yang Gao, Royal Holloway, University of London, UK
    Maxime Peyrard, École polytechnique fédérale de Lausanne (EPFL), Switzerland
    Wei Zhao, Technische Universität Darmstadt, Germany
    Eduard Hovy, Carnegie Mellon University, USA

Steering Committee:

    Ido Dagan, Bar-Ilan University, Israel
    Ani Nenkova, University of Pennsylvania, USA
    Robert West, École polytechnique fédérale de Lausanne (EPFL), Switzerland
    Mohit Bansal, University of North Carolina (UNC) Chapel Hill, USA

Program Committee:

    Daniel Cer, Google AI, USA
    Jackie Chi Kit Cheung, McGill University, Canada
    Elizabeth Clark, University of Washington, USA
    Gerard de Melo, Rutgers University, USA
    Li Dong, Microsoft Research Asia, China
    Zi-Yi Dou, Carnegie Mellon University, USA
    Rotem Dror, Israel Institute of Technology, Israel
    Orhan Firat, Google AI, USA
    George Foster, Google AI, USA
    Yang Gao, Royal Holloway, University of London, UK
    Yanjun Gao, Pennsylvania State University, USA
    Claire Gardent, CNRS & LORIA, France
    Matt Gardner, Allen Institute for AI, USA
    Kevin Gimpel, Toyota Technological Institute at Chicago, USA
    Eduard Hovy, Carnegie Mellon University, USA
    Tsz Kin Lam, University of Heidelberg, Germany
    Lucy H. Lin, University of Washington, USA
    Nelson F. Liu, University of Washington, USA
    Ana Marasović, Allen Institute for AI, USA
    Nitika Mathur, University of Melbourne, Australia
    Maxime Peyrard, École polytechnique fédérale de Lausanne (EPFL), Switzerland
    Roi Reichart, Israel Institute of Technology, Israel
    Ehud Reiter, University of Aberdeen, UK
    Leonardo F. R. Ribeiro, Technische Universität Darmstadt, Germany
    Andreas Rücklé, Technische Universität Darmstadt, Germany
    Ori Shapira, Bar-Ilan University, Israel
    Anders Sogaard, University of Copenhagen, Denmark
    Benyou Wang, University of Padova, Italy
    Shiyue Zhang, University of North Carolina (UNC) Chapel Hill, USA
    Wei Zhao, Technische Universität Darmstadt, Germany
    Markus Zopf, Technische Universität Darmstadt, Germany

Invited Speaker:

    Ido Dagan, Bar-Ilan University, Israel
    William Wang, University of California, Santa Barbara, USA

Goran Glavas, University of Mannheim, Germany
Asli Celikyilmaz, Microsoft Research, USA

Table of Contents

Conference Program

Friday, November 20, 2020

9:00–9:15   *Opening Remarks*

9:15–10:15   *Keynote Talk 1*

10:15–11:15   *Keynote Talk 2*

11:15–12:45   Poster Session 1

11:15–12:45   *Truth or Error? Towards systematic analysis of factual errors in abstractive summaries*
Klaus-Michael Lux, Maya Sappelli and Martha Larson

11:15–12:45   *Fill in the BLANC: Human-free quality estimation of document summaries*
Oleg Vasilyev, Vedant Dharnidharka and John Bohannon

11:15–12:45   *Item Response Theory for Efficient Human Evaluation of Chatbots*
João Sedoc and Lyle Ungar

11:15–12:45   *ViLBERTScore: Evaluating Image Caption Using Vision-and-Language BERT*
Hwanhee Lee, Seunghyun Yoon, Franck Dernoncourt, Doo Soon Kim, Trung Bui and Kyomin Jung

11:15–12:45   *BLEU Neighbors: A Reference-less Approach to Automatic Evaluation*
Kawin Ethayarajh and Dorsa Sadigh

11:15–12:45   *Improving Text Generation Evaluation with Batch Centering and Tempered Word Mover Distance*
Xi Chen, Nan Ding, Tomer Levinboim and Radu Soricut

11:15–12:45   *On the Evaluation of Machine Translation n-best Lists*
Jacob Bremerman, Huda Khayrallah, Douglas Oard and Matt Post

11:15–12:45   *Artemis: A Novel Annotation Methodology for Indicative Single Document Summarization*
Rahul Jha, Keping Bi, Yang Li, Mahdi Pakdaman, Asli Celikyilmaz, Ivan Zhiboedov and Kieran McDonald

14:00–15:00   *Keynote Talk 3*

15:00–16:00   *Keynote Talk 4*

16:00–17:30   **Poster Session 2**

16:00–17:30   *Probabilistic Extension of Precision, Recall, and F1 Score for More Thorough Evaluation of Classification Models*
Reda Yacouby and Dustin Axman

16:00–17:30   *A survey on Recognizing Textual Entailment as an NLP Evaluation*
Adam Poliak

16:00–17:30   *Grammaticality and Language Modelling*
Jingcheng Niu and Gerald Penn

16:00–17:30   *One of these words is not like the other: a reproduction of outlier identification using non-contextual word representations*
Jesper Brink Andersen, Mikkel Bak Bertelsen, Mikkel Hørby Schou, Manuel R. Ciosici and Ira Assent

16:00–17:30   *Are Some Words Worth More than Others?*
Shiran Dudy and Steven Bedrick

16:00–17:30   *On Aligning OpenIE Extractions with Knowledge Bases: A Case Study*
Kiril Gashteovski, Rainer Gemulla, Bhushan Kotnis, Sven Hertling and Christian Meilicke

16:00–17:30   *ClusterDataSplit: Exploring Challenging Clustering-Based Data Splits for Model Performance Evaluation*
Hanna Wecker, Annemarie Friedrich and Heike Adel

16:00–17:30   *Best Practices for Crowd-based Evaluation of German Summarization: Comparing Crowd, Expert and Automatic Evaluation*
Neslihan Iskender, Tim Polzehl and Sebastian Möller

16:00–17:30   *Evaluating Word Embeddings on Low-Resource Languages*
Nathan Stringham and Mike Izbicki

Friday, November 20, 2020 (continued)

17:30–17:45   *Concluding Remarks*

Truth or Error? Towards systematic analysis of factual errors in abstractive summaries

Klaus-Michael Lux
Radboud University
info@klauslux.de

Maya Sappelli
HAN University of Applied Sciences
maya.sappelli@han.nl

Martha Larson
Radboud University
m.larson@cs.ru.nl

Abstract

This paper presents a typology of errors produced by automatic summarization systems. The typology was created by manually analyzing the output of four recent neural summarization systems. Our work is motivated by the growing awareness of the need for better summary evaluation methods that go beyond conventional overlap-based metrics. Our typology is structured into two dimensions. First, the Mapping Dimension describes surface-level errors and provides insight into word-sequence transformation issues. Second, the Meaning Dimension describes issues related to interpretation and provides insight into breakdowns in truth, i.e., factual faithfulness to the original text. Comparative analysis revealed that two neural summarization systems leveraging pretrained models have an advantage in decreasing grammaticality errors, but not necessarily factual errors. We also discuss the importance of ensuring that summary length and abstractiveness do not interfere with evaluating summary quality.

1 Introduction

We are currently witnessing a sharp increase of research interest in neural abstractive text summarization. However, we have also seen growing concern that truth, as represented in the original document, becomes lost or twisted during the summarization process. The issue was raised recently by Kryscinski et al. (2019), who point out that widely used automatic metrics, which rely mostly on word overlap, fail to reflect factual faithfulness of a summary to the original text. Until now, work on summarization has not provided systematic analysis of factual faithfulness. Instead, the trend has been for papers to provide a few examples or general descriptions of frequent errors. An example is Falke et al. (2019), who state that *"[c]ommon mistakes are using wrong subjects or objects in a proposition [...], confusing numbers, reporting hypothetical facts as factual [...] or attributing quotes to the wrong person."*, but stop short of providing a more rigorous analysis. Recent work that breaks the trend is Durmus et al. (2020), who propose an evaluation framework for faithfulness in abstractive summarization. The summaries used to develop the framework are annotated with different types of faithfulness errors. However, the annotation scheme does not incorporate linguistic concepts, e.g., does not differentiate between semantic and pragmatic faithfulness.

The aim of our research is to go beyond existing characterizations and provide a comprehensive typology that can be used to understand errors that neural abstractive summarization systems produce, and how they affect the factual faithfulness of summaries. The contribution of this paper is an error typology that was created by analyzing the output of four abstractive summarization systems. The systems vary in their use of pre-training, their model architecture and in the integration of extractive tasks during training. We carry out a comparative analysis that demonstrates the ability of the typology to uncover interesting differences between systems that are not revealed by conventional overlap-based metrics in current use. This paper represents the main results of Lux (2020), which contains additional examples and analysis. Further, annotations used for our analysis and more detailed statistics are publicly available[1] to support future research on faithfulness errors.

2 Related work

Over the years there have been several methods to evaluate summarization methods (Lloret et al., 2018; Ermakova et al., 2019), each with their own strengths and challenges. In this section, we first

---

[1] https://tinyurl.com/truth-error-2020.

1

Proceedings of the First Workshop on Evaluation and Comparison of NLP Systems (Eval4NLP), pages 1–10,
November 20, 2020. ©2020 Association for Computational Linguistics

cover the ROUGE score, which is the main target of the criticism of overlap-based summarization metrics, such as from Kryscinski et al. (2019) mentioned in Section 1. We then provide a discussion on the relatively limited amount of work that has dealt with factual errors in summaries. Finally, we introduce the automatic summarization systems that we use in our study.

2.1 ROUGE

ROUGE is a set of metrics that measures textual overlap (Lin, 2004). The ROUGE score is almost exclusively used as the optimization and evaluation metric in neural summarization methods, even though it has been recognized to be difficult to interpret and does not correlate well with human judgement (van der Lee et al., 2019).

The major issue with the ROUGE score is its focus on textual overlap with a reference summary, which does not measure important aspects in summaries such as redundancy, relevance and informativeness (Peyrard, 2019a). Moreover, there is no clear optimal variant of ROUGE, and the exact choice can have a large impact on how a (neural) summarizer behaves when it is used as a training objective (Peyrard, 2019b). Sun et al. (2019) demonstrate another shortfall of ROUGE-based evaluation: Since the metric does not adjust for summary length, a comparison between systems can be misleading if one of them is inherently worse at the task, but better tuned to the summary length that increases ROUGE.

The shortcomings of ROUGE suggest that we should work towards metrics that are more focused on summary quality as perceived by readers. Unfortunately, quality is hard to measure, demonstated by an interactive summarization experiment by Gao et al. (2019), in which the authors show that users find it easier to give preference feedback on summaries. Simple preference ordering, however, does not give insight in the actual cause of preference. An important factor of perceived quality can be the errors being made by the summarizer. Grammatical errors can have an effect on the perceived quality, credibility and informativeness of news articles when there are many (Appelman and Schmierbach, 2018). Moreover with the rise in fake news and misinformation it seems important to have a better grip on factual errors that are a result of the summarization process.

2.2 Factual errors in summaries

Recent abstractive systems have a tendency to generate summaries that are factually incorrect, meaning that they fail to be factually faithful to the documents that they summarize. An analysis by Cao et al. (2018) of a neural summarization system finds that up to 30% of generated summaries contain "fabricated facts". Similarly, the authors of Falke et al. (2019) evaluate three different state-of-the-art systems and find that between 8 and 26% of the generated summaries contain at least one factual error, even though ROUGE scores indicate good performance.

Kryściński et al. (2019) propose a weakly supervised method for verifying factual consistency between document and summary by training a binary model that predicts whether or not a sentence is consistent. For this purpose they artificially generate a dataset with various types of errors, such as entity or number swapping, paraphrasing, pronoun swapping, sentence negation and noise injection. The authors claim the error patterns to be based on an error analysis of system output. However, it is not conclusively established that they constitute a good approximation of the actual errors that current summarization systems make.

Additionally, Goodrich et al. (2019) compare several models such as relation extraction, binary classification and end-to-end models (E2E) for estimating factual accuracy on a Wikipedia text summarization task. They show that their E2E model for factual correctness has the highest correlation with human judgements and suggest that the E2E models could benefit from a better labeling scheme.

In contrast, Lebanoff et al. (2019) are interested in what happens when summarization systems fuse sentences from the source. They automatically extract fused summary sentences generated by five different systems and conduct a manual annotation of faithfulness and grammaticality using crowd sourcing. Reference summaries are annotated as well. Generally, they find that fused sentences are often unfaithful to the source, especially when there is a marked imbalance in the contribution of multiple sentences. Surprisingly, the reference summaries achieve lower than the expected 100% faithfulness and grammaticality, which may have been due to low inter-annotator agreement or to presentation bias as suggested by the authors. Out of all five systems, See et al. (2017) and Chen and Bansal (2018) perform best, but are still more error-prone than reference summaries.

We find that previous research has not established a detailed typology of summarization errors. Most work instead relies on on a binary distinction between correct and erroneous (Cao et al., 2018; Falke et al., 2019; Lebanoff et al., 2019) or faithfulness measured on a Likert scale (Goodrich et al., 2019). However, not all errors are created equal. Some errors might be less severe than others. As mentioned in Section 1, Durmus et al. (2020) is an exceptional case that looks at different kinds of errors related to faithfulness. Our work goes further, since it recognizes linguistic differences between factual errors, providing a more detailed typology.

2.3 Neural summarization systems

Here, we describe the summarization systems that generate the summaries used to create the typology (Section 3) and to carry out our comparative analysis (Section 4). We include two older approaches trained entirely from scratch on the summarization task, namely a pointer-generator architecture (See et al., 2017), henceforth referred to as **PG** and an RL-inspired rewriting paradigm (Chen and Bansal, 2018), **FAST-ABS-RL**. Additionally, two approaches using pre-trained language models are included: The first is **TRANSFORMER-LM**, proposed by (Hoang et al., 2019), a language-modeling approach leveraging GPT (a transformer-based model trained on roughly 7,000 books). The second is **BERTSUM**, an approach leveraging pre-trained BERT encoders (another transformer-based model trained on the books and the English Wikipedia), proposed by (Liu and Lapata, 2019). All four models were trained on the same split of the non-anonymized version of the CNN/Daily Mail dataset. PG and TRANSFORMER-LM directly train on the abstractive task and do not involve extraction. In contrast, BERTSUM performs initial fine-tuning on an extractive task and FAST-ABS-RL even involves an extractive sub-step directly in the pipeline.

3 Building the typology

In this section, we describe our methods and present the typology that we created.

3.1 Methodology

We collected the output of four summarization systems varying in a number of design aspects in order to capture as much linguistic diversity of generated text as possible. All systems were trained on the CNN/Daily Mail dataset (CNN/DM), a large corpus of news articles with associated abstractive summaries (Hermann et al., 2015), which has been widely used in the summarization literature. Generated summaries of test set articles as provided by the original authors were used. We conduct sentence-level annotation, allowing us to look at fine-grained differences.

Our typology was created in two steps. First, we carried out a card sort to establish an initial set of categories. For each of the four summarization systems, we randomly sampled 30 of its summaries, ensuring that each corresponded to a different article. Each summary was divided into sentences and one sentence was printed on a card, with the respective article printed above. This yielded a total of 393 sentences. Six experts in the news domain working at a news company sorted the cards (including one of the paper authors). Cards with similar errors were placed together in a pile. Then the experts iterated over the piles together, dividing and merging them until the sentences were grouped into a stable set of categories.

Second, we carried out a review of the categories in order to ensure that the boundaries of the categories were clear and to connect the categories to linguistic concepts. The review was carried out by the authors of the paper, two of whom were working at the news company. This group differed from the card sort group in that they have had training in linguistics. It was observed that some of the categories established in the card sort focused on surface nature of the error, others dealt more with the consequences of the error. This led us to establish a two dimensional typology, described in the following section.

3.2 Typology of summarization errors

The resulting error typology distinguishes two dimensions of summary error. First, the *Mapping Dimension* describes the surface level, looking at how the summary system used words and phrases from article sentences to create the erroneous summary sentence. This dimension can help us to understand the cause of an error, potentially helping to establish how these errors can be avoided. It distinguishes the four categories in Table 1. Second, the *Meaning Dimension* describes the effect of the error on whether the sentence can be understood and how the reader interprets it. This dimension distinguishes six categories, presented in Table 2.

Omission	Copying words from an article sentence, but omitting necessary words or phrases.
Wrong combination	Copying words or phrases from multiple article sentences and combining them into an erroneous sentence.
Fabrication	Introducing one or multiple new words or phrases that cause an error.
Lack of re-writing	Failing to adequately re-write sentences, e.g., by not replacing referential expressions with their original antecedents in the text. When the antecedents are not present in the preceding summary context, this causes an error.

Table 1: The *Mapping Dimension* of summarization system errors

Malformed

Ungrammatical	A sentence that is syntactically unnatural and would not be uttered by a competent speaker. Syntactically malformed.
Semantically implausible	A sentence that is semantically unnatural and would not be uttered by a competent speaker. Nonsensical due to semantic errors.
No meaning can be inferred	A sentence that is grammatically correct, but to which no meaning can be assigned, even after accommodation.

Misleading

Meaning changed, not entailed	In the summary context, the semantic content assigned to a sentence is not entailed by the original article.
Meaning changed, contradiction	In the summary context, the semantic content assigned to a sentence is in contradiction to the article.
Pragmatic meaning changed	In the summary context, the sentence gains a pragmatic meaning not present in the original article. Or, a pragmatic meaning present in the article is lost.

Table 2: The *Meaning Dimension* of summarization system errors, seperated into errors resulting in malformed sentences and errors resulting in misleading sentences

This dimension provides insight into the interaction of linguistic concepts and factual correctness. Errors from the first three categories can be considered to be **malformed** sentences: They will cause readers to stumble and question the quality of the summary, but they do not have the potential to mislead. In contrast, the remaining three categories can be considered **misleading**: They could give rise to incorrect beliefs that would not have been produced by the article alone. Misleading errors can be equated with factual errors in traditional parlance. Examples of errors and the corresponding annotation can be found below.

To validate the typology, we computed the inter-annotator agreement of three annotators. We selected a random subset of 30 articles from the CNN/DM dataset. Three annotators (the authors) applied the typology to judge the summaries generated by all four systems for this subset of articles. The origin of the summaries was not specified and the summaries were presented in a random order for each article. Annotators could refer to the original article and no time restrictions were applied.

Each sentence that contained an error was assigned both a Meaning and a Mapping category. For cases where there was no majority agreement, arbitration was used to reach agreement.

We analyzed the sentence-level inter-annotator agreement (Cohen's κ) of each dimension separately. Both showed moderate agreement (Meaning Dimension: $\kappa = 0.44$; Mapping Dimension: $\kappa = 0.46$). Further analysis of the annotations revealed that most disagreement was not between different categories in the dimension, but rather caused by raters not agreeing whether a sentence contains an error at all.

We reviewed all cases for which we disagreed on whether an error was present. There are two likely sources of lower than expected agreement. First, the annotation task is not trivial and requires maintaining close attention: A total of 14 misleading sentences were missed entirely by at least one annotator. Often, these sentences are perfectly plausible at the surface (cf. Example 1) and only a very close reading of both the article and the summary ensures they are identified. Similarly, there is often at least some judgment involved in deciding whether a given sentence is actually misleading. We found 20 examples judged misleading by one annotator and acceptable by two others that reflected different personal views on whether certain edits had faithfully retained original meaning. Consider Example 2: It shows that it is plausible that prior knowledge that the annotators might have (here, about the football team in question) causes them to accept the sentence as faithful, while annotators without this knowledge might disagree.

4 Comparison of summarizers

In this section, we carry out a comparative analysis of the four summarization systems using the error typology. This analysis highlights the usefulness of the typology for achieving insight into the nature of summary errors. We made a random selection of 170 articles and one annotator annotated all four summaries for each article using the typology. These were combined with the previously annotated set of 30 articles. This yielded a total of 800 summaries with roughly 2600 annotated sentences. Sentence annotations were additionally aggregated to summary level: A summary is labeled as malformed if it contains at least one malformed sentence, but no misleading sentence. If it contains at least one misleading sentence, it is labeled as misleading.

4.1 Meaning dimension errors

Our comparative analysis focuses on the Meaning Dimension of the typology, starting with the sentence level errors. Figure 1 presents the distribution of errors at the level of malformed and misleading errors. Exact sentence and summary level rates are presented in Table 3. A larger table including the fine-grained categories is released with the annotations.

All systems produce both misleading and malformed errors, but the distribution is quite different. PG, which does not use pre-training, produces the fewest misleading sentences. Malformed sentences are much more common for PG and FAST-ABS-RL, which are trained from scratch, than for TRANSFORMER-LM and BERTSUM, which use pre-training.

Next, we look at summary-level errors. We see that around 40% summaries contain at least one error of any kind for three of the systems and FAST-ABS-RL faring worse at almost 75%. Between 1 in

3 and 1 in 10 summaries generated by our systems contain at least one misleading statement. Our observations are consistent with summary-level error estimates reported by Falke et al. (2019). Their estimates for PG (8%) and FAST-ABS-RL (26%) are both somewhat lower than our rates, but the general trend is reflected.

For all systems, the observed summary-level error rate is closely aligned with what would be expected if errors were distributed randomly across summaries. This means that longer summaries, such as produced by FAST-ABS-RL, will have a higher error-rate independently of the sentence-level error rate. This observation underlines the importance of our choice to carry out error analysis at the sentence-level.

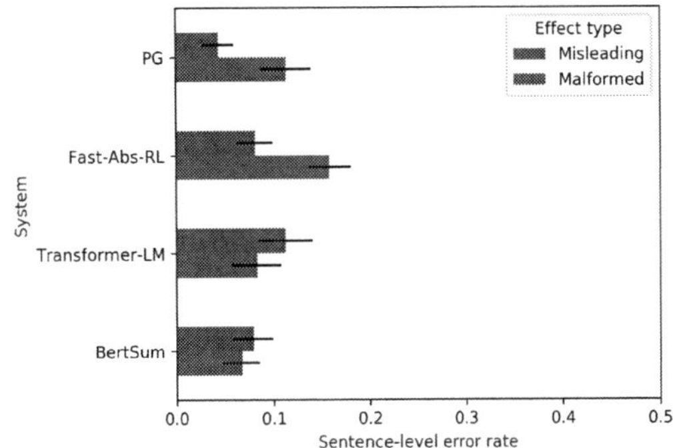

Figure 1: Sentence-level error type incidence rates by system, c.f. Table 3. 95 % CI obtained by bootstrap sampling.

4.2 Interaction of mapping and meaning

Next, we look into the interaction between the two error dimensions. Figure 2 illustrates the distribution of errors over summarization systems and the connection between the categories of the Meaning and Mapping dimensions. All systems suffer about equally from *lack of re-writing* and *wrong combinations*. However, the two pre-trained systems (TRANSFORMER-LM and BERTSUM) engage more frequently in *fabrications* and less frequently in *omissions*. FAST-ABS-RL suffers markedly from omissions.

Figure 2 also reveals that there is a correlation between the Mapping and Meaning dimension, but that essentially the dimensions are capturing two different aspects of summarization error. An important insight is that all four categories of Mapping error contribute to misleading errors, the more harmful type of Meaning error.

Headline	PICTURED: Mother-of-three who 'dropped her son in a cheetah pit' as it's revealed she is a CHILDCARE WORKER
Article excerpt	On Monday, a spokesman for Kindercare, a nationally-acclaimed education, care and resource provider, confirmed Schwab has taken a leave of absence from her management role at one of the centers in Columbus, Ohio.
Summary sentence	*Schwab* is a nationally-acclaimed education, care and resource provider.

Example 1: Wrong combination – Meaning changed, contradiction. Missed by two raters.

Headline	West Brom vs Leicester City: Team news, kick-off time, probable line-ups, odds and stats for the Premier League clash
Article excerpt	Boss Nigel Pearson has no further injury worries as his rock bottom side *continue to* fight for *Barclays Premier League* survival.
Summary sentence	Nigel Pearson has no further injury worries as his rock bottom side fight for survival.

Example 2: Omission – Pragmatic meaning changed. Two aspects of pragmatic meaning, i.e. that the fight has already started and that it was not for existence, but to avoid relegation, were resolved using background knowledge by two raters, but caused one rater to flag the sentence.

System	**PG**		**FAST-ABS-RL**		**TRANSFORMER-LM**		**BERTSUM**	
	Sent.	Sum.	Sent.	Sum.	Sent.	Sum.	Sent.	Sum.
Malformed	0.11	0.26	0.16	0.41	0.08	0.17	0.07	0.16
Misleading	0.04	0.12	0.08	0.32	0.11	0.19	0.08	0.23
Total	0.15	0.38	0.24	0.73	0.19	0.38	0.15	0.39
Avg # sentences	2.91		4.93		2.27		3.33	

Table 3: Error rates for the Meaning Dimension, sentence-level (Sent.) and summary-level (Sum.).

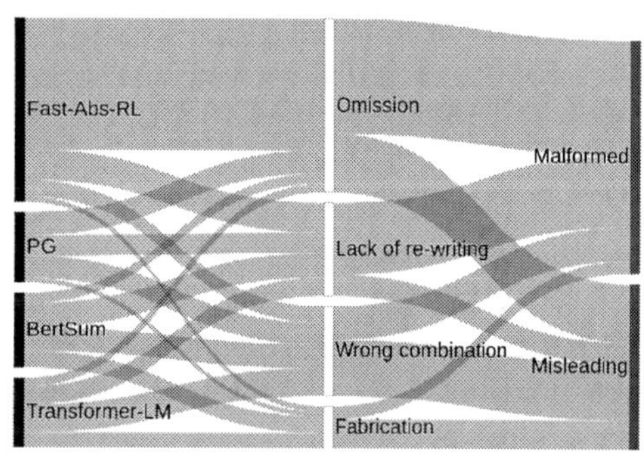

Figure 2: Sankey diagram showing the interaction of summarization systems, Mapping Dimension errors and Meaning Dimension errors.

4.3 Differences in abstractiveness

We turn now to the connection between abstractiveness and error. Improving the abstractiveness of a summary involves increasing the amount of rewriting. It could thus be expected that systems that are more abstractive are also more error-prone, unless they are inherently more capable of correctly abstracting sentences. Durmus et al. (2020) found that more abstractive systems are generally more error-prone, but did not look into the interaction of sentence-level error rates and abstractiveness. For this reason, we carry out a sentence-level analysis.

We calculate an abstractiveness score for each sentence in each summary as follows. For each sentence, we automatically select the closest document sentence in terms of word overlap. We then compute ROUGE-L. Normalizing by the length of the article sentence gives the precision of ROUGE-L and thus shows how much of the article sentence is retained. Similarly, normalizing by the summary length gives the recall of ROUGE-L, capturing how much of the summary originates from the closest document sentence. To get a combined metric, we compute ROUGE-L-F1, the harmonic mean of precision and recall for all ROUGE values. Sentences are then binned into two equal size bins, yielding a threshold of 0.705. We consider sentences about the threshold to have *high* abstractiveness and those below to have *low* abstractiveness.

Figure 3 displays the sentence-level error-rates for high and low abstractiveness summaries, separately for all four systems. Across all systems, higher abstractiveness is associated with a higher error rate. BERTSUM has a slightly lower error rate for highly abstractive sentences than the other systems with similar error rates. For

Headline	The Justice Department's questionable battle against FedEx
Article excerpt	*It turns out a corporation can indeed be prosecuted like a person.* It's a practice the Supreme Court has approved of for over a century.
Summary sentence	It's a practice the Supreme Court has approved of for over a century.

Example 3: Lack of re-writing – No meaning can be inferred. System: PG

Headline	Prince Charles leads tributes to '100-year-old teenager' Hayley Okines as hundreds gather for her funeral.
Article excerpt	She suffered from the rare disease progeria which ages the body at eight times *the normal rate.*
Summary sentence	She suffered from rare disease progeria which ages the body at eight times.

Example 4: Omission – Ungrammatical. System: FAST-ABS-RL

largely extractive sentences (low abstractiveness), PG, TRANSFORMER-LM and BERTSUM perform about equally well, while FAST-ABS-RL has a higher error rate. These findings support the observation that an absolute difference in sentence error rate between systems could be explained not by one system being inherently better, but just being less likely to write more abstractively and thus more error-prone. We also observed that sentences that score high in abstractiveness are more than twice as likely to be misleading and 50% more likely to be malformed than those that score low.

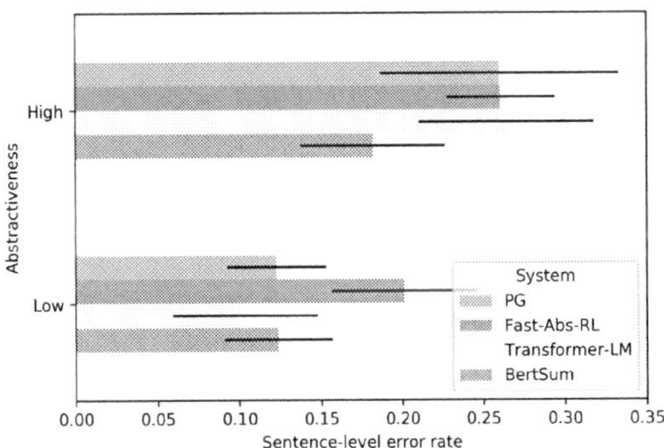

Figure 3: Binned ROUGE-F1 scores, average error rates in bins separately by system. 95 % CI obtained by bootstrap sampling.

5 Conclusion and outlook

In this section, we tie together the main contributions and insights of this paper, and discuss the avenues that it opens for future work.

5.1 Summary and discussion

In this paper, we have presented a typology of errors produced by automatic summarization systems, created by analyzing the output of four recent neural systems. The typology describes summary errors along a Mapping Dimension and a Meaning Dimensions, which are related, but are shown to capture different aspects of summary error. The Meaning Dimension is further divided into types of errors that describe malformed sentences and those that describe misleading sentences. The typology supports systematic analysis of abstractive summaries, and allows for focusing on the misleading sentences produced by automatic summarization systems. These errors are highly problematic because they impact the truth of a summary, i.e., its factual faithfulness to the original document.

Our comparative analysis has revealed the importance of using well-designed summarization metrics. With the wrong metrics, summarization systems will appear to be successful if the length of the summary or its abstractiveness has been decreased. In order to avoid these effects, and to achieve truly improved summaries, more advanced evaluation methods must be developed. The typology of errors that we have proposed here provides the basis for such methods. Metrics can become independent of length and abstractiveness if they take into account sentence-level errors and if they treat different errors differently. In particular, we recommend that misleading errors should be more important in signalling failed summaries than malformed errors.

If we consider the practical implications of improved summary evaluation, our typology makes a contribution in three related, but distinct directions: First, it can support the training of human assessors who can monitor live summarization systems in order to ensure that they do not lead to the publication of misinformation, which can have dangerous consequences. Second, it would be possible to train machine learning systems to support these human judgements. Third, it would be possible to improve automatic summarization systems in a way that

Headline	Andy Murray will jet straight from wedding with Kim Sears to run rule over prospective new assistant coach Jonas Bjorkman
Article excerpt	Mauresmo, who is to give birth some time in August, will be around eight months' pregnant during Wimbledon this summer.
Summary sentence	Mauresmo is eight months' pregnant *with her first child*.

Example 5: Fabrication – Meaning changed, not entailed. System: T-LM

Headline	Amazon removes new game that mocks anorexia sufferers by allowing players to throw food and sweets at character to fatten her up
Article excerpt	If the player misses the girl, she starts to lose weight until she eventually dies. Gamers have to throw food at the girl who appears in one of nine holes before she disappears again.
Summary sentence	Gamers have to throw food at the girl who appears in one of nine holes before she *dies*.

Example 6: Wrong combination – Meaning changed, contradiction. System: BERTSUM

allows them to specifically avoid generating misleading sentences. The work we have presented here has set down a foundation for these directions.

In terms of improving summmarization systems, our typology has supported interesting insights: The four neural summarization systems that we studied differ considerably in their error patterns (cf. Table 3 and Figure 2). For example, we see that sentence-based rewriting such as in FAST-ABS-RL leads to omission errors, resulting in a higher risk of malformed sentences. More strikingly, the two pre-trained systems are somewhat more successful at avoiding malformed sentences, indicating that pre-training helps to improve grammaticality. This finding makes intuitive sense, as learning the statistical properties of a large corpus of text can be expected to boost the ability to generate grammatical text. However, misleading sentences and fabrication errors are more common for these pre-trained systems. Overall, we observe that if any one of these systems were to be used in a real-world scenario, readers could frequently end up confused, irritated or worst of all misled to hold incorrect beliefs. Using our typology these effects can be properly understood and quantified.

5.2 Future work

The typology presented in this paper opens several avenues for future work. First, here, we used summaries from only a single data set (CNN/DM) in a single domain (news). The typology should be validated on different data from different domains, which may allow more nuance to be added to the categories of the dimensions.

Second, further research is necessary in order to determine whether it is possible to achieve higher levels of inter-annotator agreement. Recall that we saw a relatively low agreement among annotators as to whether a sentence contains an error at all. This is in line with observations made by Lebanoff et al. (2019), who noted a relatively low inter-annotator agreement for binary faithfulness annotation. However, more investigation is needed.

We point out that the inter-annotator agreement has a possible dependency with the domain and data that is being analyzed. Specific linguistic properties of the CNN/DM dataset could have negatively affected agreement about the malformedness of sentences, namely telegraphic language style and the issue of reference summaries lacking relevant context. The lack of context issue is specific to the data set, which omits the article headline, even though summaries often rely on it for interpretability. This means that some reference summaries are hard to understand in isolation, and could potentially bias systems to imitate the style. Summary sentences that suffer from these issues are a likely source of annotator disagreement.

We hope that researchers will build on and continue to refine the typology that we have presented here. For example, more detailed study of how human judgement interacts with malformed vs. misleading errors could lead to an improvement in the category descriptions or in the divisions between the categories. A refined typology would support standardization of the judgement protocols for automatically generated summaries, which would in turn help fight the adverse effects of factual errors.

Acknowledgments: We thank FD Mediagroep for conducting the Smart Journalism project which allowed us to perform this research.

References

Alyssa Appelman and Mike Schmierbach. 2018. Make no mistake? Exploring cognitive and perceptual effects of grammatical errors in news articles. *Journalism & Mass Communication Quarterly*, 95(4):930–947.

Ziqiang Cao, Furu Wei, Wenjie Li, and Sujian Li. 2018. Faithful to the original: Fact aware neural abstractive summarization. In *Proceedings of the Thirty-Second AAAI Conference on Artificial Intelligence (AAAI-18)*, pages 4784–4791.

Yen-Chun Chen and Mohit Bansal. 2018. Fast abstractive summarization with reinforce-selected sentence rewriting. In *Proceedings of the 56th Annual Meeting of the Association for Computational Linguistics (Volume 1: Long Papers)*, pages 675–686.

Esin Durmus, He He, and Mona Diab. 2020. FEQA: A question answering evaluation framework for faithfulness assessment in abstractive summarization. In *Proceedings of the 58th Annual Meeting of the Association for Computational Linguistics*, pages 5055–5070.

Liana Ermakova, Jean Valère Cossu, and Josiane Mothe. 2019. A survey on evaluation of summarization methods. *Information Processing & Management*, 56(5):1794–1814.

Tobias Falke, Leonardo F. R. Ribeiro, Prasetya Ajie Utama, Ido Dagan, and Iryna Gurevych. 2019. Ranking generated summaries by correctness: An interesting but challenging application for natural language inference. In *Proceedings of the 57th Annual Meeting of the Association for Computational Linguistics*, pages 2214–2220. Association for Computational Linguistics.

Yang Gao, Christian M Meyer, and Iryna Gurevych. 2019. Preference-based interactive multi-document summarisation. *Information Retrieval Journal*, pages 1–31.

Ben Goodrich, Vinay Rao, Peter J Liu, and Mohammad Saleh. 2019. Assessing the factual accuracy of generated text. In *Proceedings of the 25th ACM SIGKDD International Conference on Knowledge Discovery & Data Mining*, pages 166–175.

Karl Moritz Hermann, Tomas Kocisky, Edward Grefenstette, Lasse Espeholt, Will Kay, Mustafa Suleyman, and Phil Blunsom. 2015. Teaching machines to read and comprehend. In *Advances in neural information processing systems*, pages 1693–1701.

Andrew Hoang, Antoine Bosselut, Asli Celikyilmaz, and Yejin Choi. 2019. Efficient adaptation of pre-trained transformers for abstractive summarization. *arXiv:1906.00138 [cs]*. ArXiv: 1906.00138.

Wojciech Kryscinski, Nitish Shirish Keskar, Bryan McCann, Caiming Xiong, and Richard Socher. 2019. Neural text summarization: A critical evaluation. In *Proceedings of the 2019 Conference on Empirical Methods in Natural Language Processing and the 9th International Joint Conference on Natural Language Processing (EMNLP-IJCNLP)*, pages 540–551. Association for Computational Linguistics.

Wojciech Kryściński, Bryan McCann, Caiming Xiong, and Richard Socher. 2019. Evaluating the factual consistency of abstractive text summarization. *arXiv:1910.12840 [cs]*. ArXiv: 1910.12840.

Logan Lebanoff, John Muchovej, Franck Dernoncourt, Doo Soon Kim, Seokhwan Kim, Walter Chang, and Fei Liu. 2019. Analyzing sentence fusion in abstractive summarization. *arXiv:1910.00203 [cs]*. ArXiv: 1910.00203.

Chris van der Lee, Albert Gatt, Emiel van Miltenburg, Sander Wubben, and Emiel Krahmer. 2019. Best practices for the human evaluation of automatically generated text. In *Proceedings of the 12th International Conference on Natural Language Generation*, pages 355–368. Association for Computational Linguistics.

Chin-Yew Lin. 2004. Rouge: A package for automatic evaluation of summaries. In *Proceedings of the Workshop Text Summarization Branches Out*, pages 74–81. Association for Computational Linguistics.

Yang Liu and Mirella Lapata. 2019. Text summarization with pretrained encoders. In *Proceedings of the 2019 Conference on Empirical Methods in Natural Language Processing and the 9th International Joint Conference on Natural Language Processing (EMNLP-IJCNLP)*, pages 3721–3731.

Elena Lloret, Laura Plaza, and Ahmet Aker. 2018. The challenging task of summary evaluation: an overview. *Language Resources and Evaluation*, 52(1):101–148.

Klaus-Michael Lux. 2020. On the factual correctness and robustness of deep abstractive text summarization. Master's thesis, Radboud University, Nijmegen, August.

Maxime Peyrard. 2019a. A simple theoretical model of importance for summarization. In *Proceedings of the 57th Annual Meeting of the Association for Computational Linguistics*, pages 1059–1073, Florence, Italy. Association for Computational Linguistics.

Maxime Peyrard. 2019b. Studying summarization evaluation metrics in the appropriate scoring range. In *Proceedings of the 57th Annual Meeting of the Association for Computational Linguistics*, pages 5093–5100, Florence, Italy. Association for Computational Linguistics.

Abigail See, Peter J. Liu, and Christopher D. Manning. 2017. Get to the point: Summarization with pointer-generator networks. In *Proceedings of the 55th Annual Meeting of the Association for Computational Linguistics (Volume 1: Long Papers)*, pages 1073–1083.

Simeng Sun, Ori Shapira, Ido Dagan, and Ani Nenkova. 2019. How to compare summarizers without target length? Pitfalls, solutions and re-examination of the neural summarization literature. In *Proceedings of the Workshop on Methods for Optimizing and Evaluating Neural Language Generation*, pages 21–29. Association for Computational Linguistics.

Fill in the BLANC:
Human-free quality estimation
of document summaries

Oleg Vasilyev, Vedant Dharnidharka, John Bohannon

Primer Technologies Inc.

San Francisco, California

`oleg,vedant,john@primer.ai`

Abstract

We present BLANC, a new approach to the automatic estimation of document summary quality. Our goal is to measure the functional performance of a summary with an objective, reproducible, and fully automated method. Our approach achieves this by measuring the performance boost gained by a pretrained language model with access to a document summary while carrying out its language understanding task on the document's text. We present evidence that BLANC scores have as good correlation with human evaluations as do the ROUGE family of summary quality measurements. And unlike ROUGE, the BLANC method does not require human-written reference summaries, allowing for fully human-free summary quality estimation.

1 Introduction

Two most widely used methods for measuring the quality of a summary are ROUGE (Lin, 2004) and human evaluation (Kryściński et al., 2019a).

The ROUGE family of methods are well-defined and reproducible. However, these methods typically require a human-written reference summaries for comparison, completely disregarding the original document text. Even if one assumes that a reference summary is available and of optimal quality, the ROUGE method is limited to measuring a mechanical overlap of text tokens with little regard to semantics. This deficiency may be partially addressable through measurement of the similarity not of text tokens but named entities or other preprocessed features (Mao et al., 2019; Cohan and Goharian, 2016; Elghannam and El-Shishtawy, 2015; Ng and Abrecht, 2015; Ganesan, 2018) or embeddings (Zhao et al., 2019; Zhang et al., 2020; Gao et al., 2020). In the latter work (Gao et al., 2020) the references are not human-written but unsupervisedly constructed from selected salient sentences. An overlap can be measured as well

between summary and document text (Shao et al., 2017).

Human evaluation of summary quality is far more meaningful and powerful than ROUGE, but it is far less reproducible. Summary quality estimation is a cognitively demanding and highly subjective task. Humans are also vulnerable to biases, such as the preference for phrases and sentences copied directly from the document text into summaries (Ziegler et al., 2020). Improving human evaluation may require prompting labelers to pay higher attention (Hardy et al., 2019), as well as splitting quality scores into multiple dimensions such as fluency, informativeness, and factual correctness (Kryściński et al., 2019a,b; Fan et al., 2018). Even if humans can be trained to be more reliable, reproducible estimators of summary quality, they will forever remain a slow, expensive, limiting resource.

One possible route to a better automatic method for summary quality estimation is to train a model on document summaries annotated with human quality scores (Louis and Nenkova, 2009, 2013; Xenouleas et al., 2019). Such a model could be used to evaluate summaries without further human involvement. But even if such a model could achieve high agreement with human labelers, its performance would only be as objective and reproducible as the summary quality scores generated by one particular group of humans on a particular group of documents. Such a model may not generalize beyond the domain and style of the training samples unless they are a massive, representative sample of all documents of interest.

A more fundamental approach to the problem is to estimate how "helpful" a summary is for the task of understanding a text. For example this might be achieved through a series of question-answers (Eyal et al., 2019; Chen et al., 2018; Scialom et al., 2019). However, with this approach one must choose from a vast set of questions one might ask

Proceedings of the First Workshop on Evaluation and Comparison of NLP Systems (Eval4NLP), pages 11–20,
November 20, 2020. ©2020 Association for Computational Linguistics

of a text, presupposing knowledge of the document itself and seriously limiting its reproducibility.

In the following section we suggest a new approach that is fundamentally justifiable as an estimator of summary quality, as well as being conceptually simple and reproducible.

2 Methods

2.1 Introducing BLANC

An ideal estimator should directly test how helpful a summary is to its readers. It should reliably estimate quality across a broad range of document domains and styles. And yet it should achieve this without requiring ornate preconditions and presuppositions about the text being summarized. If this estimator relies upon an existing base model, that model should be well-documented, well-understood and widely used.

We propose BLANC[1] as a replacement for the ROUGE family of summary quality estimators.

We define BLANC as a measure of how well a summary helps an independent, pre-trained language model while it performs its language understanding task on a document. We focus on the masked token task, also known as the Cloze task (Taylor, 1953), in which a model is challenged to reconstruct obscured spans of text. We use the well-known BERT language model (Devlin et al., 2018) pre-trained to predict masked text tokens (words or sub-words). The BERT tokenizer represents the majority of the most frequently used words as single tokens, while splitting less common words into two or more.

We present two versions of BLANC, which we dub BLANC-help and a BLANC-tune. These measures are described in detail in the following sections. The essential difference between them:

1. BLANC-help uses the summary text by directly concatenating it to each document sentence during inference.
2. BLANC-tune uses the summary text to finetune the language model, and then processes the entire document.

---

[1] According to ancient tradition, we should adorn our newly created jargon term with a bacronymic justification. The term BLANC is a nod to its proud lineage of French color words that began with the BLEU method for evaluating machine translation and ROUGE for summarization. BLANC is also a reference to the method's core task of "filling in the blanks" in the masked token task. But to honor tradition we offer this: Bacronymic Language model Approach for summary quality estimatioN. Cool?

Thus with BLANC-help, the language model refers to the summary each time it attempts to understand a part of the document text. While with BLANC-tune, the model learns from the summary first, and then uses its gained skill to help it understand the entire document.

2.2 BLANC-help

The algorithm for obtaining BLANC-help scores is illustrated in Figure 1.

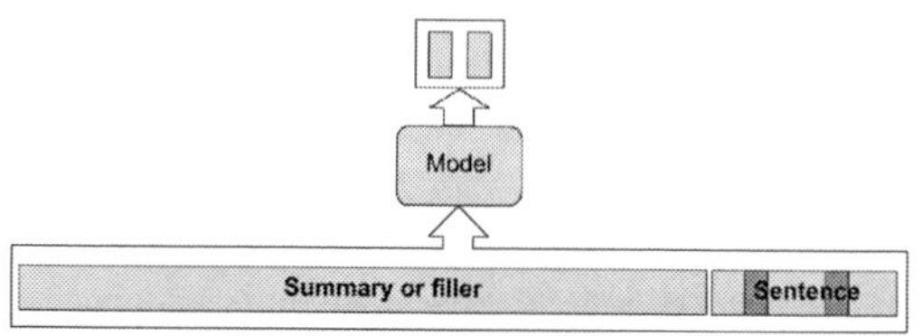

Figure 1: BLANC-help of summary quality is defined by the difference in accuracy of two reconstructions of masked tokens: with summary vs. filler concatenated in front of the sentence with masked tokens. The model input is a summary (or filler) + sentence with masked (grey) tokens. The output is the unmasked tokens.

There are many possible choices for how to mask the tokens. Our aim is to evenly cover all tokens in a sentence with a certain frequency, for the sake of full reproducibility. A random coverage is also possible, but it is not as conveniently reproducible.

The unmasking is done twice for each sentence of the text and for each allowed choice of masked tokens in the sentence. First, the unmasking is done for input composed of the summary concatenated with the sentence. Second, the unmasking is done for input composed of a "filler" concatenated with the sentence. The filler has exactly the same lengths as the summary, but each summary token is replaced by a period symbol ("."). After iterating over all sentences and over all the allowed choices of masking, we end up with four total counts of successful and unsuccessful unmasking $S_{ij}, i = 0, 1; j = 0, 1$. Here the index i equals 0 or 1 - for unsuccessful (0) or successful (1) unmasking for the filler-input. The index j is defined the same way for the summary-input. For example, S_{01} is the count of cases where the filler-input was unsuccessful and the summary-input was successful.

We define BLANC-help as the difference between the accuracy A_s of unmasking with the summary and the accuracy A_f of unmasking with the filler:

Given: $summary$; $text$; $model$;
   Parameters $M = 6$, $L_{min} = 4$

Initialise $filler = ".".* length(summary)$
Initialise $S_{00}, S_{01}, S_{10}, S_{11}$ to zero
for $sentence$ **in** $text$:
   for i_0 **in range from** 1 **to** M:
      Mask each ith word if $(i - i_0)\%M == 0$
         and if $length(word) >= L_{min}$
      $input_{base} = filler + sentence$
      $input_{help} = summary + sentence$
      $out_{base} = model(input_{base})$
      $out_{help} = model(input_{help})$
      for each position i in masked tokens:
         $k = int(out_{base}[i] == sentence[i])$
         $m = int(out_{help}[i] == sentence[i])$
         $S_{km} += 1$
$B = (S_{01} - S_{10})/(S_{00} + S_{11} + S_{01} + S_{10})$

Figure 2: BLANC-help B for quality of summary.

$$BLANC_{help} = A_s - A_f = \frac{S_{01} - S_{10}}{S_{total}}$$

The accuracies are $A_s = (S_{11} + S_{01})/S_{total}$ and $A_f = (S_{11} + S_{10})/S_{total}$. The total count is $S_{total} = S_{00} + S_{11} + S_{01} + S_{10}$. The BLANC value can range from -1 to 1, but as shown in next sections the typical values are between 0 (summary is useless) and 0.3 (summary provides 30% help).

The algorithm for BLANC-help is shown in more detail in Figure 2.

Since the BERT model deals with tokens rather than words, we can choose to mask tokens rather than words. In typical news documents only about 10% of words are split by the BERT tokenizer into two or more tokens. Such "composite" words (not existing in the BERT vocabulary) should be particularly valuable in estimating the helpfulness of a summary. In a version dealing with tokens rather than words it is natural to always allow masking of composite words regardless of their length.

The setting $L_{min} = 4$ allows the masking only of sufficiently long words (4 or more characters), because shorter words are typically easier to predict, with or without the help of a summary.

The value $M = 6$ in Figure 2 is a natural choice because the standard BERT model is trained by masking 15% of tokens, which makes about one-sixth of tokens eligible to be masked.

We found that altering the filler has a negligible effect on the measures. The reason we use the filler is to avoid any effect of the length of input on the action of the model.

2.3 BLANC-tune

The algorithm for obtaining BLANC-tune is illustrated in Figure 3.

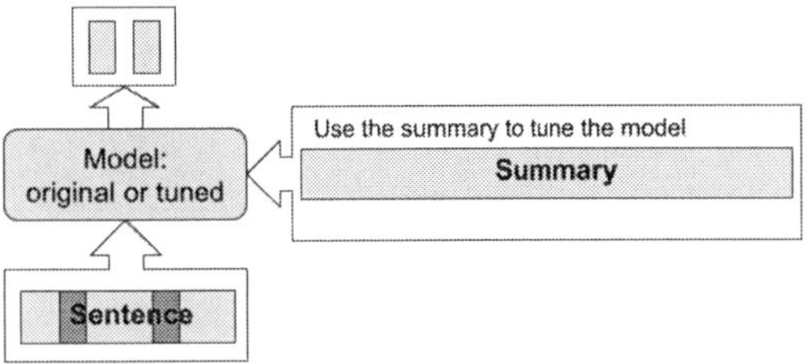

Figure 3: BLANC-tune of summary quality is defined by the difference in accuracy of two reconstructions of masked tokens: with model tuned on the summary vs. with the original model. Both models are given the same input: a sentence with masked (grey) tokens. Each model outputs the unmasked tokens.

For calculating this measure, the model first learns from the summary, and then we observe how helpful this learning was in reconstructing masked tokens in text sentences.

As in the case of BLANC-help, we define BLANC-tune by comparing the accuracy of two reconstructions: one that does use the summary, and another that does not. In the case of BLANC-help, this was the difference between placing the summary vs. placing the filler in front of a sentence. Now, in the case of BLANC-tune, we compare performance of a model fine-tuned on the summary text vs. a model that has never seen the summary.

The task, using a model to unmask tokens, is performed the same way as for BLANC-help, except that the input is simply a document sentence with masked tokens.

The tuning of the model is done on an extremely small dataset (derived from the summary text), in which each sample is the very same summary but with different tokens masked. The masking in the summary is done according to the original BERT pre-training strategy. Unmasking must be performed for 15% randomly selected tokens, of which 80% are masked, 10% are replaced by random tokens, and 10% are left unchanged. To ensure coverage of tokens, we select and shuffle all eligible tokens, and then go through them to generate samples for the BLANC-tune dataset.

The algorithm for BLANC-tune is shown in more detail in Figure 4.

Given:
   $summary$; $text$; $model$;
   probability $p_{mask} = 0.15$ of masking tuning;
   min length of word to be masked $L_{min} = 4$;
   number of tuning passes $N = 10$

 # Tune the model on the summary
N_{words} = number of words in summary
$N_{mask} = int(N_{words} * p_{mask})$
Initialize empty tuning dataset set_{tune}
for i **in range from** 1 **to** N**:**
   pos = positions of words longer than L_{min}
   Random shuffle pos
   until all position in pos are used:
      Mask words in next N_{mask} positions
      Add summary with masked words to set_{tune}
Tune $model$ on set_{tune}. Result: $model_{tuned}$

 # Compare inference with model vs. $model_{tuned}$
Initialise $S_{00}, S_{01}, S_{10}, S_{11}$ to zero
$M = integer(1/p_{mask})$
for $sentence$ **in** $text$**:**
   for i_0 **in range from** 1 **to** M**:**
      Mask each ith word if $(i - i_0)\%M == 0$
         $and\ length(word) >= L_{min}$
      $out_{base} = model(sentence)$
      $out_{help} = model_{tuned}(sentence)$
      for each position i in masked tokens:
      $k = int(out_{base}[i] == sentence[i])$
      $m = int(out_{help}[i] == sentence[i])$
      $S_{km}\mathrel{+}= 1$
$B = (S_{01} - S_{10})/(S_{00} + S_{11} + S_{01} + S_{10})$

Figure 4: BLANC-tune B for quality of summary

Similar to BLANC-help, there can be several variations of the measure. The details described in the previous section for BLANC-help are now applicable here in two parts of the algorithm where we must select masked tokens: for the tuning dataset, and for the inference. Any fixed version of the measure can be reproducible, with fixed seed for randomness at the tuning. In our tuning we used the same optimizer and learning rate as was used by the open source huggingface repository (Wolf et al., 2019) for training, and we found that dependency on the seed is very weak.

While BLANC-tune appears more complicated than BLANC-help, it is a promising method in that learning from a summary is separated completely from the task of understanding the document, with no concatenation required. While we use BLANC-help for the presentation of our approach in this paper, in future work we will systematically explore BLANC-tune. Our preliminary experiments showed that BLANC-tune and BLANC-help return similar values.

2.4 Extractive summaries: no-copy-pair guard

In the case of purely extractive summaries, the process of calculating BLANC scores may pair a summary with sentences from the text that have been copied into the summary. This exact sentence copying should be unfairly helpful in unmasking words in the original sentence. This effect may be reduced or completely eliminated by using a stronger underlying language model, especially for BLANC-tune. But a simpler solution is to include a simple guard rule into the measure: We may exclude any pairing of exact copy sentences from the calculation of the measure. In the process of iterating over text sentences, whenever a sentence contains its exact copy in the summary, it is skipped (or, alternative version, the copy is removed from the summary for this specific step in the process).

Throughout the paper we do not use the "no-copy-pair" guard, except in the corner case consideration of copying random sentences from the text, as described in the next section.

3 Basic validation of BLANC measurement

As part of the validation of these new measures we performed experiments to determine how a substitution of an obviously bad summary affects the measure. One example is a summary generated by selecting random words from the text. The random words summary is generated with the same length as the original summary. Our original summaries are generated for randomly selected daily news by three different methods: by Microsoft's abstractive UniML model (Dong et al., 2019), by semi-abstractive summarization model (based on (Vasilyev et al., 2019)), and by extractive LexRank model (based on (Erkan and Radev, 2004)). The summaries generated by these models are not flawless and vary widely in overall quality when evaluated by human labelers.

In another validation experiment, we generate a

"random sentences summary", which is constructed from the sentences of a document. For this example, we apply BLANC-help with the "no-copy-pair" guard introduced above. But we use the second version of the guard rule, because it is less exclusive of text sentences overall, and we also compensate for the length of the summary by replacing the copy-sentence of the summary with another sentence, rather than simply removing the copy-sentence.

BLANC-help results for both examples (in comparison to the measure of the original summaries) are shown in Figure 5. We can see that the

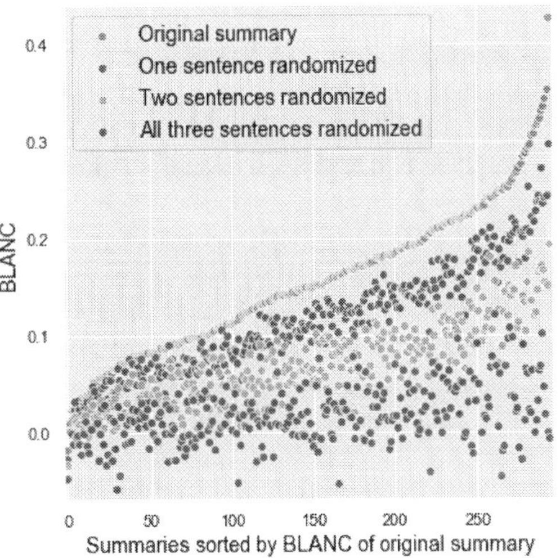

Figure 6: BLANC-help for 3-sentence summaries with one or more sentences replaced by random words from the text. The summaries are sorted by measure of the original summary.

4 Comparison with human evaluation scores

The BLANC measures do not require any "gold-labeled" data: No human-written summaries nor human-annotated quality scores are needed. Theoretically, the measures should reflect how fluent, informative, and factually correct a summary is, simply because only fluent, informative, correct summaries are helpful to the underlying language model. We now turn to the question of whether the BLANC measures correlate with summary quality scores assigned by human readers.

Human scoring is fallible; a correlation with human scores should not be considered as a full validation of our measures, but rather as an independent confirmation that the measures are sensible.

For purposes unrelated to this study, we have undertaken a series of human evaluations of many generated summaries of approximately similar length. As mentioned in the previous section, the summaries were generated by Microsoft's abstractive UniML model (Dong et al., 2019), by semi-abstractive model (Vasilyev et al., 2019), and by extractive LexRank model (Erkan and Radev, 2004). The summaries from the latter two sources were "equalized" in length to the UniML, so that at least on average the summaries from all three generation sources would be equal, and also so that most summaries would not differ significantly in length.

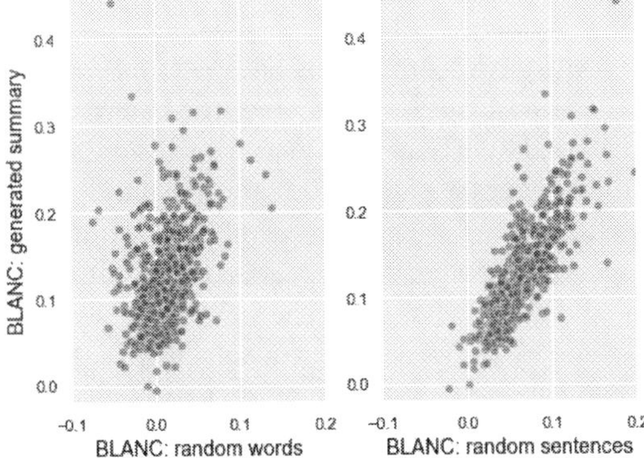

Figure 5: BLANC-help of a generated summary vs. random-words summary (left) and BLANC-help of a generated summary vs. random-sentences "summary" (right). The random-words summary is produced from random words of the same text by filling with the words the same length as the generated summary. The random-sentences summary is calculated with the no-copy-pair guard rule (version 2), but compensating for the summary length by adding more random sentences to the summary whenever needed.

BLANC value for the real generated summary is almost always higher than the value for the random-sentences summary. This confirms that the measure takes into account the context as well as the informativeness of the summary to assess the quality.

Selecting only summaries with exactly three sentences, we can observe how BLANC-help deteriorates if we spoil some of the sentences of the summary. We replace one, two or all three sentences with random words, keeping the same length of the resulting randomized summary as the original summary. We also take care to run on each possible choice of replacement sentences twice, and average the resulting BLANC-help. The result is shown up in Figure 6.

Altogether, we assembled 555 summary-text pairs for human scoring, with the texts taken from the CNN / Daily Mail dataset (Hermann et al., 2015).

We hired 10 annotators through Odetta.ai and trained them to assess the overall quality of each summary on a 5-point scale: 0 = VERY BAD, 1 = BAD, 2 = OK, 3 = GOOD or 4 = VERY GOOD. The annotators worked independently from each other and had access to only one summary-text pair at a time. The task was performed through the online text annotation tool LightTag (lighttag.io).

The values of the correlations are illustrated in Figure 7.

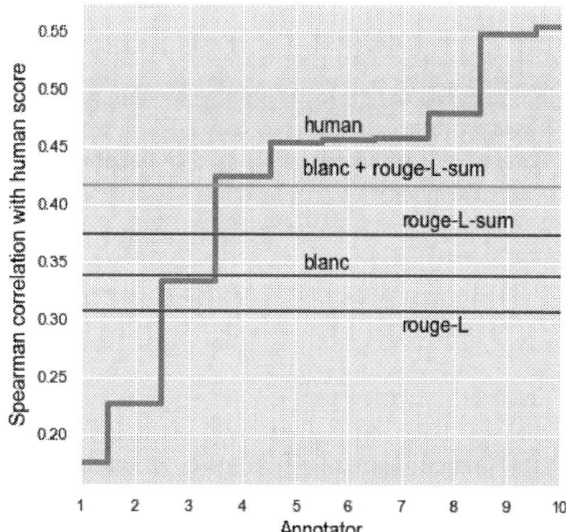

Figure 7: Spearman correlations with human annotators. The green step-line is the level of correlations of one of annotators with all other annotators. The correlation of BLANC-help with an average over all annotators is shown by the red line. The blue lines correspond to ROUGE-L and ROUGE-Lsum, and the yellow line to a simple sum "BLANC-help + ROUGE-Lsum". The summaries were generated on the CNN / DailyMail texts.

The green step-function shows the value of correlation of an annotator score (with Id ranging from 1 to 10) with the averaged score of the 9 other annotators. The number of samples used for the correlation is 555 - the summaries generated by the three models. The red and blue lines show correlations of BLANC-help and rouge correspondingly with the averaged score of all 10 annotators. The rouge here is calculated using the google-research package (github.com/google-research/google-research/tree/master/rouge) as F1 value of "rougeL" (lower blue line on the plot) and F1 value of "rougeLsum" (upper blue line). The latter is the 'summary-level LCS', with summaries split to sentences and using a union longest common subsequence (Lin, 2004)

The yellow line in the figure shows how a simplest combination of BLANC-help and ROUGE correlates with the annotators. The "BLANC-help + ROUGE-Lsum" is literally a simple sum of BLANC-help and the ROUGE-Lsum. As usual a blending of two different models produces better results, though it is not our purpose here to fit human scores, and we do not fit the weights in the sum. (For example, using a $score = 3 * blanc_{help} + rouge_{Lsum}$ with the weight 3 for BLANC-help would increase the correlation with human scores by 1%).

All shown correlations have p-values of order 10^{-6} and lower. We observe that both BLANC-help and ROUGE correlate with annotators as good as or better than about 30% of annotators.

In Figure 8 we present correlations with human scores on summaries generated for 100 typical daily news documents. The summaries were generated by the same three models; there were 300 summary-text pairs for scoring, again by 10 annotators.

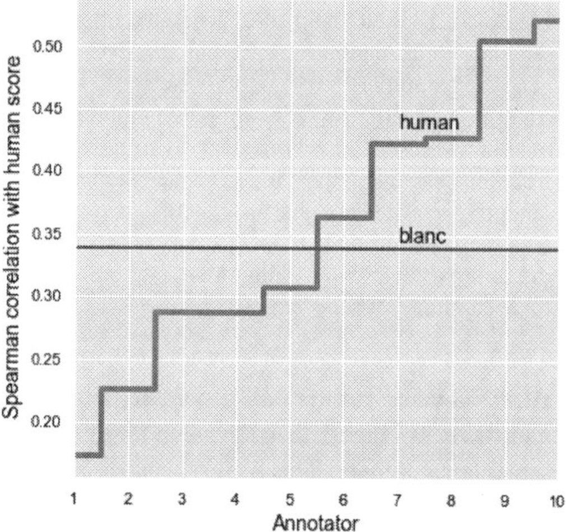

Figure 8: Spearman correlations with human annotators. The green step-line is the level of correlations of one of the annotators with all other annotators. The correlation of BLANC-help with an average over all annotators is shown by the red line. The summaries were generated on regular news documents: There are no reference summaries, and hence no ROUGE score.

Since there are no "gold-labeled" summaries for these news documents, there is no ROUGE score in the figure.

As we see in all these examples, the human-human agreement is not impressive. We have observed from yet another evaluation dataset that if the texts and the generated summaries are challenging with very low inter-annotator agreement, the correlation of our measure with human scores is similarly diminished (with borderline p-values).

The values assigned to humans scores (0,1,2,3,4) are not a perfect translation of the human perception of the corresponding labels ("very bad", "bad", "OK", "good", "very good"). From multiple evaluations unrelated to this study we know that when an evaluation is repeated, human annotators are far more likely to substitute "OK" and "good" with each other than other tags. When we obtain an averaged human score, a weighting of the values $(0, 1, 2, 3, 4)$ with $weights =$ $(3.0, 3.0, 1.0, 1.0, 2.0)$ may be more inline with human perception, but the changes to results we presented here are not essential, of order 1%.

BERTScore (Zhang et al., 2020), similarly to ROUGE, requires reference summaries, but is using overlaps of BERT embeddings rather than strings. In Figure 7 the BERTScore F1 would be at 0.35 - close to BLANC, BERTScore Precision at 0.16, and BERTScore Recall at impressive 0.47 (calculated using python package bert-score).

A few simple observations may serve as an evidence that our measure deals with the length of a summary more reasonably than either humans or ROUGE. In Table 1 we show the correlations with the summary length and with the compression factor, which is defined as the ratio of summary length to document text length. The length here is the number of characters.

Estimator	**Correlation**	**L**	**C**
BLANC-help	Pearson	0.47	0.75
	Spearman	0.51	0.76
rouge-L	Pearson	-0.27	
	Spearman	-0.22	
rouge-L-sum	Pearson	-0.23	
	Spearman	-0.15	
humans	Pearson	0.41	0.31
	Spearman	0.41	0.43

Table 1: Correlation of different quality estimators with length L of summary and with compression C. The compression is defined as length of summary divided by length of text, in characters. The no correlation cases (p-value > 0.05) are left empty. Based on CNN / Daily Mail news.

The table is based on the same data as Figure 7. The table shows that similarly to humans, our measure is helped by longer summaries in general. But unlike humans, it is much more sensitive to a summary's compression factor. A disregard for the compression factor by humans may be caused by the anchoring effect.

Table 2 gives similar insight for very different kind of documents - random daily news, same as were used for Figure 8.

Estimator	**Correlation**	**L**	**C**
BLANC-help	Pearson	0.20	0.77
	Spearman	0.19	0.73
humans	Pearson	0.42	0.41
	Spearman	0.38	0.39

Table 2: Correlation of different quality estimators with length L of summary and with compression C. Based on randomly selected daily news documents.

Whenever we used BLANC or human annotators for comparison of quality of summaries generated by different models of by different versions of a model, we generated summaries on average of the same length. It is clear that both humans and BLANC will estimate longer summary better, at least when it is a single score of overall summary quality. If the length of individual summary has to be excluded as a factor, the BLANC score should be normalized by the compression C. A longer summary adds proportionally more help, while a longer text adds proportionally more tokens for masking.

In Table 3 we show comparison of BLANC with negated Jensen-Shannon divergence (JS) which is a no-references measure showed up as the strongest in (Louis and Nenkova, 2009). The JS is a mean of text-summary and summary-text Kullback-Leibler divergences. For a purely statistical measure which we would assume misses a lot of semantics, JS works surprisingly well on CNN / Daily Mail news examples. The modest performance at first row by both measures can be explained by high variety of in styles of the summaries, which affects both the human scoring and the measures. On human-only summaries JS is still better than BLANC. In order to confirm that BLANC grasps more semantics, we considered three subsets of summaries that might have less signal from pure statistics. The summaries of similar length, close to peak of the distribution, is one example; summaries with low human scores is another one. More important example is the highly compressed summaries, with the ratio of the summary length to the text length < 0.05. In this case JS correlation value would be 0.12, but p-value=0.15 is too high. Following (Louis and Nenkova, 2009), the JS was calculated with filtering stop words and with stemming.

Selection	N	BLANC	JS
All	855	0.22	0.28
Human	300	0.34	0.37
Close length	319	0.15	0.13
Bad	141	0.23	0.21
Compressed	155	0.18	(p=0.15)

Table 3: Comparison of BLANC and Jensen-Shannon (JS) divergence correlations with averaged human score. First column specifies the summaries considered; second is the number of summaries; the last two columns are the correlations of BLANC and JS with human scores. The texts are from CNN / Daily Mail news. Row 'All' included all summaries, both human and generated by 3 methods. Row 'Human': only human-created summaries. Row 'Close length': summaries with length limited around pick of distribution, between 200 and 350 characters long. Row 'Bad' summaries with mean human score less than 2. Row 'Compressed': summaries with compression (length of summary over length of text) less than 0.05. There is no correlation in bottom JS cell, p-value=0.15.

Simple correlation with a consensus score of annotators is not an easy criterion for judging the usefulness of the measure. When annotators are tasked with scoring several different qualities of a summary, their final score for the overall quality should be more grounded, because more attention has been spent on the summary and the text. In Figure 9 we show values of correlations obtained from such evaluation.

The data used here are the same as the data for Figure 8: summaries generated on randomly selected daily news documents. For this illustration, however, we split our 10 annotators into a small group of 3 and an "others" group of the remaining 7. There are 120 ways to chose the split (on the X-axis). The circle markers show human-human correlation, i.e. the correlation between the average score of the small group and the average score of the "others" group. The plus markers show BLANC-human correlation, i.e. a correlation of the BLANC with the "others" group of annotators. Hence we see how well the BLANC measure

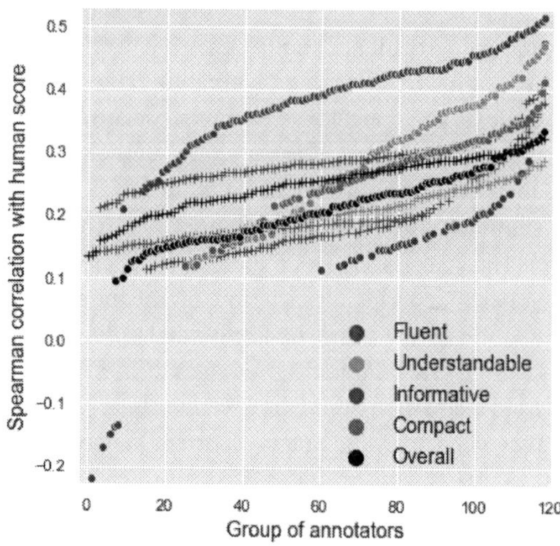

Figure 9: Spearman correlations with a group of 7 annotators. The x-axes depicts 120 ways to choose 3 annotators out of 10. The circle-markers show correlation of average score of 3 annotators with average score of 7 other annotators. The plus-markers show correlation of BLANC-help with the 7 annotators. Each type of correlation was sorted independently, left-to-right. Markers with p-values > 0.05 are not shown.

performs against the team of 3 annotators in correlating with the "others". For simplicity of the presentation, each type of correlation was sorted independently. If a correlation is unreliable (p-value > 0.05) then the marker is not shown.

We see that BLANC can be competitive to a team of three human annotators on all summary qualities, especially on the 'overall' and fluency.

5 Conclusion

In this paper we present BLANC, a new family of objective and reproducible measures of summary quality. BLANC does not require human-written reference summaries; it is based on how helpful the summary for understanding the document.

By comparison, it is difficult to suspend disbelief when considering a method like ROUGE that does not inspect the document itself when estimating the quality of a summary. It is notable that ROUGE scores are often cited even for headline generation (Ayana et al., 2016; Kiyono et al., 2017; Xu and Fung, 2019; Gu et al., 2020) where it is hard to imagine that any single headline could be regarded as the best possible headline for a document.

One may argue that ROUGE requires less processing power, unless we recall that applying it requires the processing power of a human who must write the reference summary for ROUGE. In future research we will consider variations of BLANC and, for convenience, provide a public package blanc.

We thank Charlene Chambliss (Primer) for help in preparing the design of human evaluations, and Rosanne Liu (UberAI), Nina Lopatina (In-Q-Tel) and anonymous reviewers for review of the paper and valuable feedback.

References

Ayana, Shiqi Shen, Yu Zhao, Zhiyuan Liu, and Maosong Sun. 2016. Neural headline generation with sentence-wise optimization. *arXiv*, arXiv:1604.01904v2. Version 2.

Ping Chen, Fei Wu, Tong Wang, and Wei Ding. 2018. A semantic qa-based approach for text summarization evaluation. In *Proceedings of the Thirty-Second AAAI Conference on Artificial Intelligence*, pages 4800–4807. AAAI Press (2018).

Arman Cohan and Nazli Goharian. 2016. Revisiting summarization evaluation for scientific articles. In *Proceedings of the Tenth International Conference on Language Resources and Evaluation (LREC'16)*, pages 806–813. European Language Resources Association (ELRA, 2016).

Jacob Devlin, Ming-Wei Chang, Kenton Lee, and Kristina Toutanova. 2018. Bert: Pre-training of deep bidirectional transformers for language understanding. *arXiv*, arXiv:1810.04805.

Li Dong, Nan Yang, Wenhui Wang, Furu Wei, Xiaodong Liu, Yu Wang, Ming Zhou Jianfeng Gao, and Hsiao-Wuen Hon. 2019. Unified language model pre-training for natural language understanding and generation. *arXiv*, arXiv:1905.03197.

Fatma Elghannam and Tarek El-Shishtawy. 2015. Keyphrase based evaluation of automatic text summarization. *arXiv*, arXiv:1505.06228.

Güneş Erkan and Dragomir R. Radev. 2004. Lexrank: Graph-based centrality as salience in text summarization. *Journal of Artificial Intelligence Research*, 22(1):457–479.

Matan Eyal, Tal Baumel, and Michael Elhadad. 2019. Question answering as an automatic evaluation metric for news article summarization. In *Proceedings of the 2019 Conference of the North American Chapter of the Association for Computational Linguistics: Human Language Technologies, Volume 1*, pages 3938–3948. Association for Computational Linguistics.

Lisa Fan, Dong Yu, and Lu Wang. 2018. Robust neural abstractive summarization systems and evaluation against adversarial information. *arXiv*, arXiv:1810.06065.

Kavita Ganesan. 2018. Rouge 2.0: Updated and improved measures for evaluation of summarization tasks. *arXiv*, arXiv:1803.01937.

Yang Gao, Wei Zhao, and Steffen Eger. 2020. Supert: Towards new frontiers in unsupervised evaluation metrics for multi-document summarization. *arXiv*, arXiv:2005.03724.

Xiaotao Gu, Yuning Mao, Jiawei Han, Jialu Liu, Hongkun Yu, You Wu, Cong Yu, Daniel Finnie, Jiaqi Zhai, and Nicholas Zukoski. 2020. Generating representative headlines for news stories. In *WWW '20: Proceedings of The Web Conference 2020*, pages 1773–1784. Association for Computing Machinery, New York, 2020.

Hardy, Shashi Narayan, and Andreas Vlachos. 2019. Ehighres: Highlight-based reference-less evaluation of summarization. *arXiv*, arXiv:1906.01361.

Karl Moritz Hermann, Tomáš Kočiský, Edward Grefenstette, Lasse Espeholt, Will Kay, Mustafa Suleyman, and Phil Blunsom. 2015. Teaching machines to read and comprehend. In *Advances in Neural Information Processing Systems 28*, pages 1693–1701. Curran Associates, Inc.

Shun Kiyono, Sho Takase, Jun Suzuki, Naoaki Okazaki, Kentaro Inui, and Masaaki Nagata. 2017. Source-side prediction for neural headline generation. *arXiv*, arXiv:1712.08302.

Wojciech Kryściński, Nitish Shirish Keskar, Bryan McCann, Caiming Xiong, and Richard Socher. 2019a. Neural text summarization: A critical evaluation. In *Proceedings of the 2019 Conference on Empirical Methods in Natural Language Processing and the 9th International Joint Conference on Natural Language Processing (EMNLP-IJCNLP)*, pages 540–551. Association for Computational Linguistics.

Wojciech Kryściński, Bryan McCann, Caiming Xiong, and Richard Socher. 2019b. Evaluating the factual consistency of abstractive text summarization. *arXiv*, arXiv:1910.12840.

Chin-Yew Lin. 2004. Rouge: A package for automatic evaluation of summaries. In *Proceedings of Workshop on Text Summarization Branches Out*, pages 74–81.

Annie Louis and Ani Nenkova. 2009. Automatically evaluating content selection in summarization without human models. In *Proceedings of the 2009 Conference on Empirical Methods in Natural Language Processing*, pages 306–314. Association for Computational Linguistics.

Annie Louis and Ani Nenkova. 2013. Automatically assessing machine summary content without a gold standard. *Computational Linguistics*, 39(2):267–300.

Yuning Mao, Liyuan Liu, Qi Zhu, Xiang Ren, and Ji-awei Han. 2019. Facet-aware evaluation for extractive text summarization. *arXiv*, arXiv:1908.10383.

Jun-Ping Ng and Viktoria Abrecht. 2015. Better summarization evaluation with word embeddings for rouge. In *Proceedings of the 2015 Conference on Empirical Methods in Natural Language Processing*, pages 1925–1930. Association for Computational Linguistics.

Thomas Scialom, Sylvain Lamprier, Benjamin Piwowarski, and Jacopo Staiano. 2019. Answers unite! unsupervised metrics for reinforced summarization models. In *Proceedings of the 2019 Conference on Empirical Methods in Natural Language Processing and the 9th International Joint Conference on Natural Language Processing (EMNLP-IJCNLP)*, pages 3246–3256, Hong Kong, China. Association for Computational Linguistics.

Liqun Shao, Hao Zhang, Ming Jia, and Jie Wang. 2017. Efficient and effective single-document summarizations and a word-embedding measurement of quality. *arXiv*, arXiv:1710.00284.

Wilson L Taylor. 1953. Cloze procedure: A new tool for measuring readability. *Journalism Bulletin*, 30(4):415–433.

Oleg Vasilyev, Tom Grek, and John Bohannon. 2019. Headline generation: Learning from decomposable document titles. *arXiv*, arXiv:1904.08455v3. Version 3.

Thomas Wolf, Lysandre Debut, Victor Sanh, Julien Chaumond, Clement Delangue, Anthony Moi, Pierric Cistac, Tim Rault, Rémi Louf, Morgan Funtowicz, and Jamie Brew. 2019. Huggingface's transformers: State-of-the-art natural language processing. *arXiv*, arXiv:1910.03771.

Stratos Xenouleas, Prodromos Malakasiotis, Marianna Apidianaki, and Ion Androutsopoulos. 2019. Sumqe: a bert-based summary quality estimation model. In *Proceedings of the 2019 Conference on Empirical Methods in Natural Language Processing and the 9th International Joint Conference on Natural Language Processing (EMNLP-IJCNLP)*, pages 6005–6011, Hong Kong, China. Association for Computational Linguistics.

Peng Xu and Pascale Fung. 2019. A novel repetition normalized adversarial reward for headline generation. In *ICASSP 2019 - 2019 IEEE International Conference on Acoustics, Speech and Signal Processing (ICASSP)*, pages 7325–7329, Brighton, United Kingdom. IEEE.

Tianyi Zhang, Varsha Kishore, Felix Wu, Kilian Q. Weinberger, and Yoav Artzi. 2020. Bertscore: Evaluating text generation with bert. *arXiv*, arXiv:1904.09675v3.

Wei Zhao, Maxime Peyrard, Fei Liu, Yang Gao, Christian M. Meyer, and Steffen Eger. 2019. Moverscore: Text generation evaluating with contextualized embeddings and earth mover distance. *arXiv*, arXiv:1909.02622.

Daniel M. Ziegler, Nisan Stiennon, Jeffrey Wu, Tom B. Brown, Alec Radford, Dario Amodei, Paul Christiano, and Geoffrey Irving. 2020. Fine-tuning language models from human preferences. *arXiv*, arXiv:1909.08593v2.

Item Response Theory for Efficient Human Evaluation of Chatbots

João Sedoc
New York University
jsedoc@stern.nyu.edu

Lyle Ungar
University of Pennsylvania
ungar@cs.upenn.edu

Abstract

Conversational agent quality is currently assessed using human evaluation, and often requires an exorbitant number of comparisons to achieve statistical significance. In this paper, we introduce Item Response Theory (IRT) for chatbot evaluation, using a paired comparison in which annotators judge which system responds better to the next turn of a conversation. IRT is widely used in educational testing for simultaneously assessing the ability of test takers and the quality of test questions. It is similarly well suited for chatbot evaluation since it allows the assessment of both models and the prompts used to evaluate them. We use IRT to efficiently assess chatbots, and show that different examples from the evaluation set are better suited for comparing high-quality (nearer to human performance) than low-quality systems. Finally, we use IRT to reduce the number of evaluation examples assessed by human annotators while retaining discriminative power.

1 Introduction

One of the main problems in conversation dialog modeling is evaluation. Unlike in machine translation and task-driven dialog, automated metrics for non-task driven open-domain generative conversational models (chatbots) seem not to correlate well with human judgments (Liu et al., 2016; Tao et al., 2017; Lowe et al., 2017). While the creation of new automatic metrics is an extremely active area of research (Liu et al., 2016; Tao et al., 2017; Lowe et al., 2017; Novikova et al., 2017; Galley et al., 2015; Sugiyama et al., 2019), human annotations are currently the gold standard for assessing model improvements. Prior work mainly uses straightforward approaches, such as a two-sided t-test or binomial tests (e.g., (Serban et al., 2016; Li et al., 2015; Asghar et al., 2017; Ghazvininejad

| | | Annotator | | | Net |
		1	2	3	Rating
prompt	*are you a leader or a follower?*				0
sys A	leader	-	-	-	
sys B	follower				(tie)
prompt	*do you run faster if someone chases you?*				0
sys A	i don't run	A	-		
sys B	no, i don't.			B	(tie)
prompt	*what do you think about creativity?*				3
sys A	i think that's a very good quality.				
sys B	i have a lot of ideas and a deal.	B	B	B	
prompt	*tell me something about your house?*				-3
sys A	my house is bigger than yours.	A	A	A	
sys B	i'm not sure				
prompt	*what is immoral?*				1
sys A	the fact that you have a child.	-	-		
sys B	it is a sin.			B	
prompt	*Are you a robot?*				3
sys A	and you are?				
sys B	i am a robot	B	B	B	
prompt	*spiderman*				1
sys A	i'm not batman	A			
sys B	spiderman spiderman		B	B	

Table 1: Comparison of two system responses and aggregate of three human annotator ratings. For each prompt Net Rating $= \sum_k^{annotators} \left(w_k^{sysB} - w_k^{sysA} \right)$ where w_i^{sysA} is 1 if annotator i rated system A better and 0 otherwise, and similarly for system B. "-" indicates a tie vote.

et al., 2018; Li et al., 2019b)), or pairwise bootstrap test (e.g. Baheti et al. (2018)). These methods do not assess or incorporate the effectiveness of prompts (conversational chunks used for evaluation). Given that human evaluation is necessary, it is desirable to discriminate the performance of two different systems with minimal cost.

In this paper, we present the use of Item Response Theory (IRT) (Lord et al., 1968) to compare chatbot models using a head-to-head paired experimental (A/B test) design (e.g. Table 1), which allows for statistical significance testing and item importance identification. IRT is traditionally used to assess student "ability" based on their answers ('responses') to test questions ('items') and, simultaneously, to determine how informative each question is. Throughout this paper we use the analogy of **student ∼ A/B chatbot comparison** and **question ∼ prompt**. We apply IRT

Proceedings of the First Workshop on Evaluation and Comparison of NLP Systems (Eval4NLP), pages 21–33,
November 20, 2020. ©2020 Association for Computational Linguistics

to assess chatbot model performance based on human evaluations of chatbot responses to prompts, while simultaneously assessing how informative each prompt is.

IRT is a latent variable Bayesian model, with relative chatbot model quality (or student ability) being latent variables that probabilistically produce observable responses (one chatbot response to a prompt being judged as better than another, or a student answering a question correctly or wrong). IRT is widely used in psychometric studies (Embretson and Reise, 2013), and for paired comparison in psychological studies (Maydeu-Olivares and Brown, 2010). However, it is almost entirely ignored in natural language processing (NLP), with the exception of Hopkins and May (2013); Lalor et al. (2016); Otani et al. (2016); Lalor et al. (2019); Dras (2015).

Recent work has criticized the statistical methodology used in NLP and called for use of better statistical methods (Dror et al., 2018). Here, we present IRT as a powerful method for statistical assessment of model improvements. IRT not only **assesses the relative quality between two systems**, but also **assesses the usefulness of a prompt** in comparing systems. We show that IRT can filter and choose a subset of prompts from the evaluation set efficiently, i.e. with little loss in statistical power (Figure 2), and that IRT finds different prompts to be useful for assessing high quality vs. low quality chatbots.

Our core contribution is showing how Item Response Theory (IRT) can be used for open-domain social conversational agent (chatbot) comparison. In particular, we showcase the use of IRT in comparing multiple models for neural conversational agents. Finally, we show the utility of IRT for reducing the data collection required to evaluate chatbots by filtering evaluation set prompts. To our knowledge, this is the first work to apply IRT to chatbot evaluation and to use IRT for prompt selection in the evaluation of NLP systems.

2   Related Work

The structure of our chatbot evaluation is a comparison of two chatbots responses to each prompt. This form of head-to-head pairwise block (multiple evaluations shown to one annotator) comparison dates back at least to Thurstone (1927). Subsequently, the Bradley-Terry (BT) model has become the most common model for pairwise block comparison experiments (Bradley and Terry, 1952). Dras (2015) describes further extensions and application of the BT model to machine translation. Extended BT models can correct for dependent categorical object covariates (correlated examples) as well as subject covariates (annotator ratings) (Cattelan, 2012). As Dras (2015) points out, the BT model and IRT are similar in formulation, but IRT additionally estimates the difficulty of each item using a latent variable Bayesian model. Fixed effect BT models (Borenstein et al., 2010) or bootstrapping (Koehn, 2012) could be used to compare chatbots, but IRT's ability to assess prompts is more attractive for this task where every annotation has a non-trivial cost.

An alternative straightforward approach to assess usefulness (validity) of a prompt is item-total correlation (ITC; Guilford (1953)). However, ITC does not take the student's ability into account. In general, IRT is preferred over ITC due to the more expressive formulation. ITC is mostly used for survey analysis instead of testing. However, as a sanity check, we find that indeed prompts extremely low in discriminative power (according to IRT) also have a low item-total correlation.

There is surprisingly little work on improving statistical significance testing or prompt selection in chatbot evaluation. While this is less true for machine translation, only two prior works have used IRT for model assessment (Hopkins and May, 2013; Otani et al., 2016). Our work applies IRT in a similar fashion as Otani et al. (2016), but to chatbot evaluation instead of machine translation system evaluation. We differ from Hopkins and May (2013) and Otani et al. (2016) as follows: 1. We do pairwise comparison instead of requiring baselines - this allows for improved prompt selection as models improve. Their method is focused on WMT (batch/competition) settings whereas our work focuses on perpetual evaluation. 2. We aggregate annotators - which creates much more stable predictions (their graded mean is 1-baseline, 2-tie, 3-win) whereas ours ranges from [-3,3]. 3. We explicitly assume independence of prompts and account for their correlation and thus do not overstate significance. 4. We use IRT to reduce the total number of comparisons; Otani et al. (2016) suggest this for future work.

IRT has also been applied in NLP for dataset filtering (Lalor et al., 2016). Lalor et al. (2019) uses IRT to efficiently subsample training data based on the difficulty. We differ from Lalor et al. (2019) on prompt selection: 1. We select individual prompts based on evaluations using the discriminative ability of the prompt–not just the item difficulty. 2. We use model win rank instead of item difficulty for selecting prompts for "better" models. Both of these yield more informative prompts. Kulikov et al. (2018) use a Bayesian approach for testing for significance in interactive evaluation; however, the correlation between items is not taken into account. As in Otani et al. (2016), IRT allows us to directly compare distributions; however, the correlation between the prompts still needs to be accounted for in order not to overstate significance.

Machine Translation Much effort has been placed in machine translation for correlating human annotator judgements with automatic metrics; however, Lowe et al. (2017) showed that automatic machine translation evaluation methods do not correlate with human judgments of open-domain conversational agents. This may be due to the fact that in machine translation there is a one-to-one semantic equivalence between reference and system output, whereas this is not true in the chatbot setting. Nonetheless, relevant prior work on assessing human evaluation in machine translation is relevant to chatbot evaluation. In machine translation, shared tasks offer standard evaluation sets and workshops, which have yielded standardized results (Callison-Burch et al., 2007, 2011).

Since 2015, the Workshop on Machine Translation (WMT) uses TrueSkill (Herbrich et al., 2007) for model ranking. TrueSkill can also be applied to chatbot evaluation. Sakaguchi et al. (2014) used it to efficiently pair machine translation systems and compared them using random subsets of data. They show that their non-parametric method is empirically superior in accuracy to Hopkins and May (2013). However, this comparison is limited since the non-parametric might focus only on one axis of difference similar to stochastic gradient descent. Returning to our student analogy, in an example of students taking the SAT (an English *and* a Math test), the TrueSkill method might focus on only the Math portion to discriminate between students, whereas, IRT would use both portions. Trueskill does not select examples using item utility.

Otani et al. (2016) and Hopkins and May (2013) applied IRT to machine translation. IRT is more important in chatbot evaluation than in machine translation as human evaluation is rarely reported in machine translation papers (e.g. (Sutskever et al., 2014; Vaswani et al., 2017)), but is rarely omitted in chatbot comparison (e.g. Liu et al. (2016); Serban et al. (2016); Li et al. (2017); Baheti et al. (2018); Li et al. (2019b); Zhang et al. (2019); Adiwardana et al. (2020)). Comparison of conversational generative agents using next utterance generation is in many ways similar to the evaluation of machine translation (MT); however, differentiating between chatbot models is uniquely challenging; many more responses than translations are plausible. Automated evaluation of MT is vastly better than of chatbots (Liu et al., 2016). The higher costs of human evaluation strongly encourage the use of more powerful statistical models such as IRT.

3 Chatbot Evaluation

Recently researchers tend to evaluate their methodological improvements relative to a sequence-to-sequence (Seq2Seq) baseline (Sutskever et al., 2014), as proposed for utterance generation by Shang et al. (2015); Vinyals and Le (2015); Sordoni et al. (2015) as well to compare against each other. While crowd-sourcing experiments are relatively cheap, the lack of automatic metrics means that every change in model architecture requires new evaluations. Our goal is efficient and cost-effective model assessment. Ideally, chatbots would be interactively evaluated, but due to the high cost, next utterance simulation is used as a surrogate. Although next utterance generation is a more artificial task, Logacheva et al. (2018) observed a Pearson correlation of 0.6 between conversation-level and utterance-level ratings.

Human judgments are often inconsistent for non-task driven chatbots, since there is no clear objective, which leads to low inter-annotator agreement (IAA) (Sedoc et al., 2019; Yuwono et al., 2019). However, Amidei et al. (2019) point out that even with low IAA we can still find statistical significance. There are further tensions between local coherence assessments using standard evaluation sets and human interactive evaluation. These issues are exacerbated for non task-driven dialog systems, as there is rarely a single "correct" response, leading to more local minima. Thus, there is a need to obtain the maximum possible statistical power at the minimal possible cost.

Novikova et al. (2018) found that relative rankings yield more discriminative results than absolute assessments when evaluating natural language generation. Recent work of Li et al. (2019a) introduce both human-bot as well as self-chat for interactive evaluation and show that this is more effective than conversation-level Likert scales.

4   IRT for Chatbot Evaluation

We pose chatbot human evaluation as an Item Response Theory (IRT) problem, similar to the approach of Otani et al. (2016). Again, throughout this section we consider the analogy of **student $\sim$ A/B chatbot comparison** and **question $\sim$ prompt**. In the context of educational testing, we are seeking to find the ability of a student and the effectiveness of exam questions (e.g. SAT exam) which in our setting is the comparative difference in pairs of chatbots.

As seen in Table 1, we sum the wins minus losses for each human evaluation of a pair of chatbot systems for each prompt; this net rating ranges between $[n, -n]$ where n is the number of annotators. In the student analogy, this is equivalent to an exam question worth $2n$ points. This is a well-studied problem, the so called the "graded mean" formulation of IRT (Samejima, 1969).

We first introduce the graded mean formulation of IRT required to estimate the relative assessment of chatbots and the discriminative power of the prompts. Subsequently, we describe the exact problem formulation in our setting.

4.1   Item Response Theory

The core idea behind IRT is that the probability that student i gets each question (item) j correct depends both on the ability of the student and the difficulty of the question. IRT aims to assess a latent ability trait θ_i for each student i from their answers u_j^i to items j, and, simultaneously, to determine how informative each item j is. This informativeness depends on the ability of the student; one wants to give harder questions to good students and easier questions to weaker students. IRT is a latent variable Bayesian model that can be estimated via expectation maximization (EM) or variational inference. For a comprehensive exposition of IRT see Embretson and Reise (2013).

More formally, we use the *graded mean* IRT model in which the probability that a student i

obtains a score above c (the "rated scale assignment") for question j (Andrich, 1978). $P_{ijc}(\theta_i)$, the probability that student score (or aggregate chatbot rating), $u_j^i > c$, is given by

$$
\begin{aligned}
P_{ijc}(\theta_i) &= P_{ij}(u_j^i \geq c \mid \theta_i, b_j, \alpha_j) \\
&= \sigma(\alpha_j(\theta_i - b_{jc})) \\
&= \frac{1}{1 + \exp(-\alpha_j(\theta_i - b_{jc}))},
\end{aligned}
$$

where σ is the logistic function. b_{jc} is the item (j-th question) difficulty for the score c (e.g. to score 4 or more points out of 6 on an exam question), α_j is the slope or item's *discrimination* (measuring how informative the question is for measuring the student's ability), and θ_i is the latent *ability* of student i.[1] Better questions (higher α_j) allow investigators to determine which student is better with fewer questions. We will use this same model to test which chatbot is better using fewer prompts.

In order to make this model generative, we can define

$$
\begin{aligned}
P_{ij}(u_j^i = c \mid \theta_i, b_j, \alpha_j) &= P_{ij}(u_j^i \geq c - 1 \mid \theta_i, b_j, \alpha_j) \\
&\quad - P_{ij}(u_j^i \geq c \mid \theta_i, b_j, \alpha_j).
\end{aligned}
$$

If $c \in [-3, 3]$ then $P_{ij-3}(\theta_i) = 1$ and $P_{ij4}(\theta_i) = 0$. IRT is a latent variable Bayesian model, where θ_i, b_j, and $\log(\alpha_j)$ have priors from a normal distribution. The model is estimated by gradient descent.

4.2   Problem Setting

IRT can be easily repurposed for chatbot evaluation. Rather than assessing individuals i based on their answers to exam questions j, we assess the relative rating (preference) between two chatbot models i based on their responses to conversational prompts j. Instead of teachers (or ETS) grading the students' answers, human raters now rate the chatbot responses. The overall score for a chatbot for each item is the accumulated annotator preferences for that chatbot over its competitor. The score for chatbot B compared against chatbot A for item j is

$$
u_j^{B/A} = \sum_{k=1}^{\text{num annotators}} (w_{kj}^B - w_{kj}^A),
$$

---

[1] Our formulation is slightly simpler than the canonical graded mean formulation since c is a fixed finite number. Thus, the asymptotes for the item response function (IRF) need not be estimated.

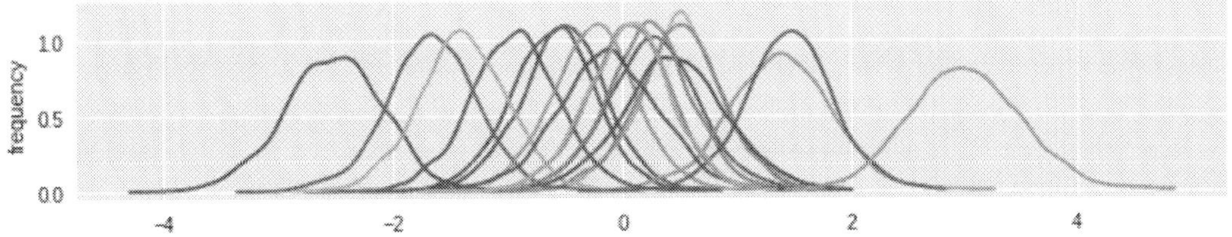

Figure 1: Each curve shows the estimated distribution of difference (inverse logit) in assessed quality between a pair of two different chatbot models produced by our Bayesian IRT model. The mode of each curve is the expected value of the quality difference, and zero means that the models are believed to be equally good.

where $w_{kj}^A = 1$ and $w_{kj}^B = 0$ if for prompt j the k-th annotator chose model A as having a better response; values are reversed if model B was preferred (see examples in Table 1).[2] The resulting *ability score* $\theta_i \in \mathbb{R}$ is then the relative "ability" (i.e. assessed quality) of models $i =$ A vs B. Figure 1 shows a distribution of ability across multiple pairwise comparisons of models.

A critical difference between our formulation and that of Otani et al. (2016) is that we explicitly account for the independence of prompts, and do not model individual annotators k. Estimating a model of individual annotators would require many annotations for each annotator, which is not practical for estimator convergence.

IRT gives an optimal way to combine item results (given the modeling assumptions). It is flexible in that one need not make comparisons for all items for all chatbot pairs. In order to avoid overstating statistical significance, we group covariate prompts using a simple correlation filter (> 0.6) over all experiments.[3] In order to keep the net rating in $[-3, 3]$, we average the scores in the group. Note that this is the most conservative possible choice. We further control for multiple testing error by analyzing all comparisons simultaneously (Miller, 1981). As more comparisons are made, more information is revealed about the prompts in the evaluation dataset.

5   Experimental Details

While human evaluation remains the gold standard for dialog research, the design of human evaluation experiments is far from standard. We restrict our analysis to designs where the annotator is shown a prompt and two possible responses and then asked to select the better one or specify a tie. We follow the setup of Sedoc et al. (2019) (see the Appendix for instruction to Amazon Mechanical Turk crowd workers).

5.1   System Descriptions

We conducted a series of experiments to establish high-quality baselines for several popular training sets to show the efficacy of our proposed method. We compared our baselines against the OpenNMT benchmark for dialog systems[4]; Cakechat[5], which is a reimplementation of the hierarchical encoder-decoder model (HRED) (Serban et al., 2016); and the Neural Conversation Model's (NCM) released responses from Vinyals and Le (2015). Cakechat was trained on Twitter data, and NCM and Open-NMT benchmark were trained on movie subtitle data from OpenSubtitles (Tiedemann, 2012). We also evaluated two state-of-the-art Transformer base models: DialoGPT[6] medium (Zhang et al., 2019) and Blender (2.7B)[7] (Roller et al., 2020). Two human baselines created by Sedoc et al. (2019) were used.

All other models were trained with OpenNMT-py (Klein et al., 2017) Seq2Seq implementation with its default parameters: two layers of LSTMs with 512 hidden neurons for the bidirectional encoder and the unidirectional decoder. We trained several models and chose the best using non-exhaustive human evaluation.[8] *OpenNMT_Seq2SeqAttn* is trained using OpenSubtitles (Tiedemann, 2012) and *Seq2SeqAttn_OpenSubtitles_Questions* is trained using pairs where the first utterance ends in a

---

[2]If the number of annotators is variable, then we scale u_j^i to a fixed range which here we set to $[-3, 3]$.

[3]We calculate the correlation of judgments u_j^i between all prompts over all annotators and evaluations.

[4]http://opennmt.net/Models-py/

[5]https://github.com/lukalabs/cakechat from Replika.ai.

[6]https://github.com/microsoft/DialoGPT

[7]https://parl.ai/

[8]We experimented with whether or not to use pre-trained word embeddings, the impact of optimizer stochasticity, and various types of data preprocessing.

question mark and the second does not. Finally, *Seq2SeqAttn_Twitter* was trained on Twitter micro-blogging data as originally done by Ritter et al. (2010).[9] All of the data was extracted and tokenized using ParlAI (Miller et al., 2017).[10]

5.2 Selection of Evaluation Set

Our evaluation set is the list of 200 questions released by Vinyals and Le (2015) in their seminal work on neural conversational models using a standard Seq2Seq framework borrowed from machine translation. The evaluation set is handcrafted and there are several correlated examples, such as the prompts *are you a follower or a leader ?* and *are you a leader or a follower ?* This quality is not unique to this evaluation dataset.

5.3 Human Evaluation Details

The evaluation prompts are split into blocks (currently defaulted to 10)[11]. We used the same experimental setup as Sedoc et al. (2019). The overall inter-annotator agreement (IAA) varies depending on the vagueness of the prompt as well as the similarity of the models. The overall IAA as measured by Fleiss' kappa (Fleiss, 1971) varies between .2 to .54 if we include tie choices. As Dras (2015) note, there is little agreement in the community on how to handle tie choices. Our IAA is similar to the findings of Yuwono et al. (2019) who also found low inter-annotator agreement when assessing conversational turns.

Unfortunately, "bad" workers accounted for roughly seven percent of all annotations, which we remove from our results. To identify such workers, we examine the worker annotation against the other two annotations. We remove annotators whose correlation is not statistically significantly greater than 0. It is important to note two things 1) the two annotations are likely more than two other workers since we have a minimum of 3 annotators and a maximum of 60, and 2) unless the "bad" worker is adversarial (i.e. labeling the opposite of the correct judgment) and instead just randomly labels, then the annotator will lower inter-annotator agreement, but IRT will not be significantly affected (Hopkins and May, 2013). How-

ever, "bad" workers will create bias in the estimate of mean difference (a.k.a. ability) of models to be closer to 0 (see the Appendix for further details).

6 Results

We used IRT to compare multiple neural models for their relative strength. Furthermore, we also included human baselines in our model comparison. Finally, we assessed the discriminative quality of the hand-crafted prompts from Vinyals and Le (2015).

6.1 Model Comparison Results

A comparison of the models described in section 5.1 is in Table 3 (all model comparisons are in the Appendix).[12] By analyzing the significance of all of the models at once using IRT, we can correct for multiple testing (Miller, 1981). I.e., given multiple comparisons, by chance a comparison might look statistically significant if naively using a p-value of 0.05.

Overall, there is a roughly uniform distribution of ratings (see the appendix for more detail). The grade is from -3 to 3 since there are 3 annotators per prompt for all but one experiment.

As seen in Table 3 the NCM (Vinyals and Le, 2015) model performance cannot be matched by any other model, even though all models are based on Seq2Seq. This indicates that either baseline models are difficult to properly train and parameterize, or that the NCM model may be overfit for the evaluation set. Interestingly, there are not enough ratings to evaluate whether NCM is worse than our human baselines. NCM also seems to outperform both Blender as well as DialoGPT; however, these results are not statistically significant. Blender is designed for multi-turn interactions, so single-turn prompts may not be a fair comparison.

Note, that IRT does not yield a total ordering of systems. In pairwise comparisons between Cakechat and Seq2SeqAttn_Twitter and Seq2SeqAttn_OpenSubtitles, Cakechat is superior to Seq2SeqAttn_Twitter. However, Seq2SeqAttn_OpenSubtitles is almost statistically significantly better than Cakechat, while Seq2SeqAttn_Twitter and Seq2SeqAttn_OpenSubtitles are rated to have equivalent performance. One possible rea-

---

[9]From `https://github.com/Marsan-Ma/chat_corpus/raw/master/`.

[10]`https://github.com/facebookresearch/ParlAI`

[11]We used the code from ChatEval `https://github.com/chateval/chateval/`

[12]We used pyStan for our IRT. Our code is available on Google Colab.

System A	System B	Mean Δ Ability	Std Δ Ability
Human2	Human1	-0.356	0.256
Human2	Seq2SeqAttn_Twitter	-2.760*	0.291
Human2	Seq2SeqAttn_OpenSubtitles_Ques	-2.015*	0.265
Human2	NCM	-0.377	0.324
Human1	Seq2SeqAttn_Twitter	-1.980*	0.269
Human1	NCM	0.224	0.262
NCM	DialoGPT	-0.223	0.245
NCM	Blender (2.7B)	-0.347	0.256
NCM	Cakechat	-0.715*	0.261
NCM	Seq2SeqAttn_Twitter	-1.426*	0.274
NCM	OpenNMT_Seq2SeqAttn	-1.034*	0.287
Cakechat	Seq2SeqAttn_Twitter	-0.529*	0.268
Cakechat	OpenNMT_Seq2SeqAttn	0.125	0.262
Cakechat	Seq2SeqAttn_OpenSubtitles	0.460	0.281
Seq2SeqAttn_OpenSubtitles	Seq2SeqAttn_OpenSubtitles_Ques	0.295	0.274
Seq2SeqAttn_OpenSubtitles	Seq2SeqAttn_Twitter	0.052	0.274
Seq2SeqAttn_OpenSubtitles	OpenNMT_Seq2SeqAttn	0.177	0.318

Table 2: The mean and standard deviation of "ability" (inverse logit) of paired comparisons of various models, where overlap with zero indicates no difference. Larger positive indicates that System B is superior in terms of rating by human annotators and similarly smaller negative numbers mean that System A is superior. (* shows significant differences $p < 0.05$ and better system is in bold.)

son for this might be that both Cakechat and Seq2SeqAttn_Twitter are trained on Twitter, so their model responses are more directly comparable.

6.2 Evaluation Set Selection

In order to minimize the numbers of evaluations required to assess the relative performance of models, we first removed redundant prompts, and then used IRT to select the prompts that were most discriminative.

IRT evaluates the discriminative ability of each prompt independently, so first we analyzed the correlation structure of responses over all evaluations and removed redundant prompts. By construction, the NCM evaluation set has correlated examples such as *my name is david . what is my name ?* and *my name is john . what is my name ?* Most models generate similar responses to both examples, and as a result, human judgments will correlate. Thus, we can use a smaller evaluation set while achieving similar significance. Defining redundancy as a correlation > 0.6 removes 6 out of 200 prompts.

To test the effect of using IRT to select prompts, we use a leave-one-out design, i.e. we keep 19 model comparisons and then select a subset of

prompts with the most discriminative power for the 20th out-of-sample comparison. It is important to note that the most discriminative prompts (α_j) are usually not the most difficult ones (b_jc). This is different from Lalor et al. (2019) who use training example difficultly.

Figure 2 shows the change in the standard error of the ability estimates as we reduced the number of prompts. Our main result is that selecting just 100 of the 200 prompts using IRT maintains the same standard error, while selecting 100 random prompts gives a significantly higher error. Thus, using IRT allows us to reliably compare methods using fewer prompts.

Different Prompts for Better Students Finally, we assessed the effect of model quality on chatbot evaluation. Intuitively, one wants harder questions for better students. Similarly, an example such as *my name is david . what is my name ?* is an easier prompt than *what is the purpose of being intelligent ?* However, two models that are closer to human parity will only be distinguishable by the latter example. Similarly, for models further from human performance, both would perform poorly for example *OpenNMT Seq2Seq: I don 't know .* and *CakeChat: i ' m not sure what to say .* Using

IRT, we were able to validate this intuition across multiple models.

We split systems into two categories "better" - (NCM, DialoGPT, Blender, and Cakechat) and the other systems (e.g. OpenNMT) by sorting using mean Δ ability (Table 3). For each set of chatbots, we re-estimate the ability and item difficulty using only the subset of comparisons within each category (i.e., better chatbots are only compared against other better chatbots). We report the average standard error of difference of ability estimates of the left-out comparisons when using IRT with the most discriminative prompts. Thus, different prompts are selected for the better chatbots than for the others. The number of prompts was reduced while maintaining discriminative power as measured by standard error of discriminative ability (Figure 2); using prompts customized to each group yields lower standard error than using the globally "best" prompts. As the number of models increases, such filtering based on model quality further improves samplewise efficiency. IRT prompt selection using model quality allows us to dynamically update the evaluation set to adapt to better models.

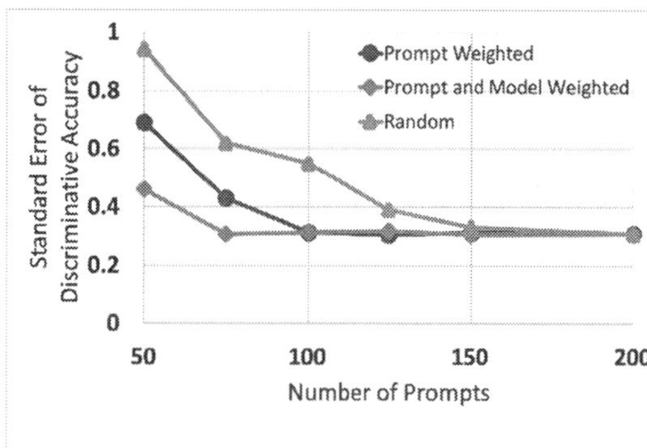

Figure 2: Standard error of discriminative accuracy as a function of the number of prompts. We compare selecting random subset (Random) to selecting prompts (Prompt Weighted), and both prompt difficulty and model performance (Prompt and Model Weighted).

Our work generalizes beyond the evaluation set from Vinyals and Le (2015). While other evaluation sets, such as random subsets of Twitter or OpenSubtitles may have fewer covariate prompts, there are many examples where further conversational context is required causing the prompts to have low discriminative power. For example, the prompt from the Twitter evaluation set (Sedoc et al., 2019), *Not really* is difficult to respond to

without conversational context causing the prompt to have low discriminative power. Also, our method is not limited to single-turn prompts; however, for this case study, we focus on the available evaluation set. Multi-turn prompts such as **A:** *Was this useful to you?* **B:** *Yes* **A:** *Ok* are not very useful since almost any future response is valid. Initial results show that we can use IRT to automatically filter such uninformative prompts instead of hand-curating an evaluation set.

7 Conclusion

We present a new method for incorporating IRT into chatbot evaluation and show that we can use IRT to adaptively and optimally weight prompts from the evaluation sets, eliminating less informative prompts. One of the strengths of our method is that prompt discriminative ability and difficulty are re-estimated as new evaluations are added. One can thus start with a larger evaluation set, such as a subset from the Cornell Movie Database (Danescu-Niculescu-Mizil and Lee, 2011) and continue refining the subset of the evaluation set. We showed that our method is effective with the NCM evaluation set. Applying it to the Cornell Movie Database evaluation set of Baheti et al. (2018), we found that we could reduce from 1000 to 150 prompts with negligible loss of accuracy. When evaluating a new model, one would start with a comparison, say against a human baseline on a large set of prompts, then against a similarly ranked model using an appropriate subset of prompts. After each evaluation, the accuracy of all comparisons will increase. IRT can also be used to adapt evaluation sets as chatbot models improve in performance, reducing annotation costs.

While our main exposition addresses single turn prompts for chatbot evaluation, our IRT model comparison method generalizes to many natural language generation tasks, including machine translation and text simplification. It also generalizes to multi-turn prompts, point-wise evaluation, pairwise conversational evaluation (e.g. Acute-Eval (Li et al., 2019a)), and interactive evaluations such as those of Kulikov et al. (2019).

Acknowledgments

We thank the reviewers for their insightful comments.

This work was partially supported by the Amazon AWS Cloud Credits for Research program. This work was supported in part by DARPA KAIROS (FA8750-19-2-0034). The views and conclusions contained in this work are those of the authors and should not be interpreted as representing official policies or endorsements by DARPA or the U.S. Government.

References

Daniel Adiwardana, Minh-Thang Luong, David R So, Jamie Hall, Noah Fiedel, Romal Thoppilan, Zi Yang, Apoorv Kulshreshtha, Gaurav Nemade, Yifeng Lu, et al. 2020. Towards a human-like open-domain chatbot. *arXiv preprint arXiv:2001.09977*.

Jacopo Amidei, Paul Piwek, and Alistair Willis. 2019. Agreement is overrated: A plea for correlation to assess human evaluation reliability. In *Proceedings of the 12th International Conference on Natural Language Generation*, pages 344–354, Tokyo, Japan. Association for Computational Linguistics.

David Andrich. 1978. A rating formulation for ordered response categories. *Psychometrika*, 43(4):561–573.

Nabiha Asghar, Pascal Poupart, Xin Jiang, and Hang Li. 2017. Deep active learning for dialogue generation. In *Proceedings of the 6th Joint Conference on Lexical and Computational Semantics (*SEM 2017)*, pages 78–83. Association for Computational Linguistics.

Ashutosh Baheti, Alan Ritter, Jiwei Li, and Bill Dolan. 2018. Generating more interesting responses in neural conversation models with distributional constraints. In *Proceedings of the 2018 Conference on Empirical Methods in Natural Language Processing*, pages 3970–3980, Brussels, Belgium. Association for Computational Linguistics.

Michael Borenstein, Larry V Hedges, Julian PT Higgins, and Hannah R Rothstein. 2010. A basic introduction to fixed-effect and random-effects models for meta-analysis. *Research synthesis methods*, 1(2):97–111.

Ralph Allan Bradley and Milton E Terry. 1952. Rank analysis of incomplete block designs: I. the method of paired comparisons. *Biometrika*, 39(3/4):324–345.

Chris Callison-Burch, Cameron Fordyce, Philipp Koehn, Christof Monz, and Josh Schroeder. 2007. (meta-) evaluation of machine translation. In *Proceedings of the Second Workshop on Statistical Machine Translation*, pages 136–158, Prague, Czech Republic. Association for Computational Linguistics.

Chris Callison-Burch, Philipp Koehn, Christof Monz, and Omar Zaidan. 2011. Findings of the 2011 workshop on statistical machine translation. In *Proceedings of the Sixth Workshop on Statistical Machine Translation*, pages 22–64, Edinburgh, Scotland. Association for Computational Linguistics.

Manuela Cattelan. 2012. Models for paired comparison data: A review with emphasis on dependent data. *Statistical Science*, pages 412–433.

Cristian Danescu-Niculescu-Mizil and Lillian Lee. 2011. Chameleons in imagined conversations: A new approach to understanding coordination of linguistic style in dialogs. In *Proceedings of the 2nd Workshop on Cognitive Modeling and Computational Linguistics*, pages 76–87, Portland, Oregon, USA. Association for Computational Linguistics.

Mark Dras. 2015. Evaluating human pairwise preference judgments. *Computational Linguistics*, 41(2):337–345.

Rotem Dror, Gili Baumer, Segev Shlomov, and Roi Reichart. 2018. The hitchhiker's guide to testing statistical significance in natural language processing. In *Proceedings of the 56th Annual Meeting of the Association for Computational Linguistics (Volume 1: Long Papers)*, pages 1383–1392. Association for Computational Linguistics.

Susan E Embretson and Steven P Reise. 2013. *Item response theory*. Psychology Press.

Joseph L Fleiss. 1971. Measuring nominal scale agreement among many raters. *Psychological bulletin*, 76(5):378.

Michel Galley, Chris Brockett, Alessandro Sordoni, Yangfeng Ji, Michael Auli, Chris Quirk, Margaret Mitchell, Jianfeng Gao, and Bill Dolan. 2015. deltaBLEU: A discriminative metric for generation tasks with intrinsically diverse targets. In *Proceedings of the 53rd Annual Meeting of the Association for Computational Linguistics and the 7th International Joint Conference on Natural Language Processing (Volume 2: Short Papers)*, pages 445–450, Beijing, China. Association for Computational Linguistics.

Marjan Ghazvininejad, Chris Brockett, Ming-Wei Chang, Bill Dolan, Jianfeng Gao, Scott Wen-tau Yih, and Michel Galley. 2018. A knowledge-grounded neural conversation model. In *AAAI*.

Joy P Guilford. 1953. The correlation of an item with a composite of the remaining items in a test. *Educational and Psychological Measurement*, 13(1):87–93.

Ralf Herbrich, Tom Minka, and Thore Graepel. 2007. Trueskill: a bayesian skill rating system. In *Advances in neural information processing systems*, pages 569–576.

Mark Hopkins and Jonathan May. 2013. Models of translation competitions. In *Proceedings of the 51st Annual Meeting of the Association for Computational Linguistics (Volume 1: Long Papers)*, pages 1416–1424, Sofia, Bulgaria. Association for Computational Linguistics.

Guillaume Klein, Yoon Kim, Yuntian Deng, Jean Senellart, and Alexander Rush. 2017. Opennmt: Open-source toolkit for neural machine translation. In *ACL, System Demonstrations*, pages 67–72. Association for Computational Linguistics.

Philipp Koehn. 2012. Simulating human judgment in machine translation evaluation campaigns. In *International Workshop on Spoken Language Translation (IWSLT) 2012*.

Ilia Kulikov, Alexander Miller, Kyunghyun Cho, and Jason Weston. 2019. Importance of search and evaluation strategies in neural dialogue modeling. In *Proceedings of the 12th International Conference on Natural Language Generation*, pages 76–87, Tokyo, Japan. Association for Computational Linguistics.

Ilya Kulikov, Alexander H Miller, Kyunghyun Cho, and Jason Weston. 2018. Importance of a search strategy in neural dialogue modelling. *arXiv preprint arXiv:1811.00907*.

John P. Lalor, Hao Wu, and Hong Yu. 2016. Building an evaluation scale using item response theory. In *Proceedings of the 2016 Conference on Empirical Methods in Natural Language Processing*, pages 648–657, Austin, Texas. Association for Computational Linguistics.

John P. Lalor, Hao Wu, and Hong Yu. 2019. Learning latent parameters without human response patterns: Item response theory with artificial crowds. In *Proceedings of the 2019 Conference on Empirical Methods in Natural Language Processing and the 9th International Joint Conference on Natural Language Processing (EMNLP-IJCNLP)*, pages 4249–4259, Hong Kong, China. Association for Computational Linguistics.

Jiwei Li, Michel Galley, Chris Brockett, Jianfeng Gao, and Bill Dolan. 2015. A Diversity-Promoting Objective Function for Neural Conversation Models.

Jiwei Li, Will Monroe, and Dan Jurafsky. 2017. Data Distillation for Controlling Specificity in Dialogue Generation.

Margaret Li, Jason Weston, and Stephen Roller. 2019a. Acute-eval: Improved dialogue evaluation with optimized questions and multi-turn comparisons. *arXiv preprint arXiv:1909.03087*.

Ziming Li, Julia Kiseleva, and Maarten de Rijke. 2019b. Dialogue generation: From imitation learning to inverse reinforcement learning. In *Proceedings of the AAAI Conference on Artificial Intelligence*, volume 33, pages 6722–6729.

Chia-Wei Liu, Ryan Lowe, Iulian Serban, Mike Noseworthy, Laurent Charlin, and Joelle Pineau. 2016. How NOT to evaluate your dialogue system: An empirical study of unsupervised evaluation metrics for dialogue response generation. In *Proceedings of the 2016 Conference on Empirical Methods in Natural Language Processing*, pages 2122–2132, Austin, Texas. Association for Computational Linguistics.

Varvara Logacheva, Mikhail Burtsev, Valentin Malykh, Vadim Poluliakh, Alexander Rudnicky, Iulian Serban, Ryan Lowe, Shrimai Prabhumoye, Alan W Black, and Yoshua Bengio. 2018. A dataset of topic-oriented human-to-chatbot dialogues.

FM Lord, MR Novick, and Allan Birnbaum. 1968. Statistical theories of mental test scores.

Ryan Lowe, Michael Noseworthy, Iulian Vlad Serban, Nicolas Angelard-Gontier, Yoshua Bengio, and Joelle Pineau. 2017. Towards an automatic turing test: Learning to evaluate dialogue responses. In *ACL*, pages 1116–1126. Association for Computational Linguistics.

Alberto Maydeu-Olivares and Anna Brown. 2010. Item response modeling of paired comparison and ranking data. *Multivariate Behavioral Research*, 45(6):935–974.

Alexander Miller, Will Feng, Dhruv Batra, Antoine Bordes, Adam Fisch, Jiasen Lu, Devi Parikh, and Jason Weston. 2017. ParlAI: A dialog research software platform. In *Proceedings of the 2017 Conference on Empirical Methods in Natural Language Processing: System Demonstrations*, pages 79–84, Copenhagen, Denmark. Association for Computational Linguistics.

Rupert G Miller. 1981. Simultaneous statistical inference.

Jekaterina Novikova, Ondřej Dušek, Amanda Cercas Curry, and Verena Rieser. 2017. Why we need new evaluation metrics for nlg.

Jekaterina Novikova, Ondřej Dušek, and Verena Rieser. 2018. RankME: Reliable human ratings for natural language generation. In *Proceedings of the 2018 Conference of the North American Chapter of the Association for Computational Linguistics: Human Language Technologies, Volume 2 (Short Papers)*, pages 72–78, New Orleans, Louisiana. Association for Computational Linguistics.

Naoki Otani, Toshiaki Nakazawa, Daisuke Kawahara, and Sadao Kurohashi. 2016. IRT-based aggregation model of crowdsourced pairwise comparison for evaluating machine translations. In *Proceedings of the 2016 Conference on Empirical Methods in Natural Language Processing*, pages 511–520, Austin, Texas. Association for Computational Linguistics.

Alan Ritter, Colin Cherry, and Bill Dolan. 2010. Unsupervised modeling of twitter conversations. In *Human Language Technologies: The 2010 Annual Conference of the North American Chapter of the Association for Computational Linguistics*, pages 172–180, Los Angeles, California. Association for Computational Linguistics.

Stephen Roller, Emily Dinan, Naman Goyal, Da Ju, Mary Williamson, Yinhan Liu, Jing Xu, Myle Ott, Kurt Shuster, Eric M Smith, et al. 2020. Recipes for building an open-domain chatbot. *arXiv preprint arXiv:2004.13637*.

Keisuke Sakaguchi, Matt Post, and Benjamin Van Durme. 2014. Efficient elicitation of annotations for human evaluation of machine translation. In *Proceedings of the Ninth Workshop on Statistical Machine Translation*, pages 1–11, Baltimore, Maryland, USA. Association for Computational Linguistics.

Fumiko Samejima. 1969. Estimation of latent ability using a response pattern of graded scores. *Psychometrika monograph supplement*.

João Sedoc, Daphne Ippolito, Arun Kirubarajan, Jai Thirani, Lyle Ungar, and Chris Callison-Burch. 2019. ChatEval: A tool for chatbot evaluation. In *Proceedings of the 2019 Conference of the North American Chapter of the Association for Computational Linguistics (Demonstrations)*, pages 60–65, Minneapolis, Minnesota. Association for Computational Linguistics.

Iulian Vlad Serban, Alessandro Sordoni, Ryan Lowe, Laurent Charlin, Joelle Pineau, Aaron Courville, and Yoshua Bengio. 2016. A Hierarchical Latent Variable Encoder-Decoder Model for Generating Dialogues.

Lifeng Shang, Zhengdong Lu, and Hang Li. 2015. Neural responding machine for short-text conversation. In *Proceedings of the 53rd ACL*, pages 1577–1586, Beijing, China. Association for Computational Linguistics.

Alessandro Sordoni, Michel Galley, Michael Auli, Chris Brockett, Yangfeng Ji, Margaret Mitchell, Jian-Yun Nie, Jianfeng Gao, and Bill Dolan. 2015. A neural network approach to context-sensitive generation of conversational responses. In *Proceedings of the 2015 Conference of the NAACL-HLT*, pages 196–205, Denver, Colorado. Association for Computational Linguistics.

Hiroaki Sugiyama, Toyomi Meguro, and Ryuichiro Higashinaka. 2019. Automatic evaluation of chat-oriented dialogue systems using large-scale multi-references. In *Advanced Social Interaction with Agents*, pages 15–25. Springer.

Ilya Sutskever, Oriol Vinyals, and Quoc V. Le. 2014. Sequence to sequence learning with neural networks. In Z. Ghahramani, M. Welling, C. Cortes, N. D. Lawrence, and K. Q. Weinberger, editors, *Advances in Neural Information Processing Systems 27*, pages 3104–3112. Curran Associates, Inc.

Chongyang Tao, Lili Mou, Dongyan Zhao, and Rui Yan. 2017. RUBER: An Unsupervised Method for Automatic Evaluation of Open-Domain Dialog Systems.

Louis L Thurstone. 1927. A law of comparative judgment. *Psychological review*, 34(4):273.

Jörg Tiedemann. 2012. Parallel data, tools and interfaces in opus. In *Lrec*, volume 2012, pages 2214–2218.

Ashish Vaswani, Noam Shazeer, Niki Parmar, Jakob Uszkoreit, Llion Jones, Aidan N Gomez, Ł ukasz Kaiser, and Illia Polosukhin. 2017. Attention is all you need. In I. Guyon, U. V. Luxburg, S. Bengio, H. Wallach, R. Fergus, S. Vishwanathan, and R. Garnett, editors, *Advances in Neural Information Processing Systems 30*, pages 5998–6008. Curran Associates, Inc.

Oriol Vinyals and Quoc V. Le. 2015. A Neural Conversational Model. *Natural Language Dialog Systems and Intelligent Assistants*, 37:233–239.

Steven Kester Yuwono, Biao Wu, and Luis Fernando DHaro. 2019. Automated scoring of chatbot responses in conversational dialogue. In *9th International Workshop on Spoken Dialogue System Technology*, pages 357–369. Springer.

Yizhe Zhang, Siqi Sun, Michel Galley, Yen-Chun Chen, Chris Brockett, Xiang Gao, Jianfeng Gao, Jingjing Liu, and Bill Dolan. 2019. Dialogpt: Large-scale generative pre-training for conversational response generation. *arXiv preprint arXiv:1911.00536*.

A Further Human Evaluation Details

Crowd workers are paid $0.01 per prompt, and on average it takes 1 minute to evaluate 10 choices with a maximum allowed time of 2 minutes. We used three evaluators per prompt, so, if there are 200 prompts, we have 600 ratings and the net cost of the experiment is $7.2. We chose 3 annotators since we can generalize enough for IAA and it is cost-effective.

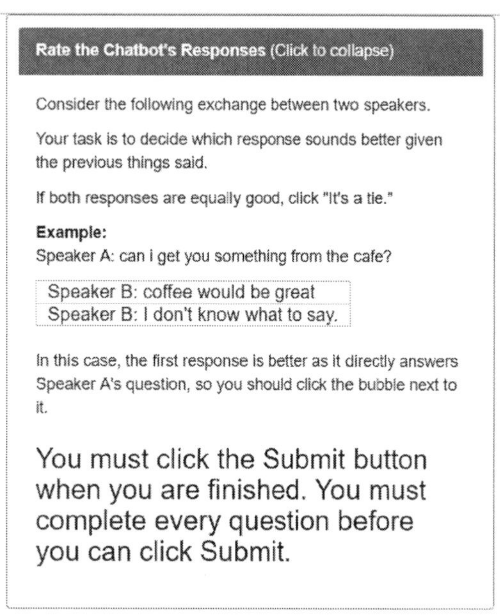

Figure 3: The instructions seen by AMT workers.

The instructions seen by AMT workers are shown in Figure 3.

We removed workers with a correlation below 0.05 with other annotators. For a worker identified as "bad", all annotations are removed. Including these workers only increases the standard error by 10%.

From the 200 NCM evaluation set prompts, each annotation task has 10 prompts; however, we do not pair the same 3 workers to the 10 prompts; instead we randomize the prompts shown, so worker 1 many compare prompts 1-10, while worker 2 compares prompts 2,3,5,7,9,11,13,17,19,23. As a result, the correlation between one worker and the others is more stable.

A full set of model comparisons on the Neural Conversation Model is available in Table 3.

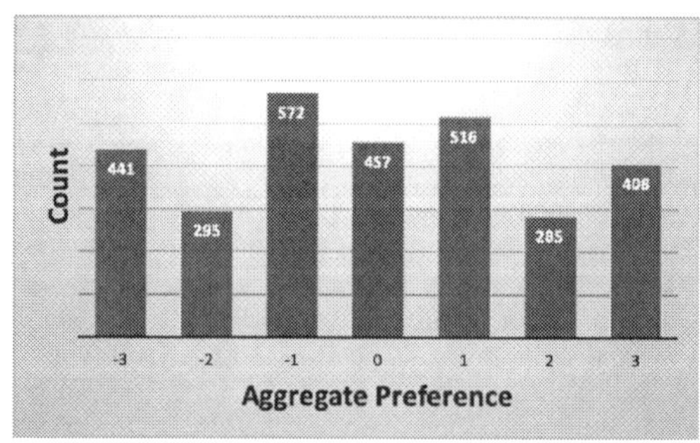

Figure 4: A histogram of aggregated preferences, $\sum_i \sum_j u_j^i$, across all prompts and model comparisons by all annotators.

A.1 Rating Distribution

Figure 4 shows a histogram of the grades over all experiments run.

System A	System B	Mean Δ Ability	Std Δ Ability
Cakechat	Seq2SeqAttn_Twitter	-0.529*	0.268
Cakechat	OpenNMT_Seq2SeqAttn	0.125	0.262
Seq2SeqAttn_OpenSubtitles	Cakechat	-0.460	0.281
Seq2SeqAttn_OpenSubtitles_wo_PTE	Seq2SeqAttn_OpenSubtitles	0.088	0.273
Seq2SeqAttn_Twitter_without_PTE	Seq2SeqAttn_Twitter	0.424	0.273
Cakechat	NCM	1.314*	0.310
Human1	Seq2SeqAttn_Twitter	-1.98*	0.269
Human1	Human2	0.356	0.256
NCM	Cakechat	-0.715*	0.261
NCM	Seq2SeqAttn_Twitter	-1.426*	0.274
NCM	OpenNMT_Seq2SeqAttn	-1.034*	0.287
NCM	Human1	-0.224	0.262
NCM	Human2	0.377	0.324
Seq2SeqAttn_OpenSubtitles	Seq2SeqAttn_OpenSubtitles	0.295	0.274
OpenNMT_Seq2SeqAttn	Seq2SeqAttn_OpenSubtitles	-0.177	0.318
Seq2SeqAttn_OpenSubtitles_Ques	Human2	2.015*	0.265
Seq2SeqAttn_OpenSubtitles	Seq2SeqAttn_Twitter	0.052	0.274
Seq2SeqAttn_Twitter	Human2	2.760*	0.291
NCM	DialoGPT	-0.223	0.245
NCM	Blender (2.7B)	-0.347	0.256

Table 3: Comparison of various models using IRT. Larger positive indicates that System B is superior in terms of rating by human annotators and similarly smaller negative numbers mean that System A is superior. (* shows significant differences.)

ViLBERTScore: Evaluating Image Caption Using Vision-and-Language BERT

Hwanhee Lee[1], Seunghyun Yoon[1,2], Franck Dernoncourt[2]
Doo Soon Kim[2], Trung Bui[2] and Kyomin Jung[1]

[1]Dept. of Electrical and Computer Engineering, Seoul National University, Seoul, Korea
[2]Adobe Research, San Jose, CA, USA
{wanted1007, mysmilesh, kjung}@snu.ac.kr
{franck.dernoncourt, dkim, bui}@adobe.com

Abstract

In this paper, we propose an evaluation metric for image captioning systems using both image and text information. Unlike the previous methods that rely on textual representations in evaluating the caption, our approach uses visiolinguistic representations. The proposed method generates image-conditioned embeddings for each token using ViLBERT from both generated and reference texts. Then, these contextual embeddings from each of the two sentence-pair are compared to compute the similarity score. Experimental results on three benchmark datasets show that our method correlates significantly better with human judgments than all existing metrics.

1 Introduction

Image captioning is a task that aims to generate a text that describes a given image. While there have been many advances for caption generation algorithms (Vinyals et al., 2015; Anderson et al., 2018) and target datasets (Fang et al., 2015; Sharma et al., 2018), few studies have focused on assessing the quality of the generated captions with consideration to the image.

Most of the previous studies on evaluating image captioning tasks rely on n-gram similarity metrics such as BLEU (Papineni et al., 2002) or CIDEr (Vedantam et al., 2015). These approaches bear limitations in dealing with the text's diverse nature, similarly found in other text generation tasks (e.g., abstractive summarization and dialog) (Kryscinski et al., 2019; Liu et al., 2016). To alleviate the issues in the n-gram based approaches, researchers proposed word embedding-based techniques (Kusner et al., 2015; Zhang et al., 2019; Zhao et al., 2019; Lo, 2019; Clark et al., 2019). These techniques shows robust performance and achieve higher correlation with human judgment than that of other previous metrics in many text

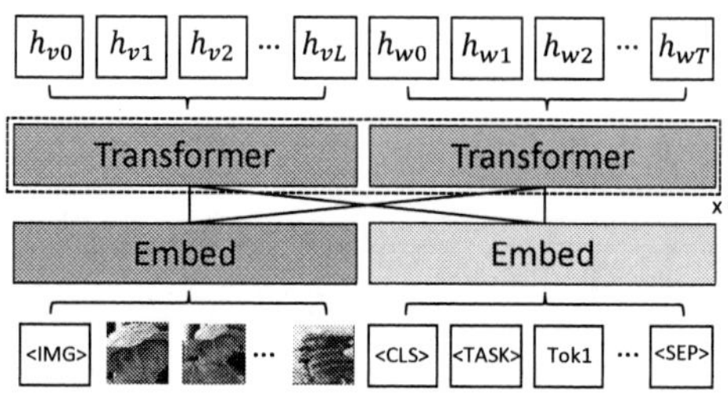

Figure 1: The overall architecture of ViLBERT. ViL-BERT consists of a self-attention based embedding layer and co-attention layer for each image and text information.

generation tasks, including image captioning. Especially, BERTScore (Zhang et al., 2019) shows that using contextualized embedding is effective for evaluating the text. As BERTScore does not utilize image content, it is still undiscovered how to effectively utilize the image content in the process of evaluating the captions.

To further reflect image context while utilizing the advantages of BERTScore, we propose ViL-BERTScore[1] by employing the ViLBERT (Lu et al., 2019), which is a task-agnostic pre-trained visiolinguistic representation. ViLBERTScore computes cosine similarity between token embeddings for reference and candidate sentences similar to BERTScore. However, different from BERTScore, the token embedding is computed with the consideration of image contexts.

We evaluate our proposed method on three benchmark datasets (i.e., Composite, Flickr8k, and PASCAL-50S). Extensive experiments show that ViLBERTScore achieves a significantly higher correlation with human judgments than previous metrics. This result demonstrates that the use of contextualized embedding from vision and language is

---

[1]https://github.com/hwanheelee1993/ViLBERTScore

Proceedings of the First Workshop on Evaluation and Comparison of NLP Systems (Eval4NLP), pages 34–39,
November 20, 2020. ©2020 Association for Computational Linguistics

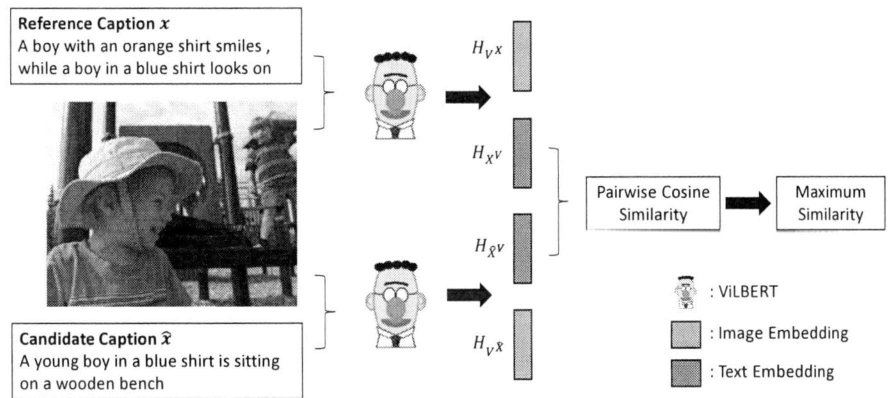

Figure 2: Overall computation of ViLBERTScore. Given the image I, reference caption x and candidate caption $\hat{x}$, we compute contextual embeddings with ViLBERT for x and $\hat{x}$ respectively. Then, we extract the text embeddings H_{Xv} and $H_{\hat{X}v}$ for each output embedding. Finally, we compute the pairwise cosine similarity between H_{Xv} and $H_{\hat{X}v}$ as in (Zhang et al., 2019).

effective in evaluating image captioning tasks.

2 Related Work

2.1 Caption Evaluation

We provide a summary of the widely used metrics for evaluating image captions such as n-gram similarity metrics, embedding based metrics, and other task-specific metrics for captioning.

N-gram Similarity Metrics The most widely used metrics for evaluating the quality of text generation tasks are n-gram similarity metrics that compute the exact number of n-gram matches between reference and generated text. One example of these metrics is BLEU (Papineni et al., 2002) that computes the precision of overlap n-gram between reference and candidate. ROUGE (Lin, 2004) is a set of commonly used metrics for text summarization. In particular, ROUGE-N, the longest common subsequence based metric, is the most frequently used variants of ROUGE. CIDEr (Vedantam et al., 2015), which is proposed for evaluating image captions, computes the tf-idf weighted n-gram similarity between reference and candidate.

Embedding Based Metrics The n-gram similarity metrics possess critical limitations; they cannot count the synonym matches of the n-gram, even though the synonyms are widely found in the generated text. To overcome this weakness, embedding based metrics such as Word Mover Distance(WMD) (Kusner et al., 2015) and BERTScore (Zhang et al., 2019) are proposed.

WMD computes minimum transportation distance among tokens using pre-trained word embeddings (i.e., GloVe (Pennington et al., 2014)). On the other hand, BERTScore computes cosine similarity among tokens using contextual embeddings from BERT (Devlin et al., 2019).

Captioning Specific Metrics After CIDEr is introduced, several metrics for image captioning are proposed. SPICE (Anderson et al., 2016) uses scene graph and LEIC (Cui et al., 2018) uses the trainable model to evaluate the captions. VIFIDEL (Madhyastha et al., 2019) is an extension of Wasserstein distance that utilizes the information from detected objects in the image. TIGEr (Jiang et al., 2019) uses the output of the visual grounding task. BERT-TBR (Yi et al., 2020) focuses on the variance of the captions and combine multiple reference captions to get improved BERTScore.

2.2 ViLBERT

To compute contextual representations from the visually-grounded text, researchers proposed a transformer-based model. One such example is ViLBERT (Lu et al., 2019), which is a task-agnostic pre-trained representation for vision and language. As shown in Fig. 1, ViLBERT employs two streams of transformer (Vaswani et al., 2017)-based architecture; one of each part processes visual and textual inputs, respectively. Specifically, the image and grounded-text inputs are fed into separate embedding layers; followed by two co-attentional transformer block that allows interaction between the two modalities. ViLBERT is pre-trained with two training objectives, masked multi-modal modeling, and multi-modal alignment. Lu et al. (2019) show that fine-tuning this pre-trained ViLBERT to vision-and-language related downstream tasks (e.g., visual question answering (Antol et al., 2015)) significantly outperforms previous approaches. Recently, Lu et al. (2020) investigate and reveal that training the ViLBERT with multi-task learning objectives provides further performance improvement for most of the vision and language tasks.

3 ViLBERTScore

We propose ViLBERTScore, a metric that utilizes visually-grounded representations for each token. The overall flow of our proposed ViLBERTScore is described in Fig. 2. Similar to BERTScore, we first compute contextual embeddings of both reference caption $X = (x_1, ..., x_n)$ and candidate caption $\hat{X} = (\hat{x}_1, ..., \hat{x}_m)$. Since we use ViLBERT, we compute the embeddings for each caption conditioning with the target image I. For the target image, we extract N region-level features $V = (v_1, ..., v_N)$ using pre-trained object detection model (see 4.2 for detailed information). Then, we feed each pair of image and caption embeddings (X, V), $(\hat{X}, V)$ to pre-trained ViLBERT and compute the contextual embeddings (H_{VX}, H_{XV}) and $(H_{V\hat{X}}, H_{\hat{X}V})$. Note that H_V and H_X are image and text embeddings, respectively. Among these embeddings, we only utilize the text embeddings, $H_{XV} = (h_{w0}, ..., h_{wT})$ and $H_{\hat{X}V} = (\hat{h}_{w0}, ..., \hat{h}_{wT})$, and compute cosine similarity among the pair of tokens from the candidate and reference caption. Finally, the greedy matching process is exercised to the pair of tokens mentioned above for finding the most similar token-match between two sentences. We can formulate ViLBERTScore as follows.

$$\text{ViLBERTScore}_P = \frac{\Sigma_{i=1}^{m} \max_{\hat{h}_{wj} \in H_{\hat{X}V}} \mathbf{h_{wi}^T \hat{h}_{wj}}}{m} \quad (1)$$

$$\text{ViLBERTScore}_R = \frac{\Sigma_{i=1}^{n} \max_{h_{wj} \in H_{XV}} \mathbf{\hat{h}_{wi}^T h_{wj}}}{n} \quad (2)$$

$$\text{ViLBERTScore}_F = 2 \cdot \frac{\text{ViLBERTScore}_P \cdot \text{ViLBERTScore}_R}{\text{ViLBERTScore}_P + \text{ViLBERTScore}_R} \quad (3)$$

4 Experiments

4.1 Dataset

Composite Composite (Aditya et al., 2015) dataset consists of 11,985 human judgments for

Metric	Flickr8k	Composite
BLEU-1[†]	0.318	0.282
BLEU-4[†]	0.140	0.199
ROUGE-L[†]	0.323	0.313
METEOR[†]	0.436	0.381
CIDEr[†]	0.447	0.387
SPICE[†]	0.458	0.418
BERTScore[†]	0.393	0.399
BERT-TBR[†]	0.481	0.423
ViLBERTScore$_P$	0.462	0.366
ViLBERTScore$_R$	0.432	0.424
ViLBERTScore$_F$	0.514	0.420
ViLBERTScore*$_P$	0.541	0.499
ViLBERTScore*$_R$	0.512	0.508
ViLBERTScore*$_F$	**0.542**	**0.514**

Table 1: Kendall Correlation between human judgments and various metrics. Note that ViLBERTScore* uses the ViLBERT model from (Lu et al., 2020), which is fine-tuned on 12 downstream tasks. Scores with † are cited from (Yi et al., 2020).

Metric	HC	HI	HM	MM	All
BLEU-1	54.5	95.0	92.0	57.7	74.8
BLEU-4	51.8	92.3	86.9	59.3	72.6
ROUGE-L	53.4	94.3	93.8	57.2	74.7
METEOR	56.3	96.9	95.1	61.2	77.4
CIDEr	53.1	98.1	92.5	63.1	76.7
SPICE	59.7	95.1	87.2	61.6	75.9
ViLBERTScore$_P$	43.4	95.3	75.4	67.7	70.4
ViLBERTScore$_R$	**66.5**	99.2	**98.3**	61.1	81.3
ViLBERTScore$_F$	50.3	98.1	91.4	69.6	77.4
ViLBERTScore*$_P$	46.0	99.5	86.2	75.3	76.8
ViLBERTScore*$_R$	61.4	**100.0**	97.1	75.0	**83.4**
ViLBERTScore*$_F$	49.9	99.6	93.1	**75.8**	79.6

Table 2: Result for PASCAL-50S dataset. The paired ways HC, HI, HM and MM respectively mean human-correct, human-incorrect, human-model and model-model. We use five reference captions among 50 reference captions for each caption pair.

each candidate caption and image pair. The images in this dataset are from Flickr8k (Hodosh et al., 2013), Flickr30k (Plummer et al., 2017), and COCO captions (Lin et al., 2014). The human judgments scores range from 1 to 5, depending on the relevance between candidate caption and image.

Flickr8k Flickr8k dataset is composed of 8,092 images with five corresponding human-generated captions. This dataset also provides three expert annotations for each image and candidate caption on 5,822 images. The score ranges from 1 to 4, depending on how well the caption and image match.

PASCAL-50S PASCAL-50S (Vedantam et al., 2015) dataset contains 1,000 images from UIUC PASCAL Sentence Dataset with 50 reference cap-

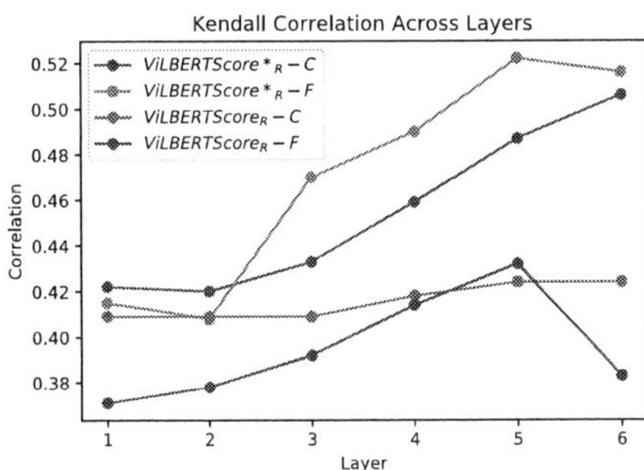

Figure 3: Kendall Correlation between human judgments across different layers. C and F are the results for Composite and Flickr8k datasets, respectively. Note that ViLBERTScore* uses the fine-tuned ViLBERT model from (Lu et al., 2020).

tions generated by humans for each image. Different from other datasets, this dataset provides 4,000 caption triplet $<A, B, C>$ composed of 50 reference captions(A) and two candidate captions(B, C) for the given image. There are human annotated answers to which is more similar to "A", "B" or "C". Candidate captions are human-written or model-generated.

4.2 Implementation Details

We use two versions of ViLBERT, one from the pre-trained ViLBERT model from (Lu et al., 2019) and the other version from (Lu et al., 2020) that are fine-tuned on 12 downstream tasks. We set N = 100 boxes for each image using image detectron model (He et al., 2017) to compute contextual embedding as in (Lu et al., 2019). We use the textual representations in the 6-th layer, the last co-attention layer, of ViLBERT for the main results in Table 1 and Table 2. For the dataset containing multiple reference captions, we average the score over the pairs of candidate caption and reference captions.

4.3 Results

Evaluation Methods We compute Kendall's correlation coefficient with human judgments for the Composite dataset and Flickr8k dataset. For the PASCAL-50S dataset, we compute the number of matches between human judgments for each candidate caption pair.

Performance Comparison We present the correlation scores for the baseline metrics and our proposed ViLBERTScore for Composite dataset and Flickr8k dataset in Table 1. ViLBERTScore shows a higher correlation than all the existing metrics. For the PASCAL-50S dataset, Table 2 shows that ViLBERTScore$_R$ is the best metric at comparing captions among all of the metrics. Interestingly, we observe that the performance of ViLBERTScore$_P$ is lower than that of ViLBERTScore$_R$ for the PASCAL-50S dataset. This is consistent behavior with the results of (Zhang et al., 2019). We speculate that the main objects in the image are the most critical words the human judgments as in (Zhang et al., 2019).

We further explore the performance of ViLBERTScore with different base model. We choose another ViLBERT model that is fine-tuned on 12 vision-and-language related tasks (see ViLBERTScore* in Table 1 and 2). This model shows better results than ViLBERTScore. We explain that some of the tasks such as image retrieval or visual entailment (Xie et al., 2019) are related to caption evaluation.

Correlation Across Layers The co-attentional block in ViLBERT is composed of six layers. To verify the effectiveness of each layer in computing the contextualized embedding of the data, we compute ViLBERTScore using the outputs of different layer. As shown in Fig. 3, the outputs of a higher layer show a better correlation with human judgments than the lower layer except for the last layer. This observation reveals that blending information among the modalities is essential in computing better contextual representations. We explain that the correlation drops in the last layer because the last layer has task specific property.

5 Conclusion

In this paper, we propose ViLBERTScore, a metric for image captioning task by using pre-trained visio-linguistic representations. Different from the BERTScore, ViLBERTScore utilizes image conditional embeddings for each token which is critical in evaluating vision-language combined task. Empirical results on Composite, Flickr8k, and PASCAL-50S datasets show that the proposed ViLBERTScore correlates better with human judgments than all of the previous metrics.

Acknowledgements

We also gratefully acknowledge support from Adobe Inc. in the form of a generous gift to Seoul

National University. K. Jung is with ASRI, Seoul National University, Korea. This work was supported by the Ministry of Trade, Industry & Energy (MOTIE, Korea) under Industrial Technology Innovation Program (No.10073144).

References

Somak Aditya, Yezhou Yang, Chitta Baral, Cornelia Fermuller, and Yiannis Aloimonos. 2015. From images to sentences through scene description graphs using commonsense reasoning and knowledge. *arXiv preprint arXiv:1511.03292*.

Peter Anderson, Basura Fernando, Mark Johnson, and Stephen Gould. 2016. Spice: Semantic propositional image caption evaluation. In *European Conference on Computer Vision*, pages 382–398. Springer.

Peter Anderson, Xiaodong He, Chris Buehler, Damien Teney, Mark Johnson, Stephen Gould, and Lei Zhang. 2018. Bottom-up and top-down attention for image captioning and visual question answering. In *Proceedings of the IEEE conference on computer vision and pattern recognition*, pages 6077–6086.

Stanislaw Antol, Aishwarya Agrawal, Jiasen Lu, Margaret Mitchell, Dhruv Batra, C Lawrence Zitnick, and Devi Parikh. 2015. Vqa: Visual question answering. In *Proceedings of the IEEE international conference on computer vision*, pages 2425–2433.

Elizabeth Clark, Asli Celikyilmaz, and Noah A Smith. 2019. Sentence mover's similarity: Automatic evaluation for multi-sentence texts. In *Proceedings of the 57th Annual Meeting of the Association for Computational Linguistics*, pages 2748–2760.

Yin Cui, Guandao Yang, Andreas Veit, Xun Huang, and Serge Belongie. 2018. Learning to evaluate image captioning. In *Proceedings of the IEEE conference on computer vision and pattern recognition*, pages 5804–5812.

Jacob Devlin, Ming-Wei Chang, Kenton Lee, and Kristina Toutanova. 2019. Bert: Pre-training of deep bidirectional transformers for language understanding. In *Proceedings of the 2019 Conference of the North American Chapter of the Association for Computational Linguistics: Human Language Technologies, Volume 1 (Long and Short Papers)*, pages 4171–4186.

Hao Fang, Saurabh Gupta, Forrest Iandola, Rupesh K Srivastava, Li Deng, Piotr Dollár, Jianfeng Gao, Xiaodong He, Margaret Mitchell, John C Platt, et al. 2015. From captions to visual concepts and back. In *Proceedings of the IEEE conference on computer vision and pattern recognition*, pages 1473–1482.

Kaiming He, Georgia Gkioxari, Piotr Dollár, and Ross Girshick. 2017. Mask r-cnn. In *Proceedings of the IEEE international conference on computer vision*, pages 2961–2969.

Micah Hodosh, Peter Young, and Julia Hockenmaier. 2013. Framing image description as a ranking task: Data, models and evaluation metrics. *Journal of Artificial Intelligence Research*, 47:853–899.

Ming Jiang, Qiuyuan Huang, Lei Zhang, Xin Wang, Pengchuan Zhang, Zhe Gan, Jana Diesner, and Jianfeng Gao. 2019. Tiger: Text-to-image grounding for image caption evaluation. In *Proceedings of the 2019 Conference on Empirical Methods in Natural Language Processing and the 9th International Joint Conference on Natural Language Processing (EMNLP-IJCNLP)*, pages 2141–2152.

Wojciech Kryscinski, Nitish Shirish Keskar, Bryan McCann, Caiming Xiong, and Richard Socher. 2019. Neural text summarization: A critical evaluation. In *Proceedings of the 2019 Conference on Empirical Methods in Natural Language Processing and the 9th International Joint Conference on Natural Language Processing (EMNLP-IJCNLP)*, pages 540–551.

Matt Kusner, Yu Sun, Nicholas Kolkin, and Kilian Weinberger. 2015. From word embeddings to document distances. In *International conference on machine learning*, pages 957–966.

Chin-Yew Lin. 2004. Rouge: A package for automatic evaluation of summaries. In *Text summarization branches out*, pages 74–81.

Tsung-Yi Lin, Michael Maire, Serge Belongie, James Hays, Pietro Perona, Deva Ramanan, Piotr Dollár, and C Lawrence Zitnick. 2014. Microsoft coco: Common objects in context. In *European conference on computer vision*, pages 740–755. Springer.

Chia-Wei Liu, Ryan Lowe, Iulian Vlad Serban, Mike Noseworthy, Laurent Charlin, and Joelle Pineau. 2016. How not to evaluate your dialogue system: An empirical study of unsupervised evaluation metrics for dialogue response generation. In *Proceedings of the 2016 Conference on Empirical Methods in Natural Language Processing*, pages 2122–2132.

Chi-kiu Lo. 2019. Yisi-a unified semantic mt quality evaluation and estimation metric for languages with different levels of available resources. In *Proceedings of the Fourth Conference on Machine Translation (Volume 2: Shared Task Papers, Day 1)*, pages 507–513.

Jiasen Lu, Dhruv Batra, Devi Parikh, and Stefan Lee. 2019. Vilbert: Pretraining task-agnostic visiolinguistic representations for vision-and-language tasks. In *Advances in Neural Information Processing Systems*, pages 13–23.

Jiasen Lu, Vedanuj Goswami, Marcus Rohrbach, Devi Parikh, and Stefan Lee. 2020. 12-in-1: Multi-task vision and language representation learning. In

Proceedings of the IEEE/CVF Conference on Computer Vision and Pattern Recognition, pages 10437–10446.

Pranava Swaroop Madhyastha, Josiah Wang, and Lucia Specia. 2019. Vifidel: Evaluating the visual fidelity of image descriptions. In *Proceedings of the 57th Annual Meeting of the Association for Computational Linguistics*, pages 6539–6550.

Kishore Papineni, Salim Roukos, Todd Ward, and Wei-Jing Zhu. 2002. Bleu: a method for automatic evaluation of machine translation. In *Proceedings of the 40th annual meeting of the Association for Computational Linguistics*, pages 311–318.

Jeffrey Pennington, Richard Socher, and Christopher D Manning. 2014. Glove: Global vectors for word representation. In *Proceedings of the 2014 conference on empirical methods in natural language processing (EMNLP)*, pages 1532–1543.

Bryan A. Plummer, Liwei Wang, Christopher M. Cervantes, Juan C. Caicedo, Julia Hockenmaier, and Svetlana Lazebnik. 2017. Flickr30k entities: Collecting region-to-phrase correspondences for richer image-to-sentence models. *IJCV*, 123(1):74–93.

Piyush Sharma, Nan Ding, Sebastian Goodman, and Radu Soricut. 2018. Conceptual captions: A cleaned, hypernymed, image alt-text dataset for automatic image captioning. In *Proceedings of the 56th Annual Meeting of the Association for Computational Linguistics (Volume 1: Long Papers)*, pages 2556–2565.

Ashish Vaswani, Noam Shazeer, Niki Parmar, Jakob Uszkoreit, Llion Jones, Aidan N Gomez, Łukasz Kaiser, and Illia Polosukhin. 2017. Attention is all you need. In *Advances in neural information processing systems*, pages 5998–6008.

Ramakrishna Vedantam, C Lawrence Zitnick, and Devi Parikh. 2015. Cider: Consensus-based image description evaluation. In *Proceedings of the IEEE conference on computer vision and pattern recognition*, pages 4566–4575.

Oriol Vinyals, Alexander Toshev, Samy Bengio, and Dumitru Erhan. 2015. Show and tell: A neural image caption generator. In *Proceedings of the IEEE conference on computer vision and pattern recognition*, pages 3156–3164.

Ning Xie, Farley Lai, Derek Doran, and Asim Kadav. 2019. Visual entailment: A novel task for fine-grained image understanding. *arXiv preprint arXiv:1901.06706*.

Yanzhi Yi, Hangyu Deng, and Jinglu Hu. 2020. Improving image captioning evaluation by considering inter references variance. In *Proceedings of the 58th Annual Meeting of the Association for Computational Linguistics*, pages 985–994.

Tianyi Zhang, Varsha Kishore, Felix Wu, Kilian Q Weinberger, and Yoav Artzi. 2019. Bertscore: Evaluating text generation with bert. *arXiv preprint arXiv:1904.09675*.

Wei Zhao, Maxime Peyrard, Fei Liu, Yang Gao, Christian M Meyer, and Steffen Eger. 2019. Moverscore: Text generation evaluating with contextualized embeddings and earth mover distance. In *Proceedings of the 2019 Conference on Empirical Methods in Natural Language Processing and the 9th International Joint Conference on Natural Language Processing (EMNLP-IJCNLP)*, pages 563–578.

BLEU Neighbors:
A Reference-less Approach to Automatic Evaluation

Kawin Ethayarajh
Stanford University
kawin@stanford.edu

Dorsa Sadigh
ILIAD Lab, Stanford University
dorsa@cs.stanford.edu

Abstract

Evaluation is a bottleneck in the development of natural language generation (NLG) models. Automatic metrics such as BLEU rely on references, but for tasks such as open-ended generation, there are no references to draw upon. Although language diversity can be estimated using statistical measures such as perplexity, measuring language *quality* requires human evaluation. However, because human evaluation at scale is slow and expensive, it is used sparingly; it cannot be used to rapidly iterate on NLG models, in the way BLEU is used for machine translation. To this end, we propose *BLEU Neighbors*, a nearest neighbors model for estimating language quality by using the BLEU score as a kernel function. On existing datasets for chitchat dialogue and open-ended sentence generation, we find that – on average – the quality estimation from a BLEU Neighbors model has a lower mean squared error and higher Spearman correlation with the ground truth than individual human annotators. Despite its simplicity, BLEU Neighbors even outperforms state-of-the-art models on automatically grading essays, including models that have access to a gold-standard reference essay.

1 Introduction

Despite recent advances on many natural language generation (NLG) tasks – including open-ended generation, chitchat dialogue, and abstractive summarization – evaluation remains a challenge. Automatic metrics such as BLEU rely on references, but for many NLG tasks, there is no single correct answer. In dialogue, the space of acceptable responses to a given prompt is often very large, yet most datasets only provide a few gold-standard references (Serban et al., 2015). In open-ended generation, where text is generated freely by a language model, there are no references at all; statistical measures such as perplexity capture language

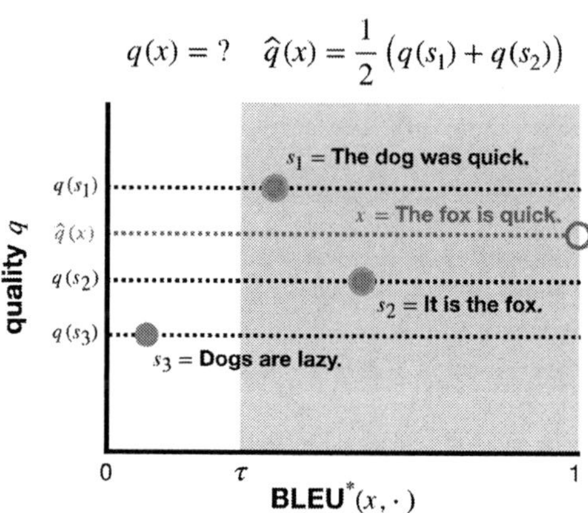

Figure 1: We want to score a sentence x given training examples $S = \{s_1, s_2, s_3\}$ with known quality scores $\{q(s_1), q(s_2), q(s_3)\}$. BLEU Neighbors works as follows: calculate BLEU$^*(x, \cdot)$, a variant of the BLEU-4 score, for each s; ignore those below $\tau = 0.08$; take the average score of those that remain to predict $\hat{q}(x)$.

diversity but not language quality (Hashimoto et al., 2019). These limitations necessitate human evaluation. However, because human evaluation at scale is slow and expensive, it is used sparingly; it cannot be used to rapidly iterate on NLG models, in the way BLEU is used for machine translation.

Prior work on automating reference-less evaluation has largely been limited in scope. Heuristic-based evaluation was found to be effective for grammatical error correction, but the methods used were problem-specific and cannot be extended to other tasks (Napoles et al., 2016; Choshen and Abend, 2018; Asano et al., 2017). Using the log-odds from a language model, Kann et al. (2018) made automatic judgments of sentence-level fluency that correlated moderately well with human judgment, but this captured only one facet of language quality. Approaches that were broader in scope found less success: although ADEM, an RNN trained to

Proceedings of the First Workshop on Evaluation and Comparison of NLP Systems (Eval4NLP), pages 40–50,
November 20, 2020. ©2020 Association for Computational Linguistics

score dialogue responses, was initially thought to correlate well with human judgment (Lowe et al., 2017), it was later found to generalize poorly, placing outsized influence on factors such as response length (Lowe, 2019).

Can we come up with a fast and simple method for reference-less evaluation of language quality, analogous to BLEU for machine translation? Note that our goal here is *not* to supplant human evaluation, but to complement it: as long as the method's predictions correlate moderately well with the ground-truth quality scores, it can be used to speed up NLG model development. Our desiderata are then as follows: simplicity, speed, and a moderately strong correlation with the ground truth. To this end, we propose *BLEU Neighbors*, a new approach to reference-less automatic evaluation.

Our approach is a nearest neighbors model that predicts language quality by using BLEU as a kernel function. We start with training examples S, where each sentence $s \in S$ has a ground-truth quality score $q(s)$. Note that these examples are not references – we do not expect the NLG model being evaluated to generate any sentence in S. In fact, S contains sentences of varying quality, including incoherent sentences with low quality scores. Given a test sentence x, we use the BLEU score to identify its neighbors in the training data: $\{s \mid \text{BLEU}^*(x, s) > \tau, s \in S\}$, where τ is a similarity threshold. Then we simply take the mean of the neighbors' known quality scores to estimate $\hat{q}(x)$, the quality of x. Consider the test sentence $x = $ *'The fox is quick'*. As seen in Figure 1, it overlaps with $s_1 = $ *'The dog was quick.'* and $s_2 = $ *'It is the fox.'* but not with $s_3 = $ *'Dogs are lazy.'*. Therefore, we estimate $\hat{q}(x)$ as the mean of $q(s_1)$ and $q(s_2)$ but not $q(s_3)$.

We test BLEU Neighbors on the datasets from HUSE (Hashimoto et al., 2019), where each sentence's ground-truth quality score is the average over 20 human judgments. On the dialogue and open-ended generation datasets, we find that – on average – the BLEU Neighbors model has a lower mean squared error (MSE) and higher Spearman correlation with the ground truth than individual annotators. The premise of our method is that past approaches to reference-less evaluation fell short because they were too ambitious – if a given test sentence is not sufficiently similar to any training example, no prediction should be made at all. Although we sacrifice some coverage in or-

der to make more accurate estimates, this sacrifice is modest: BLEU Neighbors makes predictions for 41% to 99% of sentences from the HUSE datasets. Our method is also data-efficient – none of HUSE datasets have over 400 training examples.

Our method is weakest on evaluating summaries; this is unsurprising, given that summary quality is conditioned on the source text, which the method ignores. In contrast, BLEU Neighbors is surprisingly effective at automatically grading essays, achieving a new state-of-the-art and even beating out models that have access to a gold-standard reference essay. These findings suggest that despite its simplicity, our approach has broad applicability. Although BLEU Neighbors does not measure language *diversity*, it is sufficient for it to measure quality alone. The former is easier to estimate (e.g., perplexity) and can be combined with the BLEU Neighbors score in a hybrid metric (Hashimoto et al., 2019). We conclude by providing some practical advice, such as how to prevent NLG models from explicitly optimizing for a high BLEU Neighbors score without generating high-quality output.

2   Related Work

2.1   Reference-based Evaluation

BLEU (Papineni et al., 2002), ROUGE (Lin, 2004), and METEOR (Banerjee and Lavie, 2005) are the *de facto* canonical metrics of reference-based automatic evaluation. Given a candidate sentence x and a reference sentence s, each metric assigns a score $q(x, s) \in [0, 1]$ based on how well x overlaps with s. Where the metrics differ is in how they define this overlap. Letting $\ell_n(\cdot)$ denote the list of n-grams, the n-gram precision P_n and recall R_n can be defined as follows:

$$P_n(x, s) = \frac{1}{|\ell_n(x)|} \sum_{g \in \ell_n(x)} \mathbb{1}[g \in \ell_n(s)]$$
$$R_n(x, s) = \frac{1}{|\ell_n(s)|} \sum_{g \in \ell_n(s)} \mathbb{1}[g \in \ell_n(x)]$$

$$(1)$$

BLEU   The BLEU score for (x, s) is the geometric mean of the n-gram precision P_n up to a chosen n (typically, $n = 4$). BLEU also implements clipping, such that each n-gram $g \in \ell_n(x)$ can be matched at most once. It also includes a brevity penalty to penalize shorter candidates.

METEOR   The METEOR score takes the harmonic mean of P_1 and R_1, with greater weight placed on R_1. It is laxer than BLEU, allowing words in x and s to match, for example, if they are synonyms or share the same stem (Banerjee and Lavie, 2005). Instead of looking at higher order n-grams, METEOR tries to align the tokens in x and s and penalizes alignments that are not contiguous.

ROUGE-L ROUGE-L, the variant of ROUGE we discuss in this work, measures the overlap between x and s as the size of their longest common subsequence $LCS(x, s)$. Specifically, it calculates $LCS(x, s)/P_1(x, s)$ and $LCS(x, s)/R_1(x, s)$ and takes their harmonic mean.

Although there have been advances in reference-based automatic evaluation – such as BEER (Stanojević and Sima'an, 2014) and RUSE (Vedantam et al., 2015), among others (Shimanaka et al., 2018; Ma et al., 2017; Lo et al., 2018; Zhao et al., 2019) – BLEU and METEOR are still widely used for machine translation; ROUGE, for summarization (Liu et al., 2016). This is partially because some of the newer methods are learned metrics that do not generalize well to new domains (Chaganty et al., 2018). Moreover, most do not enjoy the incumbent status that BLEU, ROUGE, and METEOR have. To our knowledge, the current state-of-the-art in reference-based evaluation metrics is BERTScore (Zhang et al., 2019), which uses BERT embeddings (Devlin et al., 2019) to compute similarity at the token-level before aggregating the similarities using importance-weighting. As it is state-of-the-art for reference-based evaluation, it is the only non-canonical metric we consider as a kernel function.

2.2 Reference-less Evaluation

Compared to reference-based evaluation, little work has been done on automating reference-less evaluation. The most successful approaches have been task-specific: heuristic-based evaluation was found to be effective for grammatical error correction (Napoles et al., 2016; Choshen and Abend, 2018; Asano et al., 2017). However, those heuristics cannot be extended to other tasks. Kann et al. (2018) proposed two metrics for judging the fluency of a sentence: sentence-level log-odds ratio (SLOR) and a Wordpiece-based variant named WP-SLOR. Although the latter correlates moderately well (Pearson's $r > 0.40$) with human judgment, it should be noted that sentence-level fluency is only one facet of language quality – a sentence may be probable according to a language model while making little sense to a human.

Approaches that were broader in scope were less successful. ADEM, an RNN trained to score dialogue responses, was initially thought to correlate well with human judgment (Lowe et al., 2017). However, the authors later found that it generalized poorly (Lowe, 2019), placing outsized influence on factors such as response length. It was also found to be vulnerable to adversarial examples (Sai et al., 2019). In any case, ADEM was not a purely reference-less method – it still required a gold-standard reference as input. Rather, its key insight was that the space of acceptable responses is much larger than the handful of gold-standard references provided in dialogue datasets, and that this should be considered when estimating quality.

3 BLEU Neighbors

Given a candidate sentence x, training examples S, and ground-truth quality scores $\{q(s) \mid s \in S\}$, we want to estimate $\widehat{q}(x)$, the language quality of x. How can we do so in a fast and simple manner such that our predictions correlate well with the ground truth? We propose a nearest neighbors model that uses a variant of the BLEU score called BLEU* as the kernel function. Once the neighbors of x have been identified, we take the mean of their known quality scores as $\widehat{q}(x)$.

Definition 3.1. The *non-unigram BLEU-4 score* is a variant of the BLEU-4 score that ignores unigram precision. Where $\beta = \exp\left(\min\left(0, 1 - \frac{|\ell_1(s)|}{|\ell_1(x)|}\right)\right)$ is the brevity penalty and P_i is defined in (1),

$$\text{BLEU}^*(x, s) = \beta \cdot \prod_{i=2}^{4} P_i(x, s)^{1/3} \qquad (2)$$

BLEU Neighbors uses this variant of BLEU as the kernel function. We ignore the unigram precision P_1 because we are not comparing candidates and their direct references, but rather candidates and training examples. It is not uncommon for two random sentences to have stopwords in common, in which case a non-zero P_1 is unexceptional. We validated this empirically as well, finding that ignoring P_1 improves correlation with the ground-truth.

Definition 3.2. Given a candidate sentence x, training examples S, and a similarity threshold $\tau \in [0, 1]$, the *BLEU neighbors* of x are

$$\mathcal{N} = \{s \in S \mid \text{BLEU}^*(x, s) \geq \tau\}$$

To ensure that the quality estimate is stable, we require that $\mathcal{N}$ have a minimum size of $a \subset \mathbb{Z}^+$.

Conversely, a candidate sentence that overlaps with many training examples in S likely does so because it contains many common n-grams. This complicates evaluation: since BLEU* does not weigh n-grams by their frequency, an abundance of common n-grams – such as *"on the"* or *"it is"*, for example – can exaggerate the similarity between the candidate and a training example. In this scenario, it is best that no prediction be made at all. Since $\mathcal{N} \subseteq \mathcal{S}$, let $b \in [0, 1]$ denote the largest fraction of S that $\mathcal{N}$ can contain. We express b as a fraction of the training set size $|S|$ because if S is very large, it would not be uncommon for even sentences with rare n-grams to have matches in S.

When $\mathcal{N}$ meets the aforementioned size constraints, the BLEU Neighbors estimate of x's quality is the average of its neighbors' quality scores:

$$
\widehat{q}(x) = \begin{cases} \dfrac{1}{|\mathcal{N}|} \sum_{s \in \mathcal{N}} q(s) & a \le |\mathcal{N}| \le b|S| \\ \text{undefined} & \text{otherwise} \end{cases}
\tag{3}
$$

In other words, $\mathcal{N} \subseteq S$ comprises all the training examples that are sufficiently similar to the candidate with respect to BLEU*. If there are fewer than a examples or more than $b|S|$ examples in $\mathcal{N}$, then no prediction is made; otherwise, the estimate $\widehat{q}(x)$ is the average quality of the examples in $\mathcal{N}$.

Although τ, a, b are parameters to be set, we find that $\tau = 0.08, a = 5, b = 0.66$ are near-optimal for all tasks (see section 5.2). This universality allows BLEU Neighbors to be used out-of-the-box, without hyperparameter tuning. Note that S should only be used to train the evaluator (i.e., BLEU Neighbors). The generator (i.e., the NLG model being evaluated) should not have access to S; otherwise, it could optimize for a high BLEU Neighbors score by including n-grams that only belong to examples with a high ground-truth quality, thus artificially inflating the quality estimates.

Definition 3.3. Given a set of candidates $\mathcal{X}$ to be evaluated, the *coverage* of $\mathcal{X}$ is the proportion of candidates for which $\widehat{q}(x)$ is defined.

This is a key distinction between BLEU Neighbors and prior approaches to reference-less evaluation: our approach does not necessarily make a prediction for all candidates. This is by design – as mentioned earlier, we surmise that past approaches fell short because they were too ambitious, trying to score sentences that simply could not be scored. There is a trade-off between coverage and prediction error, with greater coverage generally coming at the cost of greater prediction error.

4   Experiments

NLG Tasks   We test BLEU Neighbors on evaluating sentences from the following NLG tasks: chitchat dialogue, open-ended sentence generation (from a language model), and abstractive summarization. Hashimoto et al. (2019) provided a dataset for each of these tasks, which we collectively refer to as the HUSE datasets. We ignore the story generation dataset in that work because the machine-generated examples are far from human quality and can thus be trivially assigned a low quality score.

Each dataset contains a mixture of machine- and human-generated sentences, in roughly equal proportion. Each sentence in the HUSE datasets was judged by 20 human annotators, who assigned it a label based on its typicality. These labels map to an integer score from 0 to 5. We divide the raw judgment by 5 to bound it in $[0, 1]$ and then take the mean across all 20 annotators, which we treat as the ground-truth language quality $q(s)$ for each sentence s. Because these datasets are small, we use leave-one-out prediction. That is, given a candidate sentence from a particular HUSE dataset, we treat the remaining $n - 1$ sentences as S.

Grading Essays   We also test our model on automatically grading essays from the ASAP-SAS dataset[1]. Although each essay is a multi-sentence paragraph, we did not adapt our model in any way. Each essay's quality score is an integer from 0 to 3, which we divide by 3 to bound in $[0, 1]$. This normalization is done for the sake of consistency. Because there are distinct training and test sets, we draw the training examples from the training data and the candidates to be evaluated from the test data. The ASAP-SAS data is also broken down by topic. The current state-of-the-art model only evaluates on topic #3 – specifically, on essays from topic #3 that contain 5 to 15 sentences (Clark et al., 2019). Therefore, to allow for a fair comparison, we also draw test sentences from this subset.

Threshold Settings   Unless otherwise stated, for all HUSE datasets, we use $\tau = 0.08, a = 5, b = 0.66$. These settings were chosen to maximize the Spearman correlation with the ground-truth quality

---

[1] https://www.kaggle.com/c/asap-sas

	Dialogue			Open-ended Generation			Summarization		
	MSE	ρ	Coverage	MSE	ρ	Coverage	MSE	ρ	Coverage
Human (best)	0.0208	0.878	1.00	0.0177	0.861	1.00	0.0200	0.921	1.00
Human (average)	0.0807	0.456	1.00	0.0719	0.472	1.00	0.0802	0.405	1.00
BLEU Neighbors	**0.0164**	**0.470***	0.76	0.0204	**0.575***	0.41	0.0213	**0.325***	0.99
ROUGE Neighbors	0.0197	0.342*	0.86	**0.0174**	0.077	0.47	0.0226	0.245*	0.97
METEOR Neighbors	0.0165	0.382*	0.47	0.0209	0.395	0.22	**0.0180**	0.240	0.12
BERTScore Neighbors	0.0229	0.150*	0.89	0.0192	0.566*	0.32	0.0223	0.225	0.53

Table 1: The mean squared error (MSE) and Spearman's ρ of language quality predictions $\widehat{q}(\cdot)$ with respect to the ground truth $q(\cdot)$. The lowest MSE and highest ρ across all models is in bold and * signifies $p < 0.01$. For all tasks, BLEU Neighbors achieves a higher Spearman's ρ than its ROUGE, METEOR, and BERTScore counterparts. For dialogue and open-ended generation, it even has a lower MSE and higher ρ than human annotators on average.

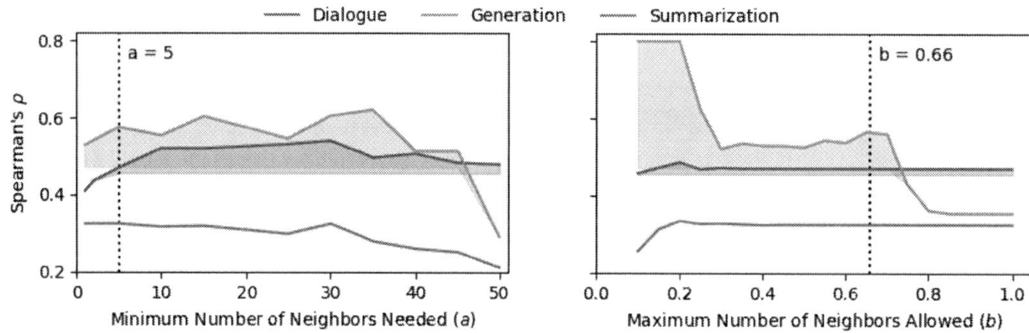

Figure 2: Spearman's ρ between BLEU Neighbors estimates $\widehat{q}(\cdot)$ and the ground-truth quality $q(\cdot)$ as each evidence threshold changes, while the other is held constant at $a = 5$ or $b = 0.66$. a is the minimum number of neighbors needed; b is the maximum allowed (as a fraction of the training set). For all tasks, increasing a improves correlation, up to a point. Only the correlation for open-ended generation is sensitive to changes in b, which decreases as b increases. The shaded area for each task indicates above-human performance (on average).

while retaining at least 40% coverage. The same settings were used for essay grading, except with no upper bound on $|\mathcal{N}|$ (i.e., $b = 1$), since each essay is a multi-sentence text that has some overlap with most essays in the training data. In section 5.2, we show how a, b can be adjusted to trade off some performance for greater coverage (and vice-versa).

Other Kernel Functions In addition to using a variant of the BLEU score as the kernel function, we try other automatic metrics, including ROUGE, METEOR, and BERTScore (Zhang et al., 2019). As with BLEU, a single value of τ for each metric works universally well: 0.06 (for ROUGE); 0.18 (for METEOR); 0.10 (for BERTScore).

5   Results

5.1   BLEU Neighbors vs. Humans

In Table 1, using mean squared error (MSE) and the Spearman correlation, we compare the language quality predictions $\widehat{q}(\cdot)$ made by our various mod-

els with the ground-truth quality $q(\cdot)$. Because the ground-truth quality is the mean over 20 annotator judgments, we provide the performance of the best human annotator and the average performance across all individual annotators. Note that not all annotators scored all the examples: the average MSE and ρ we report in Table 1 is the average over what each annotator obtained on their respective subset of the data. We find that there is a significant gap between the best- and average-case, both in terms of MSE and Spearman's ρ. For example, on the summarization task, the MSE and Spearman's ρ of the best human annnotator is 4x and 2x better than those of annotators on average.

Spearman Correlation As shown in the second section of Table 1, for all tasks, we find that BLEU Neighbors has a higher Spearman correlation with the ground truth than its ROUGE, METEOR, and BERTScore counterparts. For open-ended generation and dialogue, it even outperforms the average-case human annotator. Only on evaluating sum-

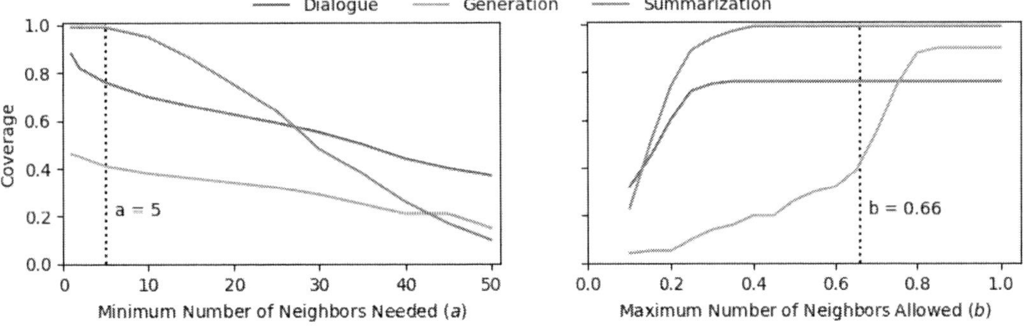

Figure 3: The coverage (i.e., the fraction of sentences for which BLEU Neighbors makes predictions) as each evidence threshold changes while the other is held constant at $a = 5$ or $b = 0.66$. a is the minimum number of neighbors needed; b is the maximum number allowed (as a fraction of the training set). For all tasks, coverage falls as a increases and b decreases (i.e., as the range for the acceptable number of neighbors gets smaller).

maries does the average-case annotator beat all nearest neighbors models with respect to Spearman's ρ; this is unsurprising, given that summary quality is strongly conditioned on the source text, which these models ignore. Despite the impressive performance of BLEU Neighbors, it should be noted that it is still well behind the *best* human annotator for each task.

Mean Squared Error   Although BLEU Neighbors achieves a much higher Spearman correlation with the ground-truth quality than its counterparts, the model that achieves the lowest MSE varies across tasks. How can we reconcile these observations? We find that the variance of the ground-truth quality is quite small for all datasets. By just predicting the mean of $q(\cdot)$ for all candidates, we can get an MSE for each task that is only slightly higher than the best annotator's. Models that obtain the lowest MSE while also having a low Spearman's ρ are thus making low-variance estimates close to the mean that do not correlate well with the ground truth. Also, annotators of the HUSE datasets assigned discrete scores (Hashimoto et al., 2019), while $q(\cdot)$, being an average over those scores, is continuous. This is conducive to human annotators having a higher MSE than the models.

5.2   Varying the Evidence Thresholds

Recall that BLEU Neighbors has two evidence thresholds: a, the minimum number of neighbors needed to make a prediction, and b, the maximum number of neighbors allowed (as a fraction of the training set S). In Figure 2, we plot the Spearman correlation between predictions $\widehat{q}(\cdot)$ and the

ground truth $q(\cdot)$ as each threshold changes, while the other is held constant at the default setting ($a = 5, b = 0.66$). In Figure 3, we plot the change in coverage as the thresholds change.

Spearman Correlation   The correlation for all tasks is sensitive to changes in a, with the correlation peaking at $a = 30$ or $a = 35$ before declining. This is intuitive: increasing the amount of evidence required yields more robust predictions, but sentences that meet the stringent requirement of having at least $a \geq 35$ neighbors likely have many common n-grams, making them harder to score. While performance on all tasks is sensitive to a, only performance on open-ended generation is sensitive to b, with the correlation decreasing as b increases (i.e., as we loosen the upper bound on the number of neighbors). This suggests that sentences in the dialogue and summarization datasets do not have many neighbors to begin with, which is why tightening the upper bound has little effect. Sentences in the open-ended generation data, on the other hand, seem to have many more neighbors on average, resulting in ρ being inversely related to b. The two sudden drops in Spearman's ρ for open-ended generation – at approximately $b = 0.2$ and $b = 0.7$ – suggests that the distribution of $|\mathcal{N}|$, the number of neighbors, is multi-modal.

Coverage within a Model   The higher a is and the lower b is, the more candidates we reject for having too few or too many neighbors. In Figure 3, the coverage falls linearly as a increases but rises linearly before plateauing as b increases. The plateau is indicative of no candidate sentence having that many neighbors to begin with.

Source Task	Target Task		
	$\to$ D	$\to$ G	$\to$ S
Dialogue (D) $\to$	**0.470**	0.206	0.032
Generation (G) $\to$	0.310	**0.575**	-0.070
Summarization (S) $\to$	0.276	0.095	**0.325**

Table 2: BLEU Neighbors performance when the training and test examples are sourced from different tasks. For example, the intersection of $G \to$ and $\to D$ means that training examples from open-ended generation are used to score dialogue data. In this setup, a moderate Spearman's ρ can still be achieved on the dialogue data.

Coverage across Models   Holding constant the evidence thresholds a and b, we see in Table 1 that coverage *across* different models is unrelated to MSE and Spearman's ρ. For all models, τ is set to minimize the MSE and maximize Spearman's ρ. However, models with the lowest MSE or highest ρ on a given task are not necessarily the most selective (i.e., those with the lowest coverage). BLEU Neighbors, which has the highest correlation on all tasks, has a coverage of 41%, 76%, and 99% on open-ended generation, dialogue, and summarization respectively. In other words, the trade-off between coverage and prediction error exists *within* a model – as a function of parameters a and b – but not *across* different types of models.

Performance vs. Coverage   As seen in Figures 2 and 3, there is a trade-off when choosing a and b. Higher a and lower b result in better performance (i.e., greater correlation with the ground truth), but they also decrease coverage. Recall the default settings: $a = 5, b = 0.66$. Even though correlation on most tasks peaks at $a = 30$ or $a = 35$, we choose $a = 5$ as the default because we want to keep the coverage as high as possible. By choosing $a > 1$, however, we still see some benefit from requiring a minimum number of neighbors. We choose $b = 0.66$ because it is near the end of a plateau past which performance on open-ended generation data drops precipitously. In other words, the default settings of a, b are near Pareto-optimal, maximizing coverage while outperforming human annotators on average. Some performance can be traded off for additional coverage by picking a different point (a, b) on the Pareto frontier.

5.3   Low-Hanging or High-Hanging Fruit?

Does BLEU Neighbors only make predictions for sentences that humans consider easy to score (i.e., low-hanging fruit)? Let $\mathcal{A}_i$ denote the set of all sentences for task i and $\mathcal{B}_i \subseteq \mathcal{A}_i$ denote the subset of those sentences for which BLEU Neighbors makes predictions. We can answer this question by comparing the average MSE of human annotators on $\mathcal{A}_i$ with their average MSE on $\mathcal{B}_i$, which we will denote as $\overline{\text{MSE}}(\mathcal{A}_i)$ and $\overline{\text{MSE}}(\mathcal{B}_i)$ respectively. We cannot use the Spearman correlation for comparison because not every annotator scored every sentence; recall that the statistics reported in Table 1 are computed over each annotator's performance on their subset of the data.

If our model were only scoring the easy-to-score sentences, then we would expect $\overline{\text{MSE}}(\mathcal{A}_i)$ to be significantly larger than $\overline{\text{MSE}}(\mathcal{B}_i)$. However, for both summarization and open-ended generation, we find that there is no statistically significant difference between these means at any level. Only on the dialogue dataset could this theory partially explain the success of our model: $\overline{\text{MSE}}(\mathcal{B}_{\text{dialogue}})$ is 15.6% lower than $\overline{\text{MSE}}(\mathcal{A}_{\text{dialogue}})$ and this difference is significant at $p < 0.01$. However, the average-case annotator MSE on the subset of the dialogue data scored by ROUGE Neighbors is only 2×10^{-4} higher than $\overline{\text{MSE}}(\mathcal{B}_{\text{dialogue}})$, yet ROUGE Neighbors performs far worse than its BLEU counterpart (see Table 1). This implies that the success of BLEU Neighbors is much more than simply picking the right sentences to score.

5.4   Cross-Task Performance

In Table 2, we report the Spearman's ρ for BLEU Neighbors when the training and test examples are drawn from different tasks. Of all the tasks, performance on dialogue is the most robust: regardless of which task is used to source the training data, it is possible to achieve a moderately strong correlation ($\rho > 0.27$), albeit with lower coverage. Performance on summarization drops to near zero in this setup – this is unsurprising, given that summary quality is strongly conditioned on the source text, which is ignored. For open-ended generation, it is still possible to achieve a weak correlation ($\rho > 0.09$) with this setup. Curiously, the coverage for open-ended generation actually improves when the training data is sourced from a different task, so it may be possible to adjust parameters a, b to trade off some coverage for a higher correlation.

5.5   How much Training Data is Needed?

In Figure 4, we plot the performance of BLEU Neighbors on the HUSE datasets for different amounts of training data. This is simulated by

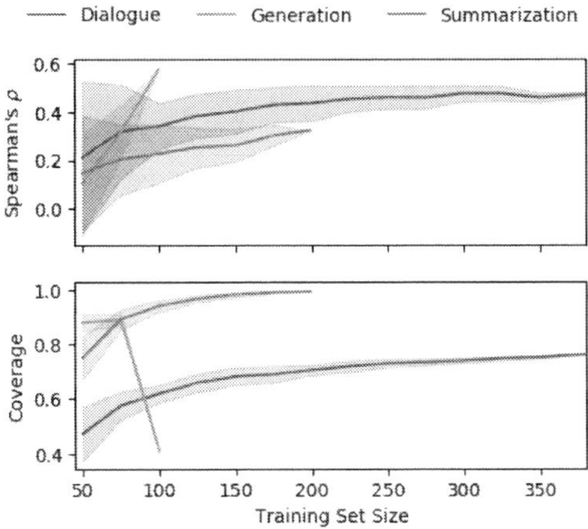

Figure 4: BLEU Neighbors performance when only a random subset of the training data is used. With more data, both coverage and the Spearman correlation with the ground truth improve, albeit with diminishing returns. The shaded area denotes one standard deviation (i.e., variation in performance across random samples).

Model	Train Topic	ρ	Coverage
ROUGE-L	3	0.441	1.0
WMS (ELMo)	3	0.443	1.0
SMS (ELMo)	3	0.451	1.0
S+WMS (ELMo)	3	0.490	1.0
	1	0.301	1.0
	2	0.392	1.0
	4	−0.128	1.0
	5	0.466*	1.0
BLEU Neighbors	6	0.383	1.0
	7	0.305	1.0
	8	**0.500***	1.0
	9	0.375	1.0
	10	0.437*	1.0
	$\tilde{3}$	0.465*	1.0

Table 3: Spearman's ρ between predicted essay quality and the ground truth, where the test essays are from Topic #3 and * denotes $p < 0.01$. When using essays from Topic #8 as the training data, BLEU Neighbors is state-of-the-art, even beating out models with access to a gold-standard reference essay for Topic #3.

drawing a random subset of the data with n examples, doing hold-one-out prediction with $n - 1$ examples, and then taking the mean performance over 20 such runs. We find that BLEU Neighbors is surprisingly robust on all tasks, with 75 training examples being sufficient to achieve a Spearman's $\rho > 0.30$ on dialogue and open-ended generation while retaining above 60% coverage. As more data is used, both coverage and the Spearman correlation improve, though there are diminishing returns. Unsurprisingly, the variation in performance across random subsets also drops as more data is used.

5.6 Automated Essay Grading

In Table 3, we report the performance on the essay grading task described in Section 4, where the goal is to score essays from Topic #3 of the ASAP-SAS dataset. Unlike the NLG tasks, every test example here is a multi-sentence paragraph, which makes scoring more difficult: ten random sentences may be high-quality on their own while making little sense when put together. The difficulty of this task is compounded by the fact that the ground-truth quality of each essay is based on a gold-standard reference for Topic #3. Since BLEU Neighbors does not use references, it is at a disadvantage compared to approaches that do, such as ROUGE-L. Excluding ROUGE-L, all the models we list in Table 3 are optimal transport methods that leverage text embeddings (Clark et al., 2019).

Despite not being given the gold-standard reference, when BLEU Neighbors is trained with sample essays from Topic #8, it achieves a new state-of-the-art: a Spearman's ρ of 0.500 between its predicted scores and the ground-truth quality judgments. However, due to the small amount of test data, this improvement over the state-of-the-art is not statistically significant at $p < 0.01$ when using a Williams test. Still, its coverage is 100%, meaning that it makes predictions for all of the test essays. As seen in the second half of Table 3, the performance of the model depends strongly on which topic the training data is sourced from. This is unsurprising, given that some topics are more related to #3 than others. Some topics (e.g., #4) are so different from the test topic that its training examples are of no use, leading to very poor quality estimates. When we use essays from all topics but topic #3 as the training data – denoted in Table 3 as $\tilde{3}$ – we still outperform most of the past approaches.

6 Limitations and Future Work

Quality + Diversity Although the BLEU Neighbors model does not measure language diversity, this is by design. Consider that if an NLG model were ideal, even the optimal discriminator could not tell whether its outputs were human- or machine-generated. Hashimoto et al. (2019) proved that such an optimal discriminator would only need two statistics, a measure of language diversity (e.g., perplexity) and a measure of language quality. The former is trivial to compute – it is the latter that is cost- and time-intensive, and which we thus try to automate using BLEU Neighbors. These two measures can be combined using a metric such as HUSE (Hashimoto et al., 2019), meaning that it is sufficient for our model to predict quality alone. The next step would be to use such a hybrid metric in rapidly evaluating NLG models during development.

Preventing "Hacks" How can we prevent the NLG model being evaluated from "hacking" a BLEU Neighbors model so as to receive inflated quality estimates for all its outputs? As mentioned in section 3, one way to prevent this is to use disjoint training sets for the NLG model and BLEU Neighbors, so that the former has no idea what the latter considers a high-quality candidate. Additionally, it would help to have a large set of training examples for BLEU Neighbors and then subsample it during each evaluation instance, as that would discourage NLG models from generating n-grams that just so happen to occur in one or two high-quality examples in the training data. Moreover, BLEU Neighbors is intended to speed up NLG model development – not supplant humans – so any attempts to inflate quality estimates during development would have poor long-term outcomes.

Metric Learning The success of BLEU Neighbors can largely be ascribed to it using BLEU*, a variant of the BLEU-4 score, as the kernel function in sentence space. Despite its simplicity, BLEU* works surprisingly well. There is likely a more convoluted variant of BLEU-4 that works even better for this purpose – one that excludes stopwords, one that places greater weight on rarer n-grams, etc. Instead of specifying a kernel function, it may also be possible to learn one. For example, instead of representing each sentence as a sequence of words, one could transform it into a sentence embedding and then learn a kernel function as a metric in the embedding space. This is one direction of future work.

Diverse Datasets Although BLEU Neighbors performs well in our experiments, because of the small size of the datasets we use, not all results are statistically significant. One limitation of the HUSE datasets in particular is that, as mentioned earlier, the annotators scored different subsets of the data. In order to more faithfully compare our method against human annotators, we need larger

datasets from a more diverse array of tasks, where every example is scored by every annotator.

Because of the leave-one-out paradigm we use on the HUSE datasets, the test examples were scored in part with the help of scored training examples that were generated by the same model. Table 2 shows that cross-task performance is generally poor, with the exception of dialogue data. Would the performance still be poor if we used model-generated training examples from the same task but used a different model to generate them? This is a possibility that should be explored. It is also unclear what exactly is driving the success of BLEU Neighbors. For example, if it is exploiting annotation artefacts, then its success would be far less impressive (Gururangan et al., 2018). Understanding these possible failure cases is an important direction for future work. Developing a theoretical understanding of BLEU Neighbors – as has been done with static word embeddings, for example (Levy and Goldberg, 2014; Ethayarajh et al., 2019a,b; Ethayarajh, 2019) – would be ideal.

7 Conclusion

The absence of a reference-less evaluation metric for language quality has been an impediment to developing NLG models. To address this problem, we proposed *BLEU Neighbors*, a nearest neighbors model that leverages the BLEU score as a kernel function in sentence space. Our simple approach worked surprisingly well: it outperformed human annotators – on average – in predicting the quality of dialogue and open-ended generation data. We also found BLEU Neighbors to be state-of-the-art on automatically grading essays, even beating out models that had access to a gold-standard reference essay. Moreover, our model is fast, data-efficient, and easy-to-use; it has only two hyperparameters and those have settings that work universally well, across various tasks. Still, BLEU Neighbors is intended to complement, not supplant, human evaluation – its speed, simplicity, and ease of use makes it ideal for rapidly iterating on NLG models long before any human evaluation is done.

Acknowledgments

Many thanks to Alex Tamkin and Peng Qi for detailed feedback. We thank Nelson Liu and Tatsunori Hashimoto for helpful discussion. KE is supported by an NSERC PGS-D.

References

Hiroki Asano, Tomoya Mizumoto, and Kentaro Inui. 2017. Reference-based metrics can be replaced with reference-less metrics in evaluating grammatical error correction systems. In *Proceedings of the Eighth International Joint Conference on Natural Language Processing (Volume 2: Short Papers)*, pages 343–348.

Satanjeev Banerjee and Alon Lavie. 2005. Meteor: An automatic metric for mt evaluation with improved correlation with human judgments. In *Proceedings of the acl workshop on intrinsic and extrinsic evaluation measures for machine translation and/or summarization*, pages 65–72.

Arun Chaganty, Stephen Mussmann, and Percy Liang. 2018. The price of debiasing automatic metrics in natural language evalaution. In *Proceedings of the 56th Annual Meeting of the Association for Computational Linguistics (Volume 1: Long Papers)*, pages 643–653.

Leshem Choshen and Omri Abend. 2018. Reference-less measure of faithfulness for grammatical error correction. In *Proceedings of the 2018 Conference of the North American Chapter of the Association for Computational Linguistics: Human Language Technologies, Volume 2 (Short Papers)*, pages 124–129.

Elizabeth Clark, Asli Celikyilmaz, and Noah A Smith. 2019. Sentence mover's similarity: Automatic evaluation for multi-sentence texts. In *Proceedings of the 57th Annual Meeting of the Association for Computational Linguistics*, pages 2748–2760.

Jacob Devlin, Ming-Wei Chang, Kenton Lee, and Kristina Toutanova. 2019. Bert: Pre-training of deep bidirectional transformers for language understanding. In *Proceedings of the 2019 Conference of the North American Chapter of the Association for Computational Linguistics: Human Language Technologies, Volume 1 (Long and Short Papers)*, pages 4171–4186.

Kawin Ethayarajh. 2019. Rotate king to get queen: Word relationships as orthogonal transformations in embedding space. In *Proceedings of the 2019 Conference on Empirical Methods in Natural Language Processing and the 9th International Joint Conference on Natural Language Processing (EMNLP-IJCNLP)*, pages 3494–3499.

Kawin Ethayarajh, David Duvenaud, and Graeme Hirst. 2019a. Towards understanding linear word analogies. In *Proceedings of the 57th Annual Meeting of the Association for Computational Linguistics*, pages 3253–3262, Florence, Italy. Association for Computational Linguistics.

Kawin Ethayarajh, David Duvenaud, and Graeme Hirst. 2019b. Understanding undesirable word embedding associations. In *Proceedings of the 57th Annual Meeting of the Association for Computational Linguistics*, pages 1696–1705.

Suchin Gururangan, Swabha Swayamdipta, Omer Levy, Roy Schwartz, Samuel Bowman, and Noah A Smith. 2018. Annotation artifacts in natural language inference data. In *Proceedings of the 2018 Conference of the North American Chapter of the Association for Computational Linguistics: Human Language Technologies, Volume 2 (Short Papers)*, pages 107–112.

Tatsunori B Hashimoto, Hugh Zhang, and Percy Liang. 2019. Unifying human and statistical evaluation for natural language generation. *arXiv preprint arXiv:1904.02792*.

Katharina Kann, Sascha Rothe, and Katja Filippova. 2018. Sentence-level fluency evaluation: References help, but can be spared! In *Proceedings of the 22nd Conference on Computational Natural Language Learning*, pages 313–323.

Omer Levy and Yoav Goldberg. 2014. Neural word embedding as implicit matrix factorization. In *Advances in neural information processing systems*, pages 2177–2185.

Chin-Yew Lin. 2004. ROUGE: A package for automatic evaluation of summaries. In *Text Summarization Branches Out*, pages 74–81, Barcelona, Spain. Association for Computational Linguistics.

Chia-Wei Liu, Ryan Lowe, Iulian Vlad Serban, Mike Noseworthy, Laurent Charlin, and Joelle Pineau. 2016. How not to evaluate your dialogue system: An empirical study of unsupervised evaluation metrics for dialogue response generation. In *Proceedings of the 2016 Conference on Empirical Methods in Natural Language Processing*, pages 2122–2132.

Chi-kiu Lo, Michel Simard, Darlene Stewart, Samuel Larkin, Cyril Goutte, and Patrick Littell. 2018. Accurate semantic textual similarity for cleaning noisy parallel corpora using semantic machine translation evaluation metric: The nrc supervised submissions to the parallel corpus filtering task. In *Proceedings of the Third Conference on Machine Translation: Shared Task Papers*, pages 908–916.

Ryan Lowe. 2019. Introducing retrospectives: 'real talk' for your past papers.

Ryan Lowe, Michael Noseworthy, Iulian Vlad Serban, Nicolas Angelard-Gontier, Yoshua Bengio, and Joelle Pineau. 2017. Towards an automatic turing test: Learning to evaluate dialogue responses. In *Proceedings of the 55th Annual Meeting of the Association for Computational Linguistics (Volume 1: Long Papers)*, pages 1116–1126.

Qingsong Ma, Yvette Graham, Shugen Wang, and Qun Liu. 2017. Blend: a novel combined mt metric based on direct assessment—casict-dcu submission to wmt17 metrics task. In *Proceedings of the second conference on machine translation*, pages 598–603.

Courtney Napoles, Keisuke Sakaguchi, and Joel Tetreault. 2016. There's no comparison: Reference-less evaluation metrics in grammatical error correction. In *Proceedings of the 2016 Conference on Empirical Methods in Natural Language Processing*, pages 2109–2115.

Kishore Papineni, Salim Roukos, Todd Ward, and Wei-Jing Zhu. 2002. Bleu: a method for automatic evaluation of machine translation. In *Proceedings of the 40th annual meeting on association for computational linguistics*, pages 311–318. Association for Computational Linguistics.

Ananya B Sai, Mithun Das Gupta, Mitesh M Khapra, and Mukundhan Srinivasan. 2019. Re-evaluating adem: A deeper look at scoring dialogue responses. In *Proceedings of the AAAI Conference on Artificial Intelligence*, volume 33, pages 6220–6227.

Iulian Vlad Serban, Ryan Lowe, Peter Henderson, Laurent Charlin, and Joelle Pineau. 2015. A survey of available corpora for building data-driven dialogue systems. *arXiv preprint arXiv:1512.05742*.

Hiroki Shimanaka, Tomoyuki Kajiwara, and Mamoru Komachi. 2018. Ruse: Regressor using sentence embeddings for automatic machine translation evaluation. In *Proceedings of the Third Conference on Machine Translation: Shared Task Papers*, pages 751–758.

Miloš Stanojević and Khalil Sima'an. 2014. Beer: Better evaluation as ranking. In *Proceedings of the Ninth Workshop on Statistical Machine Translation*, pages 414–419.

Ramakrishna Vedantam, C Lawrence Zitnick, and Devi Parikh. 2015. Cider: Consensus-based image description evaluation. In *Proceedings of the IEEE conference on computer vision and pattern recognition*, pages 4566–4575.

Tianyi Zhang, Varsha Kishore, Felix Wu, Kilian Q Weinberger, and Yoav Artzi. 2019. Bertscore: Evaluating text generation with bert. In *International Conference on Learning Representations*.

Wei Zhao, Maxime Peyrard, Fei Liu, Yang Gao, Christian M Meyer, and Steffen Eger. 2019. Moverscore: Text generation evaluating with contextualized embeddings and earth mover distance. In *Proceedings of the 2019 Conference on Empirical Methods in Natural Language Processing and the 9th International Joint Conference on Natural Language Processing (EMNLP-IJCNLP)*, pages 563–578.

Improving Text Generation Evaluation with Batch Centering and Tempered Word Mover Distance

Xi Chen[*]
Harvard University
Cambridge, MA 02138
chenx@g.harvard.edu

Nan Ding[†]
Google Research
Venice, CA 90291

Tomer Levinboim
Google Research
Venice, CA 90291

Radu Soricut
Google Research
Venice, CA 90291

{dingnan,tomerl,rsoricut}@google.com

Abstract

Recent advances in automatic evaluation metrics for text have shown that deep contextualized word representations, such as those generated by BERT encoders, are helpful for designing metrics that correlate well with human judgements. At the same time, it has been argued that contextualized word representations exhibit sub-optimal statistical properties for encoding the true similarity between words or sentences. In this paper, we present two techniques for improving encoding representations for similarity metrics: a batch-mean centering strategy that improves statistical properties; and a computationally efficient tempered Word Mover Distance, for better fusion of the information in the contextualized word representations. We conduct numerical experiments that demonstrate the robustness of our techniques, reporting results over various BERT-backbone learned metrics and achieving state of the art correlation with human ratings on several benchmarks.

1 Introduction

Automatic evaluation metrics play an important role in comparing candidate sentences generated by machines against human references. First-generation metrics such as BLEU (Papineni et al., 2002) and ROUGE (Lin, 2004) use predefined handcrafted rules to measure surface similarity between sentences and have no ability, or very little ability (Banerjee and Lavie, 2005), to go beyond word surface level. To address this problem, later work (Kusner et al., 2015; Zhelezniak et al., 2019) utilize static embedding techniques such as word2vec (Mikolov et al., 2013) and Glove (Pennington et al., 2014) to represent the words in sentences as vectors in a low-dimensional continuous space, so that word-to-word correlation can be measured by their cosine similarity. However, static embeddings cannot capture the rich syntactic, semantic, and pragmatic aspects of word usage across sentences and paragraphs.

Modern deep learning models based on the Transformer (Vaswani et al., 2017) utilize a multi-layered self-attention structure that encodes not only a global representation of each word (a word embedding), but also its contextualized information within the context considered. Such contextualized word representations have yielded significant improvements on various tasks, including machine translation (Vaswani et al., 2017), NLU tasks (Devlin et al., 2019; Liu et al., 2019; Lan et al., 2020), summarization (Zhang et al., 2019a), and automatic evaluation metrics (Reimers and Gurevych, 2019; Zhang et al., 2019b; Zhao et al., 2019; Sellam et al., 2020).

In this paper, we investigate how to better use BERT-based contextualized embeddings in order to arrive at effective evaluation metrics for generated text. We formalize a unified family of text similarity metrics, which operate either at the word/token or sentence level, and show how a number of existing embedding-based similarity metrics belong to this family. In this context, we present a tempered Word Mover Distance (TWMD) formulation by utilizing the Sinkhorn distance (Cuturi, 2013), which adds an entropy regularizer to the objective of WMD (Kusner et al., 2015). Compared to WMD, our TWMD formulation allows for a more efficient optimization using the iterative Sinkhorn algorithm (Cuturi, 2013). Although in theory the Sinkhorn algorithm may require a number of iterations to converge, we find that a single iteration is sufficient and surprisingly effective for TWMD.

Moreover, we follow (Ethayarajh, 2019) and carefully analyze the similarity between contextualized word representations along the different

---

[*] Work done during the internship at Google.
[†] Corresponding author.

Proceedings of the First Workshop on Evaluation and Comparison of NLP Systems (Eval4NLP), pages 51–59,
November 20, 2020. ©2020 Association for Computational Linguistics

layers of a BERT model. We posit three properties that multi-layered contextualized word representations should have (Section 5): (1) zero expected similarity between random words, (2) decreasing out-of-context self-similarity, and (3) increasing in-context similarity between words. As already shown by Ethayarajh (2019), cosine similarity between BERT word-embeddings does not satisfy some of these properties. To address these issues, we design and analyze several centering techniques and find one that satisfies the three properties above. The usefulness of the centering technique and TWMD formulation is validated by our empirical studies over several well-known benchmarks, where we obtain significant numerical improvements and SoTA correlations with human ratings.

2 Related Work

Recent work on learned automatic evaluation metrics leverage pretrained contextualized embeddings by building on top of BERT (Devlin et al., 2019) or variant (Liu et al., 2019) representations.

SentenceBERT (Reimers and Gurevych, 2019) uses cosine similarity of two mean-pooled sentence embedding from the top layer of BERT. BERTscore (Zhang et al., 2019b) computes the similarity of two sentences as a sum of cosine similarities between maximum-matching tokens embeddings. Mover-Score (Zhao et al., 2019) measures word distance using BERT embeddings and computes the Word Mover Distance (WMD) (Kusner et al., 2015) from the word distribution of the system text to that of the human reference.

In the next section we propose an abstract framework of embedding-based similarity metrics and show that it contains the metrics mentioned above. We then extend this family of metrics with our own improved evaluation metric.

3 A Family of Similarity Metrics

We consider a family of normalized similarity metrics for both word-level and sentence-level representations parameterized by a function C, as follows:

$$\text{Sim}(\mathbf{x}_1, \mathbf{x}_2) = \frac{C(\mathbf{x}_1, \mathbf{x}_2)}{\sqrt{C(\mathbf{x}_1, \mathbf{x}_1) C(\mathbf{x}_2, \mathbf{x}_2)}}. \quad (1)$$

Clearly, $\text{Sim}(\mathbf{x}, \mathbf{x}) = 1$, and furthermore, if $C(\mathbf{x}_1, \mathbf{x}_2)^2 \leq C(\mathbf{x}_1, \mathbf{x}_1) C(\mathbf{x}_2, \mathbf{x}_2)$, then $\text{Sim}(\mathbf{x}_1, \mathbf{x}_2) \in [-1, 1]$.

For word similarity, $\mathbf{x}$ represents a single word vector. A standard choice is defining $C(\mathbf{x}_1, \mathbf{x}_2) = \langle \mathbf{x}_1, \mathbf{x}_2 \rangle$, the inner product between the two vectors. The resulting word similarity metric $\text{Sim}(\mathbf{x}_1, \mathbf{x}_2) = \left\langle \frac{\mathbf{x}_1}{\|\mathbf{x}_1\|}, \frac{\mathbf{x}_2}{\|\mathbf{x}_2\|} \right\rangle$ becomes the cosine similarity between the two word vectors. If the word vectors are pre-normalized such that $\|\mathbf{x}\| = 1$, then $\text{Sim}(\mathbf{x}_1, \mathbf{x}_2) = \langle \mathbf{x}_1, \mathbf{x}_2 \rangle$.

For sentence similarity, we use $\mathbf{X} = \left(\mathbf{x}^1, \mathbf{x}^2, \ldots, \mathbf{x}^L \right)$ to denote a $D \times L$ matrix composed by L word vectors belonging to the sentence embedded in a D-dimensional space.

In what follows, we briefly review existing sentence similarity metrics and show that they belong to our family of similarity metrics Eq.(1) with different choices of $C(\mathbf{X}_1, \mathbf{X}_2)$ (with L_1 and L_2 denoting the sentence length for $\mathbf{X}_1$ and $\mathbf{X}_2$, respectively). Note that we do not consider word re-weighting schemes (e.g. by IDF as in (Zhang et al., 2019b)) in this paper, as their contribution does not appear to be consistent over various tasks. In addition, we assume that all word vectors are already pre-normalized.

Sentence-BERT Sentence-BERT (Reimers and Gurevych, 2019) uses the cosine-similarity between two mean-pooling sentence embeddings. This is the same as Eq.(1) when

$$C(\mathbf{X}_1, \mathbf{X}_2) = \left\langle \frac{1}{L_1} \sum_{i=1}^{L_1} \mathbf{x}_1^i, \frac{1}{L_2} \sum_{j=1}^{L_2} \mathbf{x}_2^j \right\rangle$$

$$= \frac{1}{L_1 L_2} \sum_{i=1}^{L_1} \sum_{j=1}^{L_2} \left\langle \mathbf{x}_1^i, \mathbf{x}_2^j \right\rangle.$$

Wordset-CKA Wordset-CKA (Zhelezniak et al., 2019) uses the centered kernel alignment between the two sentences represented as word sets, where

$$C(\mathbf{X}_1, \mathbf{X}_2) = \text{Tr}\left(\mathbf{X}_1 \mathbf{X}_1^\top \mathbf{X}_2 \mathbf{X}_2^\top \right)$$

$$= \sum_{i=1}^{L_1} \sum_{j=1}^{L_2} \left\langle \mathbf{x}_1^i, \mathbf{x}_2^j \right\rangle^2.$$

Here we assume each word embedding $\mathbf{x}$ is pre-centered by the mean of its own dimensions. We refer to this centering method as *dimension-mean centering*.

MoverScore MoverScore (Zhao et al., 2019) measures the sentence similarity using the Word Mover Distance (Kusner et al., 2015) from the word distribution of the hypothesis to that of the gold reference:

$$C(\mathbf{X}_1, \mathbf{X}_2) = \max_{\pi} \sum_{i=1}^{L_1} \sum_{j=1}^{L_2} \pi_{ij} \left\langle \mathbf{x}_1^i, \mathbf{x}_2^j \right\rangle$$

$$\text{s.t.} \ \sum_{i=1}^{L_1} \pi_{ij} = \frac{1}{L_2}, \ \sum_{j=1}^{L_2} \pi_{ij} = \frac{1}{L_1}. \tag{2}$$

The original MoverScore does not normalize $C(\mathbf{X}_1, \mathbf{X}_2)$ by $\sqrt{C(\mathbf{X}_1, \mathbf{X}_1) C(\mathbf{X}_2, \mathbf{X}_2)}$. In practice, we find the performance to be similar with or without such normalization.

BERTscore BERTscore (Zhang et al., 2019b) introduces three metrics corresponding to recall, precision, and F1 score. We focus the discussion here on BERTscore-Recall, as it performs most consistently across all tasks (see discussions of the precision and F1 scores in Appendix C). BERTscore-Recall uses the sum of cosine similarities between maximum-matching tokens embeddings:

$$C(\mathbf{X}_1, \mathbf{X}_2) = \frac{1}{L_1} \sum_{i=1}^{L_1} \max_{j=1...L_2} \left\langle \mathbf{x}_1^i, \mathbf{x}_2^j \right\rangle. \tag{3}$$

For BERTscore, since the words are pre-normalized, we have $C(\mathbf{X}_1, \mathbf{X}_1) = C(\mathbf{X}_2, \mathbf{X}_2) = 1$ and therefore $\text{Sim}(\mathbf{X}_1, \mathbf{X}_2) = C(\mathbf{X}_1, \mathbf{X}_2)$.

Note that BERTscore is closely related to MoverScore, since Eq.(3) is the solution of the Relaxed-WMD (Kusner et al., 2015):

$$C(\mathbf{X}_1, \mathbf{X}_2) = \max_{\pi} \sum_{i=1}^{L_1} \sum_{j=1}^{L_2} \pi_{ij} \left\langle \mathbf{x}_1^i, \mathbf{x}_2^j \right\rangle$$

$$\text{s.t.} \ \sum_{j=1}^{L_2} \pi_{ij} = \frac{1}{L_1}. \tag{4}$$

which is the same as Eq.(2) but without the first constraint.

4 Tempered Word Mover Distance

Word Mover Distance (Kusner et al., 2015) used in MoverScore (Zhao et al., 2019) is rooted in the classical optimal transport distance for probability measures and histograms of features. Despite its excellent performance and intuitive formulation, its computation involves a linear programming solver whose cost scales as $O(L^3 \log L)$ and becomes prohibitive for long sentences or documents with more than a few hundreds of words/tokens.

For this reason, (Kusner et al., 2015) proposed a Relaxed-WMD (RWMD) with only one constraint (see Eq.(4)), which can be evaluated in $O(L^2)$. However, RWMD uses the closest distance without considering there may be multiple words transforming to single words.

Inspired by the Sinkhorn distance (Cuturi, 2013) which smooths the classic optimal transport problem with an entropic regularization term, we introduce the following formulation, which we refer to as tempered-WMD (TWMD):

$$\max_{\pi} \sum_{i=1}^{L_1} \sum_{j=1}^{L_2} \pi_{ij} \left\langle \mathbf{x}_1^i, \mathbf{x}_2^j \right\rangle - T \sum_{i=1}^{L_1} \sum_{j=1}^{L_2} \pi_{ij} \log \pi_{ij}$$

$$\text{s.t.} \ \sum_{i=1}^{L_1} \pi_{ij} = \frac{1}{L_2}, \ \sum_{j=1}^{L_2} \pi_{ij} = \frac{1}{L_1}. \tag{5}$$

The temperature parameter $T \geq 0$ determines the trade-off between the two terms. When $T = 0$, Eq.(5) reduce to the original WMD as in Eq.(2). When T is larger, (5) encourages more homogeneous distributions.

The added entropy term makes Eq.(5) a strictly concave problem, which can be solved using a matrix scaling algorithm with a linear convergence rate. For example, the Sinkhorn algorithm (Cuturi, 2013) uses the initial condition $\pi_{ij}^0 = \exp\left(-\frac{1}{T} \left\langle \mathbf{x}_1^i, \mathbf{x}_2^j \right\rangle\right)$ and alternates between

$$\xi_{ij}^t = \frac{\pi_{ij}^{t-1}}{L_2 \sum_i \pi_{ij}^{t-1}}, \ \ \pi_{ij}^t = \frac{\xi_{ij}^t}{L_1 \sum_j \xi_{ij}^t}. \tag{6}$$

The computational cost for each iteration is $O(L^2)$, which is more efficient than to that of WMD. Although in theory this iterative algorithm may require a few of iterations to converge, our experiments show that a single iteration (i.e., $t = 1$) is sufficient and surprisingly effective.

Similarly, a tempered-RWMD (TRWMD) can be obtained by adding an entropy term to Eq.(4):

$$\max_{\pi} \sum_{i=1}^{L_1} \sum_{j=1}^{L_2} \pi_{ij} \left\langle \mathbf{x}_1^i, \mathbf{x}_2^j \right\rangle - T \sum_{i=1}^{L_1} \sum_{j=1}^{L_2} \pi_{ij} \log \pi_{ij}$$

$$\text{s.t.} \ \sum_{j=1}^{L_2} \pi_{ij} = \frac{1}{L_1}.$$

By taking the derivative of the Lagrangian of the above objective, the following closed-form solution is obtained:

$$\pi_{ij}^* = \frac{1}{L_1} \text{softmax}_j \left(\frac{1}{T} \left\langle \mathbf{x}_1^i, \mathbf{x}_2^j \right\rangle\right).$$

Plugging in the optimal π_{ij}^* back into the objective yields the following metric:

$$C(\mathbf{X}_1, \mathbf{X}_2) =$$

$$= \frac{T}{L_1} \sum_{i=1}^{L_1} \log \left(\sum_{j=1}^{L_2} \exp \left(\frac{1}{T} \left\langle \mathbf{x}_1^i, \mathbf{x}_2^j \right\rangle \right) \right) . \quad (7)$$

We note that as $T \to 0$, $T \log \sum_j \exp(f_j/T) \to \max_j(f_j)$, and therefore Eq.(7) reduces to Eq.(3).

5 Centered Word Vectors

Ethayarajh (2019) reports that representations obtained by deep models such as BERT exhibit high cosine similarity between any two random words in a corpus, especially at higher layers. They attribute this phenomenon to a highly anisotropic distribution of the word vectors, and further argue that such high similarity represents a bias that blurs the true similarity relationship between word (and sentence) representations and hampers performance in NLP tasks (Mu and Viswanath, 2018). We reproduce here the main results of (Ethayarajh, 2019), including the cosine similarity between two random words (baseline), same words in two different sentences (self-similarity) and two random words in the same sentence (intra-similarity). Figure 1 shows these results for several BERT and BERT-like models. As the leftmost figure shows, most of

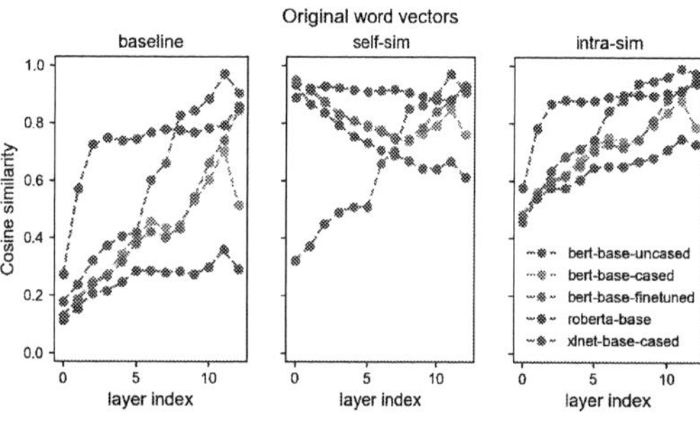

Figure 1: Cosine similarity between two random words (baseline), same words in two different sentences (self-similarity) and two random words in the same sentence (intra-similarity) for five base models, using the original layer representation of words.

these models indeed have a high baseline similarity that quickly increases with layer depth. Ethayarajh (2019) proposes to mitigate this bias by subtracting the baseline similarity from the self-similarity and intra-similarity values (per layer). However, the mathematical and statistical meaning of this solution remains unclear.

In this context, we posit the following three properties that are desirable for word vector representations in context:

1. Zero expected similarity: The word similarity between two random word vectors in the corpus is approximately zero, which indicates random words are unrelated.

2. Decreasing self-similarity: The word similarity between representations of the same word taken from different sentences decreases in higher layers, as each representation encodes more contextual information about its respective sentence.

3. Increasing intra-similarity: The word similarity between different words within the same sentence increases in higher layers, as the words encode more common information about the sentence.

Besides their intuitive appeal, our empirical results (in Section 6) do validate that word representations that obey these properties result in higher performance with respect to modeling similarity.

Since the original word representations does not satisfy these three properties, we explore three methods for centering the word vectors distribution. Consider a corpus $\mathcal{C}$ containing M sentences $\{s_i\}$, each of length N_i. Each word vector is D-dimensional, $\mathbf{w}_{i,j} = [w_{i,j}^{(1)}, ..., w_{i,j}^{(D)}]$. We propose three candidate word distribution centering approaches:

- Dimension mean centering: centering a word by subtracting the mean of the dimensions within each word vector,

$$\mathbf{v}_{i,j} = \mathbf{w}_{i,j} - \frac{1}{D} \sum_{l=1}^{D} w_{i,j}^{(l)}.$$

The second term on the RHS is a scalar, which broadcasts to all dimensions of $\mathbf{w}_{i,j}$.

- Sentence mean centering: centering a word by subtracting the mean of the words within the corresponding sentence,

$$\mathbf{v}_{i,j} = \mathbf{w}_{i,j} - \frac{1}{N} \sum_{k=1}^{N} \mathbf{w}_{i,k} .$$

- Corpus mean centering: centering a word by subtracting the mean of the words in the entire corpus,

$$\mathbf{v}_{i,j} = \mathbf{w}_{i,j} - \frac{1}{\sum_i N_i} \sum_{i=1}^{M} \sum_{k=1}^{N_i} \mathbf{w}_{i,k} \,.$$

We compare these three centering approaches in Figure 2. Due to the layer norm operation in the BERT models, the dimension mean is a small constant that has little effect after subtraction, and therefore it fails on properties 1 and 2 above. The sentence mean centering achieves approximately zero baseline (property 1), but it also reduces the intra-sim to approximately zero (failing property 3). This indicates the subtraction of sentence mean removes the common knowledge of the words about the sentence, which can have a detrimental effect on modeling similarity. Lastly, corpus-mean centering fulfills all three properties above (Fig. 2, bottom row). In this context, we note that, after applying corpus mean centering, cosine-similarity function is reduced to Pearson's correlation.

Since the computational cost of corpus mean centering can be prohibitive for a large dataset, we consider a batch-mean centering approach, which would be especially useful for fine-tuning tasks. In practice, we find that the values obtained from batch-mean–centered word vectors are very close to those of corpus-mean–centered word vectors. Therefore and henceforth, we use batch-mean centering to approximate the effect of corpus-mean centering.

Finally, it is worth noting that corpus (batch)-mean centering has recently been applied in normalizing multilingual representations (Libovický et al., 2019; Zhao et al., 2020). However, we are the first to demonstrate its superiority over various other centering methods in single-language by analyzing the inter-layer representation similarities.

6 Experiments

In order to demonstrate the effectiveness of our newly proposed approaches, we conduct extensive numerical experiments based on two commonly-used benchmarks: Semantic Textual Similarity (STS), and WMT 17-18 metrics shared task. Our experiments are designed to answer the following questions: (1) Are corpus (batch) centered word vectors better than other centered and un-centered word vectors, across different sentence similarity metrics? (2) How do tempered WMD and RWMD compare to their family-relatives MoverScore and

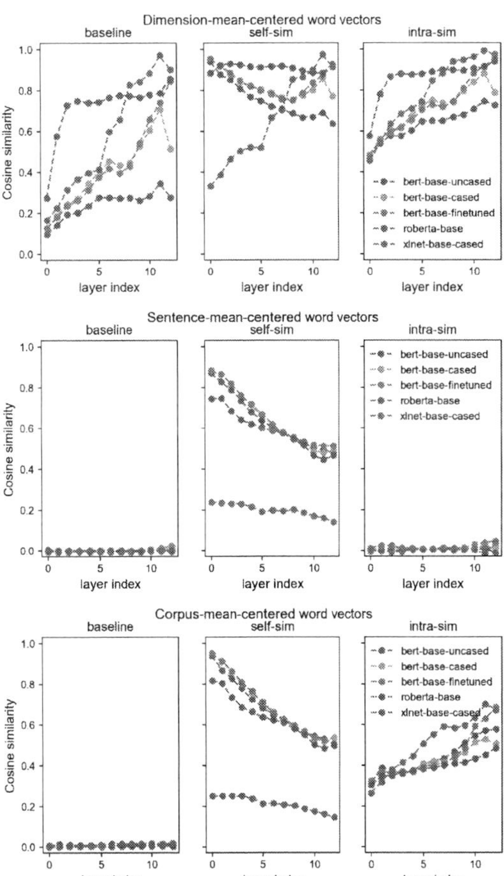

Figure 2: Comparison of the three centering approaches. Dimension mean centering has very little effect. Sentence mean centering removes too much common sentence information. Corpus mean centering shows the correct word contextualization.

BERTscore? (3) How do the temperature hyperparameter and the Sinkhorn iterations affect the performance, and how sensitive are they?

To show that our results are consistent across different BERT variants, we analyze our similarity metrics over four backbone models: bert-base-uncased, bert-large-uncased, roberta-base and roberta-large, all obtained from the Huggingface* Transformers package. (Zhang et al., 2019b) found that the better layers for evaluation metric are usually not the top layer, since the top one is greatly impacted by the pretraining task. In particular, (Zhang et al., 2019b) perform an an extensive layer sweep analysis and report that the better layers were always around Layer-10 for the base models, and Layer-19 for the large models. Therefore, in our

---

*https://huggingface.co/models

experiments, we used Layer-10 for all base models, and Layer-19 for all large models. We also present the results of evaluation metrics using different layers in the Appendix A and confirm that our main conclusion is not affected by the choice of layer.

6.1 Semantic Textual Similarity (STS)

The STS benchmark (Agirre et al., 2016) contains sentence pairs and human evaluated scores between 0 and 5 for each pair, with higher scores indicating higher semantic relatedness or similarity for the pair. From 2012 to 2016, it contains 3108, 1500, 3750, 3000, and 1186 records, respectively.

We answer the first question by comparing batch-centered word vectors with other centered and un-centered word vectors using several sentence similarity metrics, including Sentence-BERT, Wordset-CKA, BERTscore and MoverScore.

The results on STS 12-16 for various metrics are shown in Table 1. In general, for all four models (per column: base and large version of BERT and RoBERTa), batch centering gets higher Pearson and Spearman's correlation of sentence-mean cosine similarity (SBERT) and BERTscore. Dimension-mean centering has very little effect on performance, while sentence-mean improves performance for a few methods. Since Sentence-BERT uses the mean-pooling of the sentence (which would become zero after sentence mean centering), we exclude sentence-mean centering from Sentence-BERT. Overall, batch-mean centering brings an averaged +3.41 / +3.02 improvement, and sentence-mean centering brings an averaged -0.02 / +0.55 on Pearson and Spearman coefficients, across different metrics and models.

6.2 WMT metrics shared task

The WMT metrics shared task is an annual competition for comparing translation metrics against human assessments on machine-translated sentences. We use years 2017 and 2018 of the official WMT test set for evaluation. The 2017 test data includes 3,920 pairs of sentences from the news domain (including a system generated sentence and a groundtruth sentence by human) with human ratings. Similarly, the 2018 test data includes 138,188 pairs of sentences with human ratings but is reported to be much noisier (Sellam et al., 2020).

Evaluation metrics without fine-tuning

We compare the Tempered WMD (TWMD) and TRWMD with the original WMD (Moverscore)

and RWMD (BERTscore) as well as SBERT and WordSet-CKA on WMT 17 and 18. We report the results of RoBERTa-base and RoBERTa-large for WMT 17 and WMT 18, because they appear to be the best performing backbone models for these tasks.

To choose reasonable temperatures for TWMD and TRWMD, we tried a few values between 0.001 and 0.15 on WMT 15-16, and chose for each method based on the best averaged performance (details in Appendix B). The resulting temperatures for TWMD, TRWMD, TWMD-b (where "-b" stands for batch centering of word vectors) and TRWMD-b are $T = 0.02, 0.02, 0.10, 0.15$ respectively. We used a single Sinkhorn iteration for TWMD(-b).

The main results of WMT 17 and 18 are summarized in Table 2 and 3. Batch-mean centering appears to be helpful in improving the scores for all methods. TWMD-b performs the best in most of the cases. In particular, it is on average +2.3 / +2.8 higher than the WMD-based Moverscore-b in WMT-17 and +1.1 / +1.9 higher in WMT-18.

Evaluation metrics with fine-tuning

We also test the effectiveness of batch-mean centering and TWMD in the fine-tuning process. Similar to (Sellam et al., 2020), we make use of the human ratings from WMT 15-16 for training, and evaluate the fine-tuned models on WMT 17 and 18. We use the L2 loss function during fine-tuning,

$$\text{Loss} = \text{MSE}(\text{Sim}(\mathbf{X}_1, \mathbf{X}_2), \hat{y}),$$

where $\mathbf{X}_1, \mathbf{X}_2$ denotes two sentences, and $\hat{y}$ is the human score.

We present the result of TWMD based on the RoBERTa-base and RoBERTa-large backbones in Table 4. We compare the result with that of state-of-the-art BLEURT (Sellam et al., 2020) models. BLEURTbase-pre and BLEURT-pre are directly fine-tuned on WMT 15-16 (with 5344 records in total), while BLEURTbase and BLEURT are additionally pretrained on a large amount of synthetic data from Wikipedia. The scores obtained by TWMD-b not only clearly outperform BLEURTbase-pre and BLEURT-pre with the same training setting, but are comparable or better than the performance of BLEURT with the extra pre-training stage, on both base and large conditions. This last result is especially notable considering that the synthetic data and the task setup used to further pretrain BLUERT were designed with metric

Table 1: Experimental results for various metrics on STS 12-16 datasets (averaged) with BERT/Roberta pretrained checkpoints. The correlations are Pearson (left) and Spearman's rank (right).

Metric	bert-base-uncased r / ρ	bert-large-uncased r / ρ	roberta-base r / ρ	roberta-large r / ρ
SBERT	58.7 / 58.9	56.9 / 57.3	58.0 / 59.6	58.5 / 60.2
SBERT-batch	**63.8 / 62.8**	**62.8 / 62.3**	**65.9 / 65.1**	**67.1 / 66.3**
SBERT-dim	58.7 / 58.9	56.9 / 57.3	58.0 / 59.6	58.5 / 60.2
CKA	59.8 / 59.5	58.7 / 58.9	58.6 / 59.9	59.1 / 60.4
CKA-batch	**60.3 / 61.1**	58.9 / 60.0	**61.1 / 61.5**	**62.3 / 62.5**
CKA-sent	58.6 / 59.8	**59.1 / 60.5**	58.7 / 59.2	60.6 / 61.0
CKA-dim	59.8 / 59.5	58.7 / 58.9	58.6 / 59.9	59.1 / 60.4
MoverScore	56.3 / 58.2	54.4 / 56.7	54.8 / 56.2	54.5 / 56.0
MoverScore-batch	**58.0 / 60.1**	**56.2 / 58.6**	**57.2 / 59.0**	**57.7 / 59.3**
MoverScore-sent	54.2 / 57.4	54.9 / 58.3	54.1 / 56.5	55.9 / 58.1
MoverScore-dim	56.3 / 58.2	54.4 / 56.7	54.8 / 56.2	54.5 / 56.0
BERTscore	59.3 / 59.0	57.7 / 57.8	57.3 / 57.2	57.0 / 57.1
BERTscore-batch	**61.1 / 60.9**	**59.6 / 59.7**	**60.6 / 60.6**	**61.5 / 61.4**
BERTscore-sent	57.3 / 57.6	58.1 / 58.6	56.8 / 57.2	59.0 / 59.2
BERTscore-dim	59.3 / 59.0	57.7 / 57.8	57.3 / 57.2	57.0 / 57.1

Table 2: Correlation with human scores on the WMT17 Metrics Shared Task. '-b' stands for batch centering of word vectors.

Metric	cs-en τ / r	de-en τ / r	fi-en τ / r	lv-en τ / r	ru-en τ / r	tr-en τ / r	zh-en τ / r	Avg. τ / r
roberta-base								
SBERT	45.1 / 60.0	44.6 / 58.3	58.4 / 69.6	42.9 / 60.6	45.8 / 63.1	46.3 / 52.9	46.0 / 62.0	47.0 / 60.9
SBERT-b	45.2 / 63.4	45.8 / 64.1	56.8 / 74.6	45.1 / 64.9	44.9 / 64.0	47.8 / 63.4	45.4 / 66.1	47.3 / 65.8
CKA	45.0 / 60.5	44.8 / 58.8	58.3 / 70.5	42.8 / 61.0	45.9 / 63.4	46.3 / 53.9	46.1 / 62.4	47.0 / 61.5
CKA-b	48.8 / 68.4	49.1 / 69.1	61.3 / 81.3	48.5 / 69.6	49.6 / 69.6	52.1 / 71.7	49.6 / 70.8	51.3 / 71.5
MoverScore	48.5 / 66.0	47.1 / 65.9	61.6 / 80.9	48.9 / 68.2	51.6 / 69.8	53.8 / 74.2	53.4 / 74.0	52.1 / 71.3
MoverScore-b	47.9 / 66.3	47.3 / 66.1	61.6 / 81.2	48.6 / 68.6	51.4 / 69.8	54.3 / 74.9	52.2 / 72.8	51.9 / 71.3
BERTscore	47.4 / 64.7	48.0 / 66.9	61.9 / 79.9	49.7 / 69.6	50.8 / 69.5	53.4 / 71.3	50.8 / 71.7	51.7 / 70.5
BERTscore-b	47.5 / 66.4	48.8 / 68.7	61.7 / 81.3	49.9 / 70.6	50.7 / 69.8	53.8 / 73.2	49.1 / 70.1	51.6 / 71.5
TWMD	48.3 / 65.8	49.6 / 68.8	62.5 / 81.2	51.3 / 70.5	52.1 / 71.2	54.6 / 73.8	**54.7 / 75.5**	53.3 / 72.3
TWMD-b	**50.0 / 68.5**	**51.5 / 70.8**	**63.0 / 82.8**	**51.9 / 72.3**	**53.5 / 73.2**	**56.6 / 77.0**	54.0 / 75.0	**54.4 / 74.3**
TRWMD	47.4 / 64.9	47.9 / 67.0	61.8 / 80.1	49.5 / 69.3	50.9 / 69.5	53.4 / 71.8	50.7 / 71.7	51.7 / 70.7
TRWMD-b	48.5 / 66.8	49.0 / 68.5	61.1 / 81.3	49.5 / 69.3	51.4 / 69.8	54.3 / 74.7	50.2 / 70.8	52.0 / 71.6
roberta-large								
SBERT	50.9 / 67.2	53.1 / 70.8	61.3 / 73.6	51.6 / 70.5	51.4 / 69.0	52.4 / 61.4	51.9 / 68.0	53.2 / 68.6
SBERT-b	47.6 / 66.9	50.7 / 69.5	56.8 / 74.1	47.9 / 67.8	47.3 / 66.4	48.5 / 65.2	47.6 / 67.5	49.5 / 68.2
CKA	51.4 / 68.7	53.4 / 71.3	61.5 / 74.5	51.8 / 71.1	51.8 / 69.3	52.7 / 62.7	52.1 / 68.8	53.5 / 69.5
CKA-b	51.6 / 72.3	54.4 / 74.2	61.8 / 81.6	52.5 / 73.7	53.2 / 73.0	53.6 / 73.8	52.7 / 73.5	54.3 / 74.6
MoverScore	51.6 / 68.8	53.9 / 71.8	62.0 / 81.1	53.4 / 71.7	54.5 / 71.8	56.3 / 76.2	56.3 / 76.1	55.5 / 73.9
MoverScore-b	51.2 / 69.6	53.2 / 71.7	63.1 / 82.1	53.3 / 72.7	54.5 / 72.8	56.8 / 76.9	55.1 / 75.4	55.3 / 74.5
BERTscore	50.9 / 66.9	53.4 / 72.3	61.7 / 79.6	53.5 / 71.6	53.8 / 71.5	54.8 / 71.7	53.9 / 74.4	54.6 / 72.6
BERTscore-b	51.7 / 71.2	53.9 / 74.1	63.6 / 82.5	54.8 / **75.1**	54.8 / 73.7	55.6 / 75.0	52.7 / 73.6	55.3 / 75.0
TWMD	52.3 / 69.1	55.7 / 74.4	63.1 / 81.5	54.1 / 72.6	56.0 / 74.1	55.7 / 74.5	**57.5 / 77.7**	56.3 / 74.9
TWMD-b	**53.9 / 73.3**	**56.4 / 75.9**	**64.4 / 83.5**	**55.2 / 75.1**	**56.9 / 76.2**	**57.9 / 78.1**	56.8 / 77.4	**57.4 / 77.1**
TRWMD	50.8 / 67.3	53.3 / 72.1	61.5 / 79.7	53.1 / 71.3	54.0 / 71.5	54.5 / 72.0	54.0 / 74.3	54.5 / 72.6
TRWMD-b	52.5 / 71.2	53.9 / 73.4	62.7 / 82.0	53.8 / 73.4	54.8 / 72.8	55.7 / 76.1	53.4 / 74.1	55.3 / 74.7

similarity in mind (by leveraging on classical evaluation metrics for MT such as BLEU and ROUGE), whereas TWMD owes its performance solely to a better use of the representations.

Temperature dependence

The results of TWMD, TRWMD, TWMD-b, TRWMD-b in Table 2 and 3 used the fixed temperature (tuned in WMT15-16) $T = 0.02, 0.02, 0.10, 0.15$ for evaluation. A natural question to ask is how sensitive does the result depend on these hyperparameters.

Figure 3 shows the Pearson correlation vs. temperature for all four models and metrics with different temperature hyperparameters in WMT 15-18. We can see that the TWMD-b and TRWMD-b methods are robust with temperature. In compar-

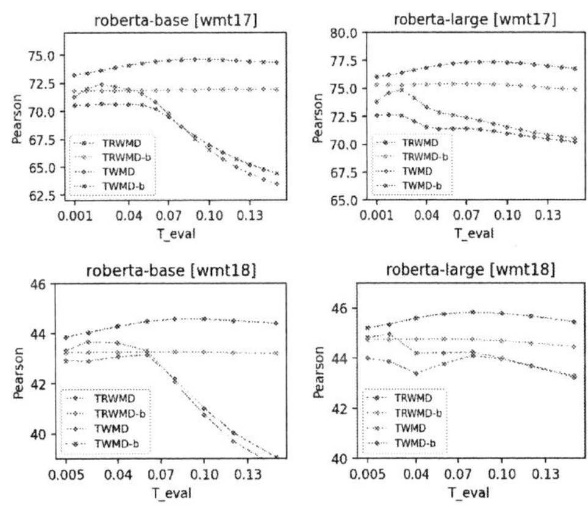

Figure 3: Pearson correlation vs. temperature in evaluation of WMT 17-18.

Table 3: Correlation with human scores on the WMT18 Metrics Shared Task. '-b' stands for batch centering of word vectors.

Metric	cs-en $\tau\,/\,r$	zh-en $\tau\,/\,r$	ru-en $\tau\,/\,r$	fi-en $\tau\,/\,r$	tr-en $\tau\,/\,r$	et-en $\tau\,/\,r$	de-en $\tau\,/\,r$	Avg. $\tau\,/\,r$
roberta-base								
SBERT	26.2 / 34.2	22.9 / 29.0	23.5 / 34.2	23.1 / 32.4	25.3 / 34.6	30.3 / 42.3	35.6 / 48.5	26.7 / 36.5
SBERT-b	28.7 / 40.6	25.8 / 35.6	26.5 / 38.4	25.1 / 36.6	28.7 / 39.8	33.4 / 46.9	38.4 / 54.1	29.5 / 41.6
CKA	26.2 / 34.6	23.0 / 29.5	23.5 / 34.5	23.2 / 32.7	25.4 / 35.1	30.4 / 42.6	35.8 / 48.9	26.8 / 36.9
CKA-b	28.9 / 41.6	26.4 / 37.4	27.2 / 39.9	25.7 / 37.8	30.0 / 42.6	34.2 / 49.3	39.0 / 55.7	30.2 / 43.5
MoverScore	28.5 / 40.6	28.2 / 37.8	27.9 / 39.4	25.1 / 35.8	31.3 / 43.4	34.3 / 48.5	38.9 / 54.2	30.5 / 42.8
MoverScore-b	28.7 / 40.6	28.1 / 37.7	27.8 / 39.2	25.2 / 36.0	31.3 / 43.2	34.4 / 48.6	38.9 / 54.2	30.5 / 42.8
BERTscore	27.6 / 39.5	27.2 / 37.5	27.6 / 39.4	24.9 / 36.0	31.1 / 43.3	34.4 / 48.6	39.3 / 56.1	30.3 / 42.9
BERTscore-b	27.8 / 39.9	26.9 / 37.5	27.5 / 39.3	25.2 / 37.1	31.1 / 43.4	34.4 / 49.0	39.5 / 56.5	30.4 / 43.2
TWMD	28.7 / 40.9	28.2 / 38.4	28.1 / 39.9	25.5 / 36.7	31.7 / 43.9	34.9 / 49.3	39.9 / 56.6	31.0 / 43.7
TWMD-b	**29.5 / 42.0**	**28.4 / 38.9**	**28.7 / 40.6**	**26.4 / 38.2**	**32.3 / 44.5**	**35.4 / 50.2**	**40.4 / 57.4**	**31.6 / 44.6**
TRWMD	27.6 / 39.4	27.3 / 37.6	27.6 / 39.3	24.9 / 35.9	31.1 / 43.3	34.4 / 48.5	39.4 / 56.2	30.3 / 42.9
TRWMD-b	28.1 / 39.9	27.6 / 37.6	27.9 / 39.2	25.3 / 36.6	31.4 / 43.2	34.6 / 49.1	39.9 / 56.7	30.7 / 43.2
roberta-large								
SBERT	29.0 / 40.4	24.9 / 33.2	26.6 / 38.2	26.2 / 37.6	28.4 / 39.3	33.9 / 44.1	39.0 / 54.3	29.7 / 41.0
SBERT-b	30.4 / 42.6	26.6 / 35.8	27.9 / 38.9	27.0 / 38.7	29.9 / 41.1	35.0 / 47.1	40.1 / 55.9	31.0 / 42.9
CKA	29.2 / 40.8	25.0 / 33.6	26.7 / 38.6	26.3 / 37.8	28.5 / 39.7	34.0 / 44.7	39.1 / 54.7	29.7 / 41.4
CKA-b	30.4 / 43.9	27.0 / 37.8	28.2 / 41.0	27.0 / 39.5	30.5 / 43.5	35.5 / 50.6	40.4 / 57.6	31.3 / 44.8
MoverScore	29.9 / 41.8	28.7 / 38.0	29.2 / 40.2	26.5 / 37.2	31.9 / 43.6	35.9 / 49.9	40.8 / 56.2	31.9 / 43.8
MoverScore-b	30.0 / 42.1	28.7 / 38.1	28.9 / 40.0	26.5 / 37.5	31.7 / 43.5	35.6 / 49.7	40.4 / 55.6	31.7 / 43.8
BERTscore	29.4 / 41.5	27.9 / 37.9	28.9 / 40.3	26.0 / 36.6	31.6 / 43.6	35.9 / 49.6	41.1 / 58.4	31.6 / 44.0
BERTscore-b	29.7 / 42.6	27.6 / 38.2	28.9 / 40.9	26.4 / 38.4	31.6 / 44.2	35.9 / 50.1	41.0 / 58.5	31.6 / 44.7
TWMD	30.5 / 42.9	**28.9 / 39.0**	29.5 / 40.9	27.2 / 38.1	32.4 / 44.4	36.5 / 50.5	**41.8 / 58.9**	32.4 / 45.0
TWMD-b	**31.1 / 44.2**	**28.9 / 39.5**	**29.7 / 41.8**	**27.6 / 39.6**	**32.6 / 45.1**	**36.7 / 51.3**	**41.8 / 59.0**	**32.7 / 45.8**
TRWMD	29.2 / 41.4	28.0 / 37.8	28.9 / 40.2	25.9 / 36.5	31.6 / 43.5	35.9 / 49.5	41.1 / 58.3	31.5 / 43.9
TRWMD-b	29.8 / 42.3	28.1 / 38.1	29.2 / 40.6	26.3 / 37.7	31.8 / 43.8	36.0 / 50.2	41.3 / 58.4	31.8 / 44.4

Table 4: Correlation with human scores on the WMT17-18 after fine-tuning on WMT15-16. BLEURTbase and BLEURT have an extra pretraining step, as described in (Sellam et al., 2020)

Metric	WMT-17 Avg.	WMT-18 Avg.
base models	($\tau\,/\,r$)	(τ)
BLEURTbase -pre	56.8 / 75.8	33.6
BLEURTbase	61.0 / 80.2	**34.9**
TWMDbase	**61.7 / 81.0**	34.7
TWMDbase-b	61.1 / 80.7	34.7
large models	($\tau\,/\,r$)	(τ)
BLEURT -pre	59.8 / 79.2	34.5
BLEURT	62.5 / 81.8	**35.6**
TWMD	62.8 / 81.7	35.5
TWMD-b	**63.4 / 82.9**	35.5

ison, TWMD and TRWMD without batch-mean centering appears sensitive to the temperature. The Kendall τ correlation follow a similar trend.

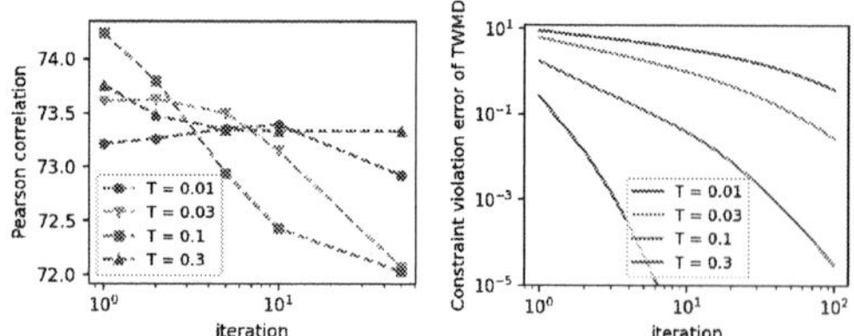

Figure 4: Left: Pearson correlation as a function of the number of iteration in Sinkhorn algorithm. Right: the convergence rate of the Sinkhorn algorithm. The underlying model in this figure is roberta-base with batch mean centered word vectors.

Sinkhorn iteration dependence for Tempered-WMD

We also investigate how the Sinkhorn iterations affect the TWMD-b. (Figure 4, left) shows the Pearson correlation vs the number of Sinkhorn iterations in four different temperatures. Somewhat surprisingly, although Sinkhorn algorithm needs more iterations to converge especially for low temperatures (Figure 4, right), the Pearson correlation of TWMD with only 1 iteration is the highest[†] of the Sinkhorn update for various temperatures.

7 Conclusion

Designing automatic evaluation metrics for text is a challenging task. Recent advances in the field leverage contextualized word representations, which are in turn generated by deep neural network models such as BERT and its variants. We present two techniques for improving such similarity metrics: a batch-mean centering strategy for word representations which addresses the statistical biases within deep contextualized word representations, and a computationally efficient tempered Word Mover Distance. Numerical experiments conducted using representations obtained from a range of BERT-like models confirm that our proposed metric consistently improves the correlation with human judgements.

[†] A minor exception appears to be for $T = 0.01$, where the 1-iter TWMD-b is slightly worse than the 10 iter TWMD b.

References

Eneko Agirre, Carmen Banea, Daniel Cer, Mona Diab, Aitor Gonzalez Agirre, Rada Mihalcea, German Rigau Claramunt, and Janyce Wiebe. 2016. Semeval-2016 task 1: Semantic textual similarity, monolingual and cross-lingual evaluation. In *SemEval-2016. 10th International Workshop on Semantic Evaluation; 2016 Jun 16-17; San Diego, CA. Stroudsburg (PA): ACL; 2016. p. 497-511. ACL (Association for Computational Linguistics).*

Satanjeev Banerjee and Alon Lavie. 2005. METEOR: An automatic metric for MT evaluation with improved correlation with human judgments. In *Proceedings of the ACL Workshop on intrinsic and extrinsic evaluation measures for machine translation and/or summarization.*

Marco Cuturi. 2013. Sinkhorn distances: Lightspeed computation of optimal transport. In *Advances in neural information processing systems*, pages 2292–2300.

Jacob Devlin, Ming-Wei Chang, Kenton Lee, and Kristina Toutanova. 2019. BERT: Pre-training of deep bidirectional transformers for language understanding. In *Proceedings of the 2019 Conference of the North American Chapter of the Association for Computational Linguistics: Human Language Technologies, Volume 1 (Long and Short Papers)*, pages 4171–4186, Minneapolis, Minnesota. Association for Computational Linguistics.

Kawin Ethayarajh. 2019. How contextual are contextualized word representations? IJCNLP.

Matt Kusner, Yu Sun, Nicholas Kolkin, and Kilian Weinberger. 2015. From word embeddings to document distances. In *International conference on machine learning*, pages 957–966.

Zhenzhong Lan, Mingda Chen, Sebastian Goodman, Kevin Gimpel, Piyush Sharma, and Radu Soricut. 2020. Albert: A lite bert for self-supervised learning of language representations.

Jindřich Libovický, Rudolf Rosa, and Alexander Fraser. 2019. How language-neutral is multilingual bert? *arXiv preprint arXiv:1911.03310.*

Chin-Yew Lin. 2004. Rouge: A package for automatic evaluation of summaries. In *Text Summarization Branches Out.*

Yinhan Liu, Myle Ott, Naman Goyal, Jingfei Du, Mandar Joshi, Danqi Chen, Omer Levy, Mike Lewis, Luke Zettlemoyer, and Veselin Stoyanov. 2019. RoBERTa: A robustly optimized BERT pretraining approach. *arXiv preprint arXiv:1907.11692.*

Tomas Mikolov, Kai Chen, Greg Corrado, and Jeff Dean. 2013. Efficient estimation of word representations in vector space. *CoRR*, abs/1301.3781.

Jiaqi Mu and Pramod Viswanath. 2018. All-but-the-top: Simple and effective postprocessing for word representations. In *International Conference on Learning Representations.*

Kishore Papineni, Salim Roukos, Todd Ward, and Wei-Jing Zhu. 2002. Bleu: A method for automatic evaluation of machine translation. In *Proceedings of ACL.*

Jeffrey Pennington, Richard Socher, and Christopher D. Manning. 2014. Glove: Global vectors for word representation. In *Proceedings of EMNLP.*

Nils Reimers and Iryna Gurevych. 2019. Sentence-bert: Sentence embeddings using siamese bert-networks. *arXiv preprint arXiv:1908.10084.*

Thibault Sellam, Dipanjan Das, and Ankur P. Parikh. 2020. Bleurt: Learning robust metrics for text generation.

Ashish Vaswani, Noam Shazeer, Niki Parmar, Jakob Uszkoreit, Llion Jones, Aidan N. Gomez, Lukasz Kaiser, and Illia Polosukhin. 2017. Attention is all you need. In *Proceedings of NeurIPS.*

Jingqing Zhang, Yao Zhao, Mohammad Saleh, and Peter J Liu. 2019a. Pegasus: Pre-training with extracted gap-sentences for abstractive summarization. *arXiv preprint arXiv:1912.08777.*

Tianyi Zhang, Varsha Kishore, Felix Wu, Kilian Q Weinberger, and Yoav Artzi. 2019b. Bertscore: Evaluating text generation with bert. *arXiv preprint arXiv:1904.09675.*

Wei Zhao, Steffen Eger, Johannes Bjerva, and Isabelle Augenstein. 2020. Inducing language-agnostic multilingual representations. *arXiv preprint arXiv:2008.09112.*

Wei Zhao, Maxime Peyrard, Fei Liu, Yang Gao, Christian M Meyer, and Steffen Eger. 2019. Moverscore: Text generation evaluating with contextualized embeddings and earth mover distance. *arXiv preprint arXiv:1909.02622.*

Vitalii Zhelezniak, April Shen, Daniel Busbridge, Aleksandar Savkov, and Nils Hammerla. 2019. Correlations between word vector sets. *arXiv preprint arXiv:1910.02902.*

On the Evaluation of Machine Translation n-best Lists

Jacob Bremerman[‡]   **Huda Khayrallah**[§]   **Douglas W. Oard**[‡] and **Matt Post**[§†]

[‡]University of Maryland, College Park
[§]Center for Language and Speech Processing, Johns Hopkins University
[†]Human Language Technology Center of Excellence, Johns Hopkins University
`{jbrem,oard}@umd.edu, {huda,post}@cs.jhu.edu`

Abstract

The standard machine translation evaluation framework measures the single-best output of machine translation systems. There are, however, many situations where n-best lists are needed, yet there is no established way of evaluating them. This paper establishes a framework for addressing n-best evaluation by outlining three different questions one could consider when determining how one would define a 'good' n-best list and proposing evaluation measures for each question. The first and principal contribution is an evaluation measure that characterizes the translation quality of an entire n-best list by asking whether many of the valid translations are placed near the top of the list. The second is a measure that uses gold translations with preference annotations to ask to what degree systems can produce ranked lists in preference order. The third is a measure that rewards partial matches, evaluating the closeness of the many items in an n-best list to a set of many valid references. These three perspectives make clear that having access to many references can be useful when n-best evaluation is the goal.

1   Introduction

Machine translation evaluation has traditionally focused on one-best translation results because many common use cases (translating a user manual, reading a news article, etc.) require only a single translation. There are, however, many scenarios in which n-best translation can be useful; examples include cross-language information retrieval, where query terms may not match in the single-best output, or language learning, where a learner is interested in whether their translation is acceptable.

Optimizing translation systems for such applications might benefit from evaluation measures that focus on choosing among systems based on which produces the best *list of translated sentences*, what

we refer to here for brevity as an n-best list. Often in these n-best scenarios, researchers first select 'good' MT systems (i.e., by BLEU) in the hope that these good systems will also produce good results beyond the top translation candidate. In this paper we test that hypothesis, using a newly available dataset to measure the quality of n-best lists directly.

To look at the problem in this way we must first decide what properties of an n-best list we would consider 'good'. In this paper we explore three questions:

1. How well does an n-best list include correct translations and rank correct translations above incorrect ones? (Section 3: *Head-weighted Precision*)

2. How well does an n-best list rank translations in preference order, with the better (e.g., more commonly used) translations ahead of those that are valid, but less preferred? (Section 4: *Preference Correlation*)

3. How close are all of the translations in an n-best list to one or more reference translations? (Section 5: *Unweighted Partial Match*)

We introduce measures for each of the three questions, using a ranking quality measure already widely used in information retrieval for question 1, correlation measures to address question 2, and variants of BLEU for question 3. In this latter study, we particularly note that n-best evaluation done in this way contrasts with a current standard used for both n-best and 1-best MT evaluation, 1-best single-reference BLEU.

However, our purpose is not to argue for a single n-best evaluation measure, but rather to highlight that different measures produce different system rankings, and therefore it is crucial that researchers

Proceedings of the First Workshop on Evaluation and Comparison of NLP Systems (Eval4NLP), pages 60–68,
November 20, 2020. ©2020 Association for Computational Linguistics

target	weight
私は気分が良くなるだろう。	0.015
私は気分が良くなるでしょう。	0.008
私はいい気分になるだろう。	0.007
気分が良くなるだろう。	0.007
私は気分が良いだろう。	0.006

Table 1: The top five valid Japanese translations for the STAPLE prompt *i will feel well*.

source	JA	PT
Europarl (Koehn, 2005)	-	2,408k
GlobalVoices[1]	822k	1,585k
OpenSubtitles (Lison and Tiedemann, 2016)	13,097k	196,960k
Tatoeba (tatoeba.org)	1,537k	1,215k
WikiMatrix (Schwenk et al., 2019)	9,013k	45,147k
JW300 (Agić and Vulić, 2019)	34,325k	39,023k
QED (Abdelali et al., 2014)	9,064k	8,542k

Table 2: English word tokens for all datasets used to train the MT models.

carefully consider what questions to ask when evaluating systems. The measures we propose are illustrative as answers to our research questions, but are not the only solutions; many others might work. We aim to provide groundwork and encourage future work on the topic.

Our investigation is made possible by the recent availability of annotations created for the Duolingo Simultaneous Translation and Paraphrase for Language Education (STAPLE) shared task, which contains an extensive (although not necessarily exhaustive) set of valid translations for each of several thousand "input prompt" sentences (Mayhew et al., 2020).

2 The STAPLE Shared Task

The Duolingo STAPLE dataset consists of thousands of English prompts, with large sets of valid translations of each, often numbering in the hundreds, each labeled with the relative frequency with which each valid translation was selected by language learners. Table 1 shows the five highest-frequency Japanese translations for the prompt "I will feel well," where the weights of all 480 translations sum to one. As this example illustrates, the prompts are relatively short and simple sentences.

In the 2020 STAPLE task, participating systems were asked to produce all and only the valid translations. Doing well at this task, which was evaluated using a variant of the F_1 measure, requires both ranking translations well and deciding where to truncate the n-best list (i.e., the choice of n). Our focus in this paper is on ranking quality, leaving the question of how best to evaluate truncation to other work.

We compare systems from Khayrallah et al. (2020)'s submission to the 2020 Duolingo STAPLE Shared Task. They were built using the data described in Table 2. In total, we compare 38 Portuguese and 44 Japanese systems. This includes some bad systems, many good ones, and many incremental variations in between, especially at the top end. These systems ranked among the best for these languages on the STAPLE leaderboard.

All were variations of the following standard training procedure. We used Transformer architectures (Vaswani et al., 2017) trained with fairseq (Ott et al., 2019). Models included 6 encoder and decoder layers, a model size of 512, a feed forward layer size of 2048, and 8 attention heads. Models were trained with the ADAM optimizer (Kingma and Ba, 2015) with a dropout size of 0.1 and an effective batch size of 200k tokens. Model training was terminated when validation perplexity failed to increase for 10 consecutive epoch-level checkpoints.

Our systems varied in the following experimental parameters:

- Training on all the data in Table 2, or just the data above the midline.

- Whether or not we fine-tuned on Duolingo STAPLE training data.

- Training on just the first million lines of each corpus.

- Varying the effective batch size.

- Limiting the training data to sentences containing at most 20% of tokens outside the Duolingo STAPLE training data vocabulary.

3 Head-weighted Precision

We begin with our first question: how well does a system produce valid translations and rank them above invalid translations?

A task that might be more aligned with such a question would be one that necessitates a strict, binary score for validity and is agnostic to where a truncation of the list might occur. For example, a language learner hoping to learn several valid possible ways to express a sentence in a target language may want to peruse many translation outputs, starting at the top of the list. It would be unknown where the user would stop, and it would be important that the translations are fully valid.

Of course the space of valid translations in this framework could be enormous, so it is important to consider the effect of incompleteness in the set of valid references. We consider that in section 3.2, but first we introduce a measure for head-weighted precision with a simplifying assumption that the set of valid references is complete. Assuming we have this, we say for the purpose of question 1 that a good n-best list would have a lot of valid translations, and that it would place them near the head (i.e., the top) of the ranked list. We refer to this framework then as *head-weighted precision*.

3.1 A Head-Weighted Precision Measure

We are not the first to need a measure for the quality of a ranked list—this is a central question in evaluation of search engines that produced ranked lists of documents. The simplest setup of the evaluation task in information retrieval is that documents are either on topic or off topic (i.e., relevant or not), and that it is only the order of the documents that matters. One widely used rank quality measure is uninterpolated Average Precision (AP), computed for a ranked list $\mathbf{L}$ of length k as follows:

$$AP(\mathbf{L}) = \frac{1}{N} \sum_{i=1}^{k} \frac{T_i}{i} s_i \qquad (1)$$

where N is the number of valid items, T_i is the number of valid items at or above rank i, and s_i is the true binary relevance for the item at rank i (0 or 1). The core of the computation is T_i/i, which in information retrieval is called precision; AP is the expected value of precision, measured only at optimal stopping points (i.e., where precision is maximized by just having added one more valid item). With this measure, ranked lists earn perfect scores for ranking all valid items at the top and are punished for invalid items occurring between valid ones (with invalid items nearer the top having a more deleterious impact). Because variance in system behavior across conditions may be high, it

is common to compare systems using Mean AP values (MAP) computed over a representative set of conditions. In information retrieval, conditions are topics, items are documents, and validity is relevance to the topic. In n-best MT, the conditions are a representative set of sentences to be translated (in the STAPLE task, the prompts), the items are system-produced translations, and validity is whether a translation is proper (i.e., present in the STAPLE gold translations).

3.2 Dealing With Incomplete Gold Data

MAP's reliance on binary validity rather than the preference order among valid translations simplified the generation of a gold standard, but the implicit assumption that the reference set of valid translations is complete is a potential concern. Due to the richness of human language, most sentences would admit an immense number of valid translations (Dreyer and Marcu, 2012). Even the STAPLE dataset used in this paper, which contains hundreds of valid reference translations for many sentences, is surely still not complete. This effect results in systems being penalized for false negatives, receiving lower MAP scores than they should.

However, when our goal is to compare systems, we are most interested in relative, not absolute, scores. So the question to be answered is whether missing data in the ground truth adversely affects comparisons between systems. Zobel (1998) introduced a clever way to characterize such an effect. The key idea is to ablate the ground truth, and to examine the effect of that ablation on system comparisons. If removing, say, half the ground truth resulted in few reversals in the preference order between systems, then one might reasonably assume that adding even more ground truth would have similarly small effects.

The art in this approach is to design the ablation in a way that removes things that are most like the things that are likely missing. Zobel, using this technique to study the stability of MAP in information retrieval test collections, ablated relevance judgments that would not have been available had less effort been devoted to generating such judgments; in information retrieval these are the documents that no participating system retrieved at high rank. For the STAPLE dataset, a natural choice is to ablate the least frequent translations, since it seems reasonable to presume that if Duolingo was not aware of the validity of some translation, that

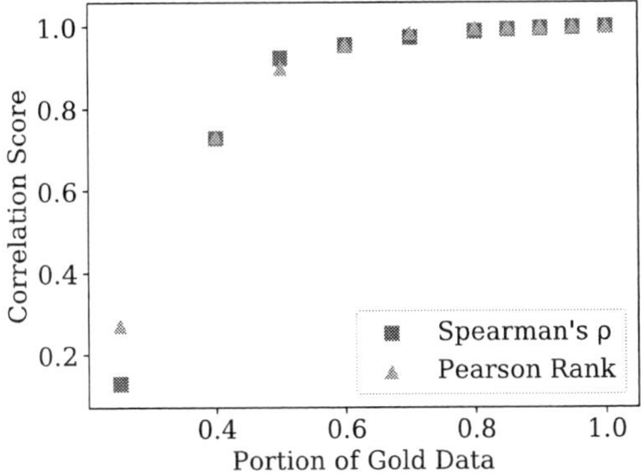 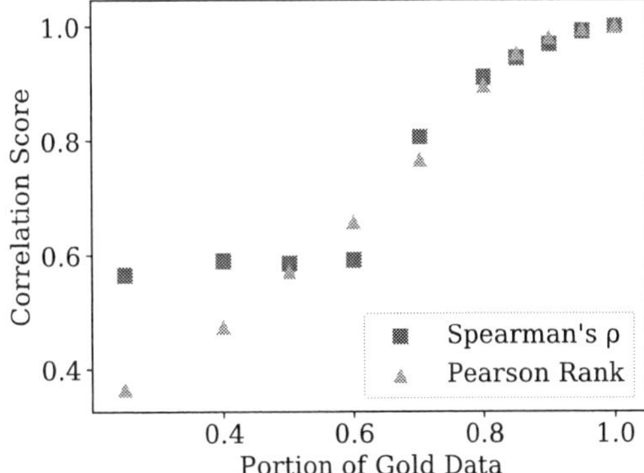

Figure 1: Spearman's ρ and Pearson Rank correlation scores for MAP system rankings for Japanese (left) and Portugese (right) under different data ablation settings. MAP results obtained for STAPLE are reliable for system ranking despite incomplete data, with results slightly more reliable for Japanese than Portuguese.

translation is likely to be rather uncommon.

Such an ablation study requires a suite of systems and a measure that characterizes the swaps between MAP scores that occur. We therefore use the aforementioned 38 Japanese MT models and 44 Portuguese MT models. From each model we generate a 1000-best list.

We can use Spearman's ρ to count the number of times the relative order of two systems is swapped. One limitation of ρ, however, is that we might care more about swaps near the top of the list of system rankings than lower down (i.e., a *head-weighted* measure). Another limitation is that we might care more about swaps between systems with very different MAP values than we do about swaps between systems with closer values (i.e., a *gap-sensitive* measure). In addition to ρ, we therefore also report Pearson Rank (Gao et al., 2016), a more recently introduced correlation measure that is head-weighted and gap-sensitive.

Figure 1 plots these correlations as progressively more common translations are ablated. The left side of the plots show how system rankings from an ablated data condition that only includes the most common translations correlate with rankings from the full data. Moving right, the correlations are compared for conditions containing more and more data, with the penultimate point representing a data condition where only the rarest translations have been removed. The flatness of the curve on the right side of the plot suggests (based on extrapolation to the right) that the presence of additional relatively uncommon translations would have been unlikely to result in many system swaps.

Pearson Rank, which accounts for head-weightedness, additionally shows that few of the system swaps are between relatively good systems. This is likely because good systems will output high-frequency translations near the top of the n-best list, so as low-frequency translations are ablated, these good systems are less likely to be affected. From this we can conclude that, at least for Japanese and Portuguese, the binarized STAPLE task ground truth is sufficiently complete to support computation of MAP scores for individual systems that can reasonably be compared, allowing us to answer Question 1 using this measure.

3.3 Comparison to the STAPLE Metric

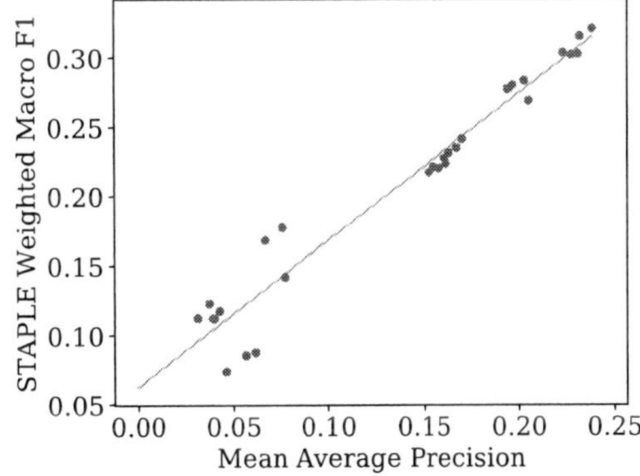

Figure 2: Correlation of system rankings based on Weighted Macro F_1 and MAP in Japanese. $r^2 = 0.836$, slope = 1.058.

As introduced earlier, the STAPLE task uses a weighted macro F_1 measure for evaluation. The weighted macro F_1 measure is the same as the standard macro-averaged F_1, but recall is replaced with weighted recall. Weighted recall is calculated by using frequency weight sums provided in the gold translation data for Weighted True Positive and Weighted False Negative terms, instead of the standard raw counts.

One difference of this measure compared to MAP is that it does not evaluate a model's ability to generate n-best lists in a pure sense (agnostic to where that list may be cut off). This is because the STAPLE systems must not only generate n-best lists, but also decide where to truncate each list, in order to maximize weighted macro F_1. This means that an n-best list that outputs hundreds of valid translations only at the top of the list, but is truncated at rank 1000, would score poorly, due to precision issues. However, MAP is robust to this, since values at the very bottom of the list have only a small effect. The definition of MAP allows it to function properly for any size lists, potentially even infinite-size lists, which weighted macro F_1 does not. This is not to argue that MAP is a better measure than F_1, but simply rather that they are different measures and may be better suited for separate goals.

Despite this, we produce a correlation plot in Figure 2 to compare system MAP scores with system weighted macro F_1 scores. For these weighted macro F_1 scores, we used a thresholding technique that truncates n-best lists at a manually tuned fraction of the top hypothesis' model probability for each prompt. We find that the weighted macro F_1 values correlate very strongly with MAP.[2] We note that the correlation is particularly strong at the top-end of systems compared to the bottom-end. This is ideal since understanding and trusting evaluation measures are particularly vital for choosing among the best of systems (often not as important for choosing among the worst). From this we conclude that MAP could have been a useful formative evaluation measure when tuning n-best MT systems for the STAPLE shared task and that these two measures may actually be answering a similar question despite the differences in their properties.

4 Preference Correlation

Our second question for n-best evaluation is how well models can rank translations in preference order. Since we have model scores from the trans-

lation model and relative prevalence from the STAPLE dataset, one type of easily computed measure of quality for the model scores would be their degree of correlation with the STAPLE score for each translation (which indicates which of the translations are more commonly used; i.e., their relative prevalence).

One interesting aspect of this type of measure is that it relies on having frequency (or some other preference score) annotation information for each reference translation. Certain tasks may be better imagined to take advantage of such data. For example, a task in which models need to generate diverse translations may want to sample from valid outputs in a way that more closely reflects natural human variance. That is, it should sample a frequent translation more often than an infrequent one. Correlating a model's scores for translations with gold frequency scores may then be useful for such a case.

We consider how these Preference Correlation scores could be used for system rankings. We calculate both Spearman's ρ and Pearson's r on all of our models in Japanese and Portuguese.[3] We then construct a scatterplot of the Preference Correlation and MAP scores for each system, as shown in Figure 3. From the near-zero slope of a linear fit and the near-zero r^2 values, it is clear that both Spearman's ρ and Pearson's r are measuring something very different from MAP. That is not to say that they are not good measures; rather, it says that they are measuring something different. MAP measures how reliably systems can place valid translations early in a ranked list; correlation to the gold standard preference order measures how reliably systems can place preferred translations ahead of less preferred translations.

Both of these measures have additional limitations, which discourage their usage. First is the requirement for more nuanced gold data. While MAP only requires access to several valid translations, these measures require either a preference order or preference scores for those translations, which may be difficult to obtain. A second limitation is the handling of missing data. Both measures compare scores or rankings of translations between

---

[2]Spearman's $\rho = 0.956$.

[3]Spearmans's ρ considers only relative rankings, while Pearson's r additionally considers the difference in scores. Neither is head-weighted. We compute Pearson's r in log space, excluding system translations not in the STAPLE references. Another option would have been to use the model to force-decode the STAPLE references. We observe similar trends when doing so.

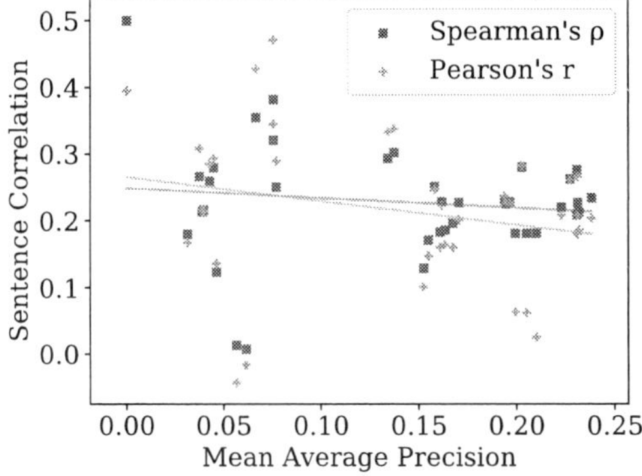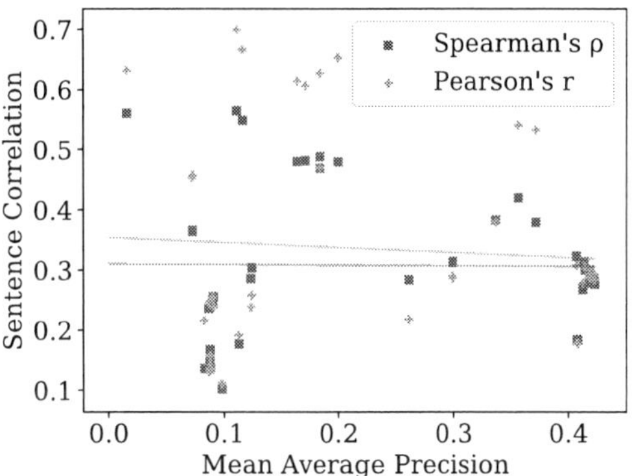

Figure 3: Correlation of system rankings based on Preference Correlation scores (Spearman's ρ and Pearson's r) vs. MAP score in Japanese (left) and Portuguese (right). Rankings do not correlate. Japanese: r^2 for Spearman's = 0.009, slope = -0.145; r^2 for Pearson's = 0.046, slope = -0.356. Portuguese: r^2 for Spearman's = -0.001, slope = -0.010; r^2 for Pearson's = -0.002, slope = -0.083. Best viewed in color.

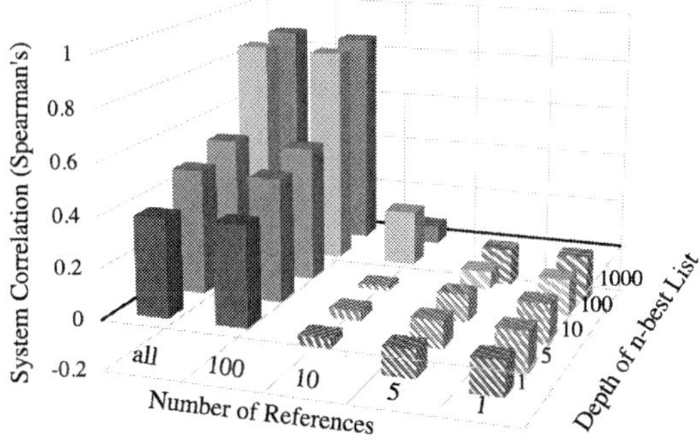

Figure 4: System ranking correlation scores (Spearman's ρ) between MAP and different configurations of BLEU (x-references and y-best outputs per source) in Japanese. Using many references and a larger depth correlates very well with MAP while 1-best 1-reference BLEU correlates poorly. Note: striped bars indicate a negative value; all references is 1536 for Japanese.

two sets. If the intersection between these two sets is very small, it limits the usefulness of the measures. Though we have many frequency scores and relative rankings in the gold translations, if the n-best lists we use to compare do not contain many of those translations, the measures could be less reliable.

5 Unweighted Partial Match

Finally, our third question is how close the translations are to the reference translations.

A task that may benefit from such a measure would be cross-language information retrieval (CLIR). In such a task, the machine translation sys-

tem would serve as an upstream component of the pipeline. It is less likely for translations to need to be fully valid to be useful as compared to some other MT tasks. CLIR could benefit from combining the terms from several translation outputs regardless of if each entire sentence is perfectly valid. In this way, a measure that can assign partial credit to translations by matching n-grams as well as weighting all translations equally may be appropriate.

For this, we turn to BLEU (Papineni et al., 2002), which computes n-gram overlap between a system's translations and the available references. This raises the question of how many references we should use when we have very many available, and which of the system translations we should be using in this computation.

The STAPLE dataset provides an opportunity to explore this question. In this section, we compute BLEU measures with different numbers of references, to different depths in the n-best list. We find that at deep depths with many references BLEU ranks systems similarly to MAP, but that with fewer references its behavior is quite different.

In order to set up various configurations for our n-best BLEU measures, we perform a grid search over $\{1,5,10,100,1000\}$-best $\{1,5,10,100,\text{all}^4\}$-reference BLEU. In what we call x-best y-reference BLEU, x refers to how many top hypotheses from the system output are used, and y refers to how many references are used. When working with multiple hypotheses in an n-best list, we simply

---

[4]all is up to 720 in Portuguese, and 1536 in Japanese

treat them as independent translations in a larger pseudo-corpus, pairing each with the relevant reference(s) for evaluation with BLEU.

After obtaining system scores under each of the BLEU configurations, we calculate the Spearman's ρ and Pearson Rank correlation coefficients between system rankings from BLEU compared to those from MAP. We find similar patterns for both languages and both correlation metrics, so we show Spearman's correlation for Japanese in Figure 4.

An important observation is our finding that 1-best, 1-reference BLEU does not correlate well with MAP. From this we conclude that when placing many valid translations near the top of the n-best list is important, as is the case in some applications, optimizing for 1-best 1-reference BLEU may be suboptimal.

This situation is not improved by adding hypotheses to the pseudo-corpus, so long as only a single reference is used. However, increasing the number of references does bring the correlation to moderate strength even when still only evaluating at 1-best. Once the evaluation has access to several references, evaluating deeper in the n-best list further improves the correlation with MAP, and correlations at moderately deep depths are quite substantial (e.g., $\rho = 0.86$ for 100-best 100-reference).

In Figure 5, we zoom in on two of these BLEU configurations. We choose 1-best 1-reference, which represents a standard BLEU evaluation framework, and also 100-best 100-reference, since it showed nearly the highest correlation with MAP (increasing the depth to 1000 and the references to 1000 yields only slightly stronger correlation). As the slope and r^2 of the linear fit indicate, 1-best 1-reference BLEU has little value for predicting MAP, whereas 100-best 100-reference BLEU has substantial preditive power. Moreover, this relationship is strongest for higher values of MAP; this is important, because when seeking to choose the best system for some task, a system builder would choose from among the best-performing ones.

To help explain this difference, we also performed a qualitative analysis. This revealed that systems with high 1-best 1-reference BLEU scores but low MAP produced valid translations at the top of the n-best list, but very poor translations (e.g., Latin characters in Japanese) deeper in the list. Systems with both higher MAP and 100-best 100-reference BLEU scores were better at producing reasonable sentences throughout the entire list.

This makes sense as a system with a great translation at rank 1 but terrible translations between ranks 2 and 100, for example, will have a great 1-best 1-reference BLEU but will be heavily punished by MAP.

6 Discussion

Access to frequency scores in STAPLE's gold data has provided a unique chance to use correlation between those scores and model scores as a way to evaluate systems. However, we see that these measures behave quite differently from MAP, and thus we would recommend use of Preference Correlation (§4) only in cases in which fine-grained distinctions between preference scores are important for the intended application.

We also looked into using BLEU for n-best evaluation. MAP and BLEU seem like quite different ways of evaluating in terms of how they approach the problem. MAP relies on binary scores, gives no partial credit, and weighs translations at the top of the list higher. BLEU on the other hand looks at closeness, allowing for partial credit, and treats all sentences equally, no matter where they appear in the n-best list. It could be expected then that these measures would differ, as we see when comparing MAP to 1-best 1-reference BLEU. However, as we increase depth and number of references for BLEU, the correlation of the resulting system rankings increases substantially and ultimately they yield quite similar system rankings. From this we can conclude that, at least for the systems we have experimented with, and for the language learning task that the STAPLE dataset models, systems that find many good translations also tend to rank those translations well. Thus, with enough references the choice between MAP and BLEU might be made based on efficiency. We suspect that the ability of many-best many-reference to work with partial matches might give it advantages over MAP when the number of available references is more limited than in STAPLE, but we leave ablation studies to test that hypothesis to future work.

Of course, the requirement for large numbers of references, which are generally expensive to obtain, is a limitation. However, this is a separate consideration; in the Duolingo dataset that was the center of our study, they were produced organically within that task; in other settings, if evaluation of n-best lists were to be important enough, the requisite investments to create the required resources

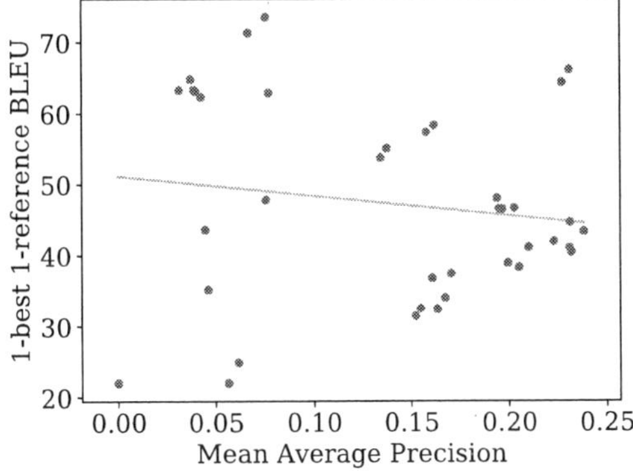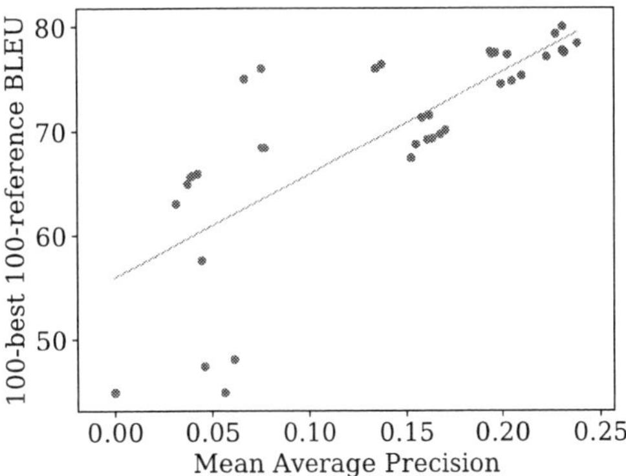

Figure 5: System scores in Japanese by MAP and BLEU (left: 1-best 1-ref, right: 100-best 100-ref). 1-best 1-reference BLEU does not correlate well with MAP ($\rho = -0.14$), but 100-best 100-reference BLEU correlates highly ($\rho = 0.86$). According to MAP, choosing the system with the highest BLEU would result in poor n-best lists in 1-best 1-ref (left) and strong n-best lists in 100-best 100-ref (right). 1-best: $r^2 = 0.022$, slope = -27.817 100-best: $r^2 = 0.487$, slope = 98.448.

could in some cases be made. In such a setting, techniques such as crowdsourcing or monolingual paraphrase generation might possibly be leveraged to reduce costs. Moreover, our ablation study indicates that the ground truth need not be completely comprehensive to be useful.

A second limitation is that our experiments were conducted on the relatively simple sentences used for the Duolingo STAPLE shared task. As with any study, it remains to be seen how well it generalizes to other settings, including other datasets. But this does not detract from our findings on the STAPLE dataset, which was after all motivated by a real language learning task that benefits large number of of people.

Perhaps our most salient general observation is that it seems that having access to more references and evaluating deeper in the list makes for better evaluation of n-best lists. Of course, this benefit must be balanced against the cost of generating the requisite number of references.

7 Conclusion

We have shown how different metrics can be used to characterize n-best list quality. In particular, we have introduced MAP as a measure for n-best list quality for machine translation systems. MAP rewards systems that place good translations near the top of the list. BLEU, computed over a pseudo-corpus built from n-best lists, and against large reference sets, ranks systems similarly to MAP. In both cases, the key distinguishing feature from

typical MT system evaluation is the use of large reference sets, which yields insights unavailable with shallower evaluations using only a single reference.

MAP is but one measure among many that have been used to characterize the quality of ranked lists in other settings. As future work, we would be interested in exploring the use of measures such as inferred average precision (infAP) that are designed to be particularly robust to missing data in the gold standard (Aslam and Yilmaz, 2007), and measures such as normalized Discounted Cumulative Gain (nDCG) (Järvelin and Kekäläinen, 2002) that represent multiple degrees of utility (thus requiring more nuanced ground truth, as what we have in STAPLE).

Acknowledgments

This research has been supported in part by the Office of the Director of National Intelligence (ODNI), Intelligence Advanced Research Projects Activity (IARPA), via contract FA8650-17-C-9117. The views and conclusions contained herein are those of the authors and should not be interpreted as necessarily representing the official policies of ODNI, IARPA, or the U.S. Government.

References

Ahmed Abdelali, Francisco Guzman, Hassan Sajjad, and Stephan Vogel. 2014. The AMARA corpus: Building parallel language resources for the educational domain. In *Proceedings of the Ninth International Conference on Language Resources and Eval-*

uation (LREC'14), pages 1856–1862, Reykjavik, Iceland. European Language Resources Association (ELRA).

Željko Agić and Ivan Vulić. 2019. JW300: A wide-coverage parallel corpus for low-resource languages. In *Proceedings of the 57th Annual Meeting of the Association for Computational Linguistics*, pages 3204–3210, Florence, Italy. Association for Computational Linguistics.

Javed A. Aslam and Emine Yilmaz. 2007. Inferring document relevance from incomplete information. In *Proceedings of the Sixteenth ACM Conference on Information and Knowledge Management, CIKM 2007, Lisbon, Portugal, November 6-10, 2007*, pages 633–642. ACM.

Markus Dreyer and Daniel Marcu. 2012. HyTER: Meaning-equivalent semantics for translation evaluation. In *Proceedings of the 2012 Conference of the North American Chapter of the Association for Computational Linguistics: Human Language Technologies*, pages 162–171, Montréal, Canada. Association for Computational Linguistics.

Ning Gao, Mossaab Bagdouri, and Douglas Oard. 2016. Pearson rank: A head-weighted gap-sensitive score-based correlation coefficient. pages 941–944.

Kalervo Järvelin and Jaana Kekäläinen. 2002. Cumulated gain-based evaluation of IR techniques. *ACM Trans. Inf. Syst.*, 20(4):422–446.

Huda Khayrallah, Jacob Bremerman, Arya D. McCarthy, Kenton Murray, Winston Wu, and Matt Post. 2020. The JHU submission to the 2020 Duolingo shared task on simultaneous translation and paraphrase for language education. In *Proceedings of the Fourth Workshop on Neural Generation and Translation*, pages 188–197, Online. Association for Computational Linguistics.

Diederik P. Kingma and Jimmy Ba. 2015. Adam: A method for stochastic optimization. In *3rd International Conference on Learning Representations, ICLR 2015, San Diego, CA, USA, May 7-9, 2015, Conference Track Proceedings*.

Philipp Koehn. 2005. Europarl: A parallel corpus for statistical machine translation. In *MT summit*, volume 5, pages 79–86.

Pierre Lison and Jörg Tiedemann. 2016. OpenSubtitles2016: Extracting large parallel corpora from movie and TV subtitles. In *Proceedings of the Tenth International Conference on Language Resources and Evaluation (LREC'16)*, pages 923–929, Portorož, Slovenia. European Language Resources Association (ELRA).

Stephen Mayhew, Klinton Bicknell, Chris Brust, Bill McDowell, Will Monroe, and Burr Settles. 2020. Simultaneous translation and paraphrase for language education. In *Proceedings of the ACL Workshop on Neural Generation and Translation (WNGT)*. ACL.

Myle Ott, Sergey Edunov, Alexei Baevski, Angela Fan, Sam Gross, Nathan Ng, David Grangier, and Michael Auli. 2019. fairseq: A fast, extensible toolkit for sequence modeling. In *Proceedings of the 2019 Conference of the North American Chapter of the Association for Computational Linguistics (Demonstrations)*, pages 48–53, Minneapolis, Minnesota. Association for Computational Linguistics.

Kishore Papineni, Salim Roukos, Todd Ward, and Wei-Jing Zhu. 2002. Bleu: a method for automatic evaluation of machine translation. In *Proceedings of the 40th Annual Meeting of the Association for Computational Linguistics*, pages 311–318, Philadelphia, Pennsylvania, USA. Association for Computational Linguistics.

Holger Schwenk, Vishrav Chaudhary, Shuo Sun, Hongyu Gong, and Francisco Guzmán. 2019. Wikimatrix: Mining 135m parallel sentences in 1620 language pairs from Wikipedia. *CoRR*, abs/1907.05791.

Ashish Vaswani, Noam Shazeer, Niki Parmar, Jakob Uszkoreit, Llion Jones, Aidan N Gomez, Ł ukasz Kaiser, and Illia Polosukhin. 2017. Attention is all you need. In I. Guyon, U. V. Luxburg, S. Bengio, H. Wallach, R. Fergus, S. Vishwanathan, and R. Garnett, editors, *Advances in Neural Information Processing Systems 30*, pages 5998–6008. Curran Associates, Inc.

Justin Zobel. 1998. How reliable are the results of large-scale information retrieval experiments? SIGIR '98, pages 307–314, New York, NY, USA. Association for Computing Machinery.

ARTEMIS: A Novel Annotation Methodology for Indicative Single Document Summarization

Rahul Jha*, **Keping Bi†**, **Yang Li***, **Mahdi Pakdaman***
Asli Celikyilmaz*, **Ivan Zhiboedov‡**, **Kieran McDonald***
* Microsoft Corporation
† Umass Amherst
‡ Facebook Inc

Abstract

We describe ARTEMIS (Annotation methodology for Rich, Tractable, Extractive, Multidomain, Indicative Summarization), a novel hierarchical annotation process that produces indicative summaries for documents from multiple domains. Current summarization evaluation datasets are single-domain and focused on a few domains for which naturally occurring summaries can be easily found, such as news and scientific articles. These are not sufficient for training and evaluation of summarization models for use in document management and information retrieval systems, which need to deal with documents from multiple domains. Compared to other annotation methods such as Relative Utility and Pyramid, ARTEMIS is more tractable because judges don't need to look at all the sentences in a document when making an importance judgment for one of the sentences, while providing similarly rich sentence importance annotations. We describe the annotation process in detail and compare it with other similar evaluation systems. We also present analysis and experimental results over a sample set of 532 annotated documents.

1 Introduction

Given an input source document, summarization systems produce a condensed summary which can be either informative or indicative. Informative summaries try to convey all the important points of the document (Kan et al., 2002, 2001b), while indicative summaries hint at the topics of the document, pointing to information alerting the reader about the document content (Saggion and Lapalme, 2002). An informative summary aims to replace the source document, so that the user does not need to read the full document (Edmundson, 1969). An indicative summary, on the other hand, aims to

---

† Work done while an intern at Microsoft.
‡ Work done while an employee of Microsoft.

Original Document
(1) This content should be viewed as reference documentation only, to inform IT business decisions ...
(2) Microsoft employees need to stay aware of new company products, services, processes, and personnel-related developments in an organization that provides them ...
(3) The SMSG Readiness team at Microsoft developed a suite of applications that delivers training and information to Microsoft employees according to employee roles ...
(4) Microsoft Information Technology (Microsoft IT) is responsible for managing one of the largest Information Technology (IT) infrastructure environments in the world.
(5) It consists of 95,000 employees working in 107 countries worldwide.
(6) The Sales, Marketing, and Services Group (SMSG) at Microsoft is responsible for servicing the needs of Microsoft customers and partners.
(7) It is essential that these 45,000 employees remain informed about products and services within their areas of expertise and, in turn, to educate and inform ...
(8) The SMSG Readiness (SMSGR) team at Microsoft is responsible for ensuring that SMSG employees have all of the tools and knowledge they require to deliver ...
(... document truncated)

Summary 1
(2) Microsoft employees need to stay aware of new company products, services, processes, and ...
(3) The SMSG Readiness team at Microsoft developed a suite of applications that delivers training and ...
(4) Microsoft Information Technology (Microsoft IT) is responsible for managing one of the largest ...

Summary 2
(3) The SMSG Readiness team at Microsoft developed a suite of applications that delivers training and ...
(6) The Sales, Marketing, and Services Group (SMSG) at Microsoft is responsible for servicing the needs of ...
(8) The SMSG Readiness (SMSGR) team at Microsoft is responsible for ensuring that SMSG employees have ...

Summary 3
(2) Microsoft employees need to stay aware of new company products, services, processes, and ...
(4) Microsoft Information Technology (Microsoft IT) is responsible for managing one of the largest ...
(8) The SMSG Readiness (SMSGR) team at Microsoft is responsible for ensuring that SMSG employees have ...

Figure 1: One of the documents from our web-crawled sample annotated dataset along with indicative summaries annotated by three different judges. The sentence numbers in round brackets are not in the original document but are added here for readability. Summary sentences are truncated for readability as well.

Proceedings of the First Workshop on Evaluation and Comparison of NLP Systems (Eval4NLP), pages 69–78,
November 20, 2020. ©2020 Association for Computational Linguistics

help the user decide whether they should consider reading the full document (Kan et al., 2002).

The content of indicative summaries can be composed in several ways. For example, it can contain sentences extracted from the source document which relate to its main topic (Barzilay and Elhadad, 1997; Kupiec et al., 1995), generated text describing how a document is different from other documents (Kan et al., 2001a), topic keywords (Hovy and Lin, 1997; Saggion and Lapalme, 2002) as well as metadata such as length and writing style (Nenkova and McKeown, 2011).

Document management systems such as Google Docs, Microsoft OneDrive and SharePoint and Dropbox can use indicative summaries to help their users decide whether a given document is relevant for them before opening the full document. Indicative summaries can also be used in information retrieval systems as previews for documents returned in search results. Document summarization systems deployed in these real-world systems need to be able to summarize documents from a wide variety of domains.

However, existing summarization datasets are highly domain-specific, with a majority of them focusing on news summarization (Nallapati et al., 2016; Grusky et al., 2018; Sandhaus, 2008; Graff et al., 2003). One of the reasons for this bias towards news summarization is the availability of naturally occurring summaries for news, which makes it easier to create large-scale summarization datasets automatically by scraping online sources. Apart from the domain bias, they are also susceptible to noise which can affect upto 5.92% of the data (Kryscinski et al., 2019).

In order to train and evaluate multi-domain summarization models for use in document management systems, we need to build representative datasets geared towards this use case. Towards this goal, we present ARTEMIS (Annotation methodology for Rich, Tractable, Extractive, Multi-domain, Indicative Summarization), a hierarchical annotation process for indicative summarization of multi-domain documents. Figure 1 shows a sample document crawled from the web with three annotated summaries obtained using ARTEMIS.

ARTEMIS's hierarchical annotation process allows judges to create indicative summaries for long documents through divide-and-conquer. Judges successively summarize larger and larger chunks of a document in multiple stages, at each stage reusing sentences selected previously. The hierarchical process means that judges only look at a small set of sentences at each stage.

Compared to previous annotation methods, where judges need to consider all the document sentences together when building a summary (Tam et al., 2007) or create expensive semantic annotations (Nenkova and Passonneau, 2004), ARTEMIS is a low-cost annotation approach that produces rich sentence importance annotations. Judges are able to use ARTEMIS to annotate documents averaging 1322 words (77 sentences) in 4.17 minutes on average, based on an initial sample of annotation tasks. This is almost twice the length of documents in summarization datasets such as CNN/Dailymail at 766 words (Nallapati et al., 2016) and NEWSROOM at 659 words (Grusky et al., 2018).

ARTEMIS's annotation process aims at selecting a set of sentences that contain relevant information about the main topics of a document rather than conveying all the relevant information in a document. Given this, summaries annotated by ARTEMIS are indicative in nature and suited for document management and information retrieval systems, where they can be used as part of document preview to help a user decide whether a document is relevant for them.

The rest of this paper is organized as follows. Section 2 describes the annotation process in detail and Section 3 relates our method to previous annotation methods for summarization. Section 4 presents a number of analyses characterizing the ARTEMIS annotation process in terms of label distribution and judge agreement by using a sample annotated document set. Section 5 presents evaluation results for a set of baseline summarization models on the sample annotated document set. Finally, Section 6 presents some concluding remarks and points to future work.

2 Annotation Methodology

Figure 2 shows a high-level diagram representing the annotation process for ARTEMIS. Given a document as input, the preprocessing step consists of first dividing the document into sections, each of which is further divided into paragraphs. The section and paragraph boundaries are computed based on a set of heuristics that depend on signals like explicit section headers as well as constraints on the number of sentences shown at each screen.

The hypothetical document in Figure 2 is di-

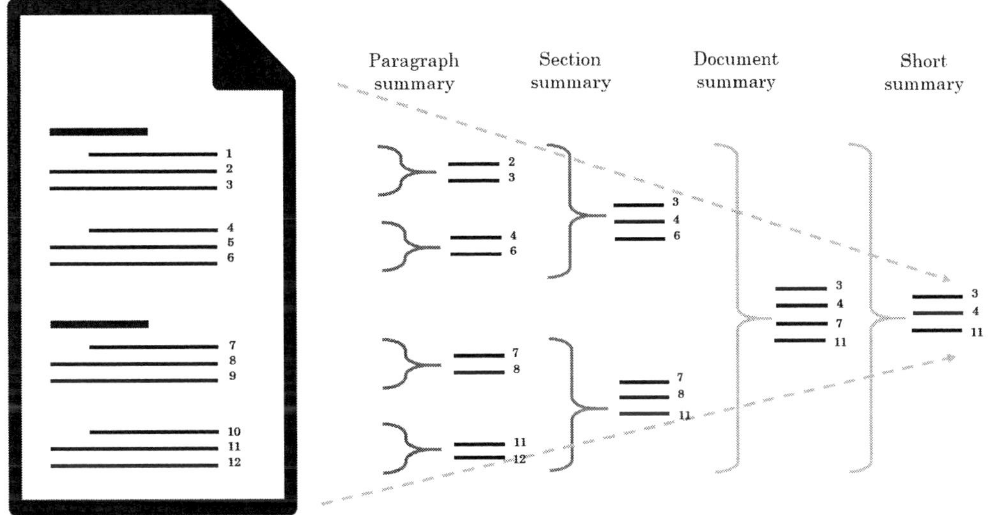

Figure 2: A schematic of ARTEMIS annotation process. A document is divided into sections and paragraphs. The judges summarize paragraphs, sections and the document hierarchically, at each step using sentences selected at the previous step.

vided into two sections with two paragraphs each. The first section contains sentences $\{1 .. 6\}$, with two paragraphs containing sentences $\{1 .. 3\}$ and $\{4 .. 6\}$ respectively. The second section contains sentences $\{7 .. 12\}$, again with two paragraphs containing sentences $\{7 .. 9\}$ and $\{10 .. 12\}$.

A salient sentence is defined as a sentence that includes a main concept or idea for summarizing the text, or a fact or an argument emphasized by the author*. Several example sentences are provided in the judge guidelines to help them distinguish salient sentences from non-salient sentences. At a high-level, the judges are trained to select sentences that allow a reader to decide whether to read the full document or not.

To summarize the document, judges proceed in a bottom-up manner starting from paragraphs (left-to-right in Figure 2). A judge is first asked to summarize each paragraph in a section by selecting a few salient sentences. A minimum number of sentences are required for each paragraph-summary [†]. Once a paragraph has been summarized, the annotation continues to the next paragraph till paragraph-level summaries are created for all the paragraphs in a section. For the document in Figure 2, the judge selected sentences $\{2, 3\}$ for the first paragraph and

sentences $\{4, 6\}$ for the second paragraph.

Once all the paragraphs in a section are summarized, the judge is asked to create a summary for the entire section. However, the judge doesn't have to look at all the sentences in the section to build the section-level summary. Instead, they only select from the set of sentences previously selected to summarize the paragraphs of the section. For example, for summarizing the first section in Figure 2, the judge only needs to select from the set of sentences $\{2, 3, 4, 6\}$, instead of the entire set of sentences $\{1 .. 6\}$ that comprise the section. In the example, the judge decided to use the sentences $\{3, 4, 6\}$ for summarizing the first section.

Once a section is summarized, the annotation proceeds to the next section in a similar manner. Once all the sections of a document are summarized, the judge is asked to build the document summary by selecting from sentences that they had previously selected to build the section-level summaries. In Figure 2, the judge selected sentences $\{3, 4, 7, 11\}$ for the document level summary. Finally, the judge is asked to build a short summary for the document by selecting three most salient sentences from their document-level summary.

ARTEMIS's hierarchical annotation process considerably reduces the cognitive load on the judges. By reusing judgements made at previous steps, judges are able to successfully summarize long documents by divide-and-conquer. For creating

---

*Authors can emphasize sentences either through formatting or discourse cues.

[†]The judge can also mark incomplete and grammatically incorrect sentences as defective, which are not counted when computing the minimum threshold for paragraph-summary.

Document Sentences	#Para	#Sec	#Doc	#Short
(1) This content should be viewed as reference documentation only, to inform IT ...	0	0	0	0
(2) Microsoft employees need to stay aware of new company products, services, processes, and personnel-related developments in an organization that provides ...	2	2	2	2
(3) The SMSG Readiness team at Microsoft developed a suite of applications that delivers training and information to Microsoft employees according to employee ...	4	4	4	3
(4) Microsoft Information Technology (Microsoft IT) is responsible for managing one of the largest Information Technology (IT) infrastructure environments in the world.	5	4	2	2
(5) It consists of 95,000 employees working in 107 countries worldwide.	0	0	0	0
(6) The Sales, Marketing, and Services Group (SMSG) at Microsoft is responsible for servicing the needs of Microsoft customers and partners.	3	1	1	1
(7) It is essential that these 45,000 employees remain informed about products and services within their areas of expertise and, in turn, to educate and inform ...	1	0	0	0
(8) The SMSG Readiness (SMSGR) team at Microsoft is responsible for ensuring that SMSG employees have all of the tools and knowledge they require to deliver ...	4	3	2	2

Table 1: Detailed view of the annotation for the web-crawled document shown in Figure 1. Against each sentence, we show the number of judges that selected the sentence at paragraph, section, document and short summary stage.

the document-level summary in the hypothetical example in Figure 2, the judge only needs to look at the 6 sentences $\{3, 4, 6, 7, 8, 11\}$ selected for the two section-level summaries, instead of having to go over the entire set of 12 sentences.

Table 1 shows a more detailed view of the annotation for an actual document annotated through ARTEMIS with five judges (This is the same document that was used in Figure 1). For each of the first eight sentences in the document, it shows the number of judges that selected the sentence at paragraph, section, document and short summary stage. This table gives an insight into the kind of information available from the annotation.

Sentences *(1)* and *(5)* were deemed by every judge as not salient. Sentence *(3)* was selected by four judges as salient up to document-summary level, but one of the judges dropped it at short-summary level. Similarly, sentence *(4)* was selected at paragraph-summary level by five judges, but only two judges kept it till the document and short-summary level. In Section 4, we present statistics on a sample annotated document set that characterize the annotation process in more detail.

3 Related Work

We now compare ARTEMIS with existing summarization evaluation methods. We start with discussing Relative Utility, which is most related to our methodology, and describe how ARTEMIS obtains similar judgments, but with a light-weight process where judges don't need to look at the entire input document when annotating a sentence. Following this, we discuss DUC evaluations, ROUGE and the Pyramid method. Finally, we discuss some of the recent trends in summarization evaluation.

3.1 Relative Utility

Tam et al. (2007) introduce Relative Utility (RU) as an evaluation metric to account for Summary Sentence Substitutability (SSS) problem in co-selection metrics. Co-selection metrics are evaluation metrics for extractive summarization that depend on text unit overlap with ideal reference summaries created by judges. The SSS problem arises because the judges only provide information about the sentences that they selected for a fixed-length summary. However, other sentences in the document might be equally good candidates for the summary. Human judges often disagree about which are the top n% of the sentences in a document (Mani, 2001).

To address the SSS problem, in RU evaluation judges are asked to assign a utility score to each sentence in a document on a scale of 0 to 10. Given these utility scores, the score for any arbitrary extractive summary can be computed based on the utility of the sentences in the summary.

In RU, to assign the utility score to a sentence in the document, a judge needs to compare the sentence with every other sentence in the document. This can be difficult for long documents. ARTEMIS is a light-weight process that achieves an approximation of this. By assigning graded importance scores to paragraph, section, document and short summary level labels, we can obtain an approximate utility score for each sentence. For example scores $\{1, 2, 3, 4\}$ could be assigned to sentences selected at paragraph, section, document and short summary level and a score of 0 could be assigned to sentences not selected at any level.

3.2 DUC evaluations and ROUGE

DUC (Document Understanding Conferences) were a series of conferences run to further progress in summarization. DUC 2001-2004 focused on single and multi-document summarization (Dang, 2005). In DUC evaluation for summary content, first a single human judge creates a model summary for each document. The model summary is split automatically into content units. For evaluating a system generated summary, a human judge compares the sentences in the system summary with model content units and estimates the fact overlap.

The use of a single model summary in DUC evaluations raised concerns in the research community and led to the proposal of Pyramid evaluation, which we describe in Section 3.3. Lin (2004a) concluded that given enough samples, the use of single model summaries was valid, but using multiple model summaries increased correlation with human judgments.

In later years, DUC experimented with ROUGE (Lin, 2004b), an automatic metric for summary evaluation that uses n-gram co-occurrence statistics for scoring system generated summaries against the model summaries. ROUGE is the standard automatic evaluation method used in recent summarization evaluations, which we describe in Section 3.4.

In ARTEMIS, the sentences selected by judges for document or short-level summary can be used as model summaries for ROUGE evaluation, as we demonstrate in Section 5. In addition, the labels for sentences at different summary levels could be used to train a pair-wise sentence ranking system such as LambdaMart (Burges, 2010) or come up with more refined evaluation metrics.

3.3 Pyramid evaluation

Nenkova and Passonneau (2004) introduced Pyramid method as a more reliable method for summary evaluation by incorporating the idea that no single best model summary exists. Given a set of human-generated model summaries for a document, the Pyramid method starts by manually identifying Summary Content Units (SCUs) in the model summaries. A SCU represents a single unit of information (e.g. "Two men were indicted") which can have different surface realizations in different summaries (e.g. "Court indicted two men", "Two men have been indicted").

The weight of an SCU is the number of model summaries it appears in. Thus, an SCU appearing in five model summaries has a higher weight than an SCU appearing in three model summaries. Given the SCU inventory over all model summaries, the Pyramid score of a system generated summary is obtained based on the number and weights of the SCUs in the summary. Nenkova and Passonneau (2004) observe that the number of SCUs grows as the number of model summaries increases, confirming a similar observation by van Halteren and Teufel (2003), supporting the claim that different judges deem different facts as important.

Finding SCUs in model summaries and then matching them to system summaries is an expensive semantic judgment task. Once created, the SCU inventory can be used to assign an importance weight to any sentence in a system generated extractive summary based on the weights of SCUs in it. Our methodology provides a cheaper method for assigning importance weight for each sentence in a document. In ARTEMIS, multiple judges select each sentence for multiple summaries at paragraph, section, document, and short-summary levels. These judgments provide a low-cost way of obtaining an importance weight for a sentence, without expensive SCU annotation.

3.4 Recent Trends in Summarization Evaluation

Recent summarization evaluations are done using large scale datasets collected automatically from the web. Most of these datasets are from the news domain, including CNN/DailyMail (Nallapati et al., 2016), NEWSROOM (Grusky et al., 2018), New York Times (Sandhaus, 2008) and Gigaword (Rush et al., 2015). Some of the other domains investigated are scientific articles (Cohan et al., 2018), patents (Sharma et al., 2019), and Reddit stories (Kim et al., 2019).

Datasets built from naturally occurring summaries found online tend to focus on domains for which manually written summaries are easily available such as news and scientific articles. These datasets are not sufficient for building a multi-domain document summarization application. Additionally, given the nature of data collection, often only a single summary is available for each document. This makes error analysis of individual examples difficult because different judges might deem different information as summary-worthy (Louis and Nenkova, 2013) as discussed in Section 3.3. ARTEMIS provides a methodology for obtaining

Partition	# Sentences	# Documents
Train	19748	266
Dev	11488	138
Test	9898	128

Table 2: Sample dataset used for the data analysis in this paper.

Partition	Average Count Per Document	Average number of sentences
Section	6.92 ± 0.91	12.04 ± 0.72
Paragraph	15.25 ± 2.17	5.46 ± 0.06

Table 3: Average number of paragraphs and sections per document and the average number of sentences in each, along with the 95% confidence interval.

rich summary annotations for open-domain documents with multiple judges.

Summaries collected from online sources are also prone to noise. Kryscinski et al. (2019) manually inspected CNN/DailyMail and NEWSROOM datasets and found that the problem of noisy data affects upto 5.92% of the summaries in different splits. Examples of noise they found include links to other articles and news sources, placeholder texts, unparsed HTML code, and non-informative passages in the reference summaries. In ARTEMIS, such noisy text is excluded from annotation by explicit labeling of defective sentences.

Hardy et al. (2019) proposed a new summarization evaluation approach called HIGHRES, which uses multiple judges to highlight salient information in original documents. Once the highlights are obtained, a system summary can be evaluated manually by asking judges to compare the system summary against highlights, or by a modified ROUGE evaluation that weighs n-grams by the number of times they were highlighted. HIGHRES is complementary to our hierarchical annotation approach and both the methods can be used together for obtaining rich summary annotations.

4   Annotated Data Analysis

We present analysis on a sample dataset of 532 Microsoft Word documents crawled from the web with no domain restrictions, thus creating an open-domain dataset. We extracted the text from the Word documents for our annotation. The annotation framework does not rely on Word document format and can be used to annotate any document for which the raw text can be extracted.

The data was annotated by a set of managed judges who were trained extensively for ARTEMIS annotation process using detailed guidelines and illustrative examples. For additional quality control, we used a set of gold documents annotated by the development team for initial qualification tests for the judges as well as their ongoing evaluation. We divided the sample dataset into train, dev and test partitions, as shown in Table 2. Unless otherwise

stated, the statistics presented are computed over the dev partition.

4.1   Distribution Statistics

Table 3 shows how the sentences of a document are divided across paragraphs and sections for the annotations. On an average, there are about 7 sections and 15 paragraphs in each document. The number of sentences in each section averages about 12, while the number of sentences in each paragraph averages about 5. Note that when summarizing a section, a judge has to look at much smaller number of sentences than 12, thanks to the hierarchical annotation process.

To understand where the salient sentences lie for the documents, we divide each document into 10 equally sized bins and plot what fraction of sentences selected for the doc-level summaries lie in each bin. Each bin on an average contains 8.34 ± 0.38 sentences. Figure 3 shows the distribution of sentences selected for the doc-level summaries across the bins. More than 50% of the selected sentences lie in the first bin and more than 90% of the sentences lie in the first five bins. This shows that there is a bias for the summary sentences to be towards the first half of a document. However, the annotators don't form summaries by just selecting the first few sentences, as shown by the poor ROUGE-F1 scores obtained by the Lead-3 baseline in Section 5.

Another characterization of the annotation system can be done based on what fraction of salient sentences selected at each stage make it to the next stage. Table 4 shows this for all the stages of annotation. Looking at the diagonal first, we see that 82.44% of the sentences selected as salient for paragraph-level summaries are also selected for section-level summaries, but only 69.57% of the sentences selected for section-level summaries are selected for document-level summaries. From document-level summaries to short summary level, again 84.57% of the salient sentences are kept. This shows that a larger number of sentences get filtered between the section and document level.

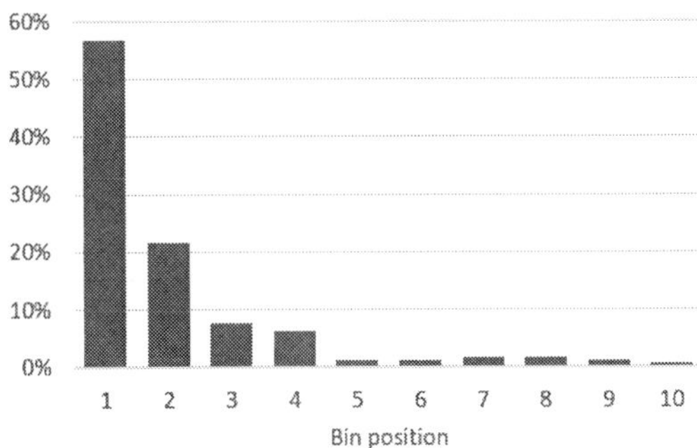

Figure 3: Distribution of sentences selected for doc-level summaries across 10 equally sized bins for each document.

	Section	Document	Short
Paragraph	82.44%	57.36%	48.51%
Section		69.57%	58.84%
Document			84.57%

Table 4: Filtration ratios for salient sentences between different stages. For example, the first row (Paragraph) shows what percentage of sentences selected at paragraph level survive till section, document and short-summary level. Table cells corresponding to filtration between same or out-of-order stages in the pipeline are colored gray.

Overall, only 48.51% of the sentences selected for paragraph-level summaries are used for the final three-sentence short summaries.

4.2 Agreement Statistics

We compute Krippendorff's alpha over the entire annotated document set by treating each of paragraph, section, document and short summary level judgements as ordinal ratings. Across the set of all judges, the Krippendorff's alpha is 0.46. This is consistent with previous findings that summary content selection is a subjective task with moderate agreement (Mani, 2001). Nenkova and Passonneau (2004) report a Krippendorff's alpha of 0.81 for their annotations. However, they measure agreement on the task of assigning SCU's to words, which is a less subjective task than assigning importance to a content unit. They also use a distance metric for computing Krippendorff's alpha that takes into account SCU size, which is not described in detail in their paper.

For additional agreement evaluation, we had 10 documents evaluated by two sets of judges. The first set of judges was comprised of 4 developers involved in the design of ARTEMIS and its guide-

#	Paragraph	Section	Document	Short
1	11.2 ± 1.0	9.4 ± 0.8	6.5 ± 0.4	5.4 ± 0.3
2	5.1 ± 0.6	4.1 ± 0.5	2.8 ± 0.3	2.4 ± 0.2
3	2.5 ± 0.4	2.0 ± 0.3	1.5 ± 0.2	1.3 ± 0.2

Table 5: Average number of salient sentences at each stage corresponding to the minimum number of judges needed to mark a sentence as salient (out of a total of five judges) along with 95% confidence intervals.

lines. The second set of judges was comprised of 5 managed judges trained for doing the annotations. For each set of judges, a sentence was considered to be selected for document-level summary if at least 2 judges selected it. Given these judgements, the Kappa score between the two sets of judges was 0.43, which is considered moderate agreement (Landis and Koch, 1977).

Table 5 shows the average number of sentences selected at the different annotation levels if we use a minimum of 1, 2, or 3 judges to mark a sentence as salient out of the 5 total judges that annotate each document. We see that with 2 judges, there is agreement for 2.4 sentences for the final short summary, which is restricted to 3 sentences per judge. Even with 3 judges, there is agreement on 1.3 sentences for the final short-summary level.

5 Experiments

We evaluate a number of baseline methods on the sample annotated document set, partitioned into train, dev and test as described in Table 2.

For these experiments, the document-level summary created by each judge for a document is treated as an independent reference summary and we evaluate the candidate summary against all the reference summaries using ROUGE-F scores.

- **Lead-3** baseline selects first three sentences of a document as the summary.

- **Oracle** scores are obtained using a jack-knifed procedure. Reference summary from each judge is considered a predicted summary and evaluated against all the other reference summaries for the document. The Oracle ROUGE score is computed by averaging the scores for all judge summaries.

- **Cheng&Lapata** (Cheng and Lapata, 2016) is an encoder-decoder summarization model where each sentence is first encoded using a CNN (Convolutional Neural Network). These sentence level encodings are then passed

Method	Rouge-1	Rouge-2	Rouge-L
Lead-3	44.94	34.37	43.39
Cheng & Lapata	60.21	49.81	58.62
SummaRunner	63.56	53.57	61.89
Seq2SeqRNN	63.89	54.22	62.36
Oracle	73.28	66.60	72.20

Table 6: Results for different baselines on the test data.

through an RNN (Recurrent Neural Network) to create contextual encodings for each sentence. The encoding for the final sentence of the document is fed into the decoder, which uses another RNN with attention over input sentence encodings to predict the label for each sentence. At each decoding step, the decoder state also depends on the probability of the previous sentence being part of summary.

- **SummaRunner** (Nallapati et al., 2017) uses a hierarchical RNN to compute contextual encodings for each sentence in the input. These encodings are average pooled and passed through a non-linear transformation to create an encoding for the document. In a second pass, a logistic layer makes a binary decision for each sentence based on the sentence encodings, the document representation as well as factors modeling previously selected summary sentences and sentence position.

- **Seq2SeqRNN** is a method introduced in Kedzie et al. (2018) that uses an RNN to encode the input sentences. A separate RNN based decoder is used to transform each sentence into a query vector which attends to the encoder output. The attention weighted encoder output and the decoder GRU output are used together to predict the output label.

We used the code released by Kedzie et al. (2018) for reproducing Cheng&Lapata, SummaRunner and Seq2SeqRNN systems. The ROUGE-F score for each system on the test data is shown in Table 6.

The Lead baseline achieves a ROUGE-1 score of 44.94, which is significantly lower than the other systems as well as the Oracle. This shows that compared to news summarization, selecting the first few sentences is a much weaker baseline for open-domain summarization.

The SummaRunner system does better than Cheng&Lapata, potentially due to its incorporating multiple signals for content, salience, novelty and position. Seq2SeqRNN performs the best, which

is consistent with the results reported in Kedzie et al. (2018). There is still a gap between these systems and the Oracle method, which achieves a ROUGE-1 score of 73.28.

6 Concluding Remarks

In this paper, we described ARTEMIS, a novel hierarchical annotation methodology for indicative, extractive summarization. We described the annotation process in detail and compared it with Relative Utility, DUC evaluation methodology, the Pyramid method as well as other recent methods for summary content evaluation. We also presented analysis over a sample annotated dataset to characterize various properties of annotation process such as distribution of salient sentences and judge agreement. Finally, we showed experimental results for a set of baseline summarization systems using the annotated dataset.

Indicative summaries are useful in a number of scenarios involving information triage such as document management and information retrieval systems. However, summarization models for such systems need to be able to summarize documents from multiple domains. Most existing summarization datasets are single-domain and focused towards news, and hence are not sufficient for training and evaluating models for these applications. ARTEMIS provides a low-cost methodology for annotating multi-domain indicative summaries compared to systems such as Pyramid and Relative Utility while producing similarly rich annotations.

ARTEMIS summary annotations contain sentences that provide information about important topics in the document. The summaries are indicative because they do not aim to convey all the important points for a given information need, but instead, give a sense of what topics are covered in the document. The set of annotations in ARTEMIS can be seen as a coarse partitioning between important and non-important sentences in an input document. Thus, models trained on these annotations can also be used as an importance signal in a larger pipeline for creating informative summaries.

References

Regina Barzilay and Michael Elhadad. 1997. Using lexical chains for text summarization. In *In Proceedings of the ACL Workshop on Intelligent Scalable Text Summarization*, pages 10 17.

Chris J.C. Burges. 2010. From ranknet to lambdarank to lambdamart: An overview. Technical Report MSR-TR-2010-82.

Jianpeng Cheng and Mirella Lapata. 2016. Neural summarization by extracting sentences and words. In *Proceedings of the 54th Annual Meeting of the Association for Computational Linguistics (Volume 1: Long Papers)*, pages 484–494, Berlin, Germany. Association for Computational Linguistics.

Arman Cohan, Franck Dernoncourt, Doo Soon Kim, Trung Bui, Seokhwan Kim, Walter Chang, and Nazli Goharian. 2018. A discourse-aware attention model for abstractive summarization of long documents. In *Proceedings of the 2018 Conference of the North American Chapter of the Association for Computational Linguistics: Human Language Technologies, Volume 2 (Short Papers)*, pages 615–621, New Orleans, Louisiana. Association for Computational Linguistics.

Hoa Trang Dang. 2005. Overview of duc 2005. In *In Proceedings of the Document Understanding Conf. Wksp. 2005 (DUC 2005) at the Human Language Technology Conf./Conf. on Empirical Methods in Natural Language Processing (HLT/EMNLP*.

H. P. Edmundson. 1969. New methods in automatic extracting. *J. ACM*, 16(2):264–285.

David Graff, Junbo Kong, Ke Chen, and Kazuaki Maeda. 2003. English gigaword. *Linguistic Data Consortium, Philadelphia*, 4(1):34.

Max Grusky, Mor Naaman, and Yoav Artzi. 2018. Newsroom: A dataset of 1.3 million summaries with diverse extractive strategies. In *Proceedings of the 2018 Conference of the North American Chapter of the Association for Computational Linguistics: Human Language Technologies*, pages 708–719, New Orleans, Louisiana. Association for Computational Linguistics.

Hans van Halteren and Simone Teufel. 2003. Examining the consensus between human summaries: initial experiments with factoid analysis. In *Proceedings of the HLT-NAACL 03 Text Summarization Workshop*, pages 57–64.

Hardy Hardy, Shashi Narayan, and Andreas Vlachos. 2019. HighRES: Highlight-based reference-less evaluation of summarization. In *Proceedings of the 57th Annual Meeting of the Association for Computational Linguistics*, pages 3381–3392, Florence, Italy. Association for Computational Linguistics.

Eduard H. Hovy and Chin-Yew Lin. 1997. Automated text summarization in summarist. In *ACL 1997*.

Min-Yen Kan, Judith L. Klavans, and Kathleen R. Mckeown. 2002. Using the annotated bibliography as a resource for indicative summarization. In *In Proceedings of LREC 2002, Las*.

Min-Yen Kan, Kathleen R. McKeown, and Judith L. Klavans. 2001a. Applying natural language generation to indicative summarization. In *In Proc. of the EACL Workshop on Natural Language Generation*, pages 1–9.

Min-Yen Kan, Kathleen R. McKeown, and Judith L. Klavans. 2001b. Domain-specific informative and indicative summarization for information retrieval. In *In: Workshop on text summarization (DUC 2001*, pages 1629–1636.

Chris Kedzie, Kathleen McKeown, and Hal Daumé III. 2018. Content selection in deep learning models of summarization. In *Proceedings of the 2018 Conference on Empirical Methods in Natural Language Processing*, pages 1818–1828, Brussels, Belgium. Association for Computational Linguistics.

Byeongchang Kim, Hyunwoo Kim, and Gunhee Kim. 2019. Abstractive summarization of Reddit posts with multi-level memory networks. In *Proceedings of the 2019 Conference of the North American Chapter of the Association for Computational Linguistics: Human Language Technologies, Volume 1 (Long and Short Papers)*, pages 2519–2531, Minneapolis, Minnesota. Association for Computational Linguistics.

Wojciech Kryscinski, Nitish Shirish Keskar, Bryan McCann, Caiming Xiong, and Richard Socher. 2019. Neural text summarization: A critical evaluation. *ArXiv*, abs/1908.08960.

Julian Kupiec, Jan Pedersen, and Francine Chen. 1995. A trainable document summarizer. In *Proceedings of the 18th Annual International ACM SIGIR Conference on Research and Development in Information Retrieval*, SIGIR 95, page 6873, New York, NY, USA. Association for Computing Machinery.

JR Landis and GG Koch. 1977. The measurement of observer agreement for categorical data. *Biometrics*, 33(1):159174.

Chin-Yew Lin. 2004a. Looking for a few good metrics: Automatic summarization evaluation - how many samples are enough?

Chin-Yew Lin. 2004b. ROUGE: A package for automatic evaluation of summaries. In *Text Summarization Branches Out*, pages 74–81, Barcelona, Spain. Association for Computational Linguistics.

Annie Louis and Ani Nenkova. 2013. Automatically assessing machine summary content without a gold standard. *Computational Linguistics*, 39(2):267–300.

Inderjeet Mani. 2001. Summarization evaluation: An overview.

Ramesh Nallapati, Feifei Zhai, and Bowen Zhou. 2017. Summarunner: A recurrent neural network based sequence model for extractive summarization of documents. In *Thirty-First AAAI Conference on Artificial Intelligence*.

Ramesh Nallapati, Bowen Zhou, Cicero dos Santos, Çağlar Gulçehre, and Bing Xiang. 2016. Abstractive text summarization using sequence-to-sequence RNNs and beyond. In *Proceedings of The 20th SIGNLL Conference on Computational Natural Language Learning*, pages 280–290, Berlin, Germany. Association for Computational Linguistics.

Ani Nenkova and Kathleen McKeown. 2011. Automatic summarization.

Ani Nenkova and Rebecca Passonneau. 2004. Evaluating content selection in summarization: The pyramid method. In *Proceedings of the Human Language Technology Conference of the North American Chapter of the Association for Computational Linguistics: HLT-NAACL 2004*, pages 145–152, Boston, Massachusetts, USA. Association for Computational Linguistics.

Alexander M. Rush, Sumit Chopra, and Jason Weston. 2015. A neural attention model for abstractive sentence summarization. In *Proceedings of the 2015 Conference on Empirical Methods in Natural Language Processing*, pages 379–389, Lisbon, Portugal. Association for Computational Linguistics.

Horacio Saggion and Guy Lapalme. 2002. Generating indicative-informative summaries with sumum. *Computational Linguistics*, 28(4):497–526.

Evan Sandhaus. 2008. he new york times annotated corpus ldc2008t19.

Eva Sharma, Chen Li, and Lu Wang. 2019. BIG-PATENT: A large-scale dataset for abstractive and coherent summarization. In *Proceedings of the 57th Annual Meeting of the Association for Computational Linguistics*, pages 2204–2213, Florence, Italy. Association for Computational Linguistics.

Daniel Tam, Dragomir R. Radev, and Gunes Erkan. 2007. Single-document and multi-document summary evaluation using relative utility. Technical Report CSE-TR-538-07, University of Michigan. Department of Electrical Engineering and Computer Science.

Probabilistic Extension of Precision, Recall, and F1 Score for More Thorough Evaluation of Classification Models

Reda Yacouby
Amazon Alexa
redaya@amazon.com

Dustin Axman
Amazon Alexa
dax@amazon.com

Abstract

In pursuit of the perfect supervised NLP classifier, razor thin margins and low-resource testsets can make modeling decisions difficult. Popular metrics such as Accuracy, Precision, and Recall are often insufficient as they fail to give a complete picture of the model's behavior. We present a probabilistic extension of Precision, Recall, and F1 score, which we refer to as confidence-Precision (cPrecision), confidence-Recall (cRecall), and confidence-F1 (cF1) respectively. The proposed metrics address some of the challenges faced when evaluating large-scale NLP systems, specifically when the model's confidence score assignments have an impact on the system's behavior. We describe four key benefits of our proposed metrics as compared to their threshold-based counterparts. Two of these benefits, which we refer to as *robustness to missing values* and *sensitivity to model confidence score assignments* are self-evident from the metrics' definitions; the remaining benefits, *generalization*, and *functional consistency* arc demonstrated empirically.

1 Introduction

Supervised machine learning classifiers are typically trained to minimize error. This error is evaluated using one or multiple metrics, the choice of which has been a continuous debate in research and industry for multiple decades (Dinga et al., 2019; Brier, 1950). Many criteria need to be considered when choosing a metric, including but not limited to: interpretability, computational cost, differentiability, and popularity in a specific field. As an example, a typical workflow of model development is to use a loss function such as cross-entropy or hinge loss during training for weight optimization, then use an easily interpretable metric such as Accuracy, Precision, or Recall when testing the model against a holdout sample of examples. This

is because the mentioned loss functions are differentiable convex functions, enabling optimization algorithms such as gradient descent to find minima with reasonable computational cost. In contrast, the test-set evaluation metrics are often required to be easy to relate to the real-world problem the classifier is designed to help solve, in order to give a concrete idea of performance or success to the stakeholders.

Essentially, all the criteria mentioned serve the same underlying purpose of driving modeling decisions. The heterogeneous nature of model evaluation illustrates how there could be no universal criteria for driving model decisions, or so-called "best metric", as each criterion could be advantageous under specific operating conditions (Hernández-Orallo et al., 2012), or even preferred by stakeholders for reasons that do not need to be scientifically driven (such as interpretability and business purposes).

In the Natural Language Processing (NLP) industry, new challenges have risen in the past few years in terms of performance evaluation, due to the complexity and scalable design of modern NLP systems such as those powering Google Assistant, Amazon Alexa, or Apple's Siri (Sarikaya, 2017). Such systems are built to support devices with a potentially limitless number of functionalities, as reflected by the Alexa Skill Developer Toolkit and Google Actions, allowing external developers to add additional functionality to the NLP system, supporting new phrases and therefore increasing the number of choices the system needs to disambiguate between.

This sharp rise in scale and complexity has made the most commonly used metrics (Accuracy, Precision, Recall, F1 score) insufficient in depicting a comprehensive picture of the impact introduced by changes in these systems. A key reason behind this gap is that classification models typically

Proceedings of the First Workshop on Evaluation and Comparison of NLP Systems (Eval4NLP), pages 79–91,
November 20, 2020. ©2020 Association for Computational Linguistics

output an n-best list of model predictions, each associated with a confidence score (or probability score), and while simple systems (and most academic use-cases) only consider the highest-score prediction, more elaborate systems tend to leverage further information from the n-best to drive decisions. Metrics such as Accuracy, Precision and Recall simply compare the highest-score prediction with the test reference, ignoring the rest of the n-best output, while this ignored information often does impact the behavior of the NLP system.

We provide 2 cases that exemplify the case of an NLP system being impacted by changes in the n-best output which are ignored by popular metrics:

1. **Arbitration:** Some specific criteria could be used to arbitrate between the n-best predictions rather than always choosing the highest-score prediction. For example, if the top prediction is un-actionable by the system (e.g. results in an error) and the second-best prediction meets some defined criteria, the system could fall-back to that prediction. In the case of a vocal assistant an example would be asking a TV to "play frozen", and the NLP model recognizes it as a request to play song called "frozen" as its top prediction, while the homonymous movie is the second-best prediction. The system could arbitrate and decide to use the second prediction specifically because the request was spoken to a TV, rather than a music player.

2. **Error correction:** It is common for large-scale NLP systems to be multi-step, having domain-specialized models receive the output of an upstream NLP model as input, then attempting to correct potential mistakes. As an example, Named Entity Recognition (NER) in the Shopping domain is challenging for general purpose NLP models due to the large size of product catalogs and potentially ambiguous product names. A downstream Shopping-specific NLP model can be applied on the upstream model's n-best for error correction, potentially re-ranking the n-best and adjusting confidence scores.

Many evaluation metrics capable of measuring changes in confidence score assignments already exist. In this document we will use the taxonomy introduced by Ferri et al. (2009), classifying metrics into 3 categories:

- Threshold-based metrics, using a qualitative understanding of error, such as Accuracy, Precision, and Recall.

- Rank-based metrics, which evaluate how well the models ranks the examples. The Area Under the ROC Curve (AUC) is the most widely used in this category.

- Probabilistic metrics, using a probabilistic understanding of error, as they consider the confidence scores assigned by the models in their measurements. Among these are Brier-score and Cross-entropy.

Among these categories, probabilistic metrics have the potential to fill the evaluation gaps we described. In this paper we are proposing a probabilistic extension of threshold-based metrics. The goal is to introduce advantages of probabilistic metrics while retaining the relatability of threshold-based metrics to the real-world operating cost function of the models, allowing for decision making that is both scientifically reliable and tied to the stakeholder's interests. We describe in Section 3 why other probabilistic metrics are not sufficient to fill the evaluation gaps we are addressing with the newly proposed metrics.

One of the primary benefits of probabilistic metrics is their ability to function more consistently in test-data sparse scenarios. It was demonstrated empirically by Wang et al. (2013) and Dinga et al. (2019) that probabilistic metrics are more reliable in discriminating between models, since they leverage the most information from the model's output. This does not necessarily make them *better* metrics, as we stated earlier how modeling decisions are closely tied to operating conditions, but allows them to be more data-efficient (require less data to reach statistically significant results). Recent developments in Transfer Learning (Pan and Yang, 2010; Conneau et al., 2020) demonstrated impressive ability to learn from small training sets (often referred to as Few-Shot Learning), showing a wide NLP community interest in improving data-efficiency during model training, but we have not found any publication related to data-efficient model testing. Usually the lack of training data would also imply a lack of test data, as they would be caused by the same underlying factor (expensive data collection and/or labelling, low-resource language), which highlights the value in developing ways to compare models with minimal test data requirements. As part of our investigation in this subject, we empirically show that our proposed metrics are more data efficient than their threshold-based counterparts, as they allow for modeling decisions with smaller test-sets.

On a side note, some of the cases in which model confidence assignments are used in production require the scores to be probabilistically calibrated, as they are interpreted by the users as probabilities of events happening (e.g. disease prevention, weather forecasts). Probabilistic calibration refers to the reliability of the scores in reflecting the true probability of the predictions being correct (e.g. if a calibrated model predicted in n cases that event X will happen with probability p, then event X should happen in approximately $p*n$ of those cases). The proposed metrics do not evaluate for probabilistic calibration. For such use-cases we suggest the combined usage of a probability calibration measure (e.g. the Expected Calibration Error (Guo et al., 2017), the reliability component of Brierscore (Murphy, 1973)) along with the proposed metrics, for a thorough evaluation of both performance and calibration.

In this document, we describe four benefits of the proposed metrics. In comparison with their threshold-based counterparts, our metrics:

A. Have an equal or lower likelihood of being NaN (*Robustness to NaN values*).

B. Are sensitive to changes in the model's confidence scores across the model's full n-best output (*Sensitivity to model confidence score assignments*).

C. Have lower variance, making their point estimates more generalizable to unseen data, and allowing for better discriminancy between models (*Generalization* hypothesis)

D. Provide the same ranking of performance of candidate models as their threshold-based counterpart's population value in the majority of cases (*Functional Consistency* hypothesis).

The first two are easily deduced from the metrics' definitions. The third and fourth benefits are demonstrated empirically in Section 6.

2 Definitions

cPrecision, cRecall, and cF1-Score have the same mathematical formulations as Precision, Recall, and F1-Score, respectively, with the only difference being the usage of continuous (as opposed to binary) definitions of Positives and Negatives, based on the confidence score (or probability assignment) a classification model yields for each label. Let's start by defining some terminology to establish a formal definition. Consider:

1. A dataset $S : (\mathbf{x_1}, y_1), ..., (\mathbf{x_n}, y_n) \in \mathbb{R}^p \times \{C_1, ..., C_m\}$, where

   - $\mathbf{x_i}$ is a vector of p features corresponding to sample i
   - y_i is the class corresponding to sample i
   - $\{C_1, ..., C_m\}$ is the set of possible classes

2. A classification model $M : \mathbb{R}^p \mapsto \{C_1, ..., C_m\}$ trained to predict label assignment given an input vector $\mathbf{x_i}$. The model assigns a *confidence score* (or *probability* if the model is probabilistically calibrated) to each possible class C_j for any given input vector $\mathbf{x_i}$, signifying the model's *confidence* that C_j is the true class for the given input vector (which can also be expressed as $C_j = y_i$). Let's call this confidence score $M(\mathbf{x_i}, C_j)$. The class with the highest confidence score will be the model's predicted class $\widehat{y_i}$.

We have, for any sample $i \in \{1, ..., n\}$:

$$\sum_{j=1}^{m} M(\mathbf{x_i}, C_j) = 1 \tag{1}$$

$$\widehat{y_i} = \arg\max_{j}(M(\mathbf{x_i}, C_j)) \tag{2}$$

By applying the model M on the full dataset S, we obtain a confidence score $M(\mathbf{x_i}, C_j)$ for each $i \in \{1, ..., n\}$ and $j \in \{1, ..., m\}$. Suppose S_j denotes the set of samples with true class C_j. We can build a probabilistic confusion matrix pCM as follows:

$$pCM(j_{ref}, j_{hyp}) = \sum_{i \in S_{j_{ref}}} M(\mathbf{x_i}, C_{j_{hyp}}) \tag{3}$$

Intuitively, each cell (j_{ref}, j_{hyp}) of the confusion matrix corresponds to the total confidence score assigned by the model to hypothesis j_{hyp} for samples for which the true class is j_{ref}. It is very similar to the usual definition of a confusion matrix, apart from the fact that we leverage all confidence scores as quantitative values as rather than just the highest-scoring class as a qualitative value. From this probabilistic confusion matrix, cRecall and cPrecision are calculated in the same way that Recall and Precision are from the non-probabilistic (regular) confusion matrix.

We can also formulate it without using a confusion matrix, by using indicator functions. The commonly used definition of *true positive for class* C_j is any model prediction for which $\widehat{y_i} = y_i = C_j$. We can formalize it as:

$$TP_{C_j} = I_{\widehat{y_i}=C_j} * I_{C_j=y_i} \qquad (4)$$

$$\text{where: } I_X = \begin{cases} 1 \text{ if } X \text{ is true} \\ 0 \text{ if } X \text{ is false} \end{cases}$$

We propose a continuous generalization as the *confidence true positive*:

$$cTP_{C_j} = M(\mathbf{x_i}, C_j) * I_{C_j=y_i} \qquad (5)$$

As shown in Equation 5, we're simply replacing the binary $I_{\widehat{y_i}=C_j}$ from Equation 4 by the continuous $M(\mathbf{x_i}, C_j)$. We can similarly define the *confidence False Positive* as

$$cFP_{C_j} = M(\mathbf{x_i}, C_j) * I_{C_j \neq y_i} \qquad (6)$$

Now that we formalized cTP and cFP, we can define $cPrecision$ and $cRecall$:

$$cPrecision = \frac{cTP}{cTP + cFP} \qquad (7)$$

$$cRecall = \frac{cTP}{TP + FN} \qquad (8)$$

Note the asymmetry between cPrecision and cRecall, as the denominator of cRecall is the same as the denominator of Recall (does not use the probabilistic extensions of FP and FN). This is because $TP + FN$ simply refers to the total number of samples labelled as the class being evaluated.

3 Related Work

In the publication Employ Decision Values for Soft-Classifier Evaluation with Crispy References, Zhu et al. (2018) have come to a similar formulation of probabilistic confusion matrix in the pursuit of a different goal. Zhu considered the use-case of soft-classification, where "the classifier outputs not only a crispy prediction about its class label, but decision values which indicate to what extent does it belong to the all the classes as well", while we're considering hard classification, where the hypothesis probabilities output by the classifier indicate a confidence score that the hypothesis is correct, rather than a measure of class membership. From the resulting confusion matrix, Zhu also formulated and empirically experimented with a probabilistic version of Precision and Recall, but only for binary classification. In our paper we dive deeper into the properties and potential of these metrics in multiclass hard classification when the model hypothesis confidence scores are impactful to the use case, especially in large-scale NLP systems.

Many publications (Dinga et al., 2019; Hossin M, 2015) have shed light on pitfalls of commonly used evaluation metrics, and introduced alternatives and best practices to avoid those pitfalls. However, the criticized metrics have maintained their status as the standard in most industries and in academia.

Ling et al. (2003) and Vanderlooy and Hüllermeier (2008) have proposed methodologies to evaluate metrics against each other. We decided however to approach this problem from a different perspective. We will only compare a metric to its proposed extended counterpart (e.g. F1 vs cF1), and will not claim our proposed metrics to be objectively better, but simply demonstrate advantages they introduce, and in which situations those advantages are useful. In many use-cases it might still be preferable to use the regular Precision and Recall.

There are many existing metrics that leverage the model's probability assignments over classes. Brier score (Brier, 1950) is an example, and is widely accepted as a standard in probabilistic weather forecasting. It is a strictly proper scoring rule, meaning it is uniquely optimized by reporting probabilistically calibrated model predictions. Using our earlier defined methodology, Brier-score can be calculated as: $BS = \frac{1}{n} \sum_{i=1}^{n} \sum_{j=1}^{m} (M(\mathbf{x_i}, C_j) - I_{C_j=y_i})^2$

which can be interpreted as a sum of squared errors between the predicted probability distribution and the true distribution. Brier-score is effective at giving a big picture of model performance beyond the top model hypothesis, along with an evaluation of probabilistic calibration.

However, Brier-score is not appropriate for large-scale NLP systems such as those described in Section 1, for two main reasons. The first one is that the data distribution is often imbalanced, as basic commands such as "stop" or "play" are dominating as compared to more niche features such as "open halo on my xbox", while the importance of a class is not reflected in its distribution (e.g. calling for emergency). This shows that these use cases require class-based measures, rather than aggregated ones like Brier-score. Secondly, it is important to be able to evaluate each class independently to understand the class tradeoffs (False Accepts and False Rejections from/towards competing classes), as different stakeholders are responsible for different functionalities. Additionally, Brier-score can be difficult to interpret and explain to non-technical stakeholders, as compared to other common metrics such as Precision and Recall. The concerns presented in this paragraph also hold for other probabilistic metrics we found in literature, such as the Probabilistic Confusion Entropy (Wang et al., 2013) and metrics usually used as loss functions during training.

Another widely popular metric is the Area Under the Receiver Operating Characteristic Curve (AUC), which is originally for binary classifiers, but has been generalized to handle multi-class (Hand and Till, 2001). AUC is taxonomized as a rank-based metric rather than a probabilistic metric, as it is only sensitive to changes in confidence scores when those changes cause a difference in the ranking of test samples. Multiple extensions of AUC have been proposed to allow it to better leverage probability score assignments, such as the pAUC (Ferri et al., 2004) and soft-AUC (Calders and Jaroszewicz, 2007) but these extensions were only defined and analyzed in the binary classification case, and were also questioned by Vanderlooy and Hüllermeier (2008) through empirical experiments indicating that the variants fail to be more effective than the original AUC.

4   Benefit A: Robustness to NaN values

Precision, Recall, and F1-Score have a denominator which in some cases can be equal to zero, making it impossible to calculate an estimate of the metric. In the case of Recall, this denominator (TP + FN) would be equal to zero for any label that is not present in the test-set (no sample in the test-set is assigned this label as its ground truth). As Recall and cRecall have the same denominator, this situation would also cause cRecall to be NaN for those labels. Precision would be NaN for any label that is not hypothesized by the model when making predictions in the test-set.

Notably, cPrecision does not fall victim to the same issue (except in the extreme case when the model never assigns any confidence to that label). This is due to the fact that cPrecision considers that the model is making soft predictions (confidence score assignments) for all labels for each test sample. This quality makes cPrecision more robust than Precision. The number of NaN values for Precision increases as the test-set size goes smaller, which also affects F1, as a NaN Precision causes a NaN F1. This makes cF1 less likely to have NaN values than F1 under small test-set sizes. Especially in imbalanced datasets or datasets with a large number of possible classes, this issue is burdensome as your test-set needs to be very large to have a high likelihood of all classes being hypothesized.

5   Benefit B: Model confidence score sensitivity

Intuitively, it appears as a good characteristic for a model to be more confident when being correct and less confident when being wrong. Even though in some use cases this might not result in better outcomes for the stakeholders since only the highest-score prediction is actually used in the final application. Nonetheless, selecting a better model can yield benefits in the long term, or when noise/out-of-sample data is introduced, as the score assignments reflect how well the model understands the underlying data. We did not deem it necessary to perform an empirical demonstration of this quality, as it is a central aspect in the definition of the proposed metrics.

In order to concretely illustrate the practical use of Benefit B in an NLP production environment, consider a case where a company is building a semi-automated text labelling pipeline, where a model automatically labels text samples when the top prediction's confidence score is higher than a chosen threshold (e.g. 0.99), and sends the remaining samples to humans for manual labelling (e.g. Amazon SageMaker Ground Truth as an NLP pipeline). In cases where the label space is large (common in large-scale NLP) human annotators cannot be familiar with all annotations. To address this, the pipeline presents the human annotator with the model's n-best output predictions as suggestions, to improve efficiency and reduce their burden. Evaluating this NLP model with threshold-based metrics would not be appropriate, as the full n-best output is used to influence the human annotator's decisions. Metrics such as Brier-score and Log-loss would be a step forward, but would not allow for a balanced class-based evaluation, and would not give visibility over the tradeoffs between classes. The latter metrics are also difficult to interpret, as the stakeholders are likely to be interested in measures they can easily relate to, and a potential break-down of which labels are more difficult to identify. In such case, cPrecision, cRecall, and cF1 would be appropriate, as they would bring the thorough evaluation of probabilistic metrics combined with the interpretability and robustness to class imbalance of Precision and Recall.

6 Empirical Results

In our experiments we directly compare each of the 3 threshold-based metrics with their probabilistic counterpart. Our goal is to support the claimed benefits of *generalization* and *functional consistency*. We present results on the SNLI dataset (Bowman et al., 2015), a dataset of paired sentences (560152 training samples and 10000 test samples) rated by annotators as either "Neutral", "Entailment", or "Contradiction" depending on how the sentences relate to each other. Please note that as SNLI does not suffer from data imbalance and only has 3 classes, this experiment is not intended to illustrate all of the advantages of the proposed metrics in large-scale commercial NLP pipelines. Instead, we simply use SNLI to experimentally support the *generalization* and *functional consistency* benefits.

6.1 Testing Hypothesis C: Generalization

We trained Sep-CNN (Denk, 2018) models (structure shown in Figure 7 in Appendix B) with different sets of randomly chosen hyperparameters and training samples. Sep-CNN was used here for its training and evaluation speed that eased speed of experimentation. More replication information can be found in Appendix A.

Generalization is directly tied to the variance of the metrics. Metrics with lower variance will have tighter confidence bounds, which implies that their point estimates are closer to the true population values. This means that a point estimate calculated from a small dataset is more likely to be generalizable to unseen data. Lower variance also implies that less data is required to reach statistically significant results in discriminating models. For this hypothesis we simply need to demonstrate that our proposed metrics have lower variance than their threshold-based counterpart. We set-up our experi-

ments also to show that our proposed metrics are better able to discriminate between models.

We introduce differences in the models by varying the percentage of the training dataset selected during subsampling for model training, and injecting noise by changing a certain percentage of the labels on that data to a random alternative label. Model 1 used 100% of the training data, Model 2 used 66.7% of the training data, 10% of which is altered to introduce noise, and finally Model 3 used 33.3% of the training data, 20% of which is altered to introduce noise. The goal of changing these two parameters is to create enough differentiation in performance between the models in order to have preliminary expectations of which models will perform best. Model 1 is expected to perform better than Model 2, which is expected to perform better than Model 3.

We then ran predictions on test-set downsamplings of 1.0, 0.5, 0.2, 0.1, 0.05, 0.02, and 0.01 ratios for each of these models and used the bootstrap method (Efron, 1979) with 1000 resamplings, to calculate the mean and 95% confidence intervals for the F1 and cF1 scores for each class, for each model, on each test data down-sampling. Figure 1 below presents a comparison of the resulting variances of cF1 and F1. Figures 5 and 6 (Appendix B) show the same comparison but for cPrecision against Precision, and cRecall against Recall respectively.

The plots show two key elements: variances get smaller as the test-set size increases, and the variance of the probabilistic metrics is always lower than the variance of their threshold-based counterpart. We also used a F-test of equality of variance, Bartlett's test, and Levene's test to reject the null hypothesis that the variance of the threshold-based metric and its probabilistic counterpart are equal, and obtained statistically significant results ($pvalues < 0.05$) in all cases.

In Figure 2 we compare F1 and cF1's abilities to discriminate between models, at different test-set sizes. The shaded region for each line represents the 95% confidence interval. The x-axis represents down-sampling ratios of the test-set used for each metric evaluation. We see the confidence intervals being further away from each other for cF1 as compared to F1, across all test-set sampling sizes, allowing for a statistically significant identification of which models have a better understanding of the underlying data. Figures 3 and 4 in Appendix B

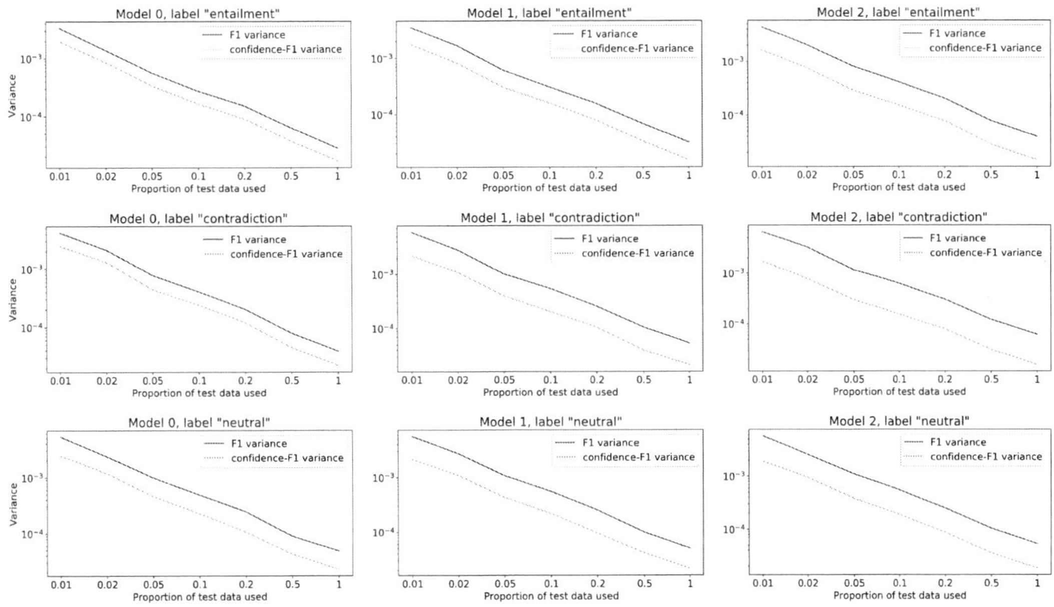

Figure 1: Empirical comparison of the variances of F1 and cF1, across different test-set sizes.

show the same but for Precision against cPrecision and Recall against cRecall respectively.

6.2 Testing Hypothesis D: Functional Consistency

We hypothesize that for most pragmatic and real-world modeling decisions, the ranking of performance of candidate models by each metric (when compared to their threshold-based counterpart) is the same when tested on a test-set similar enough to the population distribution of test data. Figure 2 illustrates it, by showing consistency in model rankings for each metric at the 1.0 subsampling (full test-set size).

In order to more empirically demonstrate this observation, we ran an experiment where we randomly generated 100 models by sampling from a selection of different possible hyperparameters. We then compared all models against each other, resulting in 4950 pairwise comparisons, using the 6 metrics considered (Precision, cPrecision, Recall, cRecall, F1, cF1). From these results, we extracted all the cases in which both the probabilistic and the thresholded metric showed a statistically significant difference between the two models being compared (t-test with p=0.01). Among the latter cases, we counted the percentage of agreement (cases where both metrics agree on which model is better). The results for each class are demonstrated in Table 1. These results indicate that comparable metrics (i.e.

Precision and cPrecision, Recall and cRecall, F1 and cF1) agree the majority of the time.

Metric Type	Class	% Sig.	% Agree
(c)F1	entailment	93.29	89.19
(c)F1	contradiction	93.61	93.75
(c)F1	neutral	90.32	84.94
(c)Precision	entailment	92.97	94.52
(c)Precision	contradiction	94.20	92.62
(c)Precision	neutral	89.78	80.11
(c)Recall	entailment	95.84	75.81
(c)Recall	contradiction	95.75	84.99
(c)Recall	neutral	91.71	81.13

Table 1: Percent of statistically significant model comparisons that agree between each pair of comparable metrics.

7 Potential Shortcomings to Consider

As mentioned in the introduction, the proposed metrics do not evaluate for probabilistic calibration. There are many cases in which model probability scores are used in production with the expectation of reflecting reliable probabilities. In such cases, probabilistic calibration would have to be evaluated separately using a strictly proper scoring rule (Gneiting and Raftery, 2007).

Another aspect to consider is interpretability.

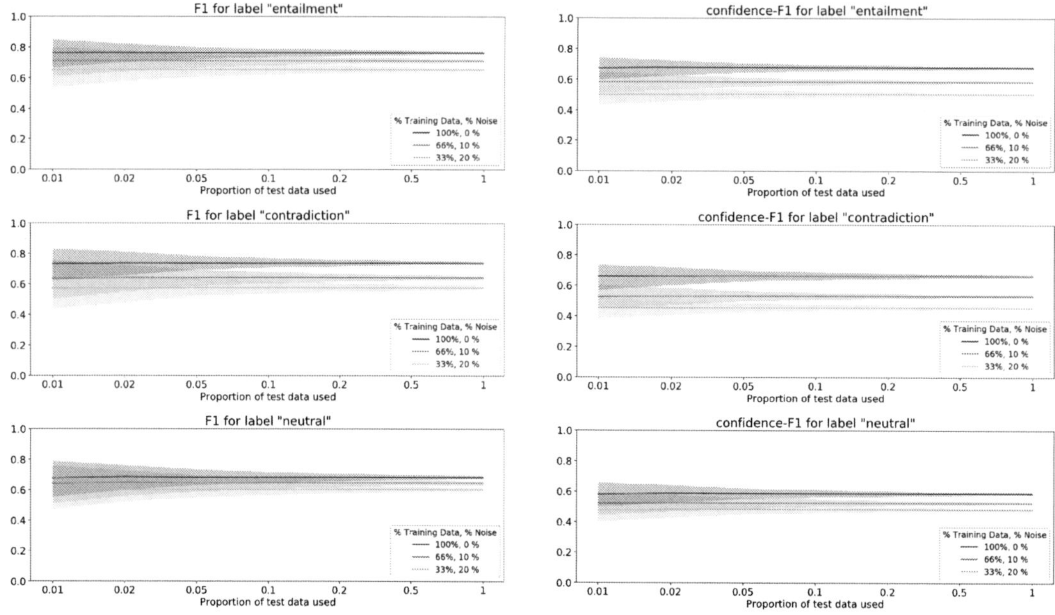

Figure 2: Empirical comparison between F1 and cF1 scores, across different levels of train-set sampling and noise, and different levels of test-set sampling. The y-axis represents the F1 and confidence-F1 values.

The proposed extensions lack the degree of direct interpretability afforded by their threshold-based counterparts. We believe that they still have a high degree of interpretability when compared to other metrics such as Brier Score and Cross-Entropy.

We believe that these downsides do not necessarily pose a problem as long as they are known to the users of the metrics, so they can take appropriate measures in cases when it is required.

8 Future Work

In this paper we only focused on classification, and not named entity recognition (NER), while NLP often requires both. Many NER specific metrics like SER (Makhoul et al., 1999) consider the possibility of having slot insertions or deletions, making them more appropriate for evaluating NER. In the future we hope to extend metrics like SER to gain these benefits.

We also hope to investigate the feasibility of altering these proposed metrics to be Strictly Proper Scoring Rules (Gneiting and Raftery, 2007) allowing for a dual assessment of probabilistic calibration and performance. Strict Proper Scoring will aid us as we plan to study the potential use of these metrics as a differentiable model loss for training.

Finally, we hope to soon address the question of how to deal with output quantization where discrete confidence bins (HIGH, MED, LOW) rather than the continuous values are used by downstream tasks or customers.

9 Conclusion

We introduced probabilistic extensions of widely used threshold-based metrics, and four benefits they provide as compared to their original counterparts. These benefits motivate the use of our proposed metrics in real-world problems where data is scarce and/or where the model confidence score assignments over its predictions are leveraged in production. We hope these metrics will allow for more reliable modeling decision-making in such cases. We hope this research will pave the way for further investigation into the challenge of model evaluation with under-representative test-sets.

Acknowledgments

The authors would like to thank Sreekar Bhaviripudi, Jack FitzGerald, Spyros Matsoukas, and Cedric Warny for reviewing this work and providing valuable feedback. The authors would also like to thank the anonymous reviewers for their insightful comments and suggestions.

References

Samuel R. Bowman, Gabor Angeli, Christopher Potts, and Christopher D. Manning. 2015. A large annotated corpus for learning natural language inference. In *Proceedings of the 2015 Conference on Empirical Methods in Natural Language Processing*, pages 632–642, Lisbon, Portugal. Association for Computational Linguistics.

Glenn W. Brier. 1950. Verification of forecasts expressed in terms of probability. *Monthly Weather Review*, 78(1):1–3.

Toon Calders and Szymon Jaroszewicz. 2007. Efficient auc optimization for classification. In *Knowledge Discovery in Databases: PKDD 2007*, pages 42–53, Berlin, Heidelberg. Springer Berlin Heidelberg.

Alexis Conneau, Kartikay Khandelwal, Naman Goyal, Vishrav Chaudhary, Guillaume Wenzek, Francisco Guzmán, Edouard Grave, Myle Ott, Luke Zettlemoyer, and Veselin Stoyanov. 2020. Unsupervised cross-lingual representation learning at scale. In *Proceedings of the 58th Annual Meeting of the Association for Computational Linguistics*, pages 8440–8451, Online. Association for Computational Linguistics.

Timo Denk. 2018. Text classification with separable convolutional neural networks.

Richard Dinga, Brenda W.J.H. Penninx, Dick J. Veltman, Lianne Schmaal, and Andre F. Marquand. 2019. Beyond accuracy: Measures for assessing machine learning models, pitfalls and guidelines. *bioRxiv*.

B. Efron. 1979. Bootstrap methods: Another look at the jackknife. *Ann. Statist.*, 7(1):1–26.

C. Ferri, J. Hernández-Orallo, and R. Modroiu. 2009. An experimental comparison of performance measures for classification. *Pattern Recogn. Lett.*, 30(1):27–38.

Cèsar Ferri, Peter Flach, José Hernández-orallo, and Athmane Senad. 2004. Modifying roc curves to incorporate predicted probabilities. In *In Second Workshop on ROC Analysis in ML*.

Tilmann Gneiting and Adrian E Raftery. 2007. Strictly proper scoring rules, prediction, and estimation. *Journal of the American Statistical Association*, 102(477):359–378.

Chuan Guo, Geoff Pleiss, Yu Sun, and Kilian Q. Weinberger. 2017. On calibration of modern neural networks. In *Proceedings of the 34th International Conference on Machine Learning - Volume 70*, ICML'17, page 1321–1330. JMLR.org.

David J. Hand and Robert J. Till. 2001. A simple generalisation of the area under the roc curve for multiple class classification problems. *Machine Learning*, 45(2):171–186.

José Hernández-Orallo, Peter Flach, and Cèsar Ferri. 2012. A unified view of performance metrics: Translating threshold choice into expected classification loss. *J. Mach. Learn. Res.*, 13(1):2813–2869.

Sulaiman M.N Hossin M. 2015. A review on evaluation metrics for data classification evaluations. *International Journal of Data Mining & Knowledge Management Process*, 5(2):1–11.

Charles X. Ling, Jin Huang, and Harry Zhang. 2003. Auc: A statistically consistent and more discriminating measure than accuracy. In *Proceedings of the 18th International Joint Conference on Artificial Intelligence*, IJCAI'03, page 519–524, San Francisco, CA, USA. Morgan Kaufmann Publishers Inc.

John Makhoul, Francis Kubala, Richard Schwartz, and Ralph Weischedel. 1999. Performance measures for information extraction. In *In Proceedings of DARPA Broadcast News Workshop*, pages 249–252.

Allan H. Murphy. 1973. A new vector partition of the probability score. *Journal of Applied Meteorology*, 12(4):595–600.

S. J. Pan and Q. Yang. 2010. A survey on transfer learning. *IEEE Transactions on Knowledge and Data Engineering*, 22(10):1345–1359.

R. Sarikaya. 2017. The technology behind personal digital assistants: An overview of the system architecture and key components. *IEEE Signal Processing Magazine*, 34(1):67–81.

Stijn Vanderlooy and Eyke Hüllermeier. 2008. A critical analysis of variants of the auc. *Machine Learning*, 72(3):247–262.

Xiao-Ning Wang, Jin-Mao Wei, Han Jin, Gang Yu, and Hai-Wei Zhang. 2013. Probabilistic confusion entropy for evaluating classifiers. *Entropy*, 15(12):4969–4992.

Lei Zhu, Tao Ban, Takeshi Takahashi, and Daisuke Inoue. 2018. Employ decision values for soft-classifier evaluation with crispy references. In *Neural Information Processing*, pages 392–402, Cham. Springer International Publishing.

A Reproducibility Information

A.1 Preprocessing

All sentences were lowercased, periods were stripped from the ends of sentences. When found in the middle of sentences the periods are space-separated so that they are separate tokens. Sentence pairs were separated with the "[SEP]" token. Tokens were given indices up to the 20000th token, after which tokens are assigned to a reserved index indicating OOV. A max sequence length of 42 was chosen for speed, based on the distribution of lengths in the SNLI dataset. Samples longer than 42 were truncated.

A.2 Model Training

All models were trained with:

- 150 epochs

- Early stopping on validation loss with 8 epochs of patience

- Randomized validation split with 9:1 train to validation ratio

- Batch size 128

- Learning rate 1e-3

- Adam optimizer

- Loss: sparse categorical cross-entropy

- 1d max pooling (pool size=1) between each convolution layer and average pooling before the dense layer output

Hyperparameter	Possible Values
Blocks	1, 2
Filters	32, 64, 128, 256
Kernel Size	2, 3, 4, 5, 6, 7, 8, 9, 10, 11, 12, 13, 14, 15, 16
Embedding Dim.	64, 128, 256
Dropout rate	0.0, 0.1, 0.2, 0.3, 0.4, 0.5

Table 2: Table of Hyperparameter choices.

When generating and training the 100 models for the testing of Hypothesis D, we randomly drew hyperparameters from the following distributions, shown in Table 2, with no two models sharing the same hyperparameters (checked for redundancy).

B   Additional Figures

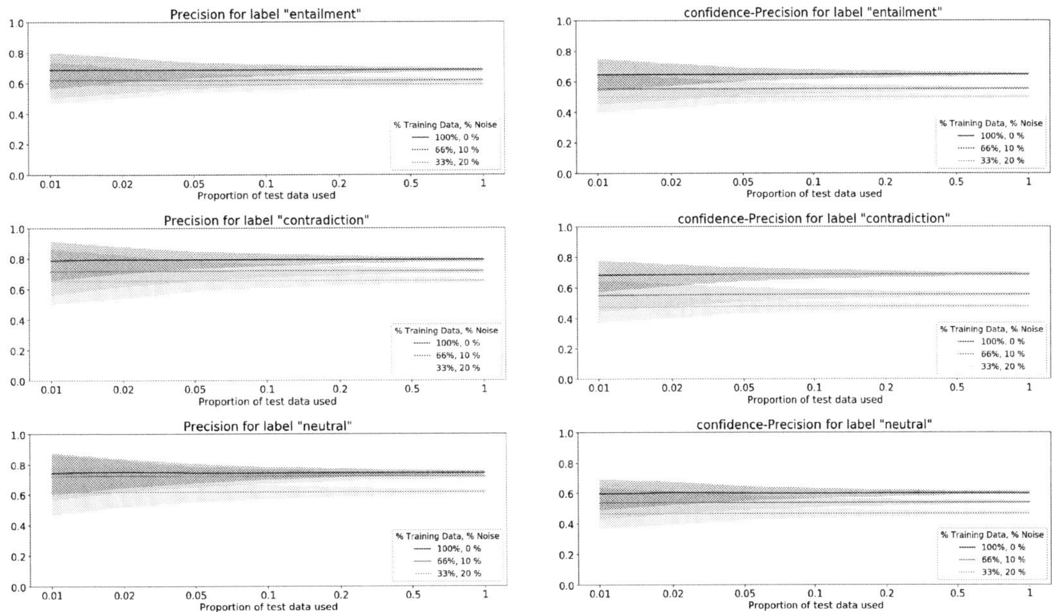

Figure 3: Empirical comparison between Precision and cPrecision scores, across different levels of train-set sampling and noise, and different levels of test-set sampling. The y-axis represents the Precision and confidence-Precision values.

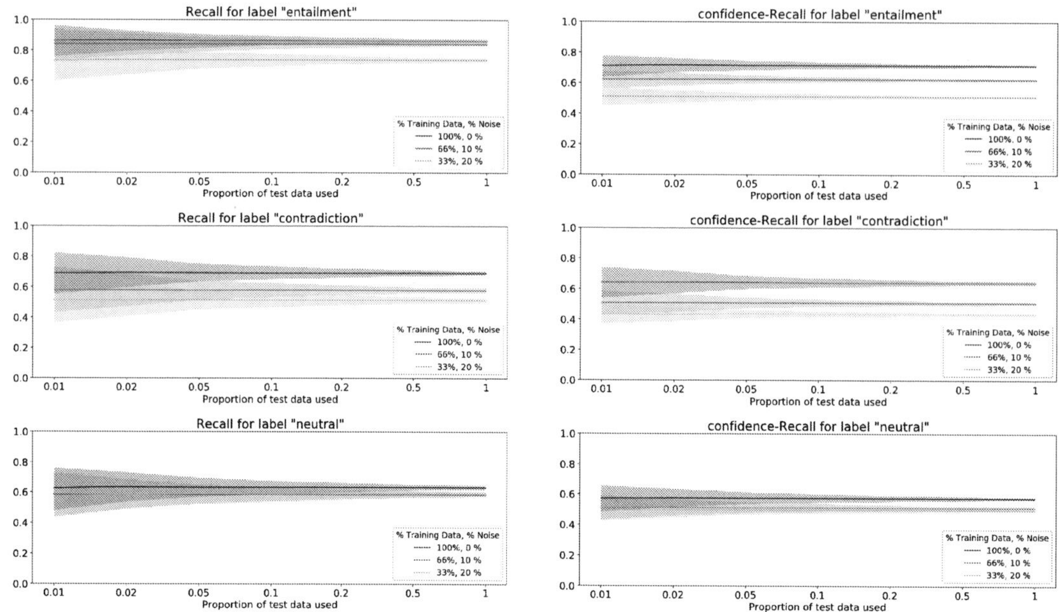

Figure 4: Empirical comparison between Recall and cRecall scores, across different levels of train-set sampling and noise, and different levels of test-set sampling. The y-axis represents the Recall and confidence-Recall values.

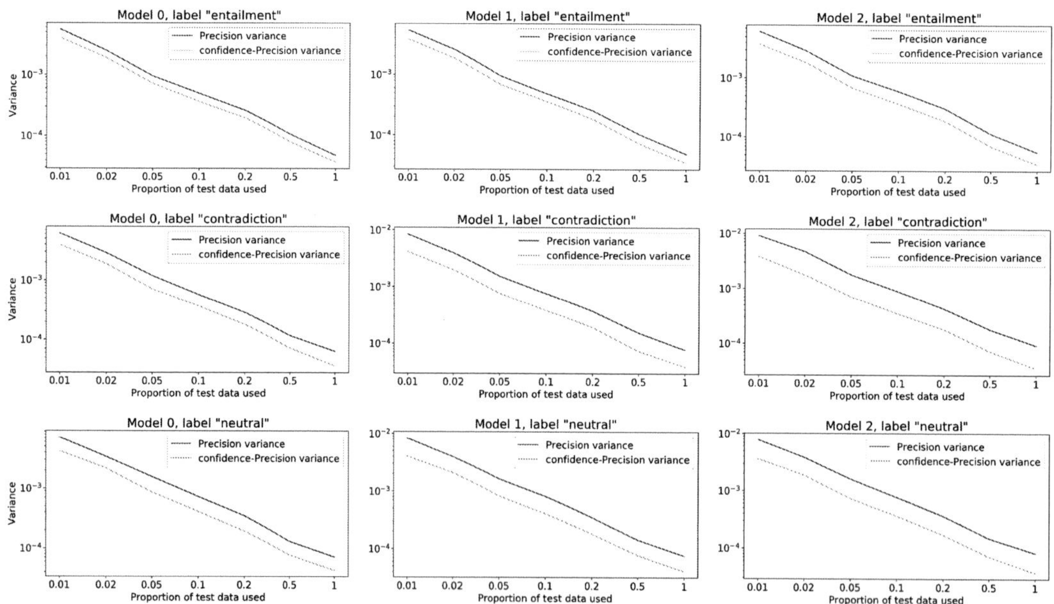

Figure 5: Empirical comparison of the variances of Precision and cPrecision, across different test-set sizes

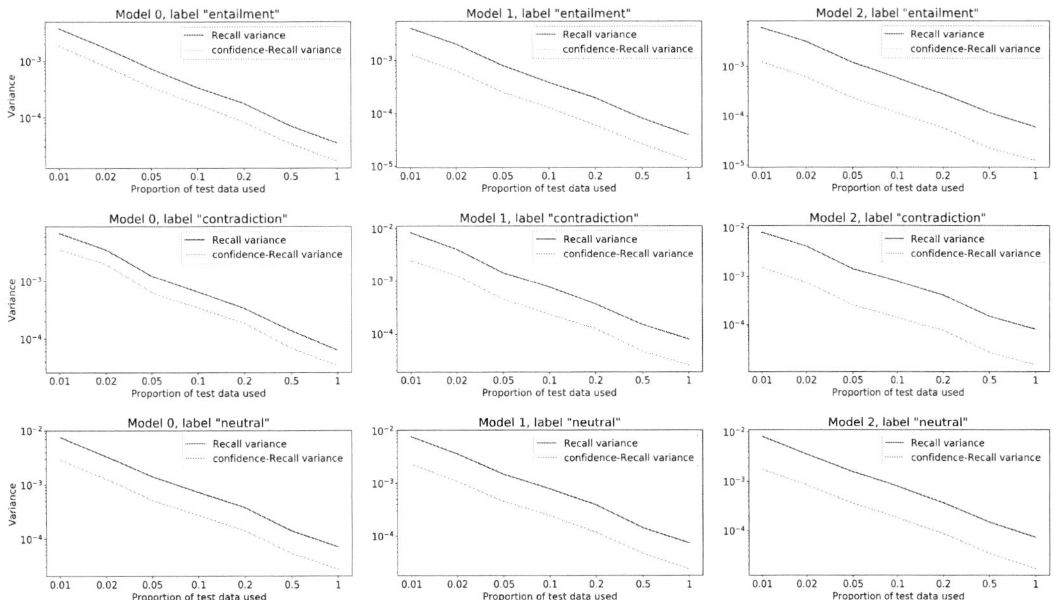

Figure 6: Empirical comparison of the variances of Recall and cRecall, across different test-set sizes

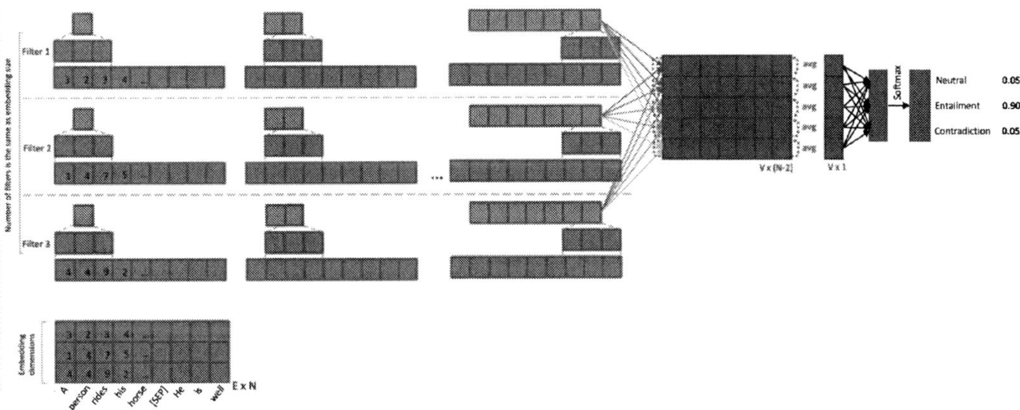

Figure 7: Sep-CNN model architecture used for experimentation on the NLP dataset

A Survey on Recognizing Textual Entailment as an NLP Evaluation

Adam Poliak

Barnard College, Data Science Institute, Columbia University

3009 Broadway, New York, NY 10027

`apoliak@barnard.ed`

Abstract

Recognizing Textual Entailment (RTE) was proposed as a unified evaluation framework to compare semantic understanding of different NLP systems. In this survey paper, we provide an overview of different approaches for evaluating and understanding the reasoning capabilities of NLP systems. We then focus our discussion on RTE by highlighting prominent RTE datasets as well as advances in RTE dataset that focus on specific linguistic phenomena that can be used to evaluate NLP systems on a fine-grained level. We conclude by arguing that when evaluating NLP systems, the community should utilize newly introduced RTE datasets that focus on specific linguistic phenomena.

1 Introduction

As NLP technologies are more widely adopted, how to evaluate NLP systems and how to determine whether one model understands language or generates text better than another is an increasingly important question. Recognizing Textual Entailment (RTE Cooper et al., 1996; Dagan et al., 2006), the task of determining whether the meaning of one sentence can likely be inferred from another was introduced to answer this question.

We begin this survey by discussing different approaches over the past thirty years for evaluating and comparing NLP systems. Next, we will discuss how RTE was introduced as a specific answer to this broad question of how to best evaluate NLP systems. This will include a broad discussion of efforts in the past three decades to build RTE datasets and use RTE to evaluate NLP models. We will then highlight recent RTE datasets that focus on specific semantic phenomena and conclude by arguing that they should be utilized for evaluating the reasoning capabilities of downstream NLP systems.

Natural Language Inference or Recognizing Textual Entailment?

The terms Natural Language Inference (NLI) and RTE are often used interchangeably. Many papers begin by explicitly mentioning that these terms are synonymous (Liu et al., 2016; Gong et al., 2018; Camburu et al., 2018).[1] The broad phrase "natural language inference" is more appropriate for a class of problems that require making inferences from natural language. Tasks like sentiment analysis, event factuality, or even question-answering can be viewed as forms of natural language inference without having to convert them into the sentence pair classification format used in RTE. Earlier works used the term *natural language inference* in this way (Schwarcz et al., 1970; Wilks, 1975; Punyakanok et al., 2004).

The leading term *recognizing* in RTE is fitting as the task is to classify or predict whether the truth of one sentence likely follows the other. The second term *textual* is similarly appropriate since the domain is limited to textual data. Critics of the name RTE often argue that the term *entailment* is inappropriate since the definition of the NLP task strays too far from the technical definition from *entailment* in linguistics (Manning, 2006). Zaenen et al. (2005) prefer the term *textual inference* because examples in RTE datasets often require a system to not only identify entailments but also conventional implicatures, conversational implicatures, and world knowledge.

If starting over, we would advocate for the phrase *Recognizing Textual Inference*. However, given the choice between RTE and NLI, we prefer RTE since it is more representative of the task at hand.

---

[1] In fact, variants of the phrase "natural language inference, also known as recognizing textual entailment" appear in many papers (Chen et al., 2017; Williams et al., 2017; Naik et al., 2018; Chen et al., 2018; Tay et al., 2018, *i.a.*).

Proceedings of the First Workshop on Evaluation and Comparison of NLP Systems (Eval4NLP), pages 92–109,
November 20, 2020. ©2020 Association for Computational Linguistics

2   Evaluating NLP Systems

The question of how best to evaluate NLP systems is an open problem intriguing the community for decades. A 1988 workshop on the evaluation of NLP systems explored key questions for evaluation. These included questions related to valid measures of "black-box" performance, linguistic theories that are relevant to developing test suites, reasonable expectations for robustness, and measuring progress in the field (Palmer and Finin, 1990). The large number of ACL workshops focused on evaluations in NLP demonstrate the lack of consensus on how to properly evaluate NLP systems. Some workshops focused on: 1) evaluations in general (Pastra, 2003); 2) different NLP tasks, e.g. machine translation (ws-, 2001; Goldstein et al., 2005) and summarization (Conroy et al., 2012; Giannakopoulos et al., 2017); or 3) contemporary NLP approaches that rely on vector space representations (Levy et al., 2016; Bowman et al., 2017; Rogers et al., 2019).

In the quest to develop an ideal evaluation framework for NLP systems, researchers proposed multiple evaluation methods, e.g. EAGLES (King et al., 1995), TSNLP (Oepen and Netter, 1995; Lehmann et al., 1996), *FraCas* (Cooper et al., 1996), SENSE-VAL (Kilgarriff, 1998), CLEF (Agosti et al., 2007), and others. These approaches are often divided along multiple dimensions. Here, we will survey approaches along two dimensions: 1) intrinsic vs. extrinsic evaluations; 2) general purpose vs task specific evaluations.[2]

2.1   Intrinsic vs Extrinsic Evaluations

> Intrinsic evaluations test the system in of itself and extrinsic evaluation test the system in relation to some other task.
>
> (Farzindar and Lapalme, 2004)

When reviewing Sparck Jones and Galliers (1996)'s textbook on NLP evaluations, Estival (1997) comments that "one of the most important distinctions that must be drawn when performing an evaluation of a system is that between *intrinsic criteria*, i.e. those concerned with the system's own objectives, and *extrinsic criteria*, i.e. those concerned with the function of the system in relation to its set-up." Resnik et al. (2006) similarly noted that "intrinsic evaluations measure the performance of an NLP component on its defined subtask,

usually against a defined standard in a reproducible laboratory setting" while "extrinsic evaluations focus on the component's contribution to the performance of a complete application, which often involves the participation of a human in the loop." Sparck Jones (1994) refers to the distinction of intrinsic vs extrinsic evaluations as the *orientation* of an evaluation.

Under these definitions, for example, "an intrinsic evaluation of a parser would analyze the accuracy of the results returned by the parser as a stand-alone system, whereas an extrinsic evaluation would analyze the impact of the parser within the context of a broader NLP application" like answer extraction (Mollá and Hutchinson, 2003). When evaluating a document summarization system, an intrinsic evaluation might ask questions related to the fluency or coverage of key ideas in the summary while an extrinsic evaluation might explore whether a generated summary was useful in a search engine (Resnik and Lin, 2010). This distinction has also been referred to as application-free versus application-driven evaluations (Kováź et al., 2016).[3]

Proper extrinsic evaluations are often infeasible in an academic lab setting. Therefore, researchers often rely on intrinsic evaluations to approximate extrinsic evaluations, even though intrinsic and extrinsic evaluations serve different goals and many common intrinsic evaluations for word vectors (Tsvetkov et al., 2015; Chiu et al., 2016; Faruqui et al., 2016), generating natural language text (Belz and Gatt, 2008; Reiter, 2018), or text mining (Caporaso et al., 2008) might not correlate with extrinsic evaluations.[4] Developing intrinsic evaluations that correlate with extrinsic evaluations remains an open problem in NLP.

---

[2]Resnik and Lin (2010) summarize other evaluation approaches and Paroubek et al. (2007) present a history and evolution of NLP evaluation methods.

[3]As another example, in the case of evaluating different methods for training word vectors, intrinsic evaluations might consider how well similarities between word vectors correlate with human evaluated word similarities. This is the basis of evaluation benchmarks like SimLex (Hill et al., 2015), Verb (Baker et al., 2014), RW (Luong et al., 2013), MEN (Bruni et al., 2012), WordSim-353 (Finkelstein et al., 2001), and others. Extrinsic evaluations for word embeddings might consider how well different word vectors help models for tasks like sentiment analysis (Petrolito, 2018; Mishev et al., 2019), machine translation (Wang et al., 2019b), or named entity recognition (Wu et al., 2015; Nayak et al., 2016).

[4]Although recent work suggest that some intrinsic evaluations for word vectors do indeed correlate with extrinsic evaluations (Qiu et al., 2018; Thawani et al., 2019).

2.2 General Purpose vs Task Specific Evaluations

General purpose evaluations determine how well NLP systems capture different linguistic phenomena. These evaluations often rely on the development of test cases that systematically cover a wide range of phenomena. Additionally, these evaluations generally do not consider how well a system under investigation performs on held out data for the task that the NLP system was trained on. In general purpose evaluations, specific linguistic phenomena should be isolated such that each test or example evaluates one specific linguistic phenomenon, as tests ideally "are controlled and exhaustive databases of linguistic utterances classified by linguistic features" (Lloberes et al., 2015).

In task specific evaluations, the goal is to determine how well a model performs on a held out test corpus. How well systems generalize on text classification problems is determined with a combination of metrics like accuracy, precision, and recall, or metrics like BLEU (Papineni et al., 2002) and ROUGE (Lin, 2004) in generation tasks. Task specific evaluations, where "the majority of benchmark datasets ... are drawn from text corpora, reflecting a natural frequency distribution of language phenomena" (Belinkov and Glass, 2019), is the common paradigm in NLP research today. Researchers often begin their research with provided training and held-out test corpora, as their research agenda is to develop systems that outperform other researchers' systems on a held-out test set based on a wide range of metrics.

The distinction between general purpose and task specific evaluations is sometimes blurred. For example, while general purpose evaluations are ideally task agnostic, researchers develop evaluations that test for a wide range of linguistic phenomena captured by NLP systems trained to perform specific tasks. These include linguistic tests targeted for systems that focus on parsing (Lloberes et al., 2015), machine translation (King and Falkedal, 1990; Koh et al., 2001; Isabelle et al., 2017; Choshen and Abend, 2019; Popović and Castilho, 2019; Avramidis et al., 2019), summarization (Pitler et al., 2010), and others (Chinchor, 1991; Chinchor et al., 1993).

Test Suites vs. Test Corpora This distinction can also be described in terms of the data used to evaluate systems. Oepen and Netter (1995) refer to this distinction as test suites versus test corpora.

They define a test suite as a "systematic collection of linguistic expressions (test items, e.g. sentences or phrases) and often includes associated annotations or descriptions." They lament the state of test suites in their time since "most of the existing test suites have been written for specific systems or simply enumerate a set of 'interesting' examples [but] does not meet the demand for large, systematic, well-documented and annotated collections of linguistic material required by a growing number of NLP applications." Oepen and Netter further delineate the difference between test corpora and test suites. Unlike "test corpora drawn from naturally occurring texts," test suites allow for 1) more control over the data, 2) systematic coverage, 3) non-redundant representation, 4) inclusion of negative data, and 5) coherent annotation. Thus, test suites "allow for a fine-grained diagnosis of system performance" (Oepen and Netter, 1995). Oepen and Netter argue that both should be used in tandem - "test suites and corpora should stand in a complementary relation, with the former building on the latter wherever possible and necessary." Hence, both test suites and test corpora are important for evaluating how well NLP systems capture linguistic phenomena and perform in practice on real world data.

2.3 Probing Deep Learning NLP Models

In recent years, interpreting and analysing NLP models has become prominent in many research agendas. Contemporary and successful deep learning NLP methods are not as interpretable as previously popular NLP approaches relying on feature engineering. Approaches for interpreting and analysing how well NLP models capture linguistic phenomena often leverage auxiliary or diagnostic classifiers. Contemporary deep learning NLP systems often leverage pre-trained encoders to represent the meaning of a sentence in a fixed-length vector representation. Adi et al. (2017) introduced the notion of using auxiliary classifiers as a general purpose methodology to diagnose what language information is encoded and captured by contemporary sentence representations. They argued for using "auxiliary prediction tasks" where, like in Dai and Le (2015), pre-trained sentence encodings are "used as input for other prediction tasks." The "auxiliary prediction tasks" can serve as diagnostics, and Adi et al. (2017)'s auxiliary, diagnostic tasks focused on how word order, word content, and sentence length are captured in pre-trained sentence representations.

As Adi et al.'s general methodology "can be applied to any sentence representation model," researchers develop other diagnostic tasks that explore different linguistic phenomenon (Ettinger et al., 2018; Conneau et al., 2018; Hupkes et al., 2018). Belinkov (2018)'s thesis relied on and popularized this methodology when exploring how well speech recognition and machine translation systems capture phenomena related to phonetics (Belinkov and Glass, 2017), morphology (Belinkov et al., 2017a), and syntax (Belinkov et al., 2017b).

The general purpose methodology of auxiliary diagnostic classifiers is also used to explore how well different pre-trained sentence representation methods perform on a broad range of NLP tasks. For example, SentEval (Conneau and Kiela, 2018) and GLUE (Wang et al., 2018) are used to evaluate how different sentence representations perform on paraphrase detection, semantic textual similarity, and a wide range of other binary and multi-class classification problems. We categorize these datasets as extrinsic evaluations since they often treat learned sentence-representations as features to train a classifier for an external task. However, most of these do not count as test suites, since the data is not tightly controlled to evaluate specific linguistic phenomena. Rather, resources like GLUE and SuperGLUE (Wang et al., 2019a) package existing test corpora for different tasks and provide an easy platform for researchers to compete on developing systems that perform well on the suite of pre-existing, and re-packaged test corpora.

3 Recognizing Textual Entailment

> NLP systems cannot be held responsible for knowledge of what goes on in the world but no NLP system can claim to "understand" language if it can't cope with textual inferences.
>
> (Zaenen et al., 2005)

Recognizing and coping with inferences is key to understanding human language. While NLP systems might be trained to perform different tasks, such as translating, answering questions, or extracting information from text, most NLP systems require understanding and making inferences from text. Therefore, RTE was introduced as a framework to evaluate NLP systems. Rooted in linguistics, RTE is the task of determining whether the meaning of one sentence can likely be inferred from another. Unlike the strict definition of entailment in linguistics that "sentence A entails sentence B if in all models in which the interpretation of A is true, also the interpretation of B is true" (Janssen, 2011), RTE relies on a fuzzier notion of entailment. For example, annotation guidelines for an RTE dataset[5] stated that

> in principle, the hypothesis must be fully entailed by the text. Judgment would be False if the hypothesis includes parts that cannot be inferred from the text. However, cases in which inference is very probable (but not completely certain) are still judged as True.
>
> (Dagan et al., 2006)

Starting with *FraCas*, we will discuss influential work that introduced and argued for RTE as an evaluation framework.

FraCas   Over a span of two years (December 1993 - January 1996), Cooper et al. (1996) developed *FraCas* as "an inference test suite for evaluating the inferential competence of different NLP systems and semantic theories". Created manually by many linguists and funded by FP3-LRE,[6] *FraCas* is a "semantic test suite" that covers a range of semantic phenomena categorized into 9 classes. These are generalized quantifiers, plurals, anaphora, ellipsis, adjectives, comparatives, temporal reference, verbs, and attitudes. Based on the descriptions in §2, we would classify *FraCas* as an intrinsic evaluation and a general purpose test suite.

Examples in *FraCas* contain a premise paired with a hypothesis. Premises are at least one sentence, though sometimes they contain multiple sentences, and most hypotheses are written in the form of a question and the answers are either *Yes*, *No*, or *Don't know*. MacCartney (2009) (specifically Chapter 7.8.1) converted the hypotheses from questions into declarative statements.[7] Table 4 (in the appendix) contains examples from *FraCas*. In total, *FraCas* only contains about 350 labeled examples, potentially limiting the ability to generalize how well models capture these phenomena. Additionally, the limited number of examples in *FraCas*

---

[5]These were the guidelines in RTE-1.

[6]https://cordis.europa.eu/programme/id/FP3-LRE

[7]`https://nlp.stanford.edu/~wcmac/downloads/fracas.xml`

Kessler 's team conducted 60,643 interviews with adults in 14 countries ► Kessler 's team interviewed more than 60,000 adults in 14 countries	entailed
Capital punishment is a catalyst for more crime ► Capital punishment is a deterrent to crime	not-entailed
Boris Becker is a former professional tennis player for Germany ► Boris Becker is a Wimbledon champion	not-entailed

Table 1: Examples from the PASCAL RTE datasets (modified for space): The first line in each example is the premise and the line starting with ► is the corresponding hypothesis. The first, second, and third examples are from the RTE1, RTE2, and RTE3 development sets respectively. The second column indicates the example's label.

prevents its use as a dataset to train data hungry deep learning models.

Pascal RTE Challenges With a similar broad goal as *FraCas*, the Pascal Recognizing Textual Entailment challenges began as a "generic evaluation framework" to compare the inference capabilities of models designed to perform different tasks, based on the intuition "that major inferences, as needed by multiple applications, can indeed be cast in terms of textual entailment" (Dagan et al., 2006). Unlike *FraCas*'s goal of determining whether a model performs distinct types of reasoning, the Pascal RTE Challenges primarily focused on using this framework to evaluate models for distinct, real-world downstream tasks. Thus, the examples in the Pascal RTE datasets were extracted from downstream tasks. The process was referred to as *recasting* in the thesis by Glickman (2006).

NLU problems were reframed under the RTE framework and candidate sentence pairs were extracted from existing NLP datasets and then labeled under variations of the RTE definition (including the quote above (Dagan et al., 2006)).[8] For example, the RTE1 data came from 7 tasks: comparable documents, reading comprehension, question answering, information extraction, machine translation, information retrieval, and paraphrase acquisition.[9] Starting with Dagan et al. (2006), there have been eight iterations of the RTE challenge, with the most recent being Dzikovska et al. (2013).

SNLI and MNLI The most popular recent RTE datasets, Stanford Natural Language Inference (SNLI; Bowman et al., 2015) and its successor Multi-NLI (Williams et al., 2017), each contain over half a million examples and enabled re-

searchers to apply data-hungry deep learning methods to RTE. Unlike the RTE datasets, these two datasets were created by eliciting hypotheses from humans. Crowd-source workers were tasked with writing one sentence each that is entailed, neutral, and contradicted by a caption extracted from the Flickr30k corpus (Young et al., 2014). Next, the label for each premise-hypothesis pair in the development and test sets were verified by multiple crowd-source workers and the majority-vote label was assigned for each example. Table 2 provides such examples for both datasets. Rudinger et al. (2017) illustrated how eliciting textual data in this fashion creates stereotypical biases in SNLI. Some of the biases are gender-, age-, and race-based. Poliak et al. (2018c) argue that this may cause additional biases enabling a hypothesis-only model to outperform the majority baseline on SNLI by 100 percent (Gururangan et al., 2018; Tsuchiya, 2018).

3.1 Entailment as a Downstream NLP Task

The datasets in the PASCAL RTE Challenges were primarily treated as test corpora. Teams participated in those challenges by developing models to achieve increasingly high scores on each challenges' datasets. Since RTE was motivated as a diagnostic, researchers analyzed the RTE challenge datasets. de Marneffe et al. (2008) argued that there exist different levels and types of contradictions. They focus on different types of phenomena, e.g. antonyms, negation, and world knowledge, that can explain why a premise contradicts a hypothesis. MacCartney (2009) used a simple bag-of-words model to evaluate early iterations of Recognizing Textual Entailment (RTE) challenge sets and noted[10] that "the RTE1 test suite is the hardest, while the RTE2 test suite is roughly 4% easier, and the RTE3 test suite is roughly 9% easier." Addi-

---

[8]See Appendix A for the annotation guidelines for RTE1, RTE2, and RTE3.

[9]Chapter 3.2 of Glickman's thesis discusses how examples from these datasets were converted into RTE.

[10]In Chapter 2.2 of his thesis

P	A woman is talking on the phone while standing next to a dog	
H1	A woman is on the phone	entailment
H2	A woman is walking her dog	neutral
H3	A woman is sleeping	contradiction
P	Tax records show Waters earned around $65,000 in 2000	
H1	Waters' tax records show clearly that he earned a lovely $65k in 2000	entailment
H2	Tax records indicate Waters earned about $65K in 2000	entailment
H3	Waters' tax records show he earned a blue ribbon last year	contradiction

Table 2: Examples from the development sets of SNLI (top) and MultiNLI (bottom). Each example contains one premise that is paired with three hypotheses in the datasets.

tionally, Vanderwende and Dolan (2006) and Blake (2007) demonstrate how sentence structure alone can provide a high signal for some RTE datasets.[11] Despite these analyses, researchers primarily built models to perform the task on the PASCAL RTE datasets rather than leveraging these datasets to evaluate models built for other tasks.

Coinciding with the recent "deep learning wave" that has taken over NLP and Machine Learning (Manning, 2015), the introduction of large scale RTE datasets, specifically SNLI and MNLI, led to a resurgence of interest in RTE amongst NLP researchers. Large scale RTE datasets focusing on specific domains, like grade-school scientific knowledge (Khot et al., 2018) or medical information (Romanov and Shivade, 2018), emerged as well. However, this resurgence did not primarily focus on using RTE as a means to evaluate NLP systems. Rather, researchers primarily used these datasets to compete with one another to achieve the top score on leaderboards for new RTE datasets.

4 Revisiting RTE as an NLP Evaluation

> There has been little evidence to suggest [that RTE models] capture the type of compositional or world knowledge tested by datasets like the FraCas test suite.
>
> (Pavlick, 2017)

As large scale RTE datasets, like SNLI and MNLI, rapidly surged in popularity, some researchers critiqued the datasets' ability to test the inferential capabilities of NLP models. A high accuracy on these datasets does not indicate which types of reasoning RTE models perform or capture. As noted by White et al. (2017), "researchers compete on which system achieves the highest score on

a test set, but this itself does not lead to an understanding of which linguistic properties are better captured by a quantitatively superior system." In other words, the single accuracy metric on these challenges indicates how well a model can recognize whether one sentence likely follows from another, but it does not illuminate how well NLP models capture different semantic phenomena that are important for general NLU.

This issue was pointed out regarding the earlier PASCAL RTE datasets. In her thesis that presented "a test suite for adjectival inference developed as a resource for the evaluation of computational systems handling natural language inference." Amoia (2008) blamed "the difficulty of defining the linguistic phenomena which are responsible for inference" as the reason why previous RTE resources "concentrated on the creation of applications coping with textual entailment" rather than "resources for the evaluation of such applications."

As current studies began exploring what linguistic phenomena are captured by neural NLP models and auxiliary diagnostic classifiers became a common tool to evaluate sentence representations in NLP systems, (§2.3), the community saw an interest in developing RTE datasets that can provide insight into what type of linguistic phenomena are captured by neural, deep learning models. In turn, the community is answering Chatzikyriakidis et al. (2017) plea to the community to test "more kinds of inference" than in previous RTE challenge sets. Here, we will highlight recent efforts in creating datasets that demonstrate how the community has started answering Chatzikyriakidis et al.'s call. We group these different datasets based on how they were created. Table 3 includes additional RTE datasets focused on specific linguistic phenomena.

---

[11] Vanderwende and Dolan (2006) explored RTE-1 and Blake (2007) analyzed RTE-2 and RTE-3.

4.1 Automatically Created

White et al. (2017) advocate for using RTE as a single framework to evaluate different linguistic phenomena. They argue for creating RTE datasets focused on specific phenomena by *recasting* existing annotations for different semantic phenomena into RTE. Poliak et al. (2018b) introduce the Diverse Natural Language Inference Collection (DNC) of over half a million RTE examples. They create the DNC by converting 7 semantic phenomena from 13 existing datasets into RTE. These phenomena include event factuality, named entity recognition, gendered anaphora resolution, sentiment analysis, relationship extraction, pun detection, and lexicosyntactic inference. Staliūnaitė (2018)'s master's thesis improved Poliak et al. (2018b)'s method used to recast annotations for factuality into RTE. Other efforts have created recast datasets in Hindi that focus on sentiment and emotion detection.[12]

Concurrent to the DNC, Naik et al. (2018) released the "NLI Stress Tests" that included RTE datasets focused on negation, word overlap between premises and hypotheses, numerical reasoning, amongst other phenomena. Naik et al. (2018) similarly create their stress tests automatically using different methods for each phenomena. They then used these datasets to evaluate how well a wide class of RTE models capture these phenomena. Other RTE datasets that target more specific phenomena were created using automatic methods, including Jeretic et al. (2020)'s "IMPRES" diagnostic RTE dataset that tests for IMPlicatures and PRESuppositions.

If not done with thorough testing and care, recasting or other automatic methods for creating these RTE datasets can lead to annotation artifacts unrelated to RTE that limit how well a dataset tests for a specific semantic phenomena. For example, to create not-entailed hypotheses, White et al. (2017) replaced a single token in a context sentence with a word that crowd-source workers labeled as not being a paraphrase of the token in the given context. In FN+ (Pavlick et al., 2015), two words might be deemed to be incorrect paraphrases in context based on a difference in the words' part of speech tags.[13] This limits the utility of the recast version of

FN+ to be used when evaluating how well models capture paraphrastic inference.

Similar to the efforts described here to recast different NLU problems as RTE, others have recast NLU problems into a question answer format (McCann et al., 2018; Gardner et al., 2019). Recasting problems into RTE, as opposed to question-answering, has deeper roots in linguistic theory (Seuren, 1998; Chierchia and McConnell-Ginet, 2000; Brinton, 2000), and continues a rich history within the NLP community.

4.2 Semi-Automatically Created

Other RTE datasets focused on specific phenomena rely on semi-automatic methods. RTE pairs are often generated automatically using well developed heuristics. Instead of automatically labeling the RTE example pairs (like in the approaches previously discussed), the automatically created examples are often labeled by crowdsource workers. For example, Kim et al. (2019) use hueristics to create RTE pairs that test for prepositions, comparatives, quantification, spacial reasoning, and negation and then present these examples to crowdsource workers on Amazon Mechanical Turk. Similarly, Ross and Pavlick (2019) generate two premise-hypothesis pairs for each RTE example in MNLI that satisfy their set of constraints. Next, they rely on crowdsource workers to annotated whether the premise likely entails the hypothesis on a 5-point Likert scale.

Some methods instead first manually annotate their data and then rely on automatic methods to construct hypotheses and label RTE pairs. When generating RTE examples testing for monotonicity, Richardson et al. (2020) first manually encode the "monotonicity information of each token in the lexicon and built sentences via a controlled set of grammar rules." They then "substitute upward entailing tokens or constituents with something 'greater than or equal to' them, or downward entailing ones with something 'less than or equal to' them."

4.3 Manually Created

While most of these datasets rely on varying degrees of automation, some RTE datasets focused on evaluating how well models capture specific phenomena rely on manual annotations. The GLUE and SuperGlue datasets include diagnostic sets where annotators manually labeled samples of examples as requiring a broad range of linguistic phenomena. The types of phenomena manu-

---

[12]https://github.com/midas-research/hindi-nli-data

[13]Table 5 (in the appendix) demonstrates such examples, and in the last example, the words "on" and "dated" in the premise and hypothesis respectively have the NN and VBN POS tag.

Proto-Roles (White et al., 2017), Paraphrastic Inference (White et al., 2017), Event Factuality (Poliak et al., 2018b; Staliūnaitė, 2018), Anaphora Resolution (White et al., 2017; Poliak et al., 2018b), Lexicosyntactic Inference (Pavlick and Callison-Burch, 2016; Poliak et al., 2018b; Glockner et al., 2018), Compositionality (Dasgupta et al., 2018), Prepositions (Kim et al., 2019), Comparatives (Kim et al., 2019; Richardson et al., 2020), Quantification/Numerical Reasoning (Naik et al., 2018; Kim et al., 2019; Richardson et al., 2020), Spatial Expressions (Kim et al., 2019), Negation (Naik et al., 2018; Kim et al., 2019; Richardson et al., 2020), Tense & Aspect (Kober et al., 2019), Veridicality (Poliak et al., 2018b; Ross and Pavlick, 2019), Monotonicity (Yanaka et al., 2019, 2020; Richardson et al., 2020), Presupposition (Jeretic et al., 2020), Implicatures (Jeretic et al., 2020), Temporal Reasoning (Vashishtha et al., 2020)

Table 3: List of different semantic phenomena tested for in recent RTE datasets.

ally labeled include lexical semantics, predicate-argument structure, logic, and common sense or world knowledge.[14]

5 Recommendations

These efforts resulted in a consistent format and framework for testing how well contemporary, deep learning NLP systems capture a wide-range of linguistic phenomena. However, so far, most of these datasets that target specific linguistic phenomena have been used to solely evaluate how well RTE models capture a wide range of phenomena, as opposed to evaluating how well systems trained for more applied NLP tasks capture these phenomena. Since RTE was introduced as a framework to evaluate how well NLP models cope with inferences, these newly created datasets have not been used to their full potential.

A limited number of studies used some of these datasets to evaluate how well models trained for other tasks capture these phenomena. Poliak et al. (2018a) evaluated how well a BiLSTM encoder trained as part of a neural machine translation system capture phenomena like semantic proto-roles, paraphrastic inference, and anaphora resolution. Kim et al. (2019) used their RTE datasets focused on function words to evaluate different encoders trained for tasks like CCG parsing, image-caption matching, predicting discourse markers, and others. Those studies relied on the use of auxiliary classifiers as a common probing technique to evaluate sentence representations. As the community's interest in analyzing deep learning systems increases, demonstrated by the recent work relying on (Linzen et al., 2018, 2019) and improving upon (Hewitt and Liang, 2019; Voita and Titov, 2020; Pimentel et al., 2020; Mu and Andreas, 2020) the popular auxiliary

classifier-based diagnostic technique, we call on the community to leverage the increasing number of RTE datasets focused on different semantic phenomena (Table 3) to thoroughly study the representations learned by downstream, applied NLP systems. The increasing number of RTE datasets focused on different phenomena can help researchers use one standard format to analyze how well models capture different phenomena, and in turn answer Sammons et al. (2010)'s challenge to make RTE "a central component of evaluation for relevant NLP tasks."

Another recent line of work uses RTE to evaluate the output of text generation systems. For example, Falke et al. (2019) explore "whether textual entailment predictions can be used to detect errors" in abstractive summarization systems and if errors "can be reduced by reranking alternative predicted summaries" with a textual entailment system trained on SNLI. While Falke et al. (2019) results demonstrated that current models might not be accurate enough to rank generated summaries, Barrantes et al. (2020) demonstrate that contemporary transformer models trained on the Adversarial NLI dataset (Nie et al., 2020) "achieve significantly higher accuracy and have the potential of selecting a coherent summary." Therefore, we are encouraged that researchers might be able to use many of these new RTE datasets focused on specific phenomena to evaluate the coherency of machine generated text based on multiple linguistic phenomena that are integral to entailment and NLU. This approach can help researchers use the RTE datasets to evaluate a wider class of models, specifically non-neural models, unlike the auxiliary classifier or probing methods previously discussed.

The overwhelming majority, if not all, of these RTE datasets targeting specific phenomena rely on categorical RTE labels, following the common for-

---

[14]https://gluebenchmark.com/diagnostics

mat of the task. However, as Chen et al. (2020) recently illustrated, categorical RTE labels do not capture the subjective nature of the task. Instead, they argue for scalar RTE labels that indicate how likely a hypothesis could be inferred by a premise. Pavlick and Kwiatkowski (2019) similarly lament how labels are currently used in RTE datasets. Pavlick and Kwiatkowski demonstrate that a single label aggregated from multiple annotations for one RTE example minimizes the "type of uncertainty present in [valid] human disagreements." Instead, they argue that a "representation should be evaluated in terms of its ability to predict the full distribution of human inferences (e.g., by reporting crossentropy against a distribution of human ratings), rather than to predict a single aggregate score (e.g., by reporting accuracy against a discrete majority label or correlation with a mean score)." Future RTE datasets targeting specific phenomena that contain scalar RTE labels from multiple annotators (following Chen et al.'s and Pavlick and Kwiatkowski's recommendations) can provide more insight into contemporary NLP models.

6 Conclusion

With the current zeitgeist of NLP research where researchers are interested in analyzing state-of-the-art deep learning models, now is a prime time to revisit RTE as a method to evaluate the inference capabilities of NLP models. In this survey, we discussed recent advances in RTE datasets that focus on specific linguistic phenomena that are integral for determining whether one sentence is likely inferred by another. Since RTE was primarily motivated as an evaluation framework, we began this survey with a broad overview of prior approaches for evaluating NLP systems. This included the distinctions between instrinsic vs extrinsic evaluations and general purpose vs task specific evaluations.

We discussed foundational RTE datasets that greatly impacted the NLP community and included critiques of why they do not fulfill the promise of RTE as an evaluation framework. We highlighted recent efforts to create RTE datasets that focus on specific linguistic phenomena. By using these datasets to evaluate sentence representations from neural models or rank generated text from NLP systems, researchers can help fulfil the promise of RTE as unified evaluation framework. Ultimately, this will help us determine how well models understand language on a fine-grained level.

Acknowledgements

The author would like to thank the anonymous reviewers for their very helpful comments, Benjamin Van Durme, Aaron Steven White, and João Sedoc for discussions that shaped this survey, Patrick Xia and Elias Stengel-Eskin for feedback on this draft, and Yonatan Belinkov and Sasha Rush for the encouragement to write a survey on RTE.

References

2001. *Workshop on MT Evaluation: Hands-On Evaluation.*

Yossi Adi, Einat Kermany, Yonatan Belinkov, Ofer Lavi, and Yoav Goldberg. 2017. Fine-grained analysis of sentence embeddings using auxiliary prediction tasks. In *ICLR*.

Maristella Agosti, Giorgio Maria Di Nunzio, Nicola Ferro, Donna Harman, and Carol Peters. 2007. The future of large-scale evaluation campaigns for information retrieval in europe. In *International Conference on Theory and Practice of Digital Libraries*, pages 509–512. Springer.

Marilisa Amoia. 2008. *Linguistic-Based Computational Treatment of Textual Entailment Recognition.* Theses, Université Henri Poincaré - Nancy 1.

Eleftherios Avramidis, Vivien Macketanz, Ursula Strohriegel, and Hans Uszkoreit. 2019. Linguistic evaluation of German-English machine translation using a test suite. In *Proceedings of the Fourth Conference on Machine Translation (Volume 2: Shared Task Papers, Day 1)*, pages 445–454, Florence, Italy. Association for Computational Linguistics.

Simon Baker, Roi Reichart, and Anna Korhonen. 2014. An unsupervised model for instance level subcategorization acquisition. In *Proceedings of the 2014 Conference on Empirical Methods in Natural Language Processing (EMNLP)*, pages 278–289, Doha, Qatar. Association for Computational Linguistics.

Roy Bar-Haim, Ido Dagan, Bill Dolan, Lisa Ferro, Danilo Giampiccolo, and Bernardo Magnini. 2006. The second pascal recognising textual entailment challenge.

Mario Barrantes, Benedikt Herudek, and Richard Wang. 2020. Adversarial nli for factual correctness in text summarisation models.

Yonatan Belinkov. 2018. *On internal language representations in deep learning: An analysis of machine translation and speech recognition.* Ph.D. thesis, Massachusetts Institute of Technology.

Yonatan Belinkov, Nadir Durrani, Fahim Dalvi, Hassan Sajjad, and James Glass. 2017a. What do neural machine translation models learn about morphology? In *Proceedings of the 55th Annual Meeting of the Association for Computational Linguistics (Volume 1: Long Papers)*, pages 861–872. Association for Computational Linguistics.

Yonatan Belinkov and James Glass. 2017. Analyzing hidden representations in end-to-end automatic speech recognition systems. In I. Guyon, U. V. Luxburg, S. Bengio, H. Wallach, R. Fergus, S. Vishwanathan, and R. Garnett, editors, *Advances in Neural Information Processing Systems 30*, pages 2441–2451. Curran Associates, Inc.

Yonatan Belinkov and James Glass. 2019. Analysis methods in neural language processing: A survey. *Transactions of the Association for Computational Linguistics*, 7:49–72.

Yonatan Belinkov, Lluís Màrquez, Hassan Sajjad, Nadir Durrani, Fahim Dalvi, and James Glass. 2017b. Evaluating layers of representation in neural machine translation on part-of-speech and semantic tagging tasks. In *Proceedings of the Eighth International Joint Conference on Natural Language Processing (Volume 1: Long Papers)*, pages 1–10, Taipei, Taiwan. Asian Federation of Natural Language Processing.

Anja Belz and Albert Gatt. 2008. Intrinsic vs. extrinsic evaluation measures for referring expression generation. In *Proceedings of ACL-08: HLT, Short Papers*, pages 197–200, Columbus, Ohio. Association for Computational Linguistics.

Catherine Blake. 2007. The role of sentence structure in recognizing textual entailment. In *Proceedings of the ACL-PASCAL Workshop on Textual Entailment and Paraphrasing*, RTE '07, pages 101–106, Stroudsburg, PA, USA. Association for Computational Linguistics.

Samuel Bowman, Yoav Goldberg, Felix Hill, Angeliki Lazaridou, Omer Levy, Roi Reichart, and Anders Søgaard, editors. 2017. *Proceedings of the 2nd Workshop on Evaluating Vector Space Representations for NLP*. Association for Computational Linguistics, Copenhagen, Denmark.

Samuel R. Bowman, Gabor Angeli, Christopher Potts, and Christopher D. Manning. 2015. A large annotated corpus for learning natural language inference. In *Proceedings of the 2015 Conference on Empirical Methods in Natural Language Processing (EMNLP)*. Association for Computational Linguistics.

L. Brinton. 2000. *The Structure of Modern English: A linguistic introduction.*

Elia Bruni, Gemma Boleda, Marco Baroni, and Nam-Khanh Tran. 2012. Distributional semantics in technicolor. In *Proceedings of the 50th Annual Meeting of the Association for Computational Linguistics (Volume 1: Long Papers)*, pages 136–145.

Oana-Maria Camburu, Tim Rocktäschel, Thomas Lukasiewicz, and Phil Blunsom. 2018. e-snli: Natural language inference with natural language explanations. In S. Bengio, H. Wallach, H. Larochelle,

K. Grauman, N. Cesa-Bianchi, and R. Garnett, editors, *Advances in Neural Information Processing Systems 31*, pages 9539–9549. Curran Associates, Inc.

J Gregory Caporaso, Nita Deshpande, J Lynn Fink, Philip E Bourne, K Bretonnel Cohen, and Lawrence Hunter. 2008. Intrinsic evaluation of text mining tools may not predict performance on realistic tasks. In *Biocomputing 2008*, pages 640–651. World Scientific.

Stergios Chatzikyriakidis, Robin Cooper, Simon Dobnik, and Staffan Larsson. 2017. An overview of natural language inference data collection: The way forward? In *Proceedings of the Computing Natural Language Inference Workshop*.

Qian Chen, Xiaodan Zhu, Zhen-Hua Ling, Diana Inkpen, and Si Wei. 2018. Neural natural language inference models enhanced with external knowledge. In *Proceedings of the 56th Annual Meeting of the Association for Computational Linguistics (Volume 1: Long Papers)*, pages 2406–2417, Melbourne, Australia. Association for Computational Linguistics.

Qian Chen, Xiaodan Zhu, Zhen-Hua Ling, Si Wei, Hui Jiang, and Diana Inkpen. 2017. Recurrent neural network-based sentence encoder with gated attention for natural language inference. In *Proceedings of the 2nd Workshop on Evaluating Vector Space Representations for NLP*, pages 36–40, Copenhagen, Denmark. Association for Computational Linguistics.

Tongfei Chen, Zhengping Jiang, Adam Poliak, Keisuke Sakaguchi, and Benjamin Van Durme. 2020. Uncertain natural language inference. In *ACL*.

Gennaro Chierchia and Sally McConnell-Ginet. 2000. *Meaning and grammar: An introduction to semantics.*

Nancy Chinchor. 1991. MUC-3 linguistic phenomena test experiment. In *Third Message Uunderstanding Conference (MUC-3): Proceedings of a Conference Held in San Diego, California, May 21-23, 1991.*

Nancy Chinchor, Lynette Hirschman, and David D. Lewis. 1993. Evaluating message understanding systems: An analysis of the third message understanding conference (MUC-3). *Computational Linguistics*, 19(3):409–450.

Billy Chiu, Anna Korhonen, and Sampo Pyysalo. 2016. Intrinsic evaluation of word vectors fails to predict extrinsic performance. In *Proceedings of the 1st Workshop on Evaluating Vector-Space Representations for NLP*, pages 1–6, Berlin, Germany. Association for Computational Linguistics.

Leshem Choshen and Omri Abend. 2019. Automatically extracting challenge sets for non-local phenomena in neural machine translation. In *Proceedings of the 23rd Conference on Computational Natural Language Learning (CoNLL)*, pages 291–303,

Hong Kong, China. Association for Computational Linguistics.

Alexis Conneau and Douwe Kiela. 2018. SentEval: An evaluation toolkit for universal sentence representations. In *Proceedings of the Eleventh International Conference on Language Resources and Evaluation (LREC 2018)*, Miyazaki, Japan. European Language Resources Association (ELRA).

Alexis Conneau, GermÃ¡n Kruszewski, Guillaume Lample, LoÃc Barrault, and Marco Baroni. 2018. What you can cram into a single $&!#* vector: Probing sentence embeddings for linguistic properties. In *Proceedings of the 56th Annual Meeting of the Association for Computational Linguistics (Volume 1: Long Papers)*, pages 2126–2136, Melbourne, Australia. Association for Computational Linguistics.

John M. Conroy, Hoa Trang Dang, Ani Nenkova, and Karolina Owczarzak, editors. 2012. *Proceedings of Workshop on Evaluation Metrics and System Comparison for Automatic Summarization*. Association for Computational Linguistics, Montréal, Canada.

Robin Cooper, Dick Crouch, Jan Van Eijck, Chris Fox, Johan Van Genabith, Jan Jaspars, Hans Kamp, David Milward, Manfred Pinkal, Massimo Poesio, et al. 1996. Using the framework.

Ido Dagan, Oren Glickman, and Bernardo Magnini. 2006. The pascal recognising textual entailment challenge. In *Machine learning challenges. evaluating predictive uncertainty, visual object classification, and recognising tectual entailment*, pages 177–190. Springer.

Andrew M Dai and Quoc V Le. 2015. Semi-supervised sequence learning. In *Advances in neural information processing systems*, pages 3079–3087.

Ishita Dasgupta, Demi Guo, Andreas Stuhlmüller, Samuel J Gershman, and Noah D Goodman. 2018. Evaluating compositionality in sentence embeddings. *arXiv preprint arXiv:1802.04302*.

Myroslava Dzikovska, Rodney Nielsen, Chris Brew, Claudia Leacock, Danilo Giampiccolo, Luisa Bentivogli, Peter Clark, Ido Dagan, and Hoa Trang Dang. 2013. Semeval-2013 task 7: The joint student response analysis and 8th recognizing textual entailment challenge. In *Second Joint Conference on Lexical and Computational Semantics (*SEM), Volume 2: Proceedings of the Seventh International Workshop on Semantic Evaluation (SemEval 2013)*, pages 263–274, Atlanta, Georgia, USA. Association for Computational Linguistics.

Dominique Estival. 1997. Karen sparck jones & julia r. galliers, evaluating natural language processing systems: An analysis and review. lecture notes in artificial intelligence 1083. *Machine Translation*, 12(4):375–379.

Allyson Ettinger, Ahmed Elgohary, Colin Phillips, and Philip Resnik. 2018. Assessing composition in sentence vector representations. In *Proceedings of the 27th International Conference on Computational Linguistics*, pages 1790–1801, Santa Fe, New Mexico, USA. Association for Computational Linguistics.

Tobias Falke, Leonardo F. R. Ribeiro, Prasetya Ajie Utama, Ido Dagan, and Iryna Gurevych. 2019. Ranking generated summaries by correctness: An interesting but challenging application for natural language inference. In *Proceedings of the 57th Annual Meeting of the Association for Computational Linguistics*, pages 2214–2220, Florence, Italy. Association for Computational Linguistics.

Manaal Faruqui, Yulia Tsvetkov, Pushpendre Rastogi, and Chris Dyer. 2016. Problems with evaluation of word embeddings using word similarity tasks. In *Proceedings of the 1st Workshop on Evaluating Vector-Space Representations for NLP*, pages 30–35, Berlin, Germany. Association for Computational Linguistics.

Atefeh Farzindar and Guy Lapalme. 2004. Letsum, an automatic legal text summarizing system. In *Legal knowledge and information systems, JURIX*.

Lev Finkelstein, Evgeniy Gabrilovich, Yossi Matias, Ehud Rivlin, Zach Solan, Gadi Wolfman, and Eytan Ruppin. 2001. Placing search in context: The concept revisited. In *Proceedings of the 10th international conference on World Wide Web*, pages 406–414.

Matt Gardner, Jonathan Berant, Hannaneh Hajishirzi, Alon Talmor, and Sewon Min. 2019. Question answering is a format; when is it useful? *arXiv preprint arXiv:1909.11291*.

Danilo Giampiccolo, Bernardo Magnini, Ido Dagan, and Bill Dolan. 2007. The third PASCAL recognizing textual entailment challenge. In *Proceedings of the ACL-PASCAL Workshop on Textual Entailment and Paraphrasing*, pages 1–9, Prague. Association for Computational Linguistics.

George Giannakopoulos, Elena Lloret, John M. Conroy, Josef Steinberger, Marina Litvak, Peter Rankel, and Benoit Favre, editors. 2017. *Proceedings of the MultiLing 2017 Workshop on Summarization and Summary Evaluation Across Source Types and Genres*. Association for Computational Linguistics, Valencia, Spain.

Oren Glickman. 2006. *Applied textual entailment*. Ph.D. thesis, Bar Ilan University.

Max Glockner, Vered Shwartz, and Yoav Goldberg. 2018. Breaking nli systems with sentences that require simple lexical inferences. In *Proceedings of the 56th Annual Meeting of the Association for Computational Linguistics (Volume 2: Short Papers)*, pages 650–655, Melbourne, Australia. Association for Computational Linguistics.

Jade Goldstein, Alon Lavie, Chin-Yew Lin, and Clare Voss, editors. 2005. *Proceedings of the ACL Workshop on Intrinsic and Extrinsic Evaluation Measures for Machine Translation and/or Summarization*. Association for Computational Linguistics, Ann Arbor, Michigan.

Yichen Gong, Heng Luo, and Jian Zhang. 2018. Natural language inference over interaction space. In *International Conference on Learning Representations*.

Suchin Gururangan, Swabha Swayamdipta, Omer Levy, Roy Schwartz, Samuel Bowman, and Noah A. Smith. 2018. Annotation artifacts in natural language inference data. In *Proceedings of the 2018 Conference of the North American Chapter of the Association for Computational Linguistics: Human Language Technologies, Volume 2 (Short Papers)*, pages 107–112, New Orleans, Louisiana. Association for Computational Linguistics.

John Hewitt and Percy Liang. 2019. Designing and interpreting probes with control tasks. In *Proceedings of the 2019 Conference on Empirical Methods in Natural Language Processing and the 9th International Joint Conference on Natural Language Processing (EMNLP-IJCNLP)*, pages 2733–2743, Hong Kong, China. Association for Computational Linguistics.

Felix Hill, Roi Reichart, and Anna Korhonen. 2015. SimLex-999: Evaluating semantic models with (genuine) similarity estimation. *Computational Linguistics*, 41(4):665–695.

Dieuwke Hupkes, Sara Veldhoen, and Willem Zuidema. 2018. Visualisation and'diagnostic classifiers' reveal how recurrent and recursive neural networks process hierarchical structure. *Journal of Artificial Intelligence Research*, 61:907–926.

Pierre Isabelle, Colin Cherry, and George Foster. 2017. A challenge set approach to evaluating machine translation. In *Proceedings of the 2017 Conference on Empirical Methods in Natural Language Processing*, pages 2486–2496, Copenhagen, Denmark. Association for Computational Linguistics.

Theo M. V. Janssen. 2011. Montague semantics. In Edward N. Zalta, editor, *The Stanford Encyclopedia of Philosophy*, winter 2011 edition. Metaphysics Research Lab, Stanford University.

Paloma Jeretic, Alex Warstadt, Suvrat Bhooshan, and Adina Williams. 2020. Are natural language inference models IMPPRESsive? Learning IMPlicature and PRESupposition. In *Proceedings of the 58th Annual Meeting of the Association for Computational Linguistics*, pages 8690–8705, Online. Association for Computational Linguistics.

Tushar Khot, Ashish Sabharwal, and Peter Clark. 2018. SciTail: A textual entailment dataset from science question answering. In *AAAI*.

Adam Kilgarriff. 1998. Senseval: an exercise in evaluating world sense disambiguation programs. In *First International Conference on language resources & evaluation: Granada, Spain, 28-30 May 1998*, pages 581–588. European Language Resources Association.

Najoung Kim, Roma Patel, Adam Poliak, Patrick Xia, Alex Wang, Tom McCoy, Ian Tenney, Alexis Ross, Tal Linzen, Benjamin Van Durme, Samuel R. Bowman, and Ellie Pavlick. 2019. Probing what different NLP tasks teach machines about function word comprehension. In *Proceedings of the Eighth Joint Conference on Lexical and Computational Semantics (*SEM 2019)*, pages 235–249, Minneapolis, Minnesota. Association for Computational Linguistics.

Maghi King, Bente MAEGAARD, Jörg SCHÜTZ, Louis des TOMBE, Annelise BECH, Ann NEVILLE, Antti ARPPE, Lorna BALKAN, Colin BRACE, Harry BUNT, Lauri CARLSON, Shona DOUGLAS, Monika HÖGE, Steven KRAUWER, Sandra MANZI, Cristina MAZZI, Ann June SIELEMANN, and Ragna STEENBAKKERS. 1995. Eagles: Evaluation of natural language processing systems. final report. Technical report.

Margaret King and Kirsten Falkedal. 1990. Using test suites in evaluation of machine translation systems. In *COLING 1990 Volume 2: Papers presented to the 13th International Conference on Computational Linguistics*.

Thomas Kober, Sander Bijl de Vroe, and Mark Steedman. 2019. Temporal and aspectual entailment. In *Proceedings of the 13th International Conference on Computational Semantics - Long Papers*, pages 103–119, Gothenburg, Sweden. Association for Computational Linguistics.

Sungryong Koh, Jinee Maeng, Ji-Young Lee, Young-Sook Chae, and Key-Sun Choi. 2001. A test suite for evaluation of english-to-korean machine translation systems. In *MT Summit'conference, Santiago de Compostela*.

Vojtźch Ková, Miloź Jakubíźek, and Aleź Horák. 2016. On evaluation of natural language processing tasks. In *Proceedings of the 8th International Conference on Agents and Artificial Intelligence*, pages 540–545. SCITEPRESS-Science and Technology Publications, Lda.

Sabine Lehmann, Stephan Oepen, Sylvie Regnier-Prost, Klaus Netter, Veronika Lux, Judith Klein, Kirsten Falkedal, Frederik Fouvry, Dominique Estival, Eva Dauphin, Herve Compagnion, Judith Baur, Lorna Balkan, and Doug Arnold. 1996. TSNLP - test suites for natural language processing. In *COLING 1996 Volume 2: The 16th International Conference on Computational Linguistics*.

Omer Levy, Felix Hill, Anna Korhonen, Kyunghyun Cho, Roi Reichart, Yoav Goldberg, and Antione Bordes, editors. 2016. *Proceedings of the 1st Workshop on Evaluating Vector-Space Representations for NLP*. Association for Computational Linguistics, Berlin, Germany.

Chin-Yew Lin. 2004. ROUGE: A package for automatic evaluation of summaries. In *Text Summarization Branches Out*, pages 74–81, Barcelona, Spain. Association for Computational Linguistics.

Tal Linzen, Grzegorz Chrupała, and Afra Alishahi, editors. 2018. *Proceedings of the 2018 EMNLP Workshop BlackboxNLP: Analyzing and Interpreting Neural Networks for NLP*. Association for Computational Linguistics, Brussels, Belgium.

Tal Linzen, Grzegorz Chrupała, Yonatan Belinkov, and Dieuwke Hupkes, editors. 2019. *Proceedings of the 2019 ACL Workshop BlackboxNLP: Analyzing and Interpreting Neural Networks for NLP*. Association for Computational Linguistics, Florence, Italy.

Yang Liu, Chengjie Sun, Lei Lin, and Xiaolong Wang. 2016. Learning natural language inference using bidirectional lstm model and inner-attention. *arXiv preprint arXiv:1605.09090*.

Marina Lloberes, Irene Castellón, and Lluís Padró. 2015. Suitability of ParTes test suite for parsing evaluation. In *Proceedings of the 14th International Conference on Parsing Technologies*, pages 61–65, Bilbao, Spain. Association for Computational Linguistics.

Thang Luong, Richard Socher, and Christopher Manning. 2013. Better word representations with recursive neural networks for morphology. In *Proceedings of the Seventeenth Conference on Computational Natural Language Learning*, pages 104–113, Sofia, Bulgaria. Association for Computational Linguistics.

Bill MacCartney. 2009. *Natural language inference*. Ph.D. thesis, Stanford University.

Christopher D Manning. 2006. Local textual inference: it's hard to circumscribe, but you know it when you see it–and nlp needs it.

Christopher D Manning. 2015. Computational linguistics and deep learning. *Computational Linguistics*, 41(4):701–707.

Marie-Catherine de Marneffe, Anna N. Rafferty, and Christopher D. Manning. 2008. Finding contradictions in text. In *Proceedings of ACL-08: HLT*, pages 1039–1047, Columbus, Ohio. Association for Computational Linguistics.

Bryan McCann, Nitish Shirish Keskar, Caiming Xiong, and Richard Socher. 2018. The natural language decathlon: Multitask learning as question answering. *arXiv preprint arXiv:1806.08730*.

Kostadin Mishev, Ana Gjorgjevikj, Riste Stojanov, Igor Mishkovski, Irena Vodenska, Ljubomir Chitkushev, and Dimitar Trajanov. 2019. Performance evaluation of word and sentence embeddings for finance headlines sentiment analysis. In *ICT Innovations 2019. Big Data Processing and Mining*, pages 161–172, Cham. Springer International Publishing.

Diego Mollá and Ben Hutchinson. 2003. Intrinsic versus extrinsic evaluations of parsing systems. In *Proceedings of the EACL 2003 Workshop on Evaluation Initiatives in Natural Language Processing: are evaluation methods, metrics and resources reusable?*, pages 43–50, Columbus, Ohio. Association for Computational Linguistics.

Jesse Mu and Jacob Andreas. 2020. Compositional explanations of neurons. In *Advances in Neural Information Processing Systems 33 (NeurIPS)*.

Aakanksha Naik, Abhilasha Ravichander, Norman Sadeh, Carolyn Rose, and Graham Neubig. 2018. Stress test evaluation for natural language inference. In *Proceedings of the 27th International Conference on Computational Linguistics*, pages 2340–2353, Santa Fe, New Mexico, USA. Association for Computational Linguistics.

Neha Nayak, Gabor Angeli, and Christopher D Manning. 2016. Evaluating word embeddings using a representative suite of practical tasks. In *Proceedings of the 1st workshop on evaluating vector-space representations for nlp*, pages 19–23.

Yixin Nie, Adina Williams, Emily Dinan, Mohit Bansal, Jason Weston, and Douwe Kiela. 2020. Adversarial NLI: A new benchmark for natural language understanding. In *Proceedings of the 58th Annual Meeting of the Association for Computational Linguistics*, pages 4885–4901, Online. Association for Computational Linguistics.

Stephan Oepen and Klaus Netter. 1995. Tsnlp - test suites for natural language processing. In *In J. Nerbonne (Ed.), Linguistic Databases (pp. 13 – 36*, pages 711–716. CSLI Publications.

Martha Palmer and Tim Finin. 1990. Workshop on the evaluation of natural language processing systems. *Computational Linguistics*, 16(3):175–181.

Kishore Papineni, Salim Roukos, Todd Ward, and Wei-Jing Zhu. 2002. Bleu: a method for automatic evaluation of machine translation. In *Proceedings of the 40th Annual Meeting of the Association for Computational Linguistics*, pages 311–318, Philadelphia, Pennsylvania, USA. Association for Computational Linguistics.

Patrick Paroubek, Stéphane Chaudiron, and Lynette Hirschman. 2007. Principles of evaluation in natural language processing. *Traitement Automatique des Langues*, 48(1):7–31.

Katerina Pastra, editor. 2003. *Proceedings of the EACL 2003 Workshop on Evaluation Initiatives in Natural Language Processing: are evaluation methods, metrics and resources reusable?* Association for Computational Linguistics, Columbus, Ohio.

Ellie Pavlick. 2017. *Compositional Lexical Entailment for Natural Language Inference.* Ph.D. thesis, University of Pennsylvania.

Ellie Pavlick and Chris Callison-Burch. 2016. Most "babies" are "little" and most "problems" are "huge": Compositional entailment in adjective-nouns. In *Proceedings of the 54th Annual Meeting of the Association for Computational Linguistics (Volume 1: Long Papers)*, pages 2164–2173. Association for Computational Linguistics.

Ellie Pavlick and Tom Kwiatkowski. 2019. Inherent disagreements in human textual inferences. *Transactions of the Association for Computational Linguistics*, 7:677–694.

Ellie Pavlick, Travis Wolfe, Pushpendre Rastogi, Chris Callison-Burch, Mark Dredze, and Benjamin Van Durme. 2015. Framenet+: Fast paraphrastic tripling of framenet. In *Proceedings of the 53rd Annual Meeting of the Association for Computational Linguistics and the 7th International Joint Conference on Natural Language Processing (Volume 2: Short Papers)*, pages 408–413, Beijing, China. Association for Computational Linguistics.

Ruggero Petrolito. 2018. Word embeddings in sentiment analysis. In *Italian Conference on Computational Linguistics*.

Tiago Pimentel, Josef Valvoda, Rowan Hall Maudslay, Ran Zmigrod, Adina Williams, and Ryan Cotterell. 2020. Information-theoretic probing for linguistic structure. In *Proceedings of the 58th Annual Meeting of the Association for Computational Linguistics*, pages 4609–4622, Online. Association for Computational Linguistics.

Emily Pitler, Annie Louis, and Ani Nenkova. 2010. Automatic evaluation of linguistic quality in multi-document summarization. In *Proceedings of the 48th Annual Meeting of the Association for Computational Linguistics*, pages 544–554, Uppsala, Sweden. Association for Computational Linguistics.

Adam Poliak, Yonatan Belinkov, James Glass, and Benjamin Van Durme. 2018a. On the evaluation of semantic phenomena in neural machine translation using natural language inference. In *Proceedings of the 2018 Conference of the North American Chapter of the Association for Computational Linguistics: Human Language Technologies, Volume 2 (Short Papers)*, pages 513–523, New Orleans, Louisiana. Association for Computational Linguistics.

Adam Poliak, Aparajita Haldar, Rachel Rudinger, J. Edward Hu, Ellie Pavlick, Aaron Steven White, and Benjamin Van Durme. 2018b. Collecting diverse natural language inference problems for sentence representation evaluation. In *Proceedings of the 2018 Conference on Empirical Methods in Natural Language Processing*, pages 67–81. Association for Computational Linguistics.

Adam Poliak, Jason Naradowsky, Aparajita Haldar, Rachel Rudinger, and Benjamin Van Durme. 2018c. Hypothesis only baselines in natural language inference. In *Proceedings of the Seventh Joint Conference on Lexical and Computational Semantics*, pages 180–191. Association for Computational Linguistics.

Maja Popović and Sheila Castilho. 2019. Challenge test sets for MT evaluation. In *Proceedings of Machine Translation Summit XVII Volume 3: Tutorial Abstracts*, Dublin, Ireland. European Association for Machine Translation.

Vasin Punyakanok, Dan Roth, and Wen-tau Yih. 2004. Natural language inference via dependency tree mapping: An application to question answering. Technical report.

Yuanyuan Qiu, Hongzheng Li, Shen Li, Yingdi Jiang, Renfen Hu, and Lijiao Yang. 2018. Revisiting correlations between intrinsic and extrinsic evaluations of word embeddings. In *Chinese Computational Linguistics and Natural Language Processing Based on Naturally Annotated Big Data*, pages 209–221. Springer.

Ehud Reiter. 2018. A structured review of the validity of bleu. *Computational Linguistics*, 44(3):393–401.

Philip Resnik and Jimmy Lin. 2010. 11 evaluation of nlp systems. *The handbook of computational linguistics and natural language processing*, 57.

Philip Resnik, Michael Niv, Michael Nossal, and Gregory Schnitzer. 2006. Using intrinsic and extrinsic metrics to evaluate accuracy and facilitation in computer-assisted coding. In *Perspectives in Health Information Management Computer Assisted Coding Conference Proceedings*.

Kyle Richardson, Hai Na Hu, Lawrence S. Moss, and Ashish Sabharwal. 2020. Probing natural language inference models through semantic fragments. In *AAAI*, volume abs/1909.07521.

Anna Rogers, Aleksandr Drozd, Anna Rumshisky, and Yoav Goldberg, editors. 2019. *Proceedings of the 3rd Workshop on Evaluating Vector Space Representations for NLP*. Association for Computational Linguistics, Minneapolis, USA.

Alexey Romanov and Chaitanya Shivade. 2018. Lessons from natural language inference in the clinical domain. In *Proceedings of the 2018 Conference on Empirical Methods in Natural Language Processing*, pages 1586–1596, Brussels, Belgium. Association for Computational Linguistics.

Alexis Ross and Ellie Pavlick. 2019. How well do NLI models capture verb veridicality? In *Proceedings of the 2019 Conference on Empirical Methods in Natural Language Processing and the 9th International Joint Conference on Natural Language Processing (EMNLP-IJCNLP)*, pages 2230–2240, Hong Kong, China. Association for Computational Linguistics.

Rachel Rudinger, Chandler May, and Benjamin Van Durme. 2017. Social bias in elicited natural language inferences. In *Proceedings of the First ACL Workshop on Ethics in Natural Language Processing*, pages 74–79, Valencia, Spain. Association for Computational Linguistics.

Mark Sammons, V.G.Vinod Vydiswaran, and Dan Roth. 2010. "ask not what textual entailment can do for you...". In *Proceedings of the 48th Annual Meeting of the Association for Computational Linguistics*, pages 1199–1208, Uppsala, Sweden. Association for Computational Linguistics.

Robert M Schwarcz, John F Burger, and Robert F Simmons. 1970. A deductive question-answerer for natural language inference. *Communications of the ACM*, 13(3):167–183.

P.A.M. Seuren. 1998. *Western Linguistics: An Historical Introduction*.

Karen Sparck Jones. 1994. Towards better NLP system evaluation. In *Human Language Technology: Proceedings of a Workshop held at Plainsboro, New Jersey, March 8-11, 1994*.

Karen Sparck Jones and Julia R. Galliers. 1996. *Evaluating Natural Language Processing Systems: An Analysis and Review*. Springer-Verlag, Berlin, Heidelberg.

Ieva Staliūnaitė. 2018. Learning about non-veridicality in textual entailment. Master's thesis, Utrecht University.

Yi Tay, Anh Tuan Luu, and Siu Cheung Hui. 2018. Compare, compress and propagate: Enhancing neural architectures with alignment factorization for natural language inference. In *Proceedings of the 2018 Conference on Empirical Methods in Natural Language Processing*, pages 1565–1575, Brussels, Belgium. Association for Computational Linguistics.

Avijit Thawani, Biplav Srivastava, and Anil Singh. 2019. SWOW-8500: Word association task for intrinsic evaluation of word embeddings. In *Proceedings of the 3rd Workshop on Evaluating Vector Space Representations for NLP*, pages 43–51, Minneapolis, USA. Association for Computational Linguistics.

Masatoshi Tsuchiya. 2018. Performance impact caused by hidden bias of training data for recognizing textual entailment. In *11th International Conference on Language Resources and Evaluation (LREC2018)*.

Yulia Tsvetkov, Manaal Faruqui, Wang Ling, Guillaume Lample, and Chris Dyer. 2015. Evaluation of word vector representations by subspace alignment. In *Proceedings of the 2015 Conference on Empirical Methods in Natural Language Processing*, pages 2049–2054, Lisbon, Portugal. Association for Computational Linguistics.

Lucy Vanderwende and William B Dolan. 2006. What syntax can contribute in the entailment task. In *Machine Learning Challenges. Evaluating Predictive Uncertainty, Visual Object Classification, and Recognising Tectual Entailment*, pages 205–216. Springer.

Siddharth Vashishtha, Adam Poliak, Yash Kumar Lal, Benjamin Van Durme, and Aaron Steven White. 2020. Temporal reasoning in natural language inference. In *Proceedings of the Findings of EMNLP*.

Elena Voita and Ivan Titov. 2020. Information-theoretic probing with minimum description length.

Alex Wang, Yada Pruksachatkun, Nikita Nangia, Amanpreet Singh, Julian Michael, Felix Hill, Omer Levy, and Samuel Bowman. 2019a. Superglue: A stickier benchmark for general-purpose language understanding systems. In *Advances in Neural Information Processing Systems*, pages 3261–3275.

Alex Wang, Amapreet Singh, Julian Michael, Felix Hill, Omer Levy, and Samuel R Bowman. 2018. Glue: A multi-task benchmark and analysis platform for natural language understanding. *arXiv preprint arXiv:1804.07461*.

Bin Wang, Angela Wang, Fenxiao Chen, Yuncheng Wang, and C-C Jay Kuo. 2019b. Evaluating word embedding models: Methods and experimental results. *APSIPA transactions on signal and information processing*, 8.

Aaron Steven White, Pushpendre Rastogi, Kevin Duh, and Benjamin Van Durme. 2017. Inference is everything: Recasting semantic resources into a unified evaluation framework. In *Proceedings of the Eighth International Joint Conference on Natural Language Processing (Volume 1: Long Papers)*, pages 996–1005, Taipei, Taiwan. Asian Federation of Natural Language Processing.

Yorick Wilks. 1975. A preferential, pattern-seeking, semantics for natural language inference. *Artificial intelligence*, 6(1):53–74.

Adina Williams, Nikita Nangia, and Samuel R Bowman. 2017. A broad-coverage challenge corpus for sentence understanding through inference. *arXiv preprint arXiv:1704.05426*.

Yonghui Wu, Jun Xu, Min Jiang, Yaoyun Zhang, and Hua Xu. 2015. A study of neural word embeddings for named entity recognition in clinical text. In *AMIA Annual Symposium Proceedings*, volume 2015, page 1326. American Medical Informatics Association.

Hitomi Yanaka, Koji Mineshima, Daisuke Bekki, and Kentaro Inui. 2020. Do neural models learn systematicity of monotonicity inference in natural language? In *ACL*.

Hitomi Yanaka, Koji Mineshima, Daisuke Bekki, Kentaro Inui, Satoshi Sekine, Lasha Abzianidze, and Johan Bos. 2019. Can neural networks understand monotonicity reasoning? In *Proceedings of the 2019 ACL Workshop BlackboxNLP: Analyzing and Interpreting Neural Networks for NLP*, pages 31–40, Florence, Italy. Association for Computational Linguistics.

Peter Young, Alice Lai, Micah Hodosh, and Julia Hockenmaier. 2014. From image descriptions to visual denotations: New similarity metrics for semantic inference over event descriptions. *Transactions of the Association for Computational Linguistics*, 2:67–78.

Annie Zaenen, Lauri Karttunen, and Richard Crouch. 2005. Local textual inference: Can it be defined or circumscribed? In *Proceedings of the ACL Workshop on Empirical Modeling of Semantic Equivalence and Entailment*, pages 31–36, Ann Arbor, Michigan. Association for Computational Linguistics.

A Pascal RTE Annotation Guidelines

In the first iteration of the PASCAL RTE challeges, the task organizers were frank in their view that they expected the task definition to change over time. They wrote that "finally, the task definition and evaluation methodologies are clearly not mature yet. We expect them to change over time and hope that participants' contributions, observations and comments will help shaping this evolving research direction." Here, we include snippets from the annotation guidelines for the first three PASCAL RTE challenges:

A.1 RTE1 Guidelines

Given that the text and hypothesis might originate from documents at different points in time, tense aspects are ignored. In principle, the hypothesis must be fully entailed by the text. Judgment would be False if the hypothesis includes parts that cannot be inferred from the text. However, cases in which inference is very probable (but not completely certain) are still judged at True. . . . To reduce the risk of unclear cases, annotators were guided to avoid vague examples for which inference has some positive probability that is not clearly very high. To keep the contexts in T and H self contained annotators replaced anaphors with the appropriate reference from preceding sentences where applicable. They also often shortened the hypotheses, and sometimes the texts, to reduce complexity.

(Dagan et al., 2006)

A.2 RTE2 Guidelines

The data collection and annotation guidelines were revised and expanded . . . We say that t entails h if, typically, a human reading t would infer that h is most likely true. This somewhat informal definition is based on (and assumes) common human understanding of language as well as common background knowledge. Textual entailment recognition is the task of deciding, given t and h, whether t entails h. Some additional judgment criteria and guidelines are listed below:

- *Entailment is a directional relation. The hypothesis must be entailed from the given text, but the text need not be entailed from the hypothesis.*

- *The hypothesis must be fully entailed by the text. Judgment would be NO if the hypothesis includes parts that cannot be inferred from the text.*

- *Cases in which inference is very probable (but not completely certain) are judged as YES. For instance, in pair #387 one could claim that although Shapiro's office is in Century City, he actually never arrives to his office, and works elsewhere. However, this interpretation of t is very unlikely, and so the entailment holds with high probability. On the other hand, annotators were guided to avoid vague examples for which inference has some positive probability which is not clearly very high.*

- *Our definition of entailment allows presupposition of common knowledge, such as: a company has a CEO, a CEO is an employee of the company, an employee is a person, etc. For instance, in pair #294, the entailment depends on knowing that the president of a country is also a citizen of that country.*

(Bar-Haim et al., 2006)

A.3 RTE3 Guidelines

As entailment is a directional relation, the hypothesis must be entailed by the given text, but the text need not be entailed by the hypothesis.

- *The hypothesis must be fully entailed by the text. Judgment must be NO if the hypothesis includes parts that cannot be inferred from the text.*

- *Cases in which inference is very probable (but not completely certain) were judged as YES.*

- *Common world knowledge was assumed, e.g. the capital of a country is situated in that country, the prime minister of a state is also a citizen of that state, and so on.*

(Giampiccolo et al., 2007)

QUANTIFIERS (14)

P	Neither leading tenor comes cheap. One of the leading tenors is Pavarotti.
Q	Is Pavarotti a leading tenor who comes cheap?
H	Pavarotti is a leading tenor who comes cheap.
A	No

PLURALS (94)

P	The inhabitants of Cambridge voted for a Labour MP.
Q	Did every inhabitant of Cambridge vote for a Labour MP?
H	Every inhabitant of Cambridge voted for a Labour MP.
A	Unknown

COMPARATIVES (243)

P	ITEL sold 3000 more computers than APCOM. APCOM sold exactly 2500 computers.
Q	Did ITEL sell 5500 computers?
H	ITEL sold 5500 computers.
A	Yes

Table 4: Examples from Fracas: **P** represents the premise(s), **Q** represents the question from *FraCas*, **H** represents the declarative statement MacCartney (2009) created and, **A** represents the label. The number in the parenthesis indicates the example ID from *FraCas*.

---

unemployment is at an all-time <u>low</u>
▶ unemployment is at an all-time <u>poor</u>

---

aeoi 's activities and <u>facility</u> have been tied to several universities
▶ aeoi 's activities and <u>local</u> have been tied to several universities

---

jerusalem fell to the ottomans in 1517 , remaining under their <u>control</u> for 400 years
▶ jerusalem fell to the ottomans in 1517 , remaining under their <u>regulate</u> for 400 years

---

usually such parking spots are <u>on</u> the side of the lot
▶ usually such parking spots are <u>dated</u> the side of the lot

---

Table 5: Not-entailed examples from FN+'s dev set where the hypotheses are ungrammatical. The first line in each section is a premise and the lines with ▶ are corresponding hypotheses. <u>Underline words</u> represent the swapped paraphrases.

Grammaticality and Language Modelling

Jingcheng Niu and **Gerald Penn**
Department of Computer Science
University of Toronto
Toronto, Canada
{niu,gpenn}@cs.toronto.edu

Abstract

Ever since Pereira (2000) provided evidence against Chomsky's (1957) conjecture that statistical language modelling is incommensurable with the aims of grammaticality prediction as a research enterprise, a new area of research has emerged that regards statistical language models as "psycholinguistic subjects" and probes their ability to acquire syntactic knowledge. The advent of The Corpus of Linguistic Acceptability (CoLA) (Warstadt et al., 2019) has earned a spot on the leaderboard for acceptability judgements, and the polemic between Lau et al. (2017) and Sprouse et al. (2018) has raised fundamental questions about the nature of grammaticality and how acceptability judgements should be elicited. All the while, we are told that neural language models continue to improve.

That is not an easy claim to test at present, however, because there is almost no agreement on how to measure their improvement when it comes to grammaticality and acceptability judgements. The GLUE leaderboard bundles CoLA together with a Matthews correlation coefficient (MCC), although probably because CoLA's seminal publication was using it to compute inter-rater reliabilities. Researchers working in this area have used other accuracy and correlation scores, often driven by a need to reconcile and compare various discrete and continuous variables with each other.

The score that we will advocate for in this paper, the point biserial correlation, in fact compares a discrete variable (for us, acceptability judgements) to a continuous variable (for us, neural language model probabilities). The only previous work in this area to choose the PBC that we are aware of is Sprouse et al. (2018), and that paper actually applied it backwards (with some justification) so that the language model probability was treated as the discrete binary variable by setting a threshold.

With the PBC in mind, we will first reappraise some recent work in syntactically targeted linguistic evaluations (Hu et al., 2020), arguing that while their experimental design sets a new high watermark for this topic, their results may not prove what they have claimed. We then turn to the task-independent assessment of language models as grammaticality classifiers. Prior to the introduction of the GLUE leaderboard, the vast majority of this assessment was essentially anecdotal, and we find the use of the MCC in this regard to be problematic. We conduct several studies with PBCs to compare several popular language models. We also study the effects of several variables such as normalization and data homogeneity on PBC.

1 Background

The three currently most popular means of evaluating a neural language model are: (1) perplexity, an information-theoretic measure that was in use long before neural networks became the preferred means of implementing language models; (2) task performance profiles, in which derivative aspects of a language model's predictions are embedded in a so-called "downstream" task, with all other aspects of the implementation held constant; and (3) targeted linguistic evaluations, the purpose of which is to demonstrate specific syntactic generalizations that a candidate model implicitly captures or does not capture. These targeted evaluations must take place on a large number of small data sets in order to control for the syntactic and lexical variations that we witness among sentences in a realistic corpus.

The purpose of this paper is ultimately to find a task-independent means of testing how well language model probabilities might serve as grammaticality regression scores. Using evidence from targeted linguistic evaluations, we argue for the point-biserial correlation as at least the basis of

110

Proceedings of the First Workshop on Evaluation and Comparison of NLP Systems (Eval4NLP), pages 110–119,
November 20, 2020. ©2020 Association for Computational Linguistics

such a task-independent measure, and then use the PBC to examine several neural models along with some important variables that affect both their evaluation and the data that we evaluate on.

Borrowing a convention from linguistic theory, Marvin and Linzen (2018) coined the use of "minimal pairs" as input to language models in order to test these fine-grained variations. For example:

(1) Reflexive pronoun in a sentential complement:

    a. The bankers thought the pilot embarrassed himself.

    b. *The bankers thought the pilot embarrassed themselves.

(2) Reflexive pronoun across an object relative clause:

    a. The manager that the architects like doubted himself.

    b. *The manager that the architects like doubted themselves.

These pairs deal with referential agreement in specific syntactic environments. If a model assigns the grammatical string in a pair a higher score than the ungrammatical string, then we say that the model made the correct prediction on that pair. Having evaluated the model over a large number of these pairs, we can compute an accuracy score, relative to a 50% random baseline.

Hu et al. (2020) have taken exception to the design of many such evaluations on that grounds that: (1) a number of English nouns are stereotypically gendered, which conditions pronoun choice, and (2) the unigram probabilities of reflexive pronouns are different, which biases the probabilities that models assign to sentences that contain them. To circumvent these shortcomings, they generalized the pairs to larger sets of strings in which multiple nouns were used in multiple positions so that lexical choice and order could be permuted across sets. They also introduced *distractors*, grammatical strings that contain material irrelevant, or distracting, to the determination of the sentence's grammaticality. One set that they use, for example, is:

(1B) The girl said that the mother saw herself.

(2B) The mother said that the girl saw herself.

(1D) The girls said that the mother saw herself.

(2D) The mothers said that the girl saw herself.

(1U) The girl said that the mothers saw herself.

(2U) The mother said that the girls saw herself.

where (B) is a baseline grammatical string, (D) is a distractor, and (U) is an ungrammatical string. This set has six strings, but sets in their experiments can have as many as 48 strings each, with as many as 75 sets in a single experiment, each one having a unique target pronoun in all of its strings. Because here it is the context that varies, rather than the pronoun, Hu et al. (2020) must rank the conditional probabilities of the pronoun in these various contexts, rather than total sentence probabilities.

Hu et al. (2020) also evaluate models with accuracies. Because there are three classes of string, rather than two, a model is said to have made the correct prediction if the ungrammatical data receive a lower score than both the baseline and distractor data. But because there are more than three strings, they do not compare individual scores from the candidate model, but rather the three means that result from averaging the conditional pronoun probabilities of the baseline, distractor and ungrammatical strings, respectively.

This alternative design not only provided better accuracies than were achieved by Marvin and Linzen (2018), but the inclusion of distractors in the design lowers the random baseline from 50% to 33.3% accuracy. Hu et al. (2020) conclude that current neural language models are learning more about the licensing of reflexive anaphora than was previously thought.

2 Theoretical Exceptions

In a typical psycholinguistics experiment, we would give human subjects a task to perform during which they would be presented with a stimulus that was labelled as either baseline, distractor or ungrammatical. The effect of the stimulus on the task could be measured by time to completion, the number of correct tokens retrieved during a fixed interval of time, etc. Regardless, the task would almost certainly be chosen so that samples of its corresponding measure of success would be normally distributed. So a within-subjects mean of these quantities is entirely justifiable.

The situation is somewhat less clear with the scores that are returned by a neural language model. Ignoring for the moment that Hu et al. (2020) are interested in conditional pronoun probabilities and not sentence probabilities, the scores are generally not regarded as measures of success on a task *per se* — there is no actual task here, apart from achieving a high rank in the evaluation. Legitimate task performance profiles are defined over separate downstream tasks, such as those in the GLUE leaderboard (Wang et al., 2018). It is rather more difficult to think of downstream tasks that depend on conditional pronoun probabilities, however. Note that for Marvin and Linzen (2018), the ratio of conditional pronoun probabilities of a set of stimuli was the same as the ratio of their total sentence probabilities because the reflexive pronoun is always the last word of the sentence, and the contexts preceding the pronouns are always identical.

Several papers by Lau et al., culminating in Lau et al. (2017), have argued instead that sentence probabilities can justifiably be interpreted as gradient grammaticality scores, rejecting the long-standing assumption in generative linguistics that grammaticality is a binary judgement. It is also possible to regard sentence probabilities as summaries of group behaviour, such as relative frequencies of binary grammaticality judgements across multiple individual participants, with no claim of gradience implied for any single participant. This in turn raises the very old question of whether neural networks in fact have any cognitive plausibility, which has recently started to be debated again (Cichy and Kaiser, 2019). Sample distributions of means converge to a normal distribution even if the underlying population distribution is not normal itself, and so whether an average would be justified in this group interpretation would depend to a great extent on the sizes of the sets of strings (relatively small, as we have seen) as well as how skewed the underlying distribution was.

3 Empirical Exceptions

3.1 Significance Test: Normality

Using Hu et al.'s (2020) publicly available experimental results, [1] we administered Levene's test of homoscedasticity to every set of probabilities, given a fixed stimulus set, model and experimental context. Levene's test attempts to reject the null hypothesis that a set of continuous data is normal. Levene's test was successful for 22.5% of Hu et al.'s (2020) sets at a confidence threshold of

---

[1] https://github.com/jennhu/reflexive-anaphor-licensing.

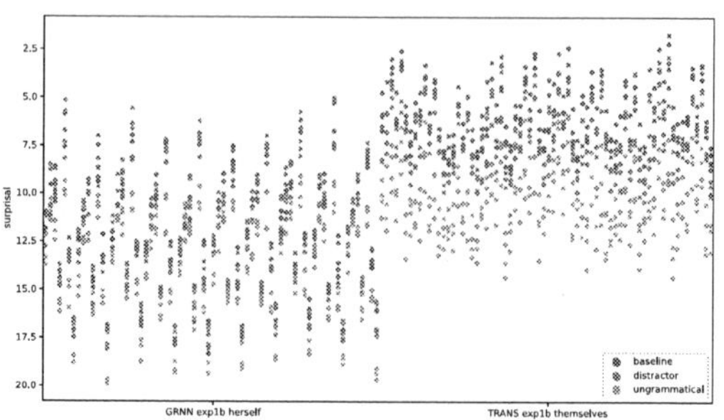

Figure 1: Surprisals (negative log probabilities) for every set in experiment 1b for the GRNN model with *herself*, on the left, and for the TransXL model with *themselves* on the right.

$\alpha = 0.05$, and marginally successful for an additional 8% at $\alpha = 0.1$. This means that somewhere between 20–30% of the sets are provably not normal. Homoscedasticity is merely one aspect of normal distributions that can be used to prove that a distribution is not normal.

3.2 Significance Test: Mean Differentials

In view of the previous section's results, we elected to use the non-parametric Mann-Whitney U-test to determine, on a set-by-set basis, whether the probability that: "the score of a grammatical (meaning baseline or distractor) string is *greater* than that of an ungrammatical string" is significantly different from the probability that it is *less*. This does not determine the difference between means because it cannot quantify effect size, nor does it even determine the sign of the difference. This is an alternative, very minimalist way of formalizing that a language model has made the correct prediction — it can simply distinguish grammatical from ungrammatical, somehow.

Let us consider part of Hu et al.'s (2020) experiment 1b as an example, shown in Figure 1. There would be little disagreement that the model on the right (Transformer-XL with the pronoun *themselves*) had made better predictions than the model on the left (an LSTM with the pronoun *herself*), and yet under both of these conditions the accuracy is 100%. Large differences involving strings at either extreme help to offset a number of smaller differences of the wrong sign when computing differences in means.

Across all experiments, 44.3% of the sets in which the mean differentials qualified for the numerator of the accuracy computation (i.e., the ungrammatical mean was less than both the baseline and distractor means) failed to show a significant difference under the criterion of the Mann-Whitney test. A further 90% of the sets in which the mean differential did not qualify for the numerator (i.e., they were taken not to have been correctly predicted) also failed to show a significant difference. Of the 60 combinations of pronoun and experimental context that we examined, 24 did not have even a single set that showed significance in the numerator. Of the 42 combinations that did not have 100% accuracies, 32 did not have even a single set that showed significance.

In our view, although we agree with every one of the design modifications made by Hu et al. (2020) to targeted evaluations such as these, the decision to continue using accuracy and to generalize it in this way seems not to be working well.

3.3 Matthews Correlation Coefficients

This is potentially a much more pervasive problem than just with Hu et al.'s (2020) experiments. MCCs have emerged as a popular alternative among language modelling enthusiasts (Liu et al., 2019; Lan et al., 2020; Raffel et al., 2019) since grammaticality classification with The Corpus of Linguistic Acceptability (CoLA) (Warstadt et al., 2019) was incorporated into the GLUE standard (Wang et al., 2018). Warstadt et al. (2019) themselves began using MCCs, initially to validate the CoLA corpus, but also to interpret Lau et al.'s (2017) gradient models. MCCs cannot be computed directly on continuous data, which means not only that they are insensitive to the magnitudes of probabilities, but also that a threshold must be set in order to impose a discrete boundary between classes. Defending that choice of boundary can be difficult. Consider Figure 2, for example. In a sample as small as a typical minimal set, cross-validating the MCC decision threshold is not realistic, so here we used the mean of both classes of data. In this particular set, two low-surprisal distractors cause a lot of damage to the distractor vs. ungrammatical MCC and the baseline-plus-distractor vs. ungrammatical MCC. Another correlation score, called the point-biserial correlation, which can be computed directly on continuous data, does not require an arbitrary threshold and produces very different values on this one example.

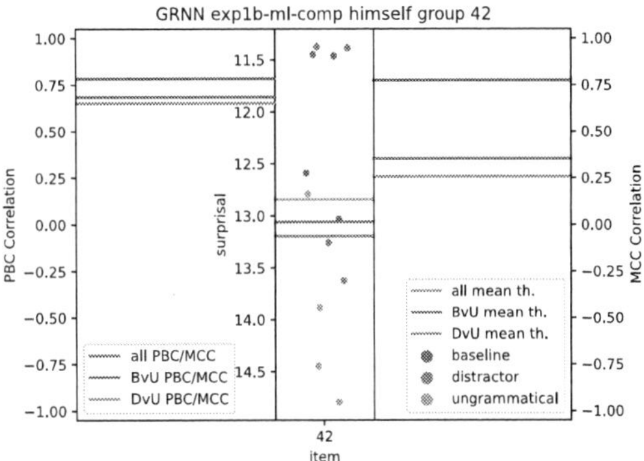

Figure 2: Surprisals (negative log probabilities), Matthews correlations and point-biserial correlations for set 42 in Hu et al.'s (2020) experiment 1b for the GRNN model with the pronoun, *himself.*

4 Aggregated Point Biserial Correlations

Our proposed alternative involves two changes. First, we propose using a point biserial correlation between the output probability of a language model and binary grammaticality judgements. Second, we propose calculating PBCs not on a set-by-set basis, but for all probabilities generated by a fixed model using all of the contexts of a fixed experiment.

To consider Figure 1 again, the model on the left has a PBC of 0.25, whereas the model on the right has one of 0.73. Correlations such as the PBC range between -1 and 1, where 1 is perfect correlation, 0 is no correlation, and -1 is perfect anti-correlation.

Our choice of PBC is perhaps the less controversial of these two changes, as our motivation for doing so is mainly due to the fact that it is *the* standard measure for correlating a continuous or interval random variable with a discrete random variable.

Our decision to "aggregate" data by ignoring the boundaries between the controlled, minimal sets that have become so widely accepted as a part of targeted syntactic evaluations is perhaps counterintuitive. But as long as the necessary distractors, permutations and lexical alternations that avoid bias appear somewhere in the context of the experiment, they will be compared to each other, although along with additional comparisons that were not made when accuracy was averaged over sets. Those additional comparisons, however, will merely corroborate the model's (in)ability to more robustly distinguish between well-formed and non-well-formed strings, and the experiment itself does restrict the variability of those comparisons to a great extent.

In our experience, aggregating makes the evaluation more resilient to choices of normalizers such as SLOR (Pauls and Klein, 2012), its results are in closer accord to our intuitive judgements, and, as expected, it handles sample bias better. Both accuracy (30–100%) and aggregate PBC (-0.01–0.81) vary widely from experiment to experiment in Hu et al.'s (2020) data, and yet the average of per-set PBCs tends to be less dispersed. The experiments in Figure 1, for example, have microaveraged PBCs of 0.77 (left) and 0.89 (right). It could therefore be argued that the effect size of the dependent variable that Hu et al. (2020) were attempting to measure is not as large as the choice of minimal set. Aggregation would then also be an effective means of utilizing the available range of correlation values.

Total (weighted) accuracy and baseline-plus-distractor vs. ungrammatical PBC have a Spearman's correlation of 0.876 ($p = 8.5 \times 10^{-25}$) across Hu et al.'s (2020) experiments and models.

5 Task-Independent Grammaticality Classification

The famous "Colorless green ideas sleep furiously" (CGISF) example (Chomsky, 1957) posited a seemingly irreconcilable divide between formal linguistics and statistical language modelling, arguing that every sequence of words not attested in the collective memory of a language's use would be considered equally "remote" by a putative instance of the latter, regardless of whether the sequence was grammatical (CGISF) or ungrammatical. The example was presented briefly and informally in order to reject statistical language modelling as an alternative approach to the one advocated and developed in greater detail by Chomsky (1957). It was only presented with one other example, the reverse of the sentence, i.e., "Furiously sleep ideas green colorless", in order to draw a contrast between two nonsensical sequences, only one of which (CGISF) is grammatical.

Pereira (2000) provides an attempt at a refutation by constructing a statistical language model based upon an agglomerative Markov process (Saul and Pereira, 1997), and then observing that CGISF is assigned a probability by the model which is roughly 200 000 times greater than the probability assigned to its reversal.

There has nevertheless been some scepticism expressed about the ensuing euphoria among computer scientists — mainly by linguists. Sprouse et al. (2015) notes that the trigram model from Lau et al. (2015) assigns different rankings to 10 different permutations of CGISF, depending on the training corpus (e.g., the *Wall Street Journal* corpus versus an example training corpus taken from Lau et al. (2015)). Can the scores assigned to these sequences be reliably construed as a regression scale of grammaticality (or perhaps acceptability), if they are so fickle? Chowdhury and Zamparelli (2018) also express concern about the ability of neural language models to generalize to more abstract grammatical phenomena than subject-verb agreement.

What we will present in this section is a more thorough appraisal of how well statistical language models perform as instruments of grammaticality testing overall, using PBCs. Previous research on grammaticality/acceptability and language models has mainly designed experiments using naturally occurring English sentences, and modifies those sentences based on various individual linguistic phenomena to manually introduce a specific source of ungrammaticality into the sentences. Notable exceptions include CoLA as well as the Linguistic Inquiry (LI) corpus of grammatical and ungrammatical sentences collected by Sprouse et al. (2013) and Sprouse and Almeida (2012), and used in Sprouse et al. (2018). Both are based upon examples found in linguistics publications. Lau et al. (2014, 2015, 2017) create ungrammatical sentences by round-trip translating natural English sentences. We will use both CoLA and the LI corpus.

5.1 CoLA

The Corpus of Linguistic Acceptability (CoLA) (Warstadt et al., 2019) is a collection of 10 657 example sentences from linguistics publications with their grammaticality judgements. It forms an integral part of the General Language Understanding Evaluation (GLUE) benchmark (Wang et al., 2018). It must be noted, however, that their linguistic acceptability task is supervised (CoLA was divided into a training set (8551), a development set (1043), and a test set (1063)), with both positive and negative samples. The ungrammatical strings in CoLA have generally been devised to illustrate a specific grammatical defect, and are often but not always sensical. Recent systems trained on these labelled data, e.g., Liu et al. (2019); Lan et al. (2020); Raffel et al. (2019), are able to attain a reported roughly 70% Matthews correlation coefficient (Matthews, 1975).

The performance of Mikolov's (2012) model, in particular, has been reported in CoLA studies as a baseline (Warstadt et al., 2019; Lau et al., 2017). Warstadt et al. (2019) did a 10-fold cross-validation on CoLA test set, which fit an optimum decision threshold to the softmax output of each fold to assign grammaticality labels, and obtained a 0.652 in-domain accuracy and 0.711 out-of-domain accuracy. This figure has been cited as a gauge for assessing the ability of statistical language models to learn grammar-related patterns in an unsupervised fashion (Lappin and Lau, 2018).

CoLA also did not include any annotations of minimal set structures, but we retained a linguist who is a native speaker of North American English to go over the first 2010 sentences in the CoLA corpus and group them into 1803 microgroups (including singletons) fashioned around the same linguistic phenomena of interest, and often very similar lexical entries. This enabled us to use CoLA as a platform to test language model performance in somewhat controlled microgroups of example sentences, although they are not as well controlled as the minimal sets of targeted evaluations. Then we ran point-biserial correlation tests within those microgroups with at least one grammatical judgement and at least one ungrammatical judgement, and calculated the median of those correlation scores. Then we split the scores into four quadrants. Below, we report the junction points of those quadrants: lower breakpoint, median, and upper breakpoint.

5.2 The LI Corpus

The LI corpus was collected by Sprouse and Almeida (2012), and contains 300 sentence structures, each expanded into 8 candidate sentences (2400 strings in total, 1192 of them grammatical). The corpus annotation shows that there are 57 pairs of sentence structures (912 strings in total) that are syntactically designed to differ on one linguistic phenomenon but have putatively opposite grammaticality. We ran the PBC test for each of the 57 pairs, and calculated the medians among the correlation scores. Sprouse and Almeida (2012) also collected 230 sentences structures from Adger's (2003) textbook. However that corpus does not include annotation indicating the minimal set struc-

ture, and therefore was ignored in this study.

5.3 Language Models

We investigated four different types of language models: Pereira's (2000) original aggregative Markov model (Saul and Pereira, 1997), Mikolov's (2012) original RNN language model (Mikolov, 2012), a QRNN-based language model (Merity et al., 2018) that we take to be representative of contemporary models, and GPT-2 (Radford et al., 2019) as the representative of large-scale pre-trained language models. Mikolov's model is also used by Clark et al. (2013); Lau et al. (2015); Sprouse et al. (2018) in their research about gradient acceptability. We chose GPT-2 over other large-scale pre-trained models such as BERT (Devlin et al., 2019) and XLNet (Yang et al., 2019), because it took the more orthodox autoregressive language modelling approach that is consistent with the remaining choices, and it is most commonly used for natural language generation for the same reason.

We obtained a publicly available implementation of each of the four language models[2]. The implementation of the tied adaptive softmax (TAS) method[3] used the unusual approach of applying softmax on already softmaxed values. For this reason, we also experiment on QRNN models trained using regular cross-entropy loss functions.

All three non-pretrained models are trained on the BNC (BNC Consortium, 2007) and WikiText-103 (WT103) (Merity et al., 2017). We used the hyperparameters described in (Pereira, 2000) to train its model, the hyperparameters described in (Lau et al., 2017; Sprouse et al., 2018) to train Mikolov's, and the hyperparameters suggested by the official SalesForce implementation of the QRNN model. The BNC corpus is tokenized based on BNC annotations, and all tokens are converted into lower case. For WT103, we used the official preprocessed corpus released on SalesForce's website[4] that has tokenization, converts low frequency words to *unk* and preserves letter case. Radford et al. (2019) re-

---

[2]For Pereira's model, we adapted the implementation of https://github.com/hsgodhia/agm_language_model; for Mikolov's model, we used the implementation of https://github.com/yandex/faster-rnnlm that is also used by Lau et al. (2017) and Sprouse et al. (2018); and for GPT-2, we used the HuggingFace's Transformers package (Wolf et al., 2020).

[3]https://github.com/salesforce/awd-lstm-lm

[4]https://blog.einstein.ai/the-wikitext-long-term-dependency-language-modeling-dataset/

Model	BNC	WT103
Pereira	362.19	460.62
Mikolov	332.04	185.82
QRNN (regular)	173.57	96.65
QRNN (TAS)	92.85	34.98
GPT-2[5]	45.61	28.34
GPT-2 XL[5]	24.92	16.28

Table 1: Perplexity achieved on test sets

leased GPT-2 models in four different parameter sizes: GPT2 (small), GPT2-medium, GPT2-large and GPT2-xl (extra large). To avoid redundancy, we experimented with GPT2, which has a similar number of parameters as the other neural language models, and GPT2-xl, which represents the maximum potential of the GPT-2 architecture. Better performance would likely be achieved through more extensive hyperparameter optimization, but our results in Table 1 are already comparable to the performance reported in the respective original publications.

5.4 Experimental Design

Our experiments consider two types of probabilities: the log probability $\ell = \log p(s)$, and the actual probability, e^ℓ, where s is a sentence. For each type of probability, we also consider two to three different types of normalization methods: no normalization (raw), normalization by length (norm) $\ell/|s|$, and SLOR (Pauls and Klein, 2012) $(\ell - \ell_u)/|s|$, where $|s|$ is the length of the sentence and ℓ_u is the log unigram probability of the sentence. For all three non-pretrained models, the unigram probability was obtained from BNC/WT103 with add-one smoothing. We used WT103 unigram probabilities for GPT-2 models since they preserve case.

5.5 Letter Case

It is a paradigm that linguists often consider semantics and pragmatics when trying to generate non-syntactic factors that attribute to language model probabilities. We also considered letter case in order to demonstrate that a more superficial fact about the writing system may affect the evaluation result. Pereira's (2000) model downcased all input tokens to speed up the training process, thus it was discarded for this experiment. We took the rest of the models that are trained on WT103 and GPT-2 models and provided them with downcased CoLA example sentences.

---

[5]GPT-2 models are evaluated on the same preprocessed BNC and WT103 test sets without any fine-tuning for the sake of consistency.

Model	Norm.	BNC		WT103	
		LOG	EXP	LOG	EXP
Pereira	Raw	0.0239	0.0139	0.0226	-0.0137
	Norm	0.0494	0.0206	0.043	-0.0012
	SLOR	0.0756	-0.0153	0.0684	0.0083
Mikolov	Raw	0.0578	0.0223	0.0574	0.0086
	Norm	0.1061	0.1161	0.106	0.1146
	SLOR	0.1896	0.1529	0.1045	0.0359
QRNN regular	Raw	0.0029	-0.0153	0.0121	-0.0093
	Norm	0.0191	0.0328	0.0124	0.0224
	SLOR	0.0496	0.0346	0.0297	0.0134
QRNN TAS	Raw	0.0067	-0.0137	0.0162	0.0047
	Norm	0.0029	-0.0153	0.0278	0.0421
	SLOR	0.0542	0.0356	0.0332	0.0112
		GPT-2		GPT-2 XL	
GPT-2 Models	Raw	0.1839	0.0117	0.1476	0.0123
	Norm	0.2498	0.1643	0.2241	0.1592
	SLOR	0.2489	0.092	0.2729	0.0872

Table 2: CoLA Point-biserial Test Results

Model	Norm.	BNC		WT103	
		LOG	EXP	LOG	EXP
Pereira	Raw	0.0231	-0.0136	-0.0027	-0.0488
	Norm	0.0758	0.0595	0.038	0.0412
Mikolov	Raw	0.0841	0.1868	0.1278	0.1914
	Norm	0.2541	0.2465	0.1955	0.2043
QRNN TAS	Raw	-0.0066	-0.2197	0.0201	0.0186
	Norm	0.068	0.0726	0.1058	0.0764
QRNN regular	Raw	-0.0135	-0.059	0.0232	0.1251
	Norm	0.042	0.0245	0.1057	0.104
		GPT-2		GPT-2 XL	
GPT-2 Models	Raw	0.4671	0.26	0.4767	0.266
	Norm	0.5233	0.487	0.5653	0.5131

Table 3: Sprouse LI Minimal Sets Results

5.6 "Sensicality"

Can we find anything that matches language model outputs better than a grammaticality judgement? Inspired by the debate over "Colorless green ideas sleep furiously" sixty years ago, we formed the hypothesis that grammatical sentences that make sense could more easily be distinguished from grammatical sentences that are nonsense. We formulated 27 nonsense sentences (including CGISF), projected their parts of speech into the BNC and found 36 exact POS matches that do not overlap with a clause or sentence boundary. The "sensicality" task is to distinguish these two sets using language model log-probabilities.

6 Experiment Results

CoLA Point-Biserial Correlation Test Table 2 shows our PBC test results. As mentioned before, every non-GPT-2-based model is trained on either BNC or WT103, and for the sake of simplicity, we report two sizes of GPT-2: small and XL.

All models show weak to no correlation. However the correlation generated by GPT-2 models does show significantly greater promise.

LI Minimal Sets Table 3 shows the language models' performance on the LI minimal scts.

Model	Norm.	Score	all group sizes ($\geq$ 2)			group size $>$ 4		
			median	up bkpt.	low bkpt.	median	up bkpt.	low bkpt.
Pereira BNC	raw	log	0.2148	0.8119	-0.4193	0.1409	0.4161	-0.0908
	raw	exp	0.3233	0.641	-0.4616	0.2501	0.3598	-0.2048
	Norm	log	0.3787	0.9026	-0.309	0.1865	0.4706	-0.1122
	Norm	exp	0.3573	0.867	-0.3238	0.2753	0.4537	-0.1087
Pereira WT103	raw	log	0.2383	0.8278	-0.3901	0.159	0.4084	-0.1335
	raw	exp	0.3254	0.6642	-0.4874	0.2244	0.3466	-0.1778
	Norm	log	0.3601	0.8849	-0.2933	0.2381	0.4849	-0.1449
	Norm	exp	0.3599	0.9023	-0.299	0.2108	0.4438	-0.0941
Mikolov BNC	raw	log	0.3838	0.8383	-0.294	0.2462	0.5453	-0.1127
	raw	exp	0.3834	0.8092	-0.3073	0.262	0.4274	-0.1617
	Norm	log	0.291	0.8411	-0.4262	0.2159	0.4823	-0.2066
	Norm	exp	0.3314	0.6903	-0.5	0.2382	0.4086	-0.0918
Mikolov WT103	raw	log	0.3651	0.8506	-0.3714	0.2701	0.4835	-0.0786
	raw	exp	0.3516	0.7988	-0.4765	0.2577	0.4199	-0.1876
	Norm	log	0.4986	0.9303	-0.1553	0.2996	0.5332	-0.0953
	Norm	exp	0.4918	0.9363	-0.1417	0.3012	0.5495	-0.0538
QRNN regular BNC	raw	log	0.0567	0.6549	-0.5812	0.0602	0.3224	-0.2602
	raw	exp	0.2	0.5	-0.5633	0.1961	0.3085	-0.2605
	Norm	log	0.0418	0.682	-0.4762	-0.0436	0.3349	-0.3539
	Norm	exp	0.0308	0.6565	-0.5317	-0.0275	0.3296	-0.3205
QRNN regular WT	raw	log	0.0249	0.6086	-0.6074	0.0534	0.4419	-0.2144
	raw	exp	0.2112	0.51	-0.5337	0.2483	0.3728	-0.1608
	Norm	log	0.0507	0.8203	-0.5342	0.0291	0.3456	-0.3227
	Norm	exp	0.084	0.8547	-0.5374	0.0428	0.3743	-0.2727
QRNN TAS BNC	raw	log	0.0456	0.5834	-0.6022	0.1171	0.4084	-0.2532
	raw	exp	0.1487	0.5	-0.5595	0.2003	0.3268	-0.2474
	Norm	log	0.0919	0.6522	-0.5106	-0.0073	0.3629	-0.3003
	Norm	exp	0.1248	0.6203	-0.5312	0.0379	0.3507	-0.3004
QRNN TAS WT103	raw	log	0.1144	0.7072	-0.622	0.1187	0.4071	-0.1658
	raw	exp	0.2524	0.5003	-0.5773	0.2212	0.3173	-0.2568
	Norm	log	0.2061	0.8411	-0.4252	0.0698	0.3924	-0.2324
	Norm	exp	0.2226	0.8138	-0.4726	0.1536	0.3975	-0.1804
GPT-2	raw	log	0.6256	0.9491	0.1424	0.4128	0.6692	0.1424
	raw	exp	0.4902	0.9999	0.2	0.2823	0.4417	0.1794
	Norm	log	0.7121	0.9914	0.0528	0.2948	0.6688	0.0259
	Norm	exp	0.6597	0.9968	0.1522	0.3294	0.6212	0.1105
GPT-2 XL	raw	log	0.6936	0.9865	0.2862	0.4503	0.7155	0.1953
	raw	exp	0.5	1.0	0.2642	0.2956	0.4714	0.2117
	Norm	log	0.6858	0.9983	0.2411	0.4537	0.6561	0.1803
	Norm	exp	0.6516	0.9987	0.2939	0.4312	0.5988	0.2477

Table 4: CoLA Microgrouping Results

Model	Norm.	LOG		EXP	
		with case	lower	with case	lower
Mikolov	Raw	0.0578	0.0574	0.0223	0.0206
	Norm	0.1061	0.0955	0.1161	0.1012
QRNN regular	Raw	0.0029	0.0086	-0.0153	-0.0186
	Norm	0.0191	0.0135	0.0328	0.0149
QRNN TAS	Raw	0.0067	0.0148	-0.0137	-0.0133
	Norm	0.0309	0.0357	0.0301	0.0146
GPT-2	Raw	0.1476	0.1129	0.0123	0.0125
	Norm	0.2241	0.1968	0.1592	0.1403
GPT-2 XL	Raw	0.1839	0.1484	0.0117	0.0149
	Norm	0.2498	0.2057	0.1643	0.1372

Table 5: Letter Case Study Results

Again, the GPT-2 models stand out, but in this case, GPT2-xl performs consistently better.

CoLA Microgroups Table 4 shows the microgrouping results. The results could be interpreted as confirming our hypothesis: that better controlled input would improve a language model's ability to focus on distinguishing grammaticality. On the other hand, it is also likely that the very small size of most microgroups is a factor, because there is a dramatic correlation drop when we evaluate on microgroups with size greater than 4. Roughly 77% of the non-singleton microgroups in CoLA are of size 2-4.

Letter Case Table 5 shows the letter case study's result. GPT-2 is once again the best, but it also suffers the most from the loss of case. The loss is

Model	Norm.	BNC	WT	GPT-2
Pereira	raw	0.8235	0.7652	
	SLOR	0.1838	0.1927	
Mikolov	raw	0.827	0.9042	
	SLOR	-0.3161	-0.1556	
QRNN	raw	0.7132	-0.3872	
	SLOR	0.089	-0.8038	
QRNN-R	raw	0.8064	0.5895	
	SLOR	0.6598	-0.7192	
GPT-2	raw			0.7574
	SLOR			0.5486
GPT-2 XL	raw			0.7642
	SLOR			0.5218

Table 6: Sensicality Results

comparable to the loss incurred by scaling the XL model's size (1542M) back to small (117M).

Sensicality The sensicality study reveals much higher PBC scores overall, although SLOR has a markedly detrimental effect overall. While this set of judgements is small, these scores are markedly higher than the PBCs for the microgroupings as well, all but one of which is smaller.

7 Discussion

In this paper, we examined the motivation and effects of using accuracy scores vs. PBC in syntactically targeted models. We also used PBC to evaluate a range of language models on curated datasets. While the results are not terribly strong, GPT-2's showing in particular suggests that a great deal of progress has been made recently.

It is nevertheless still premature to claim that the probabilities assigned by language models to sequences of words can be reliably construed as a regression scale of grammaticality. Such a claim would need to be supported by a stronger performance in more diverse settings that are larger than minimal-set or microgrouping structures, ideally with better robustness to other factors such as type case. The sensicality study suggests that language models are still overwhelmingly influenced by semantic factors. This is unsurprising: language models have been used for years as a proxy for semantics in numerous other areas such as parsing.

The best grammaticality classifiers to date are still classifiers that are constructed for the purpose of predicting grammaticality, not for the classical purpose of a language model, which is to predict the next word of input. These either use a language model output probability as their own input (Warstadt et al., 2019) or use other artefacts of the language model, such as word vectors, and discard the language model probability altogether (Liu et al., 2019).

Acknowledgments

We would like to thank Zoe McKenzie for her grammaticality judgements.

References

David Adger. 2003. *Core Syntax: A Minimalist Approach*, volume 20.

BNC Consortium. 2007. The British National Corpus, version 3 (BNC XML Edition). *Distributed by Oxford University Computing Services on behalf of the BNC Consortium.*

Noam Chomsky. 1957. *Syntactic structures*. Mouton publishers.

Shammur Absar Chowdhury and Roberto Zamparelli. 2018. RNN Simulations of Grammaticality Judgments on Long-distance Dependencies. In *Proceedings of the 27th International Conference on Computational Linguistics*, pages 133–144, Santa Fe, New Mexico, USA. Association for Computational Linguistics.

Radoslaw M. Cichy and Daniel Kaiser. 2019. Deep Neural Networks as Scientific Models. *Trends in Cognitive Sciences*, 23(4):305–317.

Alexander Clark, Gianluca Giorgolo, and Shalom Lappin. 2013. Statistical Representation of Grammaticality Judgements: The Limits of N-Gram Models. In *Proceedings of the Fourth Annual Workshop on Cognitive Modeling and Computational Linguistics (CMCL)*, pages 28–36, Sofia, Bulgaria. Association for Computational Linguistics.

Jacob Devlin, Ming-Wei Chang, Kenton Lee, and Kristina Toutanova. 2019. BERT: Pre-training of Deep Bidirectional Transformers for Language Understanding. *arXiv:1810.04805 [cs]*.

Jennifer Hu, Sherry Chen, and Roger Levy. 2020. A Closer Look at the Performance of Neural Language Models on Reflexive Anaphor Licensing. *Proceedings of the Society for Computation in Linguistics*, 3(1):382–392.

Zhenzhong Lan, Mingda Chen, Sebastian Goodman, Kevin Gimpel, Piyush Sharma, and Radu Soricut. 2020. ALBERT: A Lite BERT for Self-supervised Learning of Language Representations. In *International Conference on Learning Representations*.

Shalom Lappin and Jey Han Lau. 2018. Gradient Probabilistic Models vs Categorical Grammars: A Reply to Sprouse et al.(2018).

Jey Han Lau, Alexander Clark, and Shalom Lappin. 2014. Measuring Gradience in Speakers' Grammaticality Judgements. *Proceedings of the Annual Meeting of the Cognitive Science Society*, 36:6.

Jey Han Lau, Alexander Clark, and Shalom Lappin. 2015. Unsupervised Prediction of Acceptability Judgements. In *Proceedings of the 53rd Annual Meeting of the Association for Computational Linguistics and the 7th International Joint Conference on Natural Language Processing (Volume 1: Long Papers)*, pages 1618–1628, Beijing, China. Association for Computational Linguistics.

Jey Han Lau, Alexander Clark, and Shalom Lappin. 2017. Grammaticality, acceptability, and probability: A probabilistic view of linguistic knowledge. *Cognitive Science*, 41(5):1202–1241.

Xiaodong Liu, Pengcheng He, Weizhu Chen, and Jianfeng Gao. 2019. Multi-Task Deep Neural Networks for Natural Language Understanding. In *Proceedings of the 57th Annual Meeting of the Association for Computational Linguistics*, pages 4487–4496, Florence, Italy. Association for Computational Linguistics.

Rebecca Marvin and Tal Linzen. 2018. Targeted Syntactic Evaluation of Language Models. In *Proceedings of the 2018 Conference on Empirical Methods in Natural Language Processing*, pages 1192–1202, Brussels, Belgium. Association for Computational Linguistics.

B. W. Matthews. 1975. Comparison of the predicted and observed secondary structure of T4 phage lysozyme. *Biochimica et Biophysica Acta (BBA) - Protein Structure*, 405(2):442–451.

Stephen Merity, Nitish Shirish Keskar, and Richard Socher. 2018. An Analysis of Neural Language Modeling at Multiple Scales. *arXiv:1803.08240 [cs]*.

Stephen Merity, Caiming Xiong, James Bradbury, and Richard Socher. 2017. Pointer Sentinel Mixture Models. In *5th International Conference on Learning Representations, ICLR 2017, Toulon, France, April 24-26, 2017, Conference Track Proceedings*. OpenReview.net.

Tomáš Mikolov. 2012. Statistical language models based on neural networks. *Brno University of Technology dissertation*.

Adam Pauls and Dan Klein. 2012. Large-Scale Syntactic Language Modeling with Treelets. In *Proceedings of the 50th Annual Meeting of the Association for Computational Linguistics (Volume 1: Long Papers)*, pages 959–968, Jeju Island, Korea. Association for Computational Linguistics.

Fernando Pereira. 2000. Formal grammar and information theory: Together again? *Philosophical Transactions of the Royal Society of London. Series A: Mathematical, Physical and Engineering Sciences*, 358(1769):1239–1253.

Alec Radford, Jeff Wu, Rewon Child, David Luan, Dario Amodei, and Ilya Sutskever. 2019. Language Models are Unsupervised Multitask Learners.

Colin Raffel, Noam Shazeer, Adam Roberts, Katherine Lee, Sharan Narang, Michael Matena, Yanqi Zhou, Wei Li, and Peter J. Liu. 2019. Exploring the Limits of Transfer Learning with a Unified Text-to-Text Transformer. *arXiv e-prints*.

Lawrence Saul and Fernando Pereira. 1997. Aggregate and mixed-order Markov models for statistical language processing. In *Second Conference on Empirical Methods in Natural Language Processing*.

Jon Sprouse and Diogo Almeida. 2012. Assessing the reliability of textbook data in syntax: Adger's Core Syntax1. *Journal of Linguistics*, 48(3):609–652.

Jon Sprouse, Sagar Indurkhya, Sandiway Fong, and Robert C. Berwick. 2015. Colorless green ideas do sleep furiously: The necessity of grammar. *The 46th Annual Meeting of North East Linguistic Society (NELS 46)*.

Jon Sprouse, Carson T. Schütze, and Diogo Almeida. 2013. A comparison of informal and formal acceptability judgments using a random sample from Linguistic Inquiry 2001–2010. *Lingua*, 134:219–248.

Jon Sprouse, Beracah Yankama, Sagar Indurkhya, Sandiway Fong, and Robert C. Berwick. 2018. Colorless green ideas do sleep furiously: Gradient acceptability and the nature of the grammar. *The Linguistic Review*, 35(3):575–599.

Alex Wang, Amanpreet Singh, Julian Michael, Felix Hill, Omer Levy, and Samuel Bowman. 2018. GLUE: A Multi-Task Benchmark and Analysis Platform for Natural Language Understanding. In *Proceedings of the 2018 EMNLP Workshop BlackboxNLP: Analyzing and Interpreting Neural Networks for NLP*, pages 353–355, Brussels, Belgium. Association for Computational Linguistics.

Alex Warstadt, Amanpreet Singh, and Samuel R. Bowman. 2019. Neural Network Acceptability Judgments. *arXiv:1805.12471 [cs]*.

Thomas Wolf, Lysandre Debut, Victor Sanh, Julien Chaumond, Clement Delangue, Anthony Moi, Pierric Cistac, Tim Rault, Rémi Louf, Morgan Funtowicz, and Jamie Brew. 2020. HuggingFace's Transformers: State-of-the-art Natural Language Processing. *arXiv:1910.03771 [cs]*.

Zhilin Yang, Zihang Dai, Yiming Yang, Jaime Carbonell, Russ R Salakhutdinov, and Quoc V Le. 2019. XLNet: Generalized Autoregressive Pretraining for Language Understanding. In H. Wallach, H. Larochelle, A. Beygelzimer, F. d\textquotesingle Alché-Buc, E. Fox, and R. Garnett, editors, *Advances in Neural Information Processing Systems 32*, pages 5753–5763. Curran Associates, Inc.

One of these sp⅃OM is not like the other: a reproduction of outlier identification using non-contextual word representations

Jesper Brink Andersen[*]
Aarhus University
jesperbrink@post.au.dk

Mikkel Bak Bertelsen[*]
Aarhus University
mikkelbak@post.au.dk

Mikkel Hørby Schou[*]
Aarhus University
mikkelschou@post.au.dk

Manuel R. Ciosici
Information Sciences Institute
IT University of Copenhagen
manuelc@isi.edu

Ira Assent
Aarhus University
ira@cs.au.dk

Abstract

Word embeddings are an active topic in the NLP research community. State-of-the-art neural models achieve high performance on downstream tasks, albeit at the cost of computationally expensive training. Cost aware solutions require cheaper models that still achieve good performance. We present several reproduction studies of intrinsic evaluation tasks that evaluate non-contextual word representations in multiple languages.

Furthermore, we present 50-8-8, a new data set for the outlier identification task, which avoids limitations of the original data set, such as ambiguous words, infrequent words, and multi-word tokens, while increasing the number of test cases. The data set is expanded to contain semantic and syntactic tests and is multilingual (English, German, and Italian).

We provide an in-depth analysis of word embedding models with a range of hyper-parameters. Our analysis shows the suitability of different models and hyper-parameters for different tasks and the greater difficulty of representing German and Italian languages.

1 Introduction

Unsupervised word embeddings have largely replaced language-specific hand-designed representations of syntax and semantics (Mikolov et al., 2013a; Levy and Goldberg, 2014a; Devlin et al., 2019). Models based on deep neural networks such as the BERT family (Devlin et al., 2019; Liu et al., 2019; Sanh et al., 2019) construct contextualized word vector representations. Showing state-of-the-art results in benchmarks such as GLUE (Wang et al., 2018), they are computationally expensive for both training and inference (Devlin et al., 2019; You et al., 2020) with significant cost for the environment (Strubell et al., 2019). In this paper,

we turn our attention back to the non-contextual, less resource-hungry word representations of the word2vec family (Mikolov et al., 2013a; Levy and Goldberg, 2014a).

We contribute reproduction studies on the quality of the non-contextual word representations using outlier identification (Camacho-Collados and Navigli, 2016) and the classic word analogy task (Mikolov et al., 2013a). Replicability and reproducibility have gained increasing importance in the NLP community: focus on the publication of code and data with papers, special sections in leading journals (Branco et al., 2017), and dedicated shared tasks (Branco et al., 2020). Unfortunately, there exist opposing definitions of the terms *reproduction* and *replication* (e.g., Branco et al. (2017) and Chris (2009)), while others propose a spectrum of reproducibility (Peng, 2011). While we aim to reproduce the experiments in our target papers closely, we go beyond a straight-forward reproduction and address further questions such as effect of hyper-parameters, linear contexts (CBOW vs. skip-gram), and non-linear dependency-based contexts (word2vecf).

We also propose 50-8-8, an alternative to the 8-8-8 outlier identification data set (Camacho-Collados and Navigli, 2016) that is several times larger, includes both semantic and syntactic evaluations, and addresses result variance issues that affect the original 8-8-8 data set. Finally, our 50-8-8 data set is multilingual, covering English (EN), German (DE), and Italian (IT). The three languages are challenging for word representations due to their large vocabulary, heavy reliance on word compounding (DE), and complex grammar and sentence structure (DE and IT).

In our paper, we contribute:

- **Reproduction studies** of outlier identification and word analogy (Camacho-Collados

---

[*] Equal contribution

120

Proceedings of the First Workshop on Evaluation and Comparison of NLP Systems (Eval4NLP), pages 120–130,
November 20, 2020. ©2020 Association for Computational Linguistics

and Navigli, 2016; Köper et al., 2015; Berardi et al., 2015; Mikolov et al., 2013a) through which we find that most evaluations are reproducible, albeit some, namely outlier identification, only after taking variance into account.

- **50-8-8**, an improved outlier identification data set that addresses issues with the 8-8-8 data set used in the original outlier identification paper. 50-8-8 is multiple times larger than 8-8-8, multilingual (English, German, and Italian), excludes polysemous and rare words, and contains both semantic and syntactic tests.

- **Comparative study** and analysis of CBOW, skip-gram, word2vecf, and word2vecf without relation-suffixes, on multiple corpora and languages (English, German, and Italian), for multiple hyper-parameters, on outlier identification and analogy reasoning tasks (both semantic and syntactic). All results are based upon multiple instances of the models and quantify variation in results.

2 Related Work

Contextualized neural word embeddings (Devlin et al., 2019; Liu et al., 2019) show impressive performance in downstream NLP tasks, at the cost of training time; pre-training of the base version of BERT took four days using 16 TPU chips (Devlin et al., 2019). Efforts to reduce the training time still require significant computing power on dedicated hardware (You et al., 2020), with high environmental cost (Strubell et al., 2019). Some reduction of memory usage (Sanh et al., 2019) or of training time and memory usage (Lan et al., 2020) still does not eliminate the high resource consumption. As such, less computationally expensive models, such as word2vec (Mikolov et al., 2013a), word2vecf (Levy and Goldberg, 2014a), FastText (Bojanowski et al., 2017), and GloVe (Pennington et al., 2014), are attractive when showing good performance on NLP tasks.

Computationally cheaper models, like word2vec, have some of the same evaluation drawbacks as their more complicated and expensive counterparts: there is no generally agreed upon evaluation. Ghannay et al. (2016) compare word2vec and word2vecf on attributional similarity, extended by Li et al. (2017) for combinations of context representations and context types for CBOW, skip-gram, and GloVe. But, Faruqui et al. (2016) and

Batchkarov et al. (2016) note that attributional similarity is subjective, lacks statistical significance, and has a low correlation with extrinsic evaluation, making it inconsistent and not necessarily indicative of model properties. However, Schnabel et al. (2015) argue that different extrinsic evaluation tasks prefer different embeddings, suggesting that extrinsic tasks might not be indicators of general embedding quality either.

The outlier identification task (Camacho-Collados and Navigli, 2016) avoids subjective similarity measurements. Instead, it employs relative word vector similarity to identify an outlier from a group of otherwise semantically related words. Blair et al. (2017) expanded the outlier identification data set algorithmically based on Wikidata. However, the automatic approach has several limitations, including ambiguous, infrequent, or duplicate words in the same category, and word variants in the same category, likely due to hierarchy inconsistencies in Wikidata (Brasileiro et al., 2016). In this paper, we return to manually curated data sets with controlled quality and difficulty.

In light of recent revelations into the instability of word2vec (Antoniak and Mimno, 2018), we reproduce several word vector evaluations. We find that the original 8-8-8 data set used in the outlier identification evaluation leads to high results variance. We address this issue by proposing an expanded evaluation data set we call 50-8-8. Both the original outlier identification (Camacho-Collados and Navigli, 2016) and word similarity publications (Ghannay et al., 2016; Li et al., 2017) do not fully explore the effects of hyper-parameters and randomness. We systematically evaluate models and hyper-parameters on ten training runs and measure average performance and variance.

Finally, most evaluations of word2vec embeddings focus on English, with notable exceptions (Köper et al., 2015; Berardi et al., 2015; Svoboda and Brychcín, 2018; Venekoski and Vankka, 2017; Rodrigues et al., 2016; Chen et al., 2015; Grave et al., 2018). However, these are translations of word similarity tasks and share the weaknesses of their English language counterparts. We reproduce the evaluation of core word analogy evaluations of Köper et al. (2015) and Berardi et al. (2015) and expand them by comparing word2vec to its dependency-based counterpart, word2vecf. We use the word analogy task from Mikolov et al. (2013a) to give a reference point for model performance and ease comparison with other research, even though the pitfalls from the similarity tasks also apply to this task (Faruqui et al., 2016; Batchkarov et al., 2016). To supplement the evaluations on non-English languages, we manually translate our new 50-8-8 data set into German and Italian and thus provide a multilingual outlier identification data set and evaluation.

3 Tasks

In this section, we introduce the intrinsic tasks and data sets we use for evaluation. Furthermore, we summarize previous data sets' limitations and introduce a new data set for the outlier identification task.

3.1 Outlier identification

Evaluations of word similarity rely on a similarity score of words. Therefore it is difficult (if not impossible) to obtain a gold standard as people cannot agree on similarity scores between words (e.g., Which is more like a *cat*? a *tiger* or a *lion*?). On the other hand, outlier identification aims to identify an outlier in a set of similar words. The outlier is the word with the lowest average cosine similarity to the rest of the set. This formulation makes constructing a gold standard more straightforward as the attribution of specific similarity scores is avoided (Camacho-Collados and Navigli, 2016). Even though word embeddings cannot answer questions involving subtle similarity, they can represent outliers as sufficiently distinctive from a group of words that share some similarities (the inliers).

3.1.1 Measures for outlier identification

We use two performance measures to evaluate, **Accuracy** (Acc) and **Outlier Position Percentage** (OPP). Accuracy is the ratio of correctly identified outliers to the total number of test cases and provides a strict, narrow-focused measure of performance. OPP indicates how close the outliers are to being correctly classified. OPP is defined as:

$$OPP = \frac{\sum\limits_{W \in D} \frac{OP(W)}{|W|-1}}{|D|} \cdot 100$$

W is a word set (8 inliers and one outlier), and D is a data set consisting of $|D|$ such sets of words. Outlier Position (OP) is the outlier position in the list of words ordered by the average cosine similarity to the other words in the set. The positions

range from 0 to $|W| - 1$, where an OP equal to $|W| - 1$ indicates a correct classification of the outlier, and a lower OP indicates the computed position of the outlier in the sorted list. The lower the OP, the worse the system does at identifying the outlier. While accuracy takes a black-and-white approach to measuring performance, OPP accounts for differences in the words' rankings.

For our experiments, we modify the original evaluation script of Camacho-Collados and Navigli to address a bug. In the script, vectors are set to the zero vector for Out-Of-Vocabulary (OOV) words, resulting in an undeserved successful outlier identification. In our experiments, we instead mark such test cases as unsuccessful. Accordingly, OOV words decrease performance scores instead of increasing it. We describe the error and our fix in Appendix A and share our fixed script with our 50-8-8 data set[4].

3.1.2 Data sets for outlier identification

Camacho-Collados and Navigli (2016) provide a manually curated **8-8-8 data set** with their task; namely, 8 test groups of 8 semantically related inliers and 8 alternatives for non-related outliers, resulting in 64 test cases. The data set, however, has some limitations. First of all, its low number of test cases results in a significant change in accuracy for each misclassification. The low number also results in limited coverage of concepts in a vector space, which may not represent the semantic information encoded. Secondly, it contains ambiguous words. For example, *Smart* (used in the *German car manufacturers* test group) can denote both the car manufacturer and an unrelated adjective. Because the adjective might be more common in a corpus, it will have a higher influence on the resulting vector and might lead to its corresponding word being classified as an outlier. We claim that selecting the word "Smart" as an outlier when the adjective is prevalent is, in fact, the correct behavior. However, since this goes against the intention of the data set design (and the ground-truth labels), we consider such ambiguous words a drawback. Thirdly, multi-token words are handled by taking the average vector of all constituting tokens, which is problematic. The concept denoted by a multi-token word does not necessarily have connections to the meaning (i.e., vector) of the tokens that comprise it.[1] Finally, some words in the data set have a

---

[1]Mercedes Benz comprises two proper names. Mercedes

very low frequency in the corpora used for training in the original paper.[2] Low-frequency terms tend to have unstable word vectors, which can lead to high variance in evaluation using the 8-8-8 data set.

WikiSem500 (Blair et al., 2017) is an automatically generated extension of 8-8-8. By treating Wikidata as a graph such that semantic word similarities are distances in the graph, the authors of WikiSem500 automatically construct 500 test groups and $2\,816$ test cases. However, WikiSem500 has severe limitations. First of all, many inlier sets have a vague semantic connection that makes outliers difficult to identify (even for humans), which may be caused by Wikidata not always following structural rules from multi-level model theory (Brasileiro et al., 2016). WikiData's crowd-sourced nature causes many hierarchies spanning more than one classification level to follow known anti-patterns such as items that are simultaneously instances and subclasses other items; items that are subclasses of several items, with one of the superclasses an instance of the other, and lastly, items representing instances of several items, with one of those also an instance of the other (Brasileiro et al., 2016). Such inconsistencies in the graph are reflected in some of the test groups in WikiSem500. Take, for example, test group Q197, which consists of instances of airplanes. The inliers include various specific combat aircraft models (e.g., *B-29_Superfortress* and *F/A-18_Hornet*) and also the terms *glider* and *fighter_aircraft*, which should be subclasses rather than instances of airplanes and should therefore not be inliers. At the same time, *Mitsubishi F-1* (a Japanese combat aircraft) is an outlier, although it should be an instance of an airplane, and therefore an inlier.

Other problems include: ambiguous words, the same outliers appear several times in the same test group (thus overly impacting evaluation results), the same words with different spellings in the same test group, infrequent words, and inconsistency between using the same words or new ones in the same test group for different languages[3].

To overcome the above issues with 8-8-8 and

WikiSem500, we propose **50-8-8**[4], a manually curated data set comprising two sections: **25-8-8-Sem** and **25-8-8-Syn**. We select unambiguous single-token[5] words with a minimum frequency of 350 in each training corpus (details in Section 4.2). We determine word ambiguity using dictionaries and native speakers. Our outliers have different degrees of connectedness to the inliers for different levels of test complexity, i.e., the further down the list of outliers, the weaker the connection to the inliers, and more evidently an outlier.

For example, in the test group *Greek Gods*, the first two outliers are *Cupid* (Roman god of love) and *Odysseus* (Greek legendary king), which could be misclassified by someone with little domain knowledge. The following are *Jesus*, *Sparta*, *Delphi*, and *Rome*, all of which have only a weak connection to the inliers. The last two outliers are *wrath* and *Atlanta*, with no connection to the inliers. **25-8-8-Sem** contains 25 test groups, each comprising eight inliers and eight alternatives for outliers, resulting in 200 unique test cases, a more than 3-fold increase in size over the original 8-8-8 data set.

Please note that in preliminary experiments, we found that random selection of outliers produces trivial test cases, with all models scoring above 97.05 in accuracy and 99.15 in OPP.

The second part of our *50-8-8* data set, the syntactic **25-8-8-Syn** data set consists of 25 syntactic test groups, as defined by part-of-speech tags (PoS). We choose words with a unique PoS tag in dictionaries to avoid syntactic ambiguity[6]. Furthermore, we ensure that the words in each test case share no semantic connection, such that evaluation can focus exclusively on distinction by syntactic role.

The two distinct subsets of **50-8-8** improve the outlier identification task by allowing for evaluations that target semantics and syntax, the two core aspects that word vectors encode.

In addition to English, we also look at **German** (another West Germanic language) and **Italian** (a Romance language), which both employ a more complex grammatical structure than English, and use declension to mark gender and plurality. German also relies heavily on compound words and grammatical cases. We manually translate our 50-

---

is a popular female name in latin-language countries, not related to cars like Mercedes Benz.

[2]E.g. Nestlé, Thaddaeus, and Alpina have a frequency of 17, 24, and 27, respectively, in UMBC.

[3]e.g. Q9143, Q341, Q16970, Q23691, and Q349, respectively.

[4]The 50-8-8 data set is available for download at `https://github.com/JesperBrink/50-8-8`

[5]Except in special cases as explained in Appendix B

[6]There are minor differences in the definition of syntactic ambiguity, as explained in Appendix B

8-8 data set using dictionaries and native speakers. We address translation and language-specific challenges as follows. First of all, words that are unambiguous in one language can be ambiguous in another. We address semantic ambiguity by replacing ambiguous words in any language with words that are unambiguous in all languages, and syntactic ambiguity by replacing the ambiguous word with one belonging to the same PoS tag. Syntactic ambiguity is language-specific, e.g., when translating adverbs to German, as the suffixes *-ly* and *-mente* often distinguish adjectives from adverbs in English and Italian, respectively, but German can use the same lexical form for both[6]. In Italian, many adjectives are also nouns, and many nouns are also conjugations of verbs, which are not as prevalent in German and English. Secondly, when a word translates to two synonymous words, we use the most common, as determined by native speakers.

Furthermore, for nouns in German, we use the nominative case of the nouns to avoid the effects of different grammatical cases. For adjectives in Italian, we use the masculine gender where applicable to avoid the effects of gender. Removing syntactic variation allows the semantic tests to stay focused on semantics. Thus, all the versions of 25-8-8-Sem are identical, all versions of 25-8-8-Syn have an identical distribution of PoS tags within a given test group, and we use consistent and frequent variants of words.

3.2 Word analogy task

Our study's second task is the word analogy task, which measures how well a model captures the relational similarity between pairs of words. A high degree of relational similarity between the pairs means that the words are analogous (Mikolov et al., 2013c; Turney, 2006). It includes questions like *Berlin is to Germany as what is to France?* where the model should return *Paris*. Word analogy also has separation into semantic and syntactic tests. As we note in Section 2, there is heavy criticism of this task(Faruqui et al., 2016). We include it for easy comparison with existing work and to contextualize the outlier identification results.

3.2.1 Data set for word analogy task

We use the analogy data set of Mikolov et al. (2013a) consisting of 19 544 test cases in 14 different categories capturing different relations, nine syntactic and five semantic, resulting in 10 675 syn-

Corpus	Corpus length	Vocab. size
UMBC	3 457 177 447	1 465 802
Wiki EN	2 571 028 591	2 306 628
Wiki DE	896 693 693	2 154 939
Wiki IT	541 134 131	806 992

Table 1: Summary of corpora

tactic and 8 869 semantic test cases. For German, we use a version of the analogy data set, which has a total of 18 552 test cases (the adjective-adverb category is missing as it does not exist in German) (Köper et al., 2015). We use an Italian translation of the analogy data set (Berardi et al., 2015), with 19 791 test cases, with small changes to the data set to keep all words as single token words.

Please note that the word analogy data set is not balanced. Size varies by category, causing some relations to be over-represented, e.g., two of the semantic categories evaluate knowledge about countries and corresponding capitals and represent more than half of the total semantic tests (Gladkova et al., 2016).

4 Models and corpora

This section introduces the word embedding models and the training corpora we use for the evaluation.

4.1 Models

Word2vec consists of two types of models: CBOW (continuous-bag-of-words) and skip-gram (Mikolov et al., 2013a,b). Both models use a linear context, consisting of the n words before and n words after the current word.

Word2vecf (Levy and Goldberg, 2014a) replaces the linear context with one based on words directly connected via the dependency graph of the sentence. Thus, word2vecf eliminates the window size hyper-parameter of word2vec, increases the pool of available context tokens up to the sentence boundaries, and focuses context words selection by eliminating irrelevant words. The example *Australian scientist discovers star with a telescope* from the original paper can help understand the difference in context. For the word *discovers* and a window size of 2, word2vec would consider the words *Australian*, *scientist*, *star*, and *with* to be part of the context. There is nothing inherently Australian about discovering; hence, this word and *with* provide noise to the context of *discovers*. Word2vecf, instead, includes *scientist_nsubj*, *star_obj*, and *telescope_prepwith* into the context. Thus, word2vecf both removes noisy words (*australian*, *with*) and includes relevant terms (*telescope*) into the context.

On the downside, word2vecf requires the corpus to be dependency parsed using a dependency parser, introducing some noise (Chen and Manning, 2014). Word2vecf suffixes the dependency relation to each word in the context, which massively increases vocabulary size up to $|V| \cdot |D|$ where $|V|$ denotes the vocabulary size and $|D|$ denotes the number of relation types supported by the dependency parser. The massive vocabulary increase leads to lower frequency counts and can result in instability in vectors' values. Furthermore, the word vectors are trained on the auxiliary words with the relation as suffix instead of training word vectors directly on each other, and as such, words with dependency relations suffixed act as barriers to information flow between context words and target words.

Word2vecf+ addresses the limitations of word2vecf, more specifically the inclusion of dependency relations as word suffixes; thus, the vocabulary size does not increase. Word2vec+ maintains the vocabulary size fixed by removing the suffix from the word before training, thereby training words directly on each other and discarding the auxiliary words (Li et al., 2017). For example, the word *scientist_nsubj* from above becomes *scientist*. While the original paper calls this method *generalized skip-gram with unbound dependency-based context*, for readability, we refer to it as word2vecf+.

4.2 Training Corpora

We use multiple corpora to derive word vectors for our evaluations (see summary in Table 1). For English, we use the UMBC web-based corpus (Han et al., 2013) and the September 2019 dump of English Wikipedia. The choice of corpora aims to reproduce the experiments in the original outlier identification work (Camacho-Collados and Navigli, 2016). The newer version of Wikipedia is a super-set of the one used in the original experiments. As in the original paper, the use of two English corpora should eliminate questions of corpus-specific results.

For German, we derive vectors from the January 2020 version of Wikipedia; for Italian from the April 2020 version of Wikipedia. The three versions of Wikipedia have widely different sizes. The largest (Wiki EN) is almost five times bigger than the smallest (Wiki IT). However, even the smallest has over 500 million tokens for a vocabulary of less than one million word types (average word type frequency of 670). The smallest corpus (Wiki IT) has a larger average word type frequency (670) than the second smallest, Wiki DE (average word type frequency 416). Such large corpora, combined with repetitions of training and evaluation cycles, provide a good overview of model performance and avoid the of word2vec (Antoniak and Mimno, 2018).

We use WikiExtractor (Attardi, 2018) to extract plain text from the Wikipedia corpora, and tokenize all corpora using Stanford CoreNLP v3.9.2 (Manning et al., 2014). We remove words that appear less than five times using the original word2vec code (Mikolov et al., 2013a) or word2vecf (Levy and Goldberg, 2014a), as appropriate. We dependency parse using the Stanford neural-network dependency parser for models that require dependency relations (word2vecf, word2vecf+) (Chen and Manning, 2014). For dependency parsing Italian, we use the model trained by Palmero Aprosio and Moretti (2016).

5   Experiments

This section presents experimental results, focusing on the reproduction, new data set, window size, different corpora, and languages. In our tables and figures, we denote the different approaches as follows: **CBOW**, **SG** (skip-gram), **W2VF** (word2vecf), **W2VF+** (word2vecf+); each followed by the size of the window used. We include a detailed description of the experimental setup in Appendix C.

5.1   Reproduction results

In Table 2, we compare our reproduction results with those of Camacho-Collados and Navigli (2016). We observe a high variance in accuracy, which illustrates the small 8-8-8 data set's weakness and further underlines the importance of evaluating multiple training runs. We conclude that the original outlier identification results can be reproduced, but with the caveat that accuracy can suffer from large variance. In Section 5.2, we propose 50-8-8, a data set that alleviates this issue.

Table 3 shows the results of reproducing the

Model	Work	UMBC OPP	UMBC Acc	Wiki OPP	Wiki Acc
CBOW 5	Original	93.80	73.40	95.30	73.40
	Our	93.69 ± 0.11	71.88 ± 4.39	94.51 ± 0.09	67.66 ± 1.00
SG 10	Original	92.60	64.10	93.80	70.30
	Our	92.75 ± 0.20	62.81 ± 5.27	94.16 ± 0.05	69.53 ± 1.10
CBOW 2	Our	93.38 ± 0.06	67.97 ± 2.08	94.94 ± 0.04	68.13 ± 1.07
CBOW 10	Our	94.10 ± 0.10	**72.34** ± 2.47	94.41 ± 0.02	68.13 ± 1.07
SG 2	Our	**94.61** ± 0.04	69.53 ± 1.59	**95.41** ± 0.07	71.72 ± 1.68
SG 5	Our	94.16 ± 0.02	69.84 ± 0.51	94.59 ± 0.08	69.69 ± 2.54
W2VF	Our	89.43 ± 0.06	62.50 ± 0.00	92.83 ± 0.20	68.75 ± 0.00
W2VF+	Our	92.46 ± 0.05	66.41 ± 0.61	94.47 ± 0.04	**75.78** ± 1.10

Table 2: Outlier identification reproduction of Camacho-Collados and Navigli (2016) (10 runs, 8-8-8 data set); word2vec with different window sizes, word2vecf and word2vecf+ added for easier comparison with other results.

word analogy task[7,8]. For English, we see the same pattern as (Mikolov et al., 2013a), where skip-gram outperforms CBOW, even though our corpora and hyper-parameters differ. Comparing the German Wikipedia results to those of (Köper et al., 2015), we see a similar pattern in the semantic part, where skip-gram outperforms CBOW. However, in the syntactic part, our results differ. Köper et al. observe that CBOW outperforms skip-gram, whereas we observe the opposite, which could be due to the difference in corpora and hyper-parameters such as vector dimensionality.

Due to the different focus of this paper and that of Berardi et al. (2015), we can only compare skip-gram results with window size 10. We observe a similar semantic performance, but a significant difference in syntactic performance where Berardi et al. observe a score of 32.62 compared to our result of 44.63, which could be the result of the difference in the number of negative samples (we use 15, they use 10) and the different Wikipedia version. However, as they do not cover the CBOW model, it is difficult to get an overview of model performance.

5.2 The effect of the new 50-8-8 data set

The results of outlier identification using our proposed 50-8-8 are in Table 4. As expected, given the more comprehensive tests, on both UMBC and English Wikipedia, we see significantly lower accuracy variance for 25-8-8-Sem than 8-8-8. The only exception is word2vecf, where the accuracy variance grows slightly from 0 on 8-8-8 up to 0.15 on 25-8-8-Sem. Although word2vecf accuracy variance on 8-8-8 is 0, the ten instances do differ in

their answers, as can be observed in the OPP variance in Table 2. Except for a few individual cases, the variance on 25-8-8-Syn is also low. The performance of the best models on 25-8-8-Syn usually matches that on 25-8-8-Sem, suggesting that the two subsets of 50-8-8 are balanced in terms of difficulty. The best performing models on 25-8-8-Syn is CBOW 2 (except for Italian).

5.3 Effect of window size

Table 4 shows that window size has a limited impact on OPP for semantic tests (25-8-8-Sem), but affects the results on syntactic tests (25-8-8-Syn), where skip-gram performs best with low window size across all corpora. For the word analogy task (Table 3), the opposite is true for the semantic evaluation, where larger window sizes have improved performance. These results align with Bansal et al. (2014), who observe that larger window sizes result in more semantic information, while smaller lead to more syntactic.

The same pattern can be observed on syntactic German Wikipedia and syntactic UMBC when taking variance into account. Bansal et al. observe that CBOW and skip-gram with lower window size perform better on syntactic tests, and larger window size performs better on semantic tests. However, our results show that window size performance varies with the task. These two tasks' preferred window sizes indicate that lower window sizes better capture clusters with semantically and syntactically similar words. Larger window sizes are better suited for capturing word relations. These observations also indicate that hyper-parameters can have a big influence on the performance of the models.

5.4 Effect of context type

Table 4 casts a shadow on the superiority of the word2vecf context construction strategy. Word2vecf matches or trails the best word2vec

---

[7]Note that 5% of the questions were skipped by the German models and 10% of the questions were skipped by the Italian models due to OOV words. This was also observed by Berardi et al. (2015).

[8]We use the 3CosAdd method for solving the task, just like (Mikolov et al., 2013a). The alternative 3CosMul improves the analogy results and is discussed in Appendix D.

126

Model	UMBC Sem	UMBC Syn	EN Wiki Sem	EN Wiki Syn	DE Wiki Sem	DE Wiki Syn	IT Wiki Sem	IT Wiki Syn
CBOW 2	10.37 ± 0.03	51.92 ± 0.05	25.34 ± 0.09	43.92 ± 0.03	16.38 ± 0.07	15.28 ± 0.06	4.38 ± 0.02	21.42 ± 0.08
CBOW 5	15.96 ± 0.06	53.01 ± 0.04	35.17 ± 0.17	48.18 ± 0.06	22.36 ± 0.11	17.70 ± 0.07	5.11 ± 0.02	26.06 ± 0.02
CBOW 10	23.36 ± 0.05	54.47 ± 0.06	51.75 ± 0.02	50.95 ± 0.02	27.01 ± 0.11	18.40 ± 0.04	6.57 ± 0.03	28.06 ± 0.07
SG 2	56.29 ± 0.58	68.72 ± 0.07	72.84 ± 0.09	63.74 ± 0.09	53.93 ± 0.10	28.45 ± 0.05	28.06 ± 2.62	42.77 ± 0.11
SG 5	64.59 ± 0.13	$\mathbf{69.51} \pm 0.07$	77.70 ± 0.14	$\mathbf{64.36} \pm 0.04$	66.26 ± 0.29	31.63 ± 0.08	44.01 ± 0.07	$\mathbf{44.98} \pm 0.07$
SG 10	$\mathbf{67.59} \pm 0.56$	69.19 ± 0.80	$\mathbf{78.42} \pm 0.04$	62.36 ± 0.09	$\mathbf{68.15} \pm 0.08$	$\mathbf{32.15} \pm 0.03$	$\mathbf{50.77} \pm 0.17$	44.63 ± 0.12
W2VF	9.39 ± 0.08	54.75 ± 0.16	15.22 ± 0.22	46.05 ± 0.03	6.40 ± 0.02	12.30 ± 0.03	2.3 ± 0.01	21.38 ± 0.01
W2VF+	30.63 ± 0.23	65.82 ± 0.03	51.90 ± 0.35	62.76 ± 0.03	19.41 ± 0.17	24.49 ± 0.06	7.10 ± 0.07	33.41 ± 0.18

Table 3: Word Analogy on all training corpora; model name followed by window size.

Corpus	Model	25-8-8-Sem OPP	25-8-8-Sem Acc	25-8-8-Syn OPP	25-8-8-Syn Acc
UMBC	CBOW 2	95.67 ± 0.01	85.85 ± 0.30	$\mathbf{94.38} \pm 0.02$	73.75 ± 0.06
	CBOW 5	95.67 ± 0.40	85.50 ± 0.35	94.31 ± 0.02	75.85 ± 0.15
	CBOW 10	95.57 ± 0.10	84.75 ± 0.31	93.98 ± 0.04	75.15 ± 0.35
	SG 2	96.83 ± 0.40	87.00 ± 0.40	92.48 ± 0.13	73.35 ± 0.95
	SG 5	96.79 ± 0.01	86.15 ± 0.05	86.90 ± 0.15	62.40 ± 1.29
	SG 10	96.68 ± 0.03	86.40 ± 0.49	82.86 ± 0.24	53.55 ± 2.17
	W2VF	96.09 ± 0.03	84.65 ± 0.15	94.15 ± 0.38	$\mathbf{80.35} \pm 1.95$
	W2VF+	$\mathbf{97.41} \pm 0.01$	$\mathbf{89.45} \pm 0.32$	91.54 ± 0.70	71.55 ± 4.47
Wiki EN	CBOW 2	95.83 ± 0.01	83.60 ± 0.44	$\mathbf{95.53} \pm 0.02$	80.00 ± 0.50
	CBOW 5	96.14 ± 0.02	85.00 ± 0.20	95.26 ± 0.01	$\mathbf{80.30} \pm 0.66$
	CBOW 10	95.74 ± 0.01	83.10 ± 0.09	94.55 ± 0.02	77.05 ± 0.27
	SG 2	$\mathbf{97.68} \pm 0.01$	$\mathbf{88.75} \pm 0.41$	90.09 ± 0.25	67.00 ± 1.65
	SG 5	97.44 ± 0.01	88.50 ± 0.00	86.33 ± 0.69	59.60 ± 1.54
	SG 10	97.05 ± 0.01	87.45 ± 0.07	82.74 ± 1.01	54.00 ± 1.75
	W2VF	94.66 ± 0.03	80.45 ± 0.12	90.63 ± 0.11	70.00 ± 0.75
	W2VF+	97.07 ± 0.00	88.00 ± 0.10	84.29 ± 0.03	54.75 ± 0.41
Wiki DE	CBOW 2	92.41 ± 0.05	74.60 ± 1.34	$\mathbf{93.76} \pm 0.08$	$\mathbf{72.95} \pm 1.97$
	CBOW 5	92.24 ± 0.04	73.40 ± 0.44	92.46 ± 0.03	68.95 ± 1.02
	CBOW 10	92.48 ± 0.03	72.65 ± 0.70	91.65 ± 0.05	65.70 ± 0.51
	SG 2	$\mathbf{93.93} \pm 0.04$	$\mathbf{79.25} \pm 0.16$	89.16 ± 0.03	64.05 ± 1.22
	SG 5	$\mathbf{93.93} \pm 0.01$	78.00 ± 0.70	86.09 ± 0.12	55.40 ± 1.14
	SG 10	93.83 ± 0.03	76.90 ± 0.29	83.41 ± 0.43	51.55 ± 2.02
	W2VF	91.40 ± 0.00	69.60 ± 0.24	90.28 ± 0.02	72.80 ± 0.26
	W2VF+	93.29 ± 0.01	74.55 ± 0.57	78.58 ± 0.14	48.85 ± 0.50
Wiki IT	CBOW 2	94.29 ± 0.06	75.05 ± 0.62	93.41 ± 0.04	75.10 ± 0.84
	CBOW 5	93.88 ± 0.05	73.15 ± 0.40	93.98 ± 0.05	76.55 ± 1.67
	CBOW 10	93.21 ± 0.04	71.55 ± 0.62	93.77 ± 0.04	74.55 ± 2.17
	SG 2	$\mathbf{95.44} \pm 0.06$	$\mathbf{79.15} \pm 0.45$	81.20 ± 0.26	60.75 ± 0.51
	SG 5	95.13 ± 0.02	77.40 ± 0.39	78.69 ± 0.17	56.20 ± 0.91
	SG 10	94.93 ± 0.02	77.40 ± 0.19	75.51 ± 0.09	50.10 ± 0.29
	W2VF	92.48 ± 0.01	70.20 ± 0.06	$\mathbf{95.37} \pm 0.02$	$\mathbf{83.80} \pm 0.56$
	W2VF+	94.39 ± 0.03	75.40 ± 0.84	78.59 ± 2.15	55.10 ± 2.14

Table 4: Outlier identification on 50-8-8 (25-8-8-Sem, 25-8-8-Syn); model name followed by window size.

model on semantic tests on all corpora. However, word2vecf seems better suited to syntactic tests, where it matches or outperforms the best word2vec model on all four corpora.

We observe the same results in the word analogy task (Table 3). Despite the expected improvements in the contexts of word2vecf and word2vecf+, they consistently underperform the word2vec models, sometimes underperforming even the weakest of the word2vec models. This observation is consistent across all data sets on all languages.

5.5 Effect of relation-suffix

The results in Table 4 show that word2vecf+ outperforms word2vecf on semantic outlier identification across all corpora. On the syntactic subset, 25-8-8-Syn, word2vecf consistently outperforms word2vecf+ on all corpora. The consistent difference in performance between word2vecf and word2vecf+ on both the semantic and syntactic tests suggests that word2vecf might be better suited for encoding syntactic information and word2vecf+ might be better suited for encoding semantic information.

We observe a large drop in syntactic OPP and accuracy for both word2vecf and word2vecf+ from UMBC to Wiki EN. The drop may be due to the quality of dependency relations from the Stanford CoreNLP dependency parser, which learned from the Penn Treebank, a corpus of scientific abstracts, news stories, and bulletins (Chen and Manning, 2014; Marcus et al., 1993). Thus, Penn Treebank resembles UMBC more than English Wikipedia, which could explain the performance drop.

On the word analogy task (Table 3), word2vecf+ performs better than word2vecf. On the syntactic tests, word2vecf is comparable to CBOW, but removing the relation suffix (word2vecf+) results in scores closer to skip-gram, which is the best performing model; on the semantic tests, removing the relation suffix results in a 3-fold increase in word2vecf+ performance over word2vecf.

Based on these observations, we conclude that word2vecf+ is better able to capture semantic information as it avoids word2vecf's dramatic, artificial, increase in vocabulary. It allows word vectors to directly influence each other during training resulting in better semantically positioned related words in the embedding space and better capturing both syntactic and semantic similarities in word pairs. In contrast, the relational suffixes improve the clustering of syntactically related words.

5.6 Results across languages

Table 4 shows that the models trained on German and Italian are generally less capable than those trained on the English corpora. The difference between German and English is noticeable in syntactic analogy (Table 3). The German performance is almost half that of English across all models while Italian is better, but is still significantly lower than English. Furthermore, in the semantic part of word analogy, the performance of models trained on UMBC is closer to models trained on Wiki DE than models trained on Wiki EN. In general, Table 4 shows a drop in performance for languages other than English, in line with our expectation that German and Italian are more difficult to model.

6 Conclusions

We contribute several reproduction studies of the outlier identification task and the classic word analogy task, both intrinsic evaluations of non-contextual word representations. We provide an in-depth analysis of *word2vec*, *word2vecf*, and *word2vecf+* on the two tasks analyzing the effects of window size, context type, and context representation on English, German, and Italian. We find that the context construction strategy of word2vecf and word2vecf+ is not always effective. Sometimes the two models underperform even the weakest of the word2vec models.

Our reproduction of outlier identification shows high variance, which we attribute to the original data set's limitations. To address these limitations, we propose 50-8-8, a new data set that is multiple times larger, manually curated, multilingual, and contains syntactic and semantic tests. Besides eliminating the variance issues, 50-8-8 quantifies the drop in performance in representations of languages with more complicated grammar and morphology than English.

Acknowledgments

We would like to thank Davide Mottin for helping with the translation of 50-8-8 to Italian.

References

Maria Antoniak and David Mimno. 2018. Evaluating the stability of embedding-based word similarities. *Transactions of the Association for Computational Linguistics*, 6:107–119.

Giuseppe Attardi. 2018. Wikiextractor. `https://git.io/fARaC`.

Mohit Bansal, Kevin Gimpel, and Karen Livescu. 2014. Tailoring continuous word representations for dependency parsing. In *Proceedings of the 52nd Annual Meeting of the Association for Computational Linguistics (Volume 2: Short Papers)*, pages 809–815, Baltimore, Maryland. Association for Computational Linguistics.

Miroslav Batchkarov, Thomas Kober, Jeremy Reffin, Julie Weeds, and David Weir. 2016. A critique of word similarity as a method for evaluating distributional semantic models. In *Proceedings of the 1st Workshop on Evaluating Vector-Space Representations for NLP*, pages 7–12, Berlin, Germany. Association for Computational Linguistics.

Giacomo Berardi, Andrea Esuli, and Diego Marcheggiani. 2015. Word embeddings go to italy: A comparison of models and training datasets. In *Proceedings of the 6th Italian Information Retrieval Workshop, Cagliari, Italy, May 25-26, 2015*, volume 1404 of *CEUR Workshop Proceedings*. CEUR-WS.org.

Philip Blair, Yuval Merhav, and Joel Barry. 2017. Automated generation of multilingual clusters for the evaluation of distributed representations. In *5th International Conference on Learning Representations, ICLR 2017, Toulon, France, April 24-26, 2017, Workshop Track Proceedings*.

Piotr Bojanowski, Edouard Grave, Armand Joulin, and Tomas Mikolov. 2017. Enriching word vectors with subword information. *Transactions of the Association for Computational Linguistics*, 5:135–146.

António Branco, Nicoletta Calzolari, Piek Vossen, Gertjan Van Noord, Dieter van Uytvanck, João Silva, Luís Gomes, André Moreira, and Willem Elbers. 2020. A Shared Task of a New, Collaborative Type to Foster Reproducibility: A First Exercise in the Area of Language Science and Technology with REPROLANG2020. pages 5541–5547, Marseille, France. European Language Resources Association.

António Branco, Kevin Bretonnel Cohen, Piek Vossen, Nancy Ide, and Nicoletta Calzolari. 2017. Replicability and reproducibility of research results for human language technology: introducing an LRE special section. *Language Resources and Evaluation*, 51(1):1–5.

Freddy Brasileiro, João Paulo A. Almeida, Victorio A. Carvalho, and Giancarlo Guizzardi. 2016. Applying a multi-level modeling theory to assess taxonomic hierarchies in wikidata. In *Proceedings of the 25th International Conference Companion on World Wide Web*, WWW '16 Companion, page 975–980, Republic and Canton of Geneva, CHE. International World Wide Web Conferences Steering Committee.

José Camacho-Collados and Roberto Navigli. 2016. Find the word that does not belong: A framework for an intrinsic evaluation of word vector representations. In *Proceedings of the 1st Workshop on Evaluating Vector-Space Representations for NLP*, pages 43–50, Berlin, Germany. Association for Computational Linguistics.

Danqi Chen and Christopher Manning. 2014. A fast and accurate dependency parser using neural networks. In *Proceedings of the 2014 Conference on Empirical Methods in Natural Language Processing (EMNLP)*, pages 740–750, Doha, Qatar. Association for Computational Linguistics.

Xinxiong Chen, Lei Xu, Zhiyuan Liu, Maosong Sun, and Huan-Bo Luan. 2015. Joint learning of character and word embeddings. In *Proceedings of the Twenty-Fourth International Joint Conference on Artificial Intelligence, IJCAI 2015, Buenos Aires, Argentina, July 25-31, 2015*, pages 1236–1242. AAAI Press.

Drummond Chris. 2009. Replicability is not Reproducibility: Nor is it Good Science. In *The 4th workshop on Evaluation Methods for Machine Learning held at ICML 2009*, Montreal, Canada.

Jacob Devlin, Ming-Wei Chang, Kenton Lee, and Kristina Toutanova. 2019. BERT: Pre-training of deep bidirectional transformers for language understanding. In *Proceedings of the 2019 Conference of the North American Chapter of the Association for Computational Linguistics: Human Language Technologies, Volume 1 (Long and Short Papers)*, pages 4171–4186, Minneapolis, Minnesota. Association for Computational Linguistics.

Manaal Faruqui, Yulia Tsvetkov, Pushpendre Rastogi, and Chris Dyer. 2016. Problems with evaluation of word embeddings using word similarity tasks. In *Proceedings of the 1st Workshop on Evaluating Vector-Space Representations for NLP*, pages 30–35, Berlin, Germany. Association for Computational Linguistics.

Sahar Ghannay, Benoit Favre, Yannick Estève, and Nathalie Camelin. 2016. Word embedding evaluation and combination. In *Proceedings of the Tenth International Conference on Language Resources and Evaluation (LREC'16)*, pages 300–305, Portorož, Slovenia. European Language Resources Association (ELRA).

Anna Gladkova, Aleksandr Drozd, and Satoshi Matsuoka. 2016. Analogy-based detection of morphological and semantic relations with word embeddings: what works and what doesn't. In *Proceedings of the NAACL Student Research Workshop*, pages 8–15, San Diego, California. Association for Computational Linguistics.

Edouard Grave, Piotr Bojanowski, Prakhar Gupta, Armand Joulin, and Tomas Mikolov. 2018. Learning Word Vectors for 157 Languages. In *Proceedings of the Eleventh International Conference on Language Resources and Evaluation (LREC 2018)*, Miyazaki, Japan. European Language Resources Association (ELRA).

Lushan Han, Abhay L. Kashyap, Tim Finin, James Mayfield, and Jonathan Weese. 2013. UMBC_EBIQUITY-CORE: Semantic textual similarity systems. In *Second Joint Conference on Lexical and Computational Semantics (*SEM), Volume 1: Proceedings of the Main Conference and the Shared Task: Semantic Textual Similarity*, pages 44–52, Atlanta, Georgia, USA. Association for Computational Linguistics.

Maximilian Köper, Christian Scheible, and Sabine Schulte im Walde. 2015. Multilingual reliability and "semantic" structure of continuous word spaces. In *Proceedings of the 11th International Conference on Computational Semantics*, pages 40–45, London, UK. Association for Computational Linguistics.

Zhenzhong Lan, Mingda Chen, Sebastian Goodman, Kevin Gimpel, Piyush Sharma, and Radu Soricut. 2020. Albert: A lite bert for self-supervised learning of language representations. In *International Conference on Learning Representations*.

Omer Levy and Yoav Goldberg. 2014a. Dependency-based word embeddings. In *Proceedings of the 52nd Annual Meeting of the Association for Computational Linguistics (Volume 2: Short Papers)*, pages 302–308, Baltimore, Maryland. Association for Computational Linguistics.

Omer Levy and Yoav Goldberg. 2014b. Linguistic regularities in sparse and explicit word representations. In *Proceedings of the Eighteenth Conference on Computational Natural Language Learning*, pages 171–180, Ann Arbor, Michigan. Association for Computational Linguistics.

Omer Levy, Yoav Goldberg, and Ido Dagan. 2015. Improving distributional similarity with lessons learned from word embeddings. *Transactions of the Association for Computational Linguistics*, 3:211–225.

Bofang Li, Tao Liu, Zhe Zhao, Buzhou Tang, Aleksandr Drozd, Anna Rogers, and Xiaoyong Du. 2017. Investigating different syntactic context types and context representations for learning word embeddings. In *Proceedings of the 2017 Conference on Empirical Methods in Natural Language Processing*, pages 2421–2431, Copenhagen, Denmark. Association for Computational Linguistics.

Yinhan Liu, Myle Ott, Naman Goyal, Jingfei Du, Mandar Joshi, Danqi Chen, Omer Levy, Mike Lewis, Luke Zettlemoyer, and Veselin Stoyanov. 2019. Roberta: A robustly optimized bert pretraining approach.

Christopher Manning, Mihai Surdeanu, John Bauer, Jenny Finkel, Steven Bethard, and David McClosky. 2014. The Stanford CoreNLP natural language processing toolkit. In *Proceedings of 52nd Annual Meeting of the Association for Computational Linguistics: System Demonstrations*, pages 55–60, Baltimore, Maryland. Association for Computational Linguistics.

Mitchell P. Marcus, Mary Ann Marcinkiewicz, and Beatrice Santorini. 1993. Building a large annotated corpus of english: The penn treebank. *Comput. Linguist.*, 19(2):313–330.

Tomas Mikolov, Kai Chen, Gregory S. Corrado, and Jeffrey Dean. 2013a. Efficient estimation of word representations in vector space. *CoRR*, abs/1301.3781.

Tomas Mikolov, Ilya Sutskever, Kai Chen, Greg S Corrado, and Jeff Dean. 2013b. Distributed representations of words and phrases and their compositionality. In C. J. C. Burges, L. Bottou, M. Welling, Z. Ghahramani, and K. Q. Weinberger, editors, *Advances in Neural Information Processing Systems 26*, pages 3111–3119. Curran Associates, Inc.

Tomas Mikolov, Wen-tau Yih, and Geoffrey Zweig. 2013c. Linguistic regularities in continuous space word representations. In *Proceedings of the 2013 Conference of the North American Chapter of the Association for Computational Linguistics: Human Language Technologies*, pages 746–751, Atlanta, Georgia. Association for Computational Linguistics.

A. Palmero Aprosio and G. Moretti. 2016. Italy goes to Stanford: a collection of CoreNLP modules for Italian. *ArXiv e-prints*.

Roger D Peng. 2011. Reproducible Research in Computational Science. *Science*, 334(6060):1226–1227.

Jeffrey Pennington, Richard Socher, and Christopher Manning. 2014. Glove: Global vectors for word representation. In *Proceedings of the 2014 Conference on Empirical Methods in Natural Language Processing (EMNLP)*, pages 1532–1543, Doha, Qatar. Association for Computational Linguistics.

João Rodrigues, António Branco, Steven Neale, and João Silva. 2016. Lx-dsemvectors: Distributional semantics models for portuguese. In *Computational Processing of the Portuguese Language*, pages 259–270, Cham. Springer International Publishing.

Victor Sanh, Lysandre Debut, Julien Chaumond, and Thomas Wolf. 2019. Distilbert, a distilled version of bert: smaller, faster, cheaper and lighter. In *5th Workshop on Energy Efficient Machine Learning and Cognitive Computing (NeurIPS)*.

Tobias Schnabel, Igor Labutov, David Mimno, and Thorsten Joachims. 2015. Evaluation methods for unsupervised word embeddings. In *Proceedings of the 2015 Conference on Empirical Methods in Natural Language Processing*, pages 298–307, Lisbon, Portugal. Association for Computational Linguistics.

Emma Strubell, Ananya Ganesh, and Andrew McCallum. 2019. Energy and policy considerations for deep learning in NLP. In *Proceedings of the 57th Annual Meeting of the Association for Computational Linguistics*, pages 3645–3650, Florence, Italy. Association for Computational Linguistics.

Lukáš Svoboda and Tomáš Brychcín. 2018. New word analogy corpus for exploring embeddings of czech words. In *Computational Linguistics and Intelligent Text Processing*, pages 103–114, Cham. Springer International Publishing.

Peter D. Turney. 2006. Similarity of semantic relations. *Computational Linguistics*, 32(3):379–416.

Viljami Venekoski and Jouko Vankka. 2017. Finnish resources for evaluating language model semantics. In *Proceedings of the 21st Nordic Conference on Computational Linguistics*, pages 231–236, Gothenburg, Sweden. Association for Computational Linguistics.

Alex Wang, Amanpreet Singh, Julian Michael, Felix Hill, Omer Levy, and Samuel Bowman. 2018. GLUE: A multi-task benchmark and analysis platform for natural language understanding. In *Proceedings of the 2018 EMNLP Workshop BlackboxNLP: Analyzing and Interpreting Neural Networks for NLP*, pages 353–355, Brussels, Belgium. Association for Computational Linguistics.

Yang You, Jing Li, Sashank Reddi, Jonathan Hseu, Sanjiv Kumar, Srinadh Bhojanapalli, Xiaodan Song, James Demmel, Kurt Keutzer, and Cho-Jui Hsieh. 2020. Large batch optimization for deep learning: Training bert in 76 minutes. In *International Conference on Learning Representations*.

Are Some Words Worth More than Others?

Shiran Dudy   **Steven Bedrick**
Center for Spoken Language Understanding
Oregon Health & Science University
Portland, Oregon, USA
{dudy,bedricks}@ohsu.edu

Abstract

Current evaluation metrics for language modeling and generation rely heavily on the accuracy of predicted (or generated) words as compared to a reference ground truth. While important, token-level accuracy only captures one aspect of a language model's behavior, and ignores linguistic properties of words that may allow some mis-predicted tokens to be useful in practice. Furthermore, statistics directly tied to prediction accuracy (including perplexity) may be confounded by the Zipfian nature of written language, as the majority of the prediction attempts will occur with frequently-occurring types. A model's performance may vary greatly between high- and low-frequency words, which in practice could lead to failure modes such as repetitive and dull generated text being produced by a downstream consumer of a language model. To address this, we propose two new intrinsic evaluation measures within the framework of a simple word prediction task that are designed to give a more holistic picture of a language model's performance. We evaluate several commonly-used large English language models using our proposed metrics, and demonstrate that our approach reveals functional differences in performance between the models that are obscured by more traditional metrics.

1   Introduction

Language models are foundational components in many NLP systems, and as such it is crucial to be able to empirically evaluate their behavior. Traditionally, language models are evaluated using performance metrics that relate to the model's ability to accurately predict words given some context (e.g., perplexity). Following the paradigm described by Galliers and Spärck Jones (1993), this can be thought of as an *intrinsic* evaluation criterion (and perplexity an intrinsic metric), as it relates to the *objective* of the language model itself.

In recent years, it has become common to also evaluate language models *extrinsically*, in terms of the model's *function*. This is done by measuring a model's performance when used as a component in a downstream task. [1] For example, Devlin et al. (2019) evaluated BERT by using it as the language model component in benchmark tasks such as question answering and "commonsense inference."[2] This shift towards extrinsic and task-oriented evaluation is welcome, and has the potential to make language model evaluation more ecologically valid. [3] As useful as task-oriented evaluation metrics are, however, we believe that this approach brings with it certain practical limitations, and that there remains a strong need for robust and meaningful intrinsic evaluation metrics that can be used to characterize and compare the performance of language models.

In this work, we outline and propose a variation on the standard next-word-prediction language modeling task that is designed for use in evaluating and comparing language models and is robust to implementation differences (tokenization method, etc.) that complicate the comparison of modern models in terms of token-level predictions. Our proposed metrics are richer and more meaningful measures than traditional intrinsic metrics such as perplexity, which is insensitive to *which* tokens are matched, and as such may be

---

[1]In part, this trend has been driven by the increasing use of downstream tasks as ancillary training objective functions; this somewhat confuses the traditional notion of intrinsic and extrinsic evaluation as a binary construct.

[2]SQuAD versions 1.1 (Rajpurkar et al., 2016) and 2.0 (Rajpurkar et al., 2018), and SWAG (Zellers et al., 2018), respectively, in the case of the original BERT paper.

[3]"Ecological validity" is a dimension of experimental validity that is concerned with the question of whether an observed effect reflects "what happens in everyday life"(Brewer and Crano, 2014), i.e. beyond the artificial setting of the experiment itself. In an NLP context, a researcher working on question answering who was concerned with ecological validity would ensure that the questions on which they trained and evaluated their system were similar (in form and content) to those on which the system was designed to be used.

Proceedings of the First Workshop on Evaluation and Comparison of NLP Systems (Eval4NLP), pages 131–142,
November 20, 2020. ©2020 Association for Computational Linguistics

confounded by distributional properties of their evaluation corpora. Our approach accounts not only for the *accuracy* of a model's word predictions, but also the *diversity of types* that it predicts, across different lexical frequency bins. We further propose a formulation for the next-word-prediction task that explicitly allows for language- and task-level details to be captured in the resulting metrics, thereby blurring the line between intrinsic and extrinsic language model evaluation. Our methods provide greater ecological validity than traditional intrinsic evaluation methods, while still remaining simple to interpret and easy to calculate.

1.1 Formalities:
Language Models and Word Prediction

For our present purposes, we will consider a language model to be a model that, given a sequence W of n tokens $w_{1:n}$ from a fixed vocabulary of types V, estimates the joint probability of $P(W)$. The goal of a language models is of learning to approximate the distribution of tokens and types in some corpus.

Importantly, different models may use different units of prediction, at the level of individual character, at the word level, or (as with many modern neural models) at the level of a sub-word/sub-sentence unit (via e.g. byte-pair encoding (Sennrich et al., 2016), wordpieces (Wu et al., 2016), etc.).

Given such a model, we can typically also estimate the *conditional* probability distribution $P(w_t|w_1 \dots w_{t-1})$, over possible words occurring after a given history h consisting of $t-1$ tokens. We refer to this as the next-word-prediction problem[4] of predicting $\hat{w}_t = \text{argmax}_w P(w|h)$. Using the terminology of conditional text generation, this is akin to generating a single token via greedy decoding given a context. This is of more than theoretical interest from a language modeling perspective. Language models trained using the standard cross-entropy loss function are in effect being optimized to perform this very task, and furthermore, many NLP applications rely in practice on effective and robust word prediction.

A standard and widely-used metric for evaluating language model performance is with *perplexity* (PPX), which is closely related to this prediction task. When computed for a given token prediction event by a language model, PPX captures how "predictable" that event was for the model:

$$PPX(p,q) = -\sum_X p(x)\log q(x) \qquad (1)$$

Where X corresponds to V (the model's vocabulary of possible tokens it must choose between), $p(x)$ represents the "true" or "target" distribution and $q(x)$ the model's estimated distribution. The closer the predicted distribution matches the target distribution, the lower the perplexity. When averaged over many prediction events, and computed on a held-out test dataset, perplexity attempts to capture the degree to which the model has optimally learned to represent its target distribution. A more accurate (i.e., "better") model should result in lower average perplexity (as the model will more often predict a high probability for the correct target).

1.2 Evaluation Considerations

Perplexity is a classic example of an *intrinsic* evaluation metric, in that it is measuring the model's ability to carry out its immediate objective. As mentioned previously, modern language models are often evaluated according to their performance when used as components in a downstream task of some kind.[5] We find this increasing prevalence of *extrinsic* evaluation to be a very positive development, and do not in any way wish to argue *against* use of downstream tasks for evaluation. However, we see several limitations to an extrinsic-only evaluation paradigm, and argue for more robust intrinsic measures.[6] Extrinsic evaluation is necessarily dependent on the selection of specific benchmark tasks to include, and this process is fraught with difficulty, for several reasons. First, there are many possible benchmark tasks from which one could choose, each attempting to measure something different. Different authors will naturally choose different combinations of tasks when evaluating their language models, as they may be focused on different aspects of their models' behavior. While scientifically appropriate, this does make for a heterogeneous evaluation landscape, and complicates comparisons between published results. Second, new tasks are constantly being created, and existing tasks are regularly updated. This results in a complex and unstable evaluation landscape in which evaluation tasks change from year to year, and allows for much confusion around versions of datasets and benchmarks. Third, downstream NLP tasks and datasets often have their own issues around validity.

---

[4]Also known as the "Shannon Game" (Shannon, 1951).

[5]Galliers and Spärck Jones (1993) refer to this as the model's "function" (in contrast to its "objective.")

[6]In this, we follow Ito et al. (1999), who, writing about language models in the context of their use in ASR systems, warned against relying solely on evaluation metrics that were specific to that task (specifically, word error rate).

For example, the commonly-used SNLI natural language inference corpus (Bowman et al., 2015) was later found to have substantial issues resulting from artifacts in how its annotations were collected (Gururangan et al., 2018). How should one now assess a language model evaluated using this downstream task, knowing that the metrics may be of very limited validity? Finally, we note that widely-used and well-studied downstream evaluation tasks are often not available in "low-resource" languages, and so may not be an option in many scenarios. For these reasons, we believe that intrinsic measures should still play an important role in language model evaluation.

The question then becomes that of *what* to measure. Perplexity has the advantage of being well-understood and easy to calculate, and is closely linked to the standard cross-entropy training loss frequently used in language modeling. However, it has long been observed that perplexity itself often fails to correlate with downstream task performance (Iyer et al., 1997; Ito et al., 1999), suggesting that it may have limited external validity as a metric.

There is an additional, more subtle limitation to the use of perplexity in cross-model comparison. As previously mentioned, many modern language models use sub-word units of prediction. One of the consequences of this heterogeneity is that evaluation metrics that relate to individual base-level prediction events (as is the case with perplexity) are not comparable across models, even if they are trained and evaluated on the same corpus: different tokenizations and vocabularies will result in different numbers of prediction events, as well as a differently-sized space of possible choices at each event. From the perspective of the perplexity metric, two models with different approaches to tokenization are performing fundamentally different and numerically incomparable tasks.

Beyond this statistical problem, there is a problem with the underlying semantics of using perplexity as a measure when working with sub-word units. Any actual application of a language model that involves explicit word prediction[7] will ultimately demand not *fragments* of words, but rather *entire* words. In other words, even models whose native unit of prediction is at the sub-word level must make predictions that can *eventually* be able to be decoded into whole words at *some* point.

Given that, raw perplexity becomes a somewhat confusing evaluation metric, as the underlying phenomenon that it is measuring is quite distinct from the model's actual objective (i.e., predicting a whole word). Imagine, for instance, a model that predicts at the sub-word level, and now must predict a word given the history *"The tyrannosaurus was chased by the."* The correct continuing word is *"velociraptor,"* and under the sub-word tokenization used by this model, this will necessitate several separate prediction events (as "velociraptor" is both a long and an infrequently-occurring word). From the perspective of the perplexity metric, however, there will be no difference between the first unit or the third.[8] Whatever the perplexity metric is telling us about the model's behavior during this process will likely tell us little about the model's ability to actually predict "velociraptor" given this particular word history.

1.3 Recentering on Words

We propose that intrinsic evaluation of language models be done in terms of the *whole-word* prediction task, regardless of the specific tokenization practices of any particular model. This would have the advantage of making cross-model comparison easier, and of the resulting metric bearing a closer resemblance to what we intuitively expect such a metric to capture (i.e., the model's performance at its primary objective). While computing perplexity at the level of whole words (see section 2) is a step in the right direction, we also propose several additional intrinsic metrics relating to the word prediction task.

Word Prediction Accuracy We propose directly measuring and reporting the model's raw *accuracy* at word-level predictions (i.e., the proportion of words that were predicted correctly). This has the advantage over perplexity of grounding the number more closely to the concrete performance objective that we are concerned with. Furthermore, it is easily extended to account for various attributes of model behavior that may be of interest in terms of downstream tasks, while still remaining in the realm of intrinsic evaluation.

In the experiments we describe in section 2, we experiment with variations on this metric that capture different notions of "accuracy." For example, we explore "top n" accuracy (i.e., if the target word is in within top n most likely predictions, that prediction counts as a "hit"). This could be of use in a text entry scenario, in which the model is responsible for generating candidate words for further selection or refinement by an end-user (as in a mobile phone keyboard application). Many other possible downstream tasks for language

---

[7]For whatever definition of "word" is appropriate in the language under consideration.

[8]Or, for that matter, from the previous token, *"the."*

models involve techniques that would also benefit from having the target word given better placement in the ranked prediction space, and thus would benefit from a metric explicitly measuring this property.

"Soft-Match" Prediction Accuracy We propose extending simple prediction accuracy to allow for "near miss" predictions, where the predicted word is "similar" to the target (for a specified definition of "similar"). In many applications of language modeling, there may be multiple possible valid predictions. This problem has long been understood in the context of machine translation evaluation; in their description of the motivation behind the METEOR metric, Lavie and Denkowski (2009) addressed the "problem of reference translation variability by utilizing flexible word matching, allowing for morphological variants and synonyms to be taken into account as legitimate correspondences." In a word prediction task, we could allow an explicit synonym to count as a correct prediction; depending on the application or domain in question, one could use external language resources to model much more complex and task-specific notions of similarity (e.g., in a biomedical NLP context, one might give the model credit at evaluation time for predicting a medication that is from the same functional class as the target). In the experiments described in section 2.4.2, we use a method based on word neighborhoods in an embedding space. Depending on the nature of the task under consideration, other features could be used.

Or, consider a typing task in a morphologically rich language, in which a user might be willing to accept predictions that involve the correct lexeme but with an incorrect inflection. Allowing for this sort of flexibility in the evaluation of a word prediction model has the potential to greatly increase the ecological validity of the experiment, in that, that the experimenter is able to easily encode their own task-specific notions of relevance while still staying in a fairly constrained and easy-to-analyze evaluation setting.

Lexical Frequency & Diversity

One important limitation of raw classification accuracy as a metric is its susceptibility to being biased by imbalanced class distributions. For example, if some classes occur much more frequently than others, a model may achieve a high accuracy score by learning to focus on these frequent classes to the exclusion of infrequent ones. In written language, the distribution of classes (i.e., of word *types*) are notoriously skewed (Zipf, 1935), and exhibit a "long tail" of words that occur relatively infrequently, with a small

set of "head" words that make up a large proportion of individual *tokens* observed in the training and test data.

We observe that language models often exhibit very different performance characteristics when predicting more common types than less common types; in fact, our experiments in this paper demonstrate that, for some commonly-used language models, the actual number of infrequent types that are *ever* correctly predicted is surprisingly small (see section 3.1). This over-emphasis on frequent types, when carried forward into downstream generation tasks, may lead to the failure mode described by Holtzman et al. (2020) in which generated text is "dull and repetitive." This phenomenon is not limited to words alone; morphologically-rich languages (MRLs) exhibit a similar Zipfian distributional pattern in terms of the occurrence of different morphological phenomena, which in turn affects the performance of systems designed to process such features of language (Czarnowska et al., 2019; Tsarfaty et al., 2020). We believe that this behavior can be explained through the lens of the bias-variance tradeoff common to all statistical learning problems. As observed by Lazaridou et al. (2015), neural models have a tendency towards the "bias" end of that tradeoff, which in the context of language modeling results in a strong preference for head words and against tail words.

This is a serious enough problem in machine translation and text generation systems that there is a growing body of literature looking at ways to increase the lexical diversity in model output. Some authors (Li et al., 2016; Welleck et al., 2020) have examined training strategies and loss functions that optimize for diverse output, while others (Vijayakumar et al., 2016; Ippolito et al., 2019) focus on alternatives to greedy decoding and identify several ways to generate more diverse sequences of words. Questions of evaluation arise, as the construct of "diversity" itself is surprisingly difficult to characterize, as pointed out by Tevet and Berant (2020).

In the context of our word prediction task, we propose two evaluation measures that account for the Zipfian skew in type distributions, and illuminate differences in model performance across the type frequency spectrum. First, we propose *stratifying* our evaluation of prediction accuracy by frequency, such that we separately measure the model's ability to predict occurrences of high-, mid-, and low-frequency types (stratified *token* coverage). Second, we propose measuring the *overall proportion of possible types* that the model was able to predict at least once during evaluation (*type* coverage, also stratified by frequency).

2 Methods

In this section we describe a series of experiments in which we use our proposed evaluation metrics to explore the behavior of several widely-used and large-scale language models (obtained using the HuggingFace (Wolf et al., 2019) Transformers library). Specifically, we examine GPT-2 (Alec et al., 2019) (`gpt-2`), GPT (Alec et al., 2018) (`openai-gpt`), RoBERTa (Liu et al., 2019) (`roberta-base`), and BERT (Devlin et al., 2019) (`bert-base-uncased`).

2.1 Training & Datasets

Since the pre-trained models were all trained in widely varying ways on different corpora, we ran each model through a single pass of fine-tuning on a common corpus to attempt to bring them more closely into alignment. For this fine-tuning (and for the ensuing experiments), we used WikiText 103 (Merity et al., 2016), which consists of a large ($n = 28{,}475$) training set of English-language Wikipedia articles and a small ($n = 60$) test set of 60 articles, with one sentence per line. The fine-tuning task was on a word prediction task in a unidirectional fashion, in which the context is based only past history (i.e., not on future tokens).[9] We note that for BERT and RoBERTa, this usage does differ somewhat from the prediction paradigm under which they were trained, which is implicitly bidirectional.

2.2 Whole-word decoding

As previously described, modern language models typically use sub-word/sub-sentences units as their native unit of prediction. In order to perform a meaningful evaluation of cross-model word prediction accuracy, it is necessary to obtain word-level predictions, which for the mentioned models may involve more than one model-level prediction event. The models we worked with in this set of experiments used two different tokenization strategies (wordpieces for GPT and BERT, and BPE for GPT-2 and RoBerta), and as such we developed algorithms for decoding whole words by sequentially decoding individual sub-word units. While the algorithms differ slightly in their implementation between the model families, the overall method is similar.

Our single-word decoding algorithm extracts the first word candidate by the model through con-

catenating tokens until *end-of-word* is indicated, [10] and then compared with a target word (see App. B, Algorithm 1). To extract multiple candidate words, given a target word we run a Depth-First Search to find whether a valid path of tokens exist, having each model prediction spanning its top ten guesses (App. B, Algorithm 2). This is not a typical beam-search based on likelihoods, but rather is based on the existence of valid units (in the first K options) for a given target word, simulating user choices given a context. [11]

In addition to decoding whole words, we would like to be able to obtain a probability estimate of the resulting prediction, for use in computing a word-level perplexity measure. We approximate this by taking the product of the prediction-level probabilities (i.e., the model's estimate of the probability of each constituent unit in a given decoded word), which we can then use for a perplexity-like score:

$$ppx = -\sum^{words} p(w)\log(\prod^{units} q(u)) \qquad (2)$$

2.3 Experiments

We performed a word-level prediction experiment on the test dataset described in Section 2.2, using each of the models in Section 2. For each test example, we performed incremental unidirectional word prediction using Algorithm 1 to generate whole-word predictions. In other words, for each test example W comprised of $w_1...w_n$ words, we queried the model $n - 1$ times, to predict $\hat{w}_i = \underset{w}{\mathrm{argmax}} P(w_i|w_{1:i-1})$ for $i \in [2,n]$. Additionally, we used Algorithm 2 to decode the top k ranked word predictions (for $k = 10$), $\hat{\mathbf{w}}_t^k$. In other words, for the test input "the dinosaur ate the ..." we would sequentially predict $p(w_2|\text{"the"})$, $p(w_3|\text{"the dinosaur"})$, and so on. At each prediction event, we compared the predicted $\hat{w}_t$ to the ground-truth w_t according to the various metrics described in the next section. We counted as "hits" word-level prediction events where the comparison matched (for the different definitions of "matched"), and "misses" otherwise.

---

[10]The code is available for all model types we present in this paper, and for the different tokenization approaches by which they are trained.

[11]Code at `https://github.com/shiranD/word_level_evaluation`

---

[9]Bert and Roberta were given a '[MASK]' token at the end on a sequence to ensure unidirectional prediction.

2.4 Calculation of Metrics

2.4.1 Prediction Accuracy

We measure token-level prediction accuracy[12] using an exact-match criterion, top_1. In other words, if $w_t = \hat{w}_t$, a "hit" is counted; otherwise, a miss. We also computed a higher-recall metric top_k, in which a "hit" is counted if $w_t \in \hat{\mathbf{w}}_t^k$ — i.e., if the target word is in the top k predictions, it counts as a "hit." For our experiments, we computed top_{10} (i.e., $k=10$).

2.4.2 Soft-Match Accuracy

As described in section 1.3, there are a number of criteria by which one might implement a soft-matching algorithm. From the perspective of evaluation, the key is to design a criterion in such a way as to capture the aspect of user behavior that one may wish to support.

We performed our soft-matching experiments with a text entry scenario in mind, in which a user is able to choose among the language model's top n predictions. Under this scenario, if the model fails to predict the target word but instead predicts a *related* word (a synonym, perhaps), the user may still be able to convey their message. To simulate this, we may define the soft-match operation as follows:

$$SoftMatch(a,b,s) = \begin{cases} True & \text{if } a=b \\ s(a,b) & \text{otherwise} \end{cases}$$

Where the arguments to $SoftMatch$ are two candidate words a and b, as well as a similarity function $s : (a,b) \to X \in \{True, False\}$. $Softmatch(a,b,s)$ is true if a and b are a match, or if s indicates similarity. For our experiments here, we used a method based on similarity in word embedding space, under the theory that words with similar embeddings may be (relatively) appropriate substitutions in a word prediction task.

We used the word2vec algorithm (Mikolov et al., 2013) to train 50-dimensional word embeddings on the "train" subset of the WikiText-103 corpus. We then defined our softmatch similarity function $s_{knn}(a,b) = a \in knn(b)$, where $knn(b,k)$ retrieves the k nearest neighbors of target word b in the embedding space. Using our softmatch function, we then re-scored the prediction accuracy such that a positive softmatch counted as a "hit." We used the Annoy library (Bernhardsson, 2018) to perform efficient nearest-neighbor retrieval. We conducted experiments in which we varied the k parameter; in other words, by

allowing a match deeper into the k-nearest neighbors of the target. Our motivation for this was that, ceteris paribus, a model that mis-predicts a target but at least guesses something that lies in the right semantic neighborhood is more useful than one that does not.

2.4.3 Lexical Diversity

In order to measure type diversity given all the hits in top_1/top_{10}, we counted how many unique types were correctly predicted for the first and top-ten guesses and present it in T_1 (T_{10}) respectively. To illustrate the utility of measuring the rate of unique types that were correctly predicted, consider a hypothetical dataset in which 20% of the tokens consist of the word *the*, and that the model at hand predicts only this word for every sample in the test set. In this scenario, top_1 accuracy will be 20%, as *the* is a correct prediction for 20% of the times, yet T_1 is based on only one type [13] as there was only a single type that was correctly predicted— suggesting sub-optimal learning of the input distribution, or a lack on the model's ability to reflect that distribution during test.

3 Results

3.1 Diversity Evaluation

model	top_1 (top_{10})	T_1 (T_{10})	ppx
GPT-2	35.63 (67.76)	26.60 (47.27)	34.8
GPT	29.37 (60.89)	15.96 (30.80)	37.9
RoBerta	28.18 (59.55)	24.73 (42.63)	42.2
Bert	22.11 (50.98)	15.59 (29.61)	50.7

Table 1: Experimental results on Wiki-103 corpus

Table 1 describes the results on the different models. GPT-2, and GPT, that were pre-trained for word prediction task exhibited the lowest ppx. GPT-2 had the highest hit rate, and type diversity. However, when comparing GPT, to RoBerta, while accuracy seems to present a similar performance, and the ppx is lower for GPT, RoBerta is found to be much more diverse than GPT, suggesting that the similar hit rates (28.18, 29.37) can be attributed to different reasons as shown by their different performance over T_x metric. On the other hand, we can also learn that while Bert, and GPT share similar diversity rate (prediction diversity), GPT exhibits a higher prediction accuracy making for a different accuracy/diversity ratio than Bert, which may also suggest a different prediction

---

[12] For tokens— i.e., words— in the test set, as opposed to tokens from the perspective of the model being evaluated.

[13] T_1 is the relative percentage of one over the overall number of types

behavior than of `Bert`'s. To understand type diversity we must explore which types were predicted well and which types were harder. To this end, we stratified both T_1, and top_1 as a function of frequency; *high*, *mid*, and *low*, for $x \in [10^3, \text{inf})$, $x \in [10^2, 10^3)$, $x \in [10^1, 10^2)$ where x is each target type's frequency.

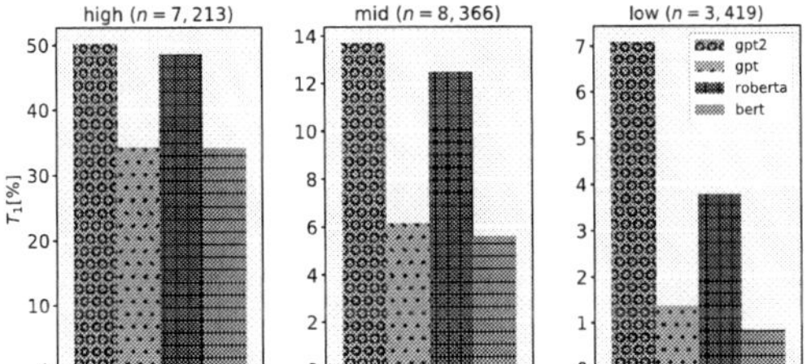

Figure 1: Wiki-103 *type* coverage by training frequency bin. n: number of items in each bin; y-axes are percentages over n (note different scales).

Figure 1 describes the type distribution reflecting high diversity for both `GPT-2`, and `RoBerta`, while having `GPT-2` picking on the low-bin twice as many than `RoBerta`. Notice the stark difference between `RoBerta`, and `GPT`, `RoBerta` outperformed `GPT` across every bin, illustrating its diversity strength (given the similar hit rate shown earlier). While performing worse, both `GPT`, and `Bert`, seem to share similar rates of diversity, with `GPT`, performing almost twice as many on the lowest bin. Finally, even `GPT-2` that attained the highest diversity, was covering only 50%, 14%, and 7% of the trained types we evaluated on. This shows there is room for improvement to reflect more optimally the input data's distribution.

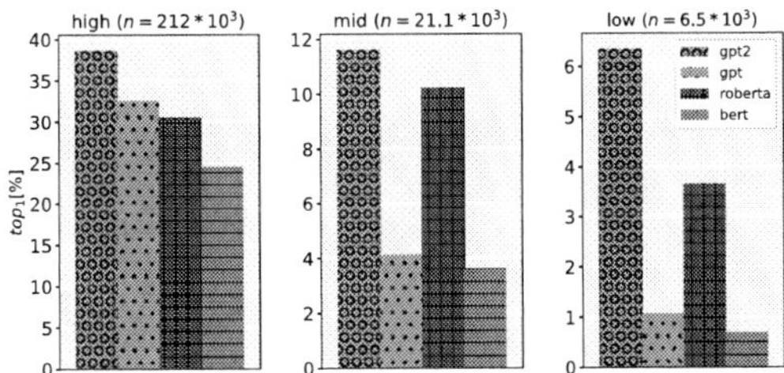

Figure 2: Wiki-103 *token* coverage by training frequency bin. n: number of items in each bin; y-axes are percentages over n (note different scales).

Figure 2 presents the hit rate distribution. This figure explains the gaps of `GPT-2`, and `RoBerta`, showing that while not so different in diversity, `RoBerta` is missing the hits mostly from the most frequent bin 10% gap, and a sub-optimal prediction in the mid- and low-bins. The similar hit rate of `RoBerta`, and `GPT`, clearly is distributed differently having `RoBerta` reaching parts of the long tail of the distribution more often than `GPT`. `Bert`, and `GPT`, also exhibit the biggest gap in the most frequent bin with 8% difference, while the mid and low bins are similar. Overall evaluating prediction diversity can inform us about the model's priorities. Through measuring type diversity, we learn that models that share similar hit rates, can be vary immensely in diversity, which later on may impact downstream tasks. Evaluating diversity could not only inform us to what degree the learned distribution is reflected, but could directly point at the missing types, and the weaknesses of the model. Since all these models are shown to be weaker in the lower bins, or biased by frequency, our community can benefit if we start addressing this problem, which indirectly would contribute to higher accuracies as well. In Section 4 we illustrate in a case study why learning diverse types, and low-frequency types in particular can be useful. Next, we present a way to further understand our models, even if the target word was not found directly in a prediction.

3.2 Soft-Match Evaluation

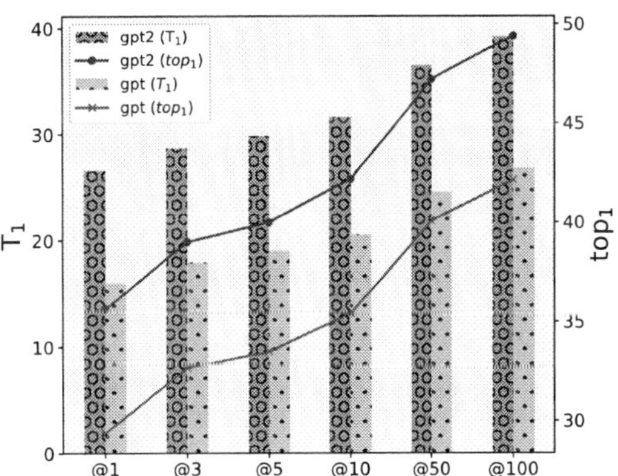

Figure 3: Soft-Match for `GPT-2`, and `GPT` (Wiki-103)

Figure 3 illustrates `GPT-2`, and `GPT`'s T_1, and top_1 performance on left (bars) and right (line) axes. Both models gradually (@3-@100) capture more types as the beam of k in knn was increased (considering more target-neighbors), leading to increased hits. This evaluation shows that `GPT-2` exact match (@1) are higher, but that its misses can enrich the pool of unique types with 14% (@100) additional unique types (light blue), whereas, `GPT-2` covered only 11% more types (light pink), while both models increase in accuracy is similar. This reinforces that the models' prediction mechanism is slightly different, as similar gains in accuracy are translated to either more of learned high types or more diverse patterns shown for the models in Figures 1, 2. This analysis teaches us that even if there were mis-matches some of them were actual near misses, and are related to what it was expected to predict, which as mentioned can be of practical use for different users, or for analyzing how wrong were the mis-matches as part of an error analysis process.

4 A case study of Paraphrasing

In this section we will look at the impact of model inference performance on the particular downstream task of paraphrasing. To this end we employed a SotA algorithm, Bertscore (Zhang et al., 2019), to compute similarity scores of sentence pairs in part by comparing embeddings derived from a language model. Under Bertscore, higher similarity scores indicate greater semantic similarity of a pair of sentences, such that one is a closer *paraphrase* of the other. We would like to stress that the critique that may be risen at the end of this section is not about Bertscore tool as such, but are rather about a certain type of pattern that the models that are employed by this tool may have insufficiently learned.

Why Paraphrasing? We choose the downstream task of paraphrasing to measure semantic similarity of sentence pairs as it can be easily manipulated to consider a single word modification. Consider the following example sentence involving the word triple: (poodle, dog, cat) [14]

(a) which `dog` has longer hair ?

(b) which `cat` has longer hair ?

(c) which `poodle` has longer hair ?

The pair (a, b) ought to score lower (i.e., be considered by Bertscore to be more dissimilar) than the pair (a,c), as a is a valid paraphrase of c while b is not. This, of course, assumes that the language model being used as the underlying source of embeddings for the Bertscore algorithm has accurately captured the semantic meaning of the three words under consideration. If not, we may see an inversion of results such that (a,b) appears (incorrectly) more similar than (a,c), suggesting that the model in question should perhaps not be used for paraphrase-related tasks.

To explore the impact of word frequency on model representations with our fine-tuned models, we have generated 50 rare, and 50 common triples elicited

from wiki-103 trainset. Each of the triples contains a rare/common word, its hypernym, and a sibling hypernym extracted from WordNet (Miller, 1995) (using `nltk` (Loper and Bird, 2002)) (x_r, x_h, x_a), (x_c, x_h, x_a) respectively. For each word in a triple, we identified a sentence in which the rare word naturally occurs, and generated probe sentences in which we replace the rare word with x_h and x_a [15]. We then used *bertscore* to compare our sentences in terms of their similarity. In principle, we expect that $bertscore(s(x_h), s(x_r)) > bertscore(s(x_h), s(x_a))$. In other words, a similarity score for the pair made of a sentence with `dog` and the sentence with `poodle` is expected to be higher than than the pair made of a sentence with `dog` and a sentence with `cat`, as `dog` and a `poodle` are closer semantically, than a `dog` and a `cat`, and therefore would be a closer paraphrase of each other. Alternatively, if the model's word representations are being confounded by lexical frequency, we may instead observe the opposite pattern (i.e., the sentences with the more common words mistakenly appearing to be more similar to one another, despite their semantic difference). We consider cases in which the model correctly identifies the paraphrase (e.g., if $bertscore(s(\text{dog}), s(\text{poodle})) > bertscore(s(\text{dog}), s(\text{cat}))$) as hits, and mis-identifications as misses. Our "null hypothesis" is that there should not be any difference in hit rate between high- and low-frequency words (i.e., word frequency should not affect the model's ability to identify paraphrases). Furthermore, we compare the performance of two fine-tuned models trained on wiki-103, `Bert` and `RoBerta`, and (given the results of our earlier experiments) we hypothesize that if there is a difference in hit rate, `RoBerta` will prove more robust to the rare words condition, given its superior performance at predicting (and thus representing) rare words.

model	hits	misses	total
`Bert`$_{rare}$	14	36	50
`RoBerta`$_{rare}$	11	39	50
`Bert`$_{common}$	40	10	50
`RoBerta`$_{common}$	39	11	50

Table 2: Paraphrasing sentences with wiki-103 words

We note that this is something of a "toy" experiment, given its small size, which limits the conclusions that we can draw. However, in Table 2, we do see a greater difference in performance

---

[14]Note that the word `poodle` occurs much less frequently in English than either `dog` or `cat`.

[15]see Appendix C for details on sentence selection and generation.

between the rare set of words to the common, such that the models do appear to be failing to capture the semantics of rare words, as reflected in the greater number of $misses$ (χ^2; $p < 0.001$ for both models).

We found that `RoBerta` and `Bert` did not differ greatly in their performance, suggesting that with this method the strong effect of word frequency outweighed the between-model difference observed in our earlier experiments. This null result could easily be an artifact of our very small sample size of 100 probe sentences, though, and we also did notice a substantial number of $misses$ with the set of common words. Overall, despite this being based only on a small sample, it does seem that the lower performance of both models on the rare words is unlikely to be a coincidence. We hope to be able to experiment with a greater sample size to begin learning more about the degree to which rare-word inferences are reliable to produce outcomes aligned with human semantics on various downstream tasks.

5   Future Work

The paraphrasing task should be conducted at a larger scale. Furthermore, we hope to continue evaluating language models' prediction diversity and its effects on additional downstream tasks (for example, tasks where human speech is anticipated), since prediction diversity evaluation may vary between one task to another. The unit of evaluation can go beyond words, and may be defined at various textual granularities, such as phrases, for instance, depending on prediction diversity desired. We also leave for future work questions of to what degree different tokenization approaches, or model size effect prediction diversity.

In our experiments, we did observe differences in performance between models with different tokenization strategies (e.g. `GPT-2` and `RoBerta` as compared with their architectural counterparts); however, these models also varied substantially from one another in other respects (size, etc.) and as such it is difficult to attribute this performance gap to tokenization alone. It may also be the case that the bigger the model (in terms of number of parameters), the more diverse it is likely to be; under this hypothesis, we would expect today's ever-larger models (e.g. `GPT-3`) to outperform their predecesors in terms of diversity. However, we do not believe that it is sustainable (Strubell et al., 2019; Schwartz et al., 2019) to rely on increasing model complexity as an approach to addressing the frequency-related challenges that we observed in our experiments, and believe that fundamentally different approaches to language model training are needed.

6   Conclusion

We presented two types of evaluation techniques to learn about the performance of the model across its input distribution, revealing the easier and the challenging areas to learn. Through this analysis we showed that current models are susceptible to frequency bias during training, and as a result under-performing when less frequent examples are encountered at test time, hurting the overall performance. In addition, we proposed a way to learn about the degree to which a model's prediction is semantically close to a target in cases where an exact match was not predicted, which may more accurately reflect a model's usefulness. Thirdly, we showed how a downstream task of paraphrasing may be rendered less reliable, as the models employed struggle to produce semantically-useful representations when rare words are involved.

We believe that language models should reflect the trained distribution more optimally than what we observed in our evaluation, and we should recognize their bias to frequency - making them unfair towards some words, and potentially harmful for our downstream tasks. We also believe it is important to take part in setting benchmarks for models' diversity. Finally, distributional representation goes beyond words, and we hope to address more complicated representational tasks as well.

Acknowledgments

We thank the anonymous reviewers for their insightful comments and suggestions. This work was supported by the National Institute on Deafness and Other Communication Disorders of the National Institutes of Health under award number R01DC015999.

References

Radford Alec, Wu Jeffrey, Child Rewon, Luan David, Amodei Dario, and Sutskever Ilya. 2019. Language models are unsupervised multitask learners.

Radford Alec, Narasimhan Karthik, Salimans Tim, and Sutskever Ilya. 2018. Improving language understanding by generative pre-training.

Erik Bernhardsson. Annoy [online]. 2018.

Samuel R. Bowman, Gabor Angeli, Christopher Potts, and Christopher D. Manning. 2015. A large annotated corpus for learning natural language inference. In *Proceedings of the 2015 Conference on Empirical Methods in Natural Language Processing*, pages 632–642, Lisbon, Portugal. Association for Computational Linguistics.

Marilynn B. Brewer and William D. Crano. 2014. *Research Design and Issues of Validity*, 2 edition, pages 11–26. Cambridge University Press.

Paula Czarnowska, Sebastian Ruder, Edouard Grave, Ryan Cotterell, and Ann Copestake. 2019. Don't forget the long tail! a comprehensive analysis of morphological generalization in bilingual lexicon induction. In *Proceedings of the 2019 Conference on Empirical Methods in Natural Language Processing and the 9th International Joint Conference on Natural Language Processing (EMNLP-IJCNLP)*, pages 974–983, Hong Kong, China. Association for Computational Linguistics.

Jacob Devlin, Ming-Wei Chang, Kenton Lee, and Kristina Toutanova. 2019. BERT: Pre-training of deep bidirectional transformers for language understanding. In *Proceedings of the 2019 Conference of the North American Chapter of the Association for Computational Linguistics: Human Language Technologies, Volume 1 (Long and Short Papers)*, pages 4171–4186, Minneapolis, Minnesota. Association for Computational Linguistics.

J.R. Galliers and Kare Spärck Jones. 1993. Evaluating natural language processing systems. Technical Report UCAM-CL-TR-291, University of Cambridge, Computer Laboratory.

Suchin Gururangan, Swabha Swayamdipta, Omer Levy, Roy Schwartz, Samuel Bowman, and Noah A. Smith. 2018. Annotation artifacts in natural language inference data. In *Proceedings of the 2018 Conference of the North American Chapter of the Association for Computational Linguistics: Human Language Technologies, Volume 2 (Short Papers)*, pages 107–112, New Orleans, Louisiana. Association for Computational Linguistics.

Ari Holtzman, Jan Buys, Li Du, Maxwell Forbes, and Yejin Choi. 2020. The curious case of neural text degeneration. In *International Conference on Learning Representations*.

Daphne Ippolito, Reno Kriz, João Sedoc, Maria Kustikova, and Chris Callison-Burch. 2019. Comparison of diverse decoding methods from conditional language models. In *Proceedings of the 57th Annual Meeting of the Association for Computational Linguistics*, pages 3752–3762, Florence, Italy. Association for Computational Linguistics.

Akinori Ito, Masaki Kohda, and Mari Ostendorf. 1999. A new metric for stochastic language model evaluation. In *Sixth European Conference on Speech Communication and Technology*, pages 1591–1594.

R. Iyer, M. Ostendorf, and M. Meteer. 1997. Analyzing and predicting language model improvements. In *1997 IEEE Workshop on Automatic Speech Recognition and Understanding Proceedings*, pages 254–261.

Alon Lavie and Michael J Denkowski. 2009. The METEOR Metric for Automatic Evaluation of Machine Translation. *Machine translation*, 23(2-3):105–115.

Angeliki Lazaridou, Georgiana Dinu, and Marco Baroni. 2015. Hubness and Pollution: Delving into Cross-Space Mapping for Zero-Shot Learning. In *Proceedings of the 53rd Annual Meeting of the Association for Computational Linguistics and the 7th International Joint Conference on Natural Language Processing (Volume 1: Long Papers)*, volume 1, pages 270–280.

Jiwei Li, Michel Galley, Chris Brockett, Jianfeng Gao, and Bill Dolan. 2016. A diversity-promoting objective function for neural conversation models. In *Proceedings of the 2016 Conference of the North American Chapter of the Association for Computational Linguistics: Human Language Technologies*, pages 110–119, San Diego, California. Association for Computational Linguistics.

Yinhan Liu, Myle Ott, Naman Goyal, Jingfei Du, Mandar Joshi, Danqi Chen, Omer Levy, Mike Lewis, Luke Zettlemoyer, and Veselin Stoyanov. 2019. Roberta: A robustly optimized bert pretraining approach. *arXiv preprint arXiv:1907.11692*.

Edward Loper and Steven Bird. 2002. Nltk: The Natural Language Toolkit. In *Proceedings of the ACL-02 Workshop on Effective Tools and Methodologies for Teaching Natural Language Processing and Computational Linguistics*, pages 63–70.

Stephen Merity, Caiming Xiong, James Bradbury, and Richard Socher. 2016. Pointer Sentinel Mixture Models. *arXiv preprint arXiv:1609.07843*.

Tomas Mikolov, Ilya Sutskever, Kai Chen, Greg S Corrado, and Jeff Dean. 2013. Distributed Representations of Words and Phrases and their Compositionality. In *Advances in neural information processing systems*, pages 3111–3119.

George A. Miller. 1995. Wordnet: A lexical database for english. *Commun. ACM*, 38(11):39–41.

Pranav Rajpurkar, Robin Jia, and Percy Liang. 2018. Know what you don't know: Unanswerable questions for SQuAD. In *Proceedings of the 56th Annual Meeting of the Association for Computational Linguistics (Volume 2: Short Papers)*, pages 784–789, Melbourne, Australia. Association for Computational Linguistics.

Pranav Rajpurkar, Jian Zhang, Konstantin Lopyrev, and Percy Liang. 2016. SQuAD: 100,000+ questions for machine comprehension of text. In *Proceedings of the 2016 Conference on Empirical Methods in Natural Language Processing*, pages 2383–2392, Austin, Texas. Association for Computational Linguistics.

Roy Schwartz, Jesse Dodge, Noah A Smith, and Oren Etzioni. 2019. Green AI. *arXiv preprint arXiv:1907.10597*.

Rico Sennrich, Barry Haddow, and Alexandra Birch. 2016. Neural Machine Translation of Rare Words with Subword Units. In *Proceedings of the 54th Annual Meeting of the Association for Computational Linguistics (Volume 1: Long Papers)*, pages 1715–1725.

Claude Shannon. 1951. Prediction and entropy of printed English. *Bell System Technical Journal*, 30:51–64.

Emma Strubell, Ananya Ganesh, and Andrew McCallum. 2019. Energy and Policy Considerations for Deep Learning in NLP. *arXiv preprint arXiv:1906.02243*.

Guy Tevet and Jonathan Berant. 2020. Evaluating the Evaluation of Diversity in Natural Language Generation. *arXiv preprint arXiv:2004.02990*.

Reut Tsarfaty, Dan Bareket, Stav Klein, and Amit Seker. 2020. From SPMRL to NMRL: What did we learn (and unlearn) in a decade of parsing morphologically-rich languages (MRLs)? *arXiv preprint arXiv:2005.01330*.

Ashwin K Vijayakumar, Michael Cogswell, Ramprasath R. Selvaraju, Qing Sun, Stefan Lee, David Crandall, and Dhruv Batra. 2016. Diverse beam search: Decoding diverse solutions from neural sequence models. *arXiv preprint arXiv:1610.02424*.

Sean Welleck, Ilia Kulikov, Stephen Roller, Emily Dinan, Kyunghyun Cho, and Jason Weston. 2020. Neural text generation with unlikelihood training. In *International Conference on Learning Representations*.

Thomas Wolf, Lysandre Debut, Victor Sanh, Julien Chaumond, Clement Delangue, Anthony Moi, Pierric Cistac, Tim Rault, R'emi Louf, Morgan Funtowicz, and Jamie Brew. 2019. HuggingFace's Transformers: State-of-the-art Natural Language Processing. *ArXiv*, abs/1910.03771.

Yonghui Wu, Mike Schuster, Zhifeng Chen, Quoc V. Le, Mohammad Norouzi, Wolfgang Macherey, Maxim Krikun, Yuan Cao, Qin Gao, Klaus Macherey, Jeff Klingner, Apurva Shah, Melvin Johnson, Xiaobing Liu, Łukasz Kaiser, Stephan Gouws, Yoshikiyo Kato, Taku Kudo, Hideto Kazawa, Keith Stevens, George Kurian, Nishant Patil, Wei Wang, Cliff Young, Jason Smith, Jason Riesa, Alex Rudnick, Oriol Vinyals, Greg Corrado, Macduff Hughes, and Jeffrey Dean. 2016. Google's neural machine translation system: Bridging the gap between human and machine translation.

Rowan Zellers, Yonatan Bisk, Roy Schwartz, and Yejin Choi. 2018. SWAG: A large-scale adversarial dataset for grounded commonsense inference. In *Proceedings of the 2018 Conference on Empirical Methods in Natural Language Processing*, pages 93–104, Brussels, Belgium. Association for Computational Linguistics.

Tianyi Zhang, Varsha Kishore, Felix Wu, Kilian Q Weinberger, and Yoav Artzi. 2019. Bertscore: Evaluating Text Generation with BERT. In *International Conference on Learning Representations*.

G. K. Zipf. 1935. *The psycho-biology of language*. Houghton, Mifflin, Oxford, England.

A   Stratified Bins

The bin's assignment is based on the words' frequency of the trainset, but the bins can only be based on the intersection of the high-freq words in train, and all the words in test set. Any high/mid/low-freq train word that occurs in the test will be assigned to its appropriate bin. Code is provided.

B   Algorithms for computing first and first ten guesses

Algorithm 1 Top1 Target Word Search

1: **procedure** TARGETFIND1($w_{<t}$, w_t, *model*)
2:     $cxt \leftarrow w_{<t}$
3:     $word \leftarrow empty$
4:     **while** str($word$) in str(w_t) **do**
5:         $cxt \leftarrow$ Cat(cxt,$word$)
6:         $P_{wpc_t} \leftarrow$ Predict(cxt,$model$)
7:         $top_1 \leftarrow$ ArgMax(P_{wpc_t})
8:         $word \leftarrow$ Cat($word$,top_1)
9:         **if** str($word$) = str(w_t) **then**
10:             return True
11:         **end if**
12:         **if** str($word$) not in str(w_t) **then**
13:             return False
14:         **end if**
15:     **end while**
16: **end procedure**

C   Protocol to elicit paraphrase pairs

We provide here the guidelines to elicit rare/common paraphrase sentences. First, a simple routine extracts possible triples that constructs the linguistic relationship desired of hypo/hypernym and a hypernym-sibling ((x_r,x_h,x_a)). We begin by taking the intersection of the vocabulary seen in the training

Algorithm 2 TopK Depth-First Search

1: **procedure** TARGETFIND2($w_{<t}$, w_t, $model$)
2:    $cxt \leftarrow w_{<t}$
3:    $P_{wpc_t} \leftarrow \texttt{Predict}(cxt, model)$
4:    $top_{10} \leftarrow \texttt{Top10}(P_{wpc_t})$
5:    **for** $root$ in top_{10} **do**
6:       $roots.append(root)$
7:    **end for**
8:    **for** $root$ in $roots$ **do**
9:       $paths \leftarrow \texttt{List}(root)$
10:      **while** $paths$ **do**
11:         $path \leftarrow \texttt{Pop}(paths)$
12:         $basic_{cxt} \leftarrow w_{<t}$
13:         $cxt \leftarrow \texttt{Cat}(basic_{cxt}, path)$
14:         $P_{wpc_t} \leftarrow \texttt{Predict}(cxt, model)$
15:         $top_{10} \leftarrow \texttt{Top10}(P_{wpc_t})$
16:         **for** wpc_t in top_{10} **do**
17:            $word \leftarrow \texttt{str}(wpc_{pre}, wpc_t)$
18:            **if** $word = \texttt{str}(w_t)$ **then**
19:               return True
20:            **else if** $word$ in $\texttt{str}(w_t)$ **then**
21:               $new \leftarrow \texttt{Cat}(path, wpc_t)$
22:               $paths.append(new)$
23:            **end if**
24:         **end for**
25:      **end while**
26:    **end for**
27:    return False
28: **end procedure**

---

is a mixture of carbon dioxide and carbon monoxide.

(b) The `gas` occurring in such situations is a mixture of carbon dioxide and carbon monoxide.

(c) The `liquid` occurring in such situations is a mixture of carbon dioxide and carbon monoxide.

Here is a common-word triple example following (x_c, x_h, x_a) order

(a) Because of the poor economy, the factory will immediately `discontinue` operations.

(b) Because of the poor economy, the factory will immediately `cease` operations.

(c) Because of the poor economy, the factory will immediately `continue` operations.

The complete sentence list can be found at `https:// github.com/shiranD/word_level_evaluation`.

partition of the Wiki-103 corpus with that found in WordNet (using the NLTK package (Loper and Bird, 2002)), and then further filtered for vocabulary items with WordNet entries exhibiting the desired linguistic relationship. (A synonym/antonym construction could also have been chosen alternatively).

The frequency dynamic for the rare/common triples $(x_r/x_c, x_h, x_a)$ was (low, mid/high, mid/high) and for the common (mid/high, mid/high, mid/high) respectively. Words occurring fewer than 50 times in the Wiki-103 training partition were categorized as "low," and were categorized as "mid/high" otherwise. Finally, a human annotator manually identified an appropriate context sentence for each target word via online search across the following web-based dictionaries: `merriam-webster.com`, `thesaurus.com`, `sentencedict.com`, and `dictionary.cambridge.org`. Here is a rare-word triple example following (x_r, x_h, x_a) order.

(a) The `afterdamp` occurring in such situations

On Aligning OpenIE Extractions with Knowledge Bases: A Case Study

Kiril Gashteovski[1,2], **Rainer Gemulla**[1], **Bhushan Kotnis**[2], **Sven Hertling**[1], **Christian Mcilicke**[1]

[1]University of Mannheim, Germany, [2]NEC Labs Europe GmbH, Germany

`{k.gashteovski,rgemulla}@uni-mannheim.de, bhushan.kotnis@neclab.eu`
`{sven,christian}@informatik.uni-mannheim.de`

Abstract

Open information extraction (OIE) is the task of extracting relations and their corresponding arguments from natural language text in unsupervised manner. Outputs of such systems are used for downstream tasks such as question answering and automatic knowledge base (KB) construction. Many of these downstream tasks rely on aligning OIE triples with reference KBs. Such alignments are usually evaluated w.r.t. a specific downstream task and, to date, no direct manual evaluation of such alignments has been performed. In this paper, we directly evaluate how OIE triples from the OPIEC corpus are related to the DBpedia KB w.r.t. information content. First, we investigate OPIEC triples and DBpedia facts having the same arguments by comparing the information on the OIE surface relation with the KB relation. Second, we evaluate the expressibility of general OPIEC triples in DBpedia. We investigate whether—and, if so, how—a given OIE triple can be mapped to a single KB fact. We found that such mappings are not always possible because the information in the OIE triples tends to be more specific. Our evaluation suggests, however, that significant part of OIE triples can be expressed by means of KB formulas instead of individual facts.

1 Introduction

Open Information Extraction (OIE) systems extract relations and their corresponding arguments from natural language text in unsupervised manner (Banko et al., 2007). Consider the sentence *"Bell, which is a telecommunication company, is located in L. A."*; an OIE system may extract the triples: *("Bell"; "is"; "telecommunication company")* and *("Bell"; "is located in"; "L. A.")*. Such triples are used in downstream tasks, such as word embeddings generation (Stanovsky et al., 2015), information retrieval (Kadry and Dietz, 2017) and entity aspect linking (Nanni et al., 2019).

OIE triples contain surface relations, which often makes their semantics ambiguous (Gashteovski et al., 2019). This poses difficulties for OIE triples to be used in downstream tasks (Broscheit et al., 2017). By contrast, KB relations have precise semantics and are machine-readable (Banko and Etzioni, 2008). To bridge this gap between OIE and KBs, many methods were proposed for aligning OIE triples with reference KBs. In such work, the goal is to associate an OIE triple with an *existing* KB fact (assuming they have the same disambiguated arguments), such that both triples have the same semantics; e.g., the OIE triple *(Jeff Bezos; "be CEO of"; Amazon.com)* and the KB fact (Jeff Bezos; dbo:ceo; Amazon.com). These methods are primarily used for bootstrapping OIE systems (Lockard et al., 2019), but also for other tasks such as link prediction (Gupta et al., 2019). Other methods map any OIE triple to a KB schema (Zhang et al., 2019); e.g. the OIE triple *(Emmanuel Macron; "be president of"; France)* could be mapped to (E. M.; dbo:president; France) even if this fact is not present in the reference KB. Such methods are used for downstream tasks such as automatic KB construction (Dong et al., 2014).

To date, alignments between OIE triples and KBs are evaluated automatically w.r.t. downstream task. Such automatic evaluations, however, do not provide insights about the information content between the alignments, which require expert manual evaluation. In this paper, we manually compare the information content of an OIE corpus—OPIEC (Gashteovski et al., 2019)—and reference KB—DBpedia (Auer et al., 2007)—under optimal alignments.[1] Both resources are automatically generated from Wikipedia, making them comparable resources for evaluation.

---

[1]All resources of the study are available on
`https://www.uni-mannheim.de/dws/research/`
`resources/opiec/`

Proceedings of the First Workshop on Evaluation and Comparison of NLP Systems (Eval4NLP), pages 143–154,
November 20, 2020. ©2020 Association for Computational Linguistics

First, we study the properties of the alignments between OPIEC triples and DBpedia facts which have the same argument pair. Consider the OIE triple t: *(Jeff Bezos; "is CEO of"; Amazon.com)* and two possible KB alignments f_1: (J. B.; dbo:ceo; Amazon.com) and f_2: (J. B.; dbo:employer; Amazon.com). The fact f_1 has same semantics as the OIE triple t. However, t is semantically more specific than f_2, since it provides additional information about J. B. being employed as CEO. Therefore, f_2 expresses *some* information in t, but not all information. In our evaluation, we consider the best possible alignment (e.g., f_1 is considered to be the best alignment) and we investigate its semantics. Note that our goal is *not* to compare different alignment strategies. Rather, *we consider the best possible alignment* and the goal is to *investigate the limits* of such alignments. We found that these alignments are usually semantically related, but quite often the open relation is more specific, thus carrying more information than the KB fact.

Second, we evaluate the expressibility of any OPIEC triple w.r.t. DBpedia by studying whether a given OIE triple can be mapped to a KB fact. In this case, there might not be a known relation in DBpedia between the arguments of the OPIEC triple. We evaluate whether an OPIEC triple can be expressed with a DBpedia fact. Consider the OIE triple *(Emmanuel Macron; "be president of"; France)*. DBpedia does not contain this fact, nevertheless, it can be fully expressed with (E. M.; dbo:president; France) and partially expressed with (E. M.; dbo:nationality; France). We found that most OPIEC triples can be expressed with DBpedia facts, but many of them only partially. Moreover, large fraction of the partially expressible triples can be fully expressed with KB formulas; e.g. OIE triple *(J. F. Kennedy; "be grandchild of"; P. J. Kennedy)* can be partially expressed with the KB fact (J. F. K.; dbo:relative; P. J. K.) and fully expressed with KB formula $\exists x$: (J. F. K.; dbo:parent; x) $\wedge$ (x; dbo:parent; P. J. K.).

Our evaluations focus on the OPIEC corpus, which was extracted with the OIE system MinIE. This makes the evaluation focused on one particular OIE system. To gain insight into transferability, we studied how the findings of our evaluations transfer to OIE triples produced by other OIE systems. We found that the results generally transfer over, though some OIE systems tend to produce more specific output.

2 Analysis of OPIEC Triples and DBpedia Facts with Same Arguments

In this section, we evaluate the semantics of alignments between OPIEC triples and DBpedia facts with the same arguments. Such alignments are inspired by the Distant Supervision Assumption (DSA), which is originally used for traditional information extraction tasks (Mintz et al., 2009). The DSA asserts that whenever there is a KB fact and a sentence mentioning the entity pair of the KB fact, then that sentence expresses the information contained in the KB fact. Similarly, the DSA within OIE context asserts that whenever there is an OIE triple for which there is a KB fact having the same arguments, then the OIE triple expresses the information of the KB fact.

DSA is key assumption used for bootstrapping OIE extractors (Pal and Mausam, 2016). By using the DSA, some methods bootstrap a training set that is used either for learning OIE extraction rules (Gotti and Langlais, 2019) or learning a neural model for extracting OIE triples (Cui et al., 2018; Kolluru et al., 2020). Wu and Weld (2010) used Wikipedia infoboxes (via DBpedia) as source for distant supervision: if there is Wikipedia sentence that contains an entity pair and a corresponding DBpedia entry with the same entity pair, then they store the syntactic patterns (e.g., shortest path in the dependency parse tree) between the two entities. These syntactic patterns are used for learning OIE extraction rules. The assumption is that the KB relation and the syntactic pattern instance (i.e., the *open* relation) express same information. Other OIE methods exploit the DSA similarly, including OLLIE (Mausam et al., 2012), ReNoun, (Yahya et al., 2014), NestIE (Bhutani et al., 2016), BONIE (Saha et al., 2017) and OpenCeres (Lockard et al., 2019).

2.1 KB Hits

For some OIE triples with disambiguated arguments, there are corresponding KB facts with the same argument pairs. Gashteovski et al. (2019) used this principle—which they called *KB hit*—to roughly measure the amount of OIE triples for which there is information in a reference KB. In particular, consider an OIE triple *(s, r_{open}, o)* where s, o are disambiguated and r_{open} is the open relation of the triple. Then, if there is at least one KB fact such that (s, r_{KB}, o) or (o, r_{KB}, s)—where r_{KB} is a KB relation—we say that the OIE triple

Figure 1: Hit categories indicate semantic relatedness between OIE triple and its KB hits.

has a KB hit. Note that one OIE triple may have more than one KB hit.

A single KB hit indicates an OIE triple for which a KB fact exists. However, it says nothing about *how* the OIE triple and the KB fact are semantically related. The DSA goes a step further and indicates semantic relatedness: if there is an OIE triple with a KB hit, then the OIE triple expresses the information of the KB triple. We study the semantic relatedness between an OIE triple and its KB hit using four *hit categories: Same, OIE-More-Specific, KB-More-Specific* and *Different*.

Same: OIE triple and KB fact are semantically equivalent, i.e., they express the same information. In Fig. 1, the OIE triple *(Jeff Bezos; "is CEO of"; Amazon.com)* expresses the same information as the KB fact (Amazon.com; dbo:ceo; Jeff Bezos).

OIE-More-Specific: OIE triple is semantically more specific than the KB fact, i.e., it expresses the KB fact along with additional information not present in the KB fact. In Fig. 1, the OIE triple is more specific than the KB hit (Jeff Bezos; dbo:employer; Amazon.com), because the OIE triple implies the KB fact and additionally expresses that Jeff Bezos is a CEO.

KB-More-Specific: KB fact is semantically more specific than the OIE triple, i.e., it expresses the OIE triple along with additional information not present in the OIE triple; e.g., OIE triple *(Angela Merkel; "is politician from"; Germany)* and its KB hit (A. M.; dbo:chancellor; Germany). Contrary to *OIE-More-Specific*, KB relations in such cases cannot be inferred from the OIE triple.

Different: OIE triple is semantically different than the KB fact, i.e., it expresses conceptually different information than the KB fact. Such KB hits cannot be compared in terms of more-general or more-specific relatedness. In Fig. 1, the KB hit (Amazon.com; dbo:foundedBy; Jeff Bezos) expresses different information w.r.t. the OIE triple, because *CEO* and *founder* are different concepts.

In case there are several KB hits for one OIE triple, each KB hit is assigned a separate category (Fig. 1). We assign only one label—*best hit*—describing the best possible semantic relatedness of the OIE triple w.r.t. all KB hits. Particularly, the best hit label is the first hit-category label appearing in the following order: *Same, OIE-More-Specific, KB-More-Specific* and *Different* (e.g., in Fig. 1, the best hit is *Same*). In our evaluation, we consider the best hits only, because we are interested in the best possible alignment of OIE triples with KB facts.

2.2 Study Design

The goal of the study is to *investigate the limits* of semantic relatedness between OPIEC triples and DBpedia facts having the same arguments. We study this by investigating what can be achieved if: (1) arguments are correctly disambiguated, (2) OIE triples are correctly extracted, (3) OIE relations are disambiguated. To this end, we used a subset of OPIEC-Linked: the largest OIE corpus to date, having 6M OIE triples with disambiguated arguments. Since we focus only on OIE triples that are correctly extracted, we filtered out triples from OPIEC-Linked that we found to be noisy, which left us with around 3M triples.[2] Details about the data are discussed in Appendix A.

Next, we constructed a random sample of 100 correctly extracted OIE triples from OPIEC which also have KB hits in DBpedia. We show to human annotator the OIE triple and the relevant KB hit information: 1) KB hits: every possible KB hit; 2) KB types: to assure the labeler that the types of the OIE triple's arguments match the domain/range constraints of the KB relation counterpart; 3) KB relation information: domain, range, description, etc., to help the labeler understand the exact semantics of the KB relation. Each KB hit of the OIE triple was labeled with one of the four hit categories. For each OIE triple, we keep the label of the best hit.

We split the OPIEC data into two subsets—*All relations* and *Is-a relation*—which are studied separately. The reason is that we have a substantial amount of triples having *Is-a relation* form *(subject; "be"; object)*, which express types; e.g., *(Berlin; "be"; City)*. We treat such triples differently to evaluate how the type information extracted from OIE compares with current KB information. The subset *All relations* are all OPIEC triples except the triples with *Is-a relation*. Both sub-studies follow the procedure explained in the previous two paragraphs.

---

[2]In the remainder of the paper, we refer to this dataset as OPIEC for simplicity

2.3 Experimental Results and Discussion

All-relations. We observed that in 88% of the cases, the OIE triple from OPIEC is able to semantically express its best hit KB fact from DBpedia (Fig. 2a). However, in almost half of these cases (40% of all triples) the OIE triple is more specific, meaning that it expresses the information of the KB fact along with additional information. Consider the OIE triple: *(All We Grow; "be debut album of"; S. Carey)* and its KB hit (All We Grow; dbo:artist; S. C.), whereas the OIE triple expresses the information of the KB hit fact, but it contains additional information about the album. In 12% of the cases, the OIE triple is not able to express its best hit; i.e., either the KB triple is more specific—meaning, the KB triple cannot be inferred by the OIE triple—or the semantics of the OIE triple is different than the semantics of the KB fact. More precisely, in 7% of the cases the OIE triple is more generic than its KB hit; e.g., OIE triple *(Rhacophorus annamensis; "be species of"; Frog)* and KB hit (R. a.; dbo:order; Frog). Judging from the OIE triple only, it is not enough to infer the relation between the two entities (e.g., order, genus, kingdom, etc.). Finally, 5% of the triples have different semantics than their KB hit; e.g., *(Saab Automobile; "test V8 in"; Saab 99)* v.s. (Saab 99; dbo:manufacturer; Saab A.).

Is-a relation. We observed that OIE triples with *Is-a* relation are more specific than DBpedia types in roughly 2/3 of the cases (Fig. 2b). In only 1/3 of the OIE triples, the KB contains an equivalent type. There are almost no cases where either the OIE type is more generic than the KB type, nor when they are different. This suggests that OIE triples with *Is-a relation* can provide more fine-grained types for the KB; e.g. OIE triple *(Tony Blair; "be"; Prime minister)* is more fine-grained than DBpedia type (Tony Blair; type; OfficeHolder). From the type "Prime minister" one can infer the type "OfficeHolder", but not the other way around.

2.4 Qualitative Study

Argument type information within the OIE relation is frequent reason for an OPIEC triple to be more specific than its KB hit in DBpedia. In particular, the details in the relation refer to more fine grained types for the argument(s); e.g., OIE triple *(Strul; "is Swedish film directed by"; Jonas Frick)* and its KB hit (Strul; dbo:director; Jonas Frick). The type available for Strul is "film". If there was a type "Swedish film" in DBpedia, then this align-

ment would have been equivalent. For the cases where the OIE triple represents different information than the KB hit, we found that usually the information on both sides is somehow semantically related; e.g., OIE triple *(s; "be CEO of"; o)* and its KB hit (s; dbo:founder; o). In this example, "CEO" and "founder" are related concepts, but they are semantically different.

3 Expressibility of OPIEC triples with DBpedia

In the previous section, we evaluated the limits of aligning OIE triples from OPIEC for which KB facts exist in DBpedia. Such cases, however, comprise only $\frac{1}{4}$ of the data. In this section, we evaluate all cases: the limits of aligning *any* OPIEC triple with a DBpedia fact. Our goal is to answer the question of whether any OPIEC triple contains information which is relevant for DBpedia and, if so, *how* can it be expressed with the KB. We measured relevance by quantifying the information that can be expressed with KB language and we study how can such information be expressed.

3.1 One Triple Assumption

Many methods use large-scale outputs of OIE systems for downstream tasks by trying to express *one* OIE triple with *one* KB fact. This includes mapping open relations to a KB relation for improving slot filling (Soderland et al., 2013, 2015; Angeli et al., 2015; Yu et al., 2017), unifying open relations into a single KB schema (Bovi et al., 2015), canonicalizing open relations into relational synsets that are mapped to a KB relation (Galárraga et al., 2014), mapping open relations to lexical KBs (Grycner and Weikum, 2014), and mapping OIE triples to KB facts (Soderland et al., 2010; Zhang et al., 2019; Putri et al., 2019) which are used for KB population (Soderland et al., 2013; Dutta et al., 2013, 2015). Such methods implicitly make the *One Triple Assumption (OTA): "Any OIE triple can be expressed with one KB fact"*. For example, the OIE triple *(Emmanuel Macron; "be president of"; France)* can be expressed with the KB relation dbo:president: (Emmanuel Macron; dbo:president; France). Note that such mapping is possible even if this particular instance does not exist in the KB (e.g. in DBpedia, there is no KB fact stating that Emmanuel Macron is president of France).

Sometimes, an OIE triple cannot be expressed by a single KB fact, but it can be expressed by multiple

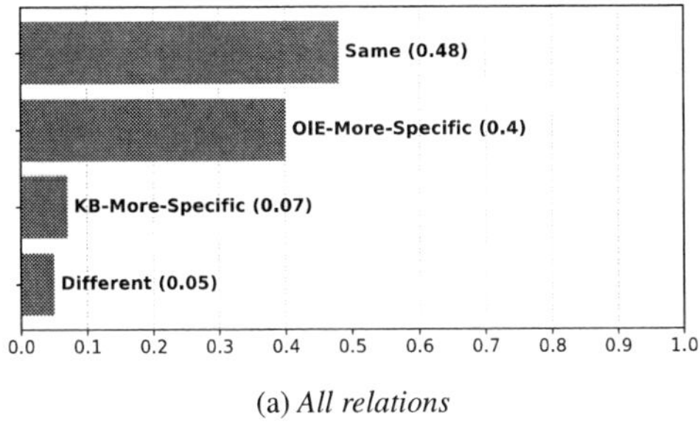

(a) *All relations*

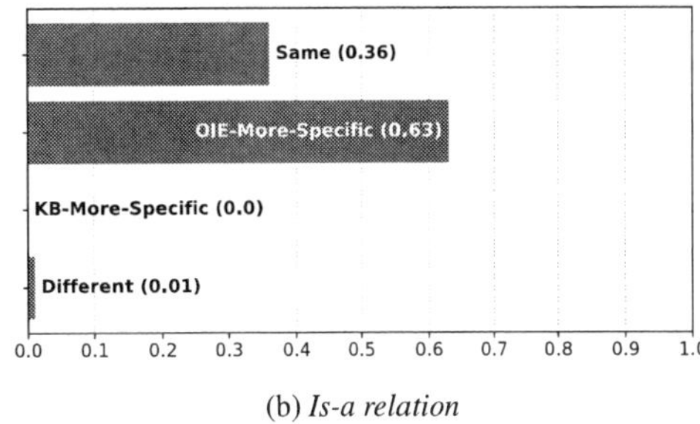

(b) *Is-a relation*

Figure 2: Semantic relatedness between OIE triples from OPIEC and their DBpedia hits

KB facts or a first-order logic KB formula. Consider the OIE triple *(J. F. Kennedy; "be grandchild of"; P.J. Kennedy)*. This triple can be represented with the KB formula $\exists x$: (J. F. K.; dbo:parent; x) $\wedge$ (x; dbo:parent; P. J. K.), because there is no KB relation expressing "grandchild" relationship between two entities. Similarly, Das et al. (2016) use multi-hop reasoning between two entities in a KB to infer new relations, while Fu et al. (2019) do multi-hop reasoning over OIE data.

3.2 Expressibility Levels

To understand the semantic expressibility of an OIE triple w.r.t. KB facts, we differentiate three possible expressibility levels: *Fully-Expressible, Partly-Expressible* or *Not-Expressible*.

Fully-Expressible: Semantics of an OIE triple can be completely expressed with one KB fact; e.g., OIE triple *(E. Schmidt; "be chairman of"; Google)* and KB fact (Google; dbo:chairman; E. S.).

Partly-Expressible: The semantics of an OIE triple can be partly expressed with one KB fact, i.e. the OIE triple contains additional information which is not present in the KB fact. For example, the OIE triple *(Steffi Graf; "defeated"; Natasha Zvereva)* is *Partly-Expressible*, because there is no KB relation about one athlete defeating another; though it can be partly expressed with the KB fact (Steffi Graf; dbo:opponent; Natasha Zvereva).

Not-Expressible: The semantics of an OIE triple cannot be expressed with one KB fact, i.e. it is neither *Fully-Expressible* nor *Partly-Expressible*. For example, the OIE triple *(IBM; "has Color Paint for"; IBM PCjr)* cannot be expressed with a single KB fact, because the KB does not possess schemas for expressing such information in a single fact.

We make use of the above-defined expressibility levels to understand the semantic expressibility of an OIE triple w.r.t. KB formulas as well. For ex-

ample, the OIE triple *(IBM; "has Color Paint for"; IBM PCjr)* is *Not-Expressible* w.r.t. a single KB fact, but it is *Fully-Expressible* w.r.t. KB formulas, because we can represent that OIE triple with the KB formula: (IBM; dbo:product; Color Paint) $\wedge$ (Color Paint; dbo:computingPlatform; IBM PCjr), i.e., two KB facts.

3.3 Study Design

The goal of the study is to evaluate whether the information found in any OPIEC triple is relevant for DBpedia. We do this by measuring the amount of OIE information which can be expressed with KB language and we study the different levels of expressibility. We constructed a random sample of 100 correctly extracted OIE triples from OPIEC with disambiguated arguments and an expert labeler evaluated the expressibility level for each OIE triple w.r.t. DBpedia fact and w.r.t. KB formula. First, we measured in how many cases an OPIEC triple can be expressed with *one* DBpedia fact fully or partially. Then, when the OPIEC triple is *Partly-Expressible* (or *Not-Expressible*), we investigate if it can become *Fully-Expressible* (or *Partly-Expressible/Fully-Expressible*) with a KB formula.

3.3.1 Expressibility of OPIEC Triple with a Single DBpedia Fact

Each OIE triple is presented to a human annotator along with: 1) argument types from DBpedia of the OIE triple, 2) a list of candidate DBpedia relations, 3) relevant information about the candidate DBpedia relations (descriptions, domain/range types, ...), 4) all other relevant information from DBpedia. The question asked was *"Can the OIE triple be expressed with one KB fact?"* Given all KB information available, the human annotator then assigned one of the three possible labels: *Fully-Expressible, Partly-Expressible* and *Not-Expressible*. Note that

147

the assumption here is that we have a *perfect mapping* from OIE triple to KB fact. Thus, the labeler assigns the best possible mapping as a final label. The goal is to evaluate—given perfect mapping—the expressibility of an OIE triple via KB fact.

The KB relation candidates are generated by two methods: *KB hit counts* (aggregates *hit relations*) and *any relation* (uses any DBpedia relation satisfying the type constraints of the OIE arguments).

Hit relation. When possible, we aligned every OPIEC triple to DBpedia via KB hit statistics. In previous step, for every open relation, we counted the corresponding KB relations obtained from the KB hits. The counts are sorted in descending order.

Any relation. For aligning the OIE triples to KB facts, it is important that we go beyond the KB hits statistics, because such statistically-based methods are useful only for frequent open relations. To this end, we generate more candidates by additionally considering the DBpedia relations that fit the domain/range constraints imposed by the types of the OPIEC triple. In case the DBpedia types for the OIE arguments themselves are wrong or missing, the labeler corrects them with the appropriate DBpedia type. With this strategy, we ensure that we show every possible fitting candidate to the labeler.

3.3.2 Expressibility of OPIEC Triple with KB Formula

Since for many cases OPIEC triples cannot be fully expressed with a single DBpedia fact, an expert labeler manually generated KB formulas (when possible) that switch the expressibility level from *Partly-Expressible* to *Fully-Expressible* or from *Not-Expressible* to *Fully/Partly-Expressible*. For example, the OIE triple *(Garrett Davis; "is Representative from"; Kentucky)* is *Partly-Expressible* with DBpedia fact (G. D.; dbo:region; Kentucky), but it is fully expressible with KB formula: (G. D.; dbo:profession; State rep.) ∧ (G. D.; dbo:state; K.).

3.4 Results and Discussion

If we consider only the hit relation candidates (light-blue bars, Fig. 3a), only 29% of the OPIEC triples can be fully expressed with a single DBpedia fact; partly expressed another 29%; and 42% of the OPIEC triples cannot be expressed at all. This suggests that KB hit relation counts contain signal for KB expressibility, but not enough to express all OPIEC triples. The main reason is that KB hit relation counts work well only for the triples having open relations with high frequency. Higher

frequency of an open relation implies higher likelihood for a KB hit, thus higher likelihood for capturing the semantic content (fully or partially) of an OIE triple by one of the candidates. Many open relations are not frequent enough, which is the main reason why in 42% of the OIE triples the KB hit relations are not enough to express the OIE triple.

When we extend the limits of the candidates by including any DBpedia relation which respects the constraints of the argument types (represented as blue bars in the middle), then we significantly reduce the amount of OPIEC triples which cannot be expressed with one DBpedia fact (from 42% down to 17%). More precisely, 42% of the triples can be fully expressed and 41% can be partly expressed with one DBpedia fact. This study shows that most of the OPIEC triples are relevant for DBpedia, because more than 80% of them can be expressed with a single DBpedia fact. However, we observed that nearly half of these cases are only partly expressible, since the OPIEC triples contain additional details which cannot be expressed in DBpedia. The reason for this is because KB relations have very strict semantics, while open relations have the expressibility of natural language.

When we introduce KB formulas, the expressibility of the OPIEC triples is significantly improved. We observed that the number of OPIEC triples that can be fully expressed with DBpedia increased from 42% to 66%. This was mostly on the expense of the cases where an OPIEC triple is partly expressible w.r.t. DBpedia fact (it reduced these cases from 41% to 20%). Less significantly, the KB formulas allowed for some OPIEC triples that are not expressible via DBpedia to be expressible (percentage went down from 17% to 14%). We illustrate the expressibility of OIE triples with KB formulas in a few examples in Tab. 1.

Finally, 14% of the OPIEC triples cannot be expressed with DBpedia vocabulary neither with single DBpedia facts nor with KB formulas. Reasons include cases with tertiary relations or open relations which can be expressed via natural language, but not with DBpedia; e.g. OIE triple *(X; "sponsored"; Y)* cannot be expressed with DBpedia.

3.5 New Information for DBpedia

To evaluate how much of the OPIEC information is new for DBpedia, we used the OPIEC triples from the expressibility study. Based on the information content of the OIE triple and the content of DBpe-

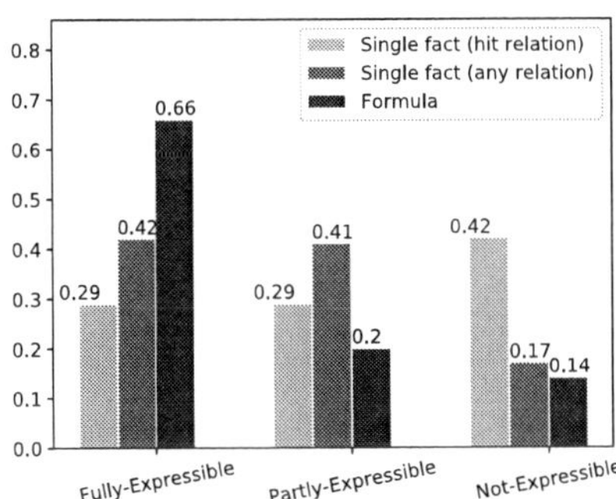

(a) Can an OPIEC triple be expressed in DBpedia?

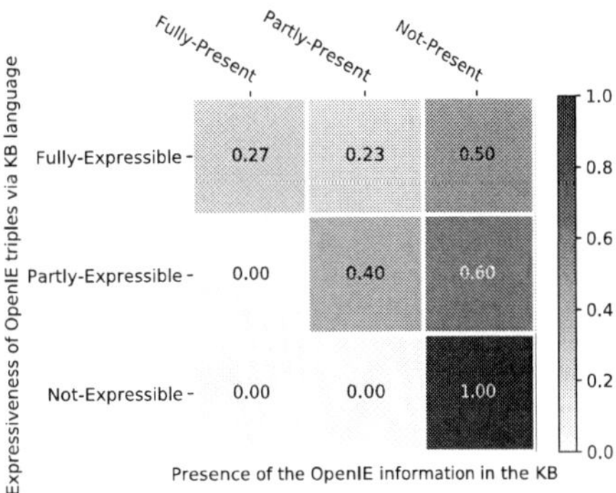

(b) Does DBpedia contain information from the OPIEC triple?

Figure 3: Expressibility and presence of OIE information within the KB

#	OIE triple	KB formula
t_1	Temporal annotation *(Coral Fang; "was released by"; Sire Records)* *Time: (in, 2003)*	(Coral Fang; dbo:recordLabel; Sire Records) ∧ (Coral Fang; dbo:releaseDate; 2003)
t_2	Complex formula *(Garrett Davis; "was Rep. from"; Kentucky)*	(G. D.; dbo:profession; State representative) ∧ [(G. D.; dbo:region; K.) ∨ (G. D.; dbo:state; K.)]
t_3	Existential quantification *(Franz Liszt; "transcribed piece for"; Piano solo)*	$\exists x$: (F. L.; dbo:write; x) ∧ (x; dbo:genre; P. solo)
t_4	Conjunctive formula *(Dick Ket; "was Dutch magic realist painter noted for"; Still life)*	(Dick Ket; dbo:nationality; Netherlands) ∧ (Dick Ket; dbo:genre; Magic realism) ∧ (Dick Ket; dbo:occupation; Painter) ∧ (Dick Ket; dbo:knownFor; Still life)

Table 1: Selected examples of OPIEC triples expressed with KB formulas

dia, an expert labeled each OIE triple with one of the three possible options: 1) completely present in the KB: there exists DBpedia fact or formula which fully expresses the OIE triple; 2) partly present in the KB: there exists DBpedia fact or formula which partly expresses the OIE triple; 3) not present in the KB: there is no existing DBpedia fact or formula which can fully or partially express the OIE triple.

We found that in 59% of the OIE triples the content is not present in DBpedia at all, in 23% is partly present and only in 18% it is fully present. This suggests that most OIE triples contain information which is either not present or not fully present in DBpedia. To investigate new *relevant*[3] information for DBpedia, we compared expressibility w.r.t. presence of the OIE information content in DBpedia (Fig. 3b). In general, we observed that most OIE information that is relevant for the KB is either not present or only partly present in DBpedia, showing the potential of such triples for downstream

[3]OIE triple: *relevant* for KB if it is expressible in that KB

tasks such as KB population (Lin et al., 2020).

4 Transferability

In this section, we study whether and to what extent the results of the evaluations transfer to other OIE systems. We used three other popular OIE systems: Stanford OIE (Angeli et al., 2015), RnnOIE (Stanovsky et al., 2018) and OpenIE 5 (Saha et al., 2018). We ran these OIE systems on the provenance sentences of the sampled triples used in our evaluations—explained in Sec. 2 and Sec. 3—and compared their outputs to their OPIEC counterparts (extracted with MinIE (Gashteovski et al., 2017)).

Consider the OPIEC triple *(Turf Buccaneers; "be album by"; Mac Dre)*. We use the provenance sentence from which this triple was extracted and we run the other OIE systems on the same sentence. Then, we select the triples that match the argument pair of the OPIEC triple; i.e. *(Turf Buccaneers, Mac Dre)* in the example. As before, we keep only the triples that are correctly extracted. Then, an anno-

Label	Stanford	OpenIE 5	RnnOIE	All
	OIE triples and KB facts with same args.			
Hit category	0.98	0.84	0.77	0.86
	Expressibility of OIE triples with DBpedia			
Single fact (hit relation)	0.92	0.93	0.85	0.90
Single fact (any KB rel.)	0.88	0.86	0.77	0.84
KB formula	0.98	0.89	0.89	0.92

Table 2: Label equivalence ratio of the evaluations: labels from OPIEC triples (produced by MinIE) v.s. labels from triples produced by other OIE systems. *All* column considers all the labels for the triples produced by the other OIE systems combined.

tator evaluates these OIE triples w.r.t. DBpedia for either hit category (Sec. 2) or expressibility level (Sec. 3). Finally, we compared these labels with the original labels of our evaluations for OPIEC.

In Sec. 4.3 we examine to what extent other OIE systems extract different entities (and entity pairs) than MinIE, given the same provenance sentences used in our study. In particular, we measure how many entities each OIE system extracts in general, how similar they are w.r.t. the entities extracted by MinIE, and to what extent the entities extracted by other OIE systems are also extracted by MinIE. Such study is important for evaluating whether other systems extract different entities, which would influence the findings of our study.

4.1 Hit Categories

We compared the newly assigned labels for hit categories from the other OIE systems with the original labels of our evaluation presented in Sec. 2 (Tab. 2). Overall, we found that in 86% of the cases the labels were equivalent (*label equivalence ratio*). In most cases for which there was a mismatch of the labels, the OPIEC triple has same semantics as the KB fact, while the triple by the other OIE system is more specific than the KB fact. Hence, when moving to other OIE systems, one should expect that they may produce more specific OIE triples.

We also observed the label equivalence ratio of the OPIEC triples w.r.t. the other OIE systems individually (Tab. 2). We found that RnnOIE has lowest label equivalence ratio (77%). Again, the main reason for mismatch is because RnnOIE extracts more specific triples than MinIE. This is because the goal of MinIE is to produce shorter extractions, while RnnOIE does not aim at reducing the length

of the extractions, thus producing more specific triples. Consequently, in many cases MinIE extracts triple having same semantics as the KB fact, while RnnOIE extracts a more specific triple.

On the other hand, Stanford OIE produced triples that have almost the same labels as OPIEC (98% of the labels are equivalent). The reason is that Stanford OIE was constructed with the slot filling task in mind, which results in producing shorter extractions (same goal as MinIE). Therefore, the specificity levels with MinIE are similar. OpenIE 5 is in between: it produces more specific triples than Stanford and less specific triples than RnnOIE.

4.2 Expressibility Levels

Following the same strategy as the labels for hit categories, we compared the newly assigned labels for expressibility levels from other OIE systems with the original labels of our evaluation for expressibility of OIE triples with DBpedia (Sec.3). We compared the labels for single fact (hit relation), single fact (any KB rel.) and KB formula (Tab. 2).

Our findings for the expressibility levels are similar to the findings discussed in Sec. 4.1. Overall, we found that the label equivalence ratio of the OPIEC triples and the triples produced by other OIE systems is relatively high. Again, most mismatches are because other OIE systems tend to produce more specific triples. Consequently, in such cases, when MinIE extracts triple that is *Fully-Expressible*, the other OIE systems extract triple that is *Partly-Expressible* with the KB.

4.3 Extracted Entities

To compare the entities extracted by MinIE with the entities extracted by the other OIE systems, we used the same provenance sentences from OPIEC's triples used in our studies (Sec. 2 and 3). From them, we extracted OIE triples with MinIE and the other OIE systems. Again, we kept only the triples generated by all systems that contain disambiguated arguments on both the subject and the object. We did not consider triples that contain more than one entity link per argument (e.g. some systems generate whole clauses as an object, which may contain more than one entity). For such extractions, it is not clear to which entity the argument is referring to. Finally, for each entity and entity pair, we computed counts, Jaccard distance w.r.t. MinIE and coverage by MinIE (Tab. 3).

For both the DSA and OTA sentences, we observed that MinIE extracts more arguments (and

DSA / OTA	Entities			Entity pairs		
	Count	Jaccard w.r.t. MinIE	Coverage by MinIE	Count	Jac. w.r.t. MinIE	Cov. by MinIE
MinIE	272 / 235	1.0 / 1.0	1.0 / 1.0	221 / 169	1.0 / 1.0	1.0 / 1.0
Stanford	156 / 120	0.44 / 0.45	0.83 / 0.92	99 / 80	0.23 / 0.29	0.61 / 0.70
OpenIE 5	70 / 81	0.21 / 0.32	0.83 / 0.95	38 / 47	0.11 / 0.21	0.68 / 0.81
RnnOIE	49 / 69	0.15 / 0.27	0.84 / 0.94	27 / 41	0.07 / 0.17	0.63 / 0.73

Table 3: Extracted entities by MinIE and other OIE systems for both studies: DSA (Sec. 2) / OTA (Sec. 3).

argument pairs) than other OIE systems. This is consistent with the findings of Gashteovski et al. (2017), where the authors report high recall for MinIE. Moreover, Lin et al. (2020) reported that MinIE extracts entities that are easier to disambiguate to KBs compared to other OIE systems, which is another reason why the number of extracted entities is lower in other systems.

Because of the lower amount of entities extracted by the other systems, the Jaccard distance between the entities extracted by MinIE and other systems is relatively low. If we turn to coverage by MinIE, however, we observed that most entities extracted by other OIE systems are also extracted by MinIE. This suggests that the extractions made by other OIE systems that are relevant for KBs were likely going to be extracted by MinIE as well. Based on these results, we conjecture that the findings of our study largely transfer over to other OIE systems.

4.4 Discussion

Overall, we found that OIE triples produced by other OIE systems tend to have very similar hit categories (as well as expressibility levels) with the OPIEC triples. Due to the fact that MinIE—OPIEC's underlying OIE system—is designed to produce less specific extractions, we observed that if one uses other OIE systems, it should be expected the extractions to be more specific. This, in turn, results in 1) producing larger fraction of triples that are more specific than the KB triple with the same argument pair; 2) producing larger fraction of triples that are *Partially-Expressible.*

As for the entities extracted by MinIE and other OIE systems, we found that MinIE extracts most of the entities that are extracted by the other OIE systems as well as additional entities. The reason for this observation is the high recall of MinIE as well as the compact extractions made by MinIE that contribute to extracting more KB-centric entities.

A limitation of this study is that we focus on the most common form of OIE extractions: OIE triples. Some OIE systems extract more complex structures—e.g. nested extractions (Bhutani et al., 2016)—which are not covered by this paper and require a separate study.

5 Main Findings and Conclusions

In this paper, we evaluated how OIE triples from the OPIEC corpus are related to the DBpedia KB w.r.t. information content. Both resources are automatically generated from same domain—OPIEC from the textual data and DBpedia from the semi-structured data of Wikipedia—which makes them compatible resources for evaluation.

First, we evaluated the semantic relatedness between OIE triples from OPIEC and DBpedia facts having the same arguments; i.e. the Distant Supervision Assumption (DSA). Such cases are important for downstream tasks and for bootstrapping OIE systems. In general, we found that such OPIEC triples are semantically related to the DBpedia facts, but quite often the OIE triples are more specific, thus capturing more information than the KB facts. Second, we evaluated the expressibility of any OPIEC triple w.r.t. DBpedia: whether (and *how*) an OPIEC triple can be expressed with a *single* DBpedia fact; i.e. the One Triple Assumption (OTA). OTA is an implicit assumption used in tasks such as slot filling. We found that expressing an OPIEC triple with a single DBpedia fact is often limited, and that the use of KB formulas improves the expressibility of OIE triples with KB language significantly. Third, we found that most OPIEC triples contain information which is not present in DBpedia, thus showing the potential of OIE triples for tasks such as KB population. Finally, we found that the findings of our case study—which was based on the OIE system MinIE—are likely to transfer over to other OIE systems.

Our study suggests that most information found in OIE triples is not present in the KB. One way to harvest such knowledge is to add OIE triples to a KB with universal schema (Riedel et al., 2013). We leave such evaluations for future work.

References

Gabor Angeli, Melvin Jose Johnson Premkumar, and Christopher D. Manning. 2015. Leveraging Linguistic Structure for Open Domain Information Extraction. In *Proc. of the Annual Meeting of the Association for Computational Linguistics (ACL)*, pages 344–354.

Sören Auer, Christian Bizer, Georgi Kobilarov, Jens Lehmann, Richard Cyganiak, and Zachary Ives. 2007. DBpedia: A Nucleus for a Web of Open Data. In *The Semantic Web*, pages 722–735.

Michele Banko, Michael J Cafarella, Stephen Soderland, Matthew Broadhead, and Oren Etzioni. 2007. Open Information Extraction from the Web. In *Proc. of the International Joint Conference on Artificial Intelligence (IJCAI)*, pages 2670–2676.

Michele Banko and Oren Etzioni. 2008. The Tradeoffs between Open and Traditional Relation Extraction. In *Proc. of the Annual Meeting of the Association for Computational Linguistics (ACL)*, pages 28–36.

Nikita Bhutani, HV Jagadish, and Dragomir Radev. 2016. Nested Propositions in Open Information Extraction. In *Proc. of the Conference on Empirical Methods in Natural Language Processing (EMNLP)*, pages 55–64.

Christian Bizer, Jens Lehmann, Georgi Kobilarov, Sören Auer, Christian Becker, Richard Cyganiak, and Sebastian Hellmann. 2009. DBpedia - a Crystallization Point for the Web of Data. *Journal of Web Semantics*, 7(3):154–165.

Claudio Delli Bovi, Luis Espinosa Anke, and Roberto Navigli. 2015. Knowledge Base Unification via Sense Embeddings and Disambiguation. In *Proc. of the Conference on Empirical Methods in Natural Language Processing (EMNLP)*, pages 726–736.

Samuel Broscheit, Kiril Gashteovski, and Martin Achenbach. 2017. OpenIE for Slot Filling at TAC KBP 2017-System Description. In *Proc. of the Text Analysis Conference (TAC)*.

Samuel Broscheit, Kiril Gashteovski, Yanjie Wang, and Rainer Gemulla. 2020. Can We Predict new Facts with Open Knowledge Graph Embeddings? A Benchmark for Open Link Prediction. In *Proc. of the Annual Meeting of the Association for Computational Linguistics (ACL)*, pages 2296–2308.

Lei Cui, Furu Wei, and Ming Zhou. 2018. Neural Open Information Extraction. *Proc. of the Annual Meeting of the Association for Computational Linguistics (ACL)*, pages 407–413.

Rajarshi Das, Arvind Neelakantan, David Belanger, and Andrew McCallum. 2016. Incorporating Selectional Preferences in Multi-hop Relation Extraction. In *Proc. of the Workshop on Automated Knowledge Base Construction (AKBC)*, pages 18–23.

Xin Dong, Evgeniy Gabrilovich, Geremy Heitz, Wilko Horn, Ni Lao, Kevin Murphy, Thomas Strohmann, Shaohua Sun, and Wei Zhang. 2014. Knowledge Vault: A Web-scale Approach to Probabilistic Knowledge Fusion. In *Proc. of the International Conference on Knowledge Discovery and Data Mining (KDD)*, pages 601–610.

Arnab Dutta, Christian Meilicke, Mathias Niepert, and Simone Paolo Ponzetto. 2013. Integrating Open and Closed Information Extraction: Challenges and First Steps. In *Proc. of Workshop NLP-DBPEDIA@ISWC*.

Arnab Dutta, Christian Meilicke, and Heiner Stuckenschmidt. 2015. Enriching Structured Knowledge with Open Information. In *Proc. of International Conf. on World Wide Web (WWW)*, pages 267–277.

Cong Fu, Tong Chen, Meng Qu, Woojeong Jin, and Xiang Ren. 2019. Collaborative Policy Learning for Open Knowledge Graph Reasoning. *Proc. of the Conference on Empirical Methods in Natural Language Processing (EMNLP)*, pages 2672–2681.

Luis Galárraga, Geremy Heitz, Kevin Murphy, and Fabian M. Suchanek. 2014. Canonicalizing Open Knowledge Bases. In *Proc. of the International Conference on Information and Knowledge Management (CIKM)*, pages 1679–1688.

Kiril Gashteovski, Rainer Gemulla, and Luciano Del Corro. 2017. MinIE: Minimizing Facts in Open Information Extraction. In *Proc. of the Conference on Empirical Methods in Natural Language Processing (EMNLP)*, pages 2630–2640.

Kiril Gashteovski, Sebastian Wanner, Sven Hertling, Samuel Broscheit, and Rainer Gemulla. 2019. OPIEC: An Open Information Extraction Corpus. In *Proc. of the Conference on Automated Knowledge Base Construction (AKBC)*.

Fabrizio Gotti and Philippe Langlais. 2019. Weakly Supervised, Data-Driven Acquisition of Rules for Open Information Extraction. In *Proc. of the Canadian Conference on Artificial Intelligence (CCAI)*, pages 16–28.

Adam Grycner and Gerhard Weikum. 2014. HARPY: Hypernyms and Alignment of Relational Paraphrases. In *Proc. of the International Conference on Computational Linguistics (COLING)*, pages 2195–2204.

Swapnil Gupta, Sreyash Kenkre, and Partha Talukdar. 2019. CaRe: Open Knowledge Graph Embeddings. In *Proc. of the Conference on Empirical Methods in Natural Language Processing and the International Joint Conference on Natural Language Processing (EMNLP-IJCNLP)*, pages 378–388.

Amina Kadry and Laura Dietz. 2017. Open Relation Extraction for Support Passage Retrieval: Merit and Open Issues. In *Proc. of International Conference on Research and Development in Information Retrieval (SIGIR)*, pages 1149–1152.

Keshav Kolluru, Samarth Aggarwal, Vipul Rathore, Soumen Chakrabarti, et al. 2020. IMoJIE: Iterative Memory-Based Joint Open Information Extraction. In *Proc. of the Annual Meeting of the Association for Computational Linguistics (ACL)*, pages 5871–5886.

Xueling Lin, Haoyang Li, Hao Xin, Zijian Li, and Lei Chen. 2020. KBPearl: A Knowledge Base Population System Supported by Joint Entity and Relation Linking. In *Proc. of the Very Large Data Base Endowment (PVLDB)*, pages 1035–1049.

Colin Lockard, Prashant Shiralkar, and Xin Luna Dong. 2019. OpenCeres: When Open Information Extraction Meets the Semi-Structured Web. In *Proc. of the Conference of the North American Chapter of the Association for Computational Linguistics: Human Language Technologies (NAACL-HLT)*, pages 3047–3056.

Mausam, Michael Schmitz, Robert Bart, Stephen Soderland, and Oren Etzioni. 2012. Open Language Learning for Information Extraction. In *Proc. of the Joint Conference on Empirical Methods in Natural Language Processing and Computational Natural Language Learning (EMNLP-CoNLL)*, pages 523–534.

Mike Mintz, Steven Bills, Rion Snow, and Dan Jurafsky. 2009. Distant Supervision for Relation Extraction without Labeled Data. In *Proc. of the Joint Conference of the Annual Meeting of the Association for Computational Linguistics and the International Joint Conference on Natural Language Processing (ACL-IJCNLP)*, pages 1003–1011.

Federico Nanni, Jingyi Zhang, Ferdinand Betz, and Kiril Gashteovski. 2019. EAL: A Toolkit and Dataset for Entity-Aspect Linking. In *Proc. of the Joint Conference on Digital Libraries (JCDL)*.

Harinder Pal and Mausam. 2016. Demonyms and Compound Relational Nouns in Nominal Open IE. In *Proc. of the Workshop on Automated Knowledge Base Construction (AKBC@NAACL-HLT)*, pages 35–39.

Rifki Afina Putri, Giwon Hong, and Sung-Hyon Myaeng. 2019. Aligning Open IE Relations and KB Relations using a Siamese Network Based on Word Embedding. In *Proc. of the International Conference on Computational Semantics (ICCS)*, pages 142–153.

Sebastian Riedel, Limin Yao, Andrew McCallum, and Benjamin M Marlin. 2013. Relation Extraction with Matrix Factorization and Universal Schemas. In *Proc. of the Conference of the North American Chapter of the Association for Computational Linguistics: Human Language Technologies (NAACL-HLT)*, pages 74–84.

Swarnadeep Saha, Harinder Pal, and Mausam. 2017. Bootstrapping for Numerical Open IE. In *Proc. of the Annual Meeting of the Association for Computational Linguistics (ACL)*, pages 317–323.

Swarnadeep Saha et al. 2018. Open Information Extraction from Conjunctive Sentences. In *Proceedings of the International Conference on Computational Linguistics (COLING)*, pages 2288–2299.

Stephen Soderland, John Gilmer, Robert Bart, Oren Etzioni, and Daniel S. Weld. 2013. Open Information Extraction to KBP Relations in 3 Hours. In *Proc. of the Text Analysis Conference (TAC)*.

Stephen Soderland, Natalie Hawkins, John Gilmer, and Daniel S. Weld. 2015. Combining Open IE and Distant Supervision for KBP Slot Filling. In *Proc. of the Text Analysis Conference (TAC)*.

Stephen Soderland, Brendan Roof, Bo Qin, Shi Xu, Mausam, and Oren Etzioni. 2010. Adapting Open Information Extraction to Domain-Specific Relations. *AI magazine*, 31(3):93–102.

Gabriel Stanovsky, Ido Dagan, et al. 2015. Open IE as an Intermediate Structure for Semantic tasks. In *Proceedings of the Annual Meeting of the Association for Computational Linguistics (ACL)*, pages 303–308.

Gabriel Stanovsky, Julian Michael, Luke Zettlemoyer, and Ido Dagan. 2018. Supervised open information extraction. In *Proceedings of the 2018 Conference of the North American Chapter of the Association for Computational Linguistics: Human Language Technologies, Volume 1 (Long Papers)*, pages 885–895.

Fei Wu and Daniel S. Weld. 2010. Open Information Extraction using Wikipedia. In *Proc. of the Annual Meeting of the Association for Computational Linguistics (ACL)*, pages 118–127.

Mohamed Yahya, Steven Whang, Rahul Gupta, and Alon Halevy. 2014. ReNoun: Fact Extraction for Nominal Attributes. In *Proc. of the Conference on Empirical Methods in Natural Language Processing (EMNLP)*, pages 325–335.

Dian Yu, Lifu Huang, and Heng Ji. 2017. Open Relation Extraction and Grounding. In *Proc. of the International Joint Conference on Natural Language Processing (IJCNLP)*, pages 854–864.

Dongxu Zhang, Subhabrata Mukherjee, Colin Lockard, Xin Luna Dong, and Andrew McCallum. 2019. OpenKI: Integrating Open Information Extraction and Knowledge Bases with Relation Inference. *Proc. of the Conference of the North American Chapter of the Association for Computational Linguistics - Human Language Technologies (NAACL-HLT)*.

A Reference Corpora and Methodology

A.1 OIE Data and Methodology

OIE Corpus. One of the major problems of aligning OIE triples with KB facts is that the OIE triples are consisted of surface patterns, which makes the triples highly ambiguous. To make such alignments possible, it is necessary that the arguments of the OIE triples are disambiguated. For these reasons, we chose OPIEC-Linked (Gashteovski et al., 2019) as an OIE corpus for our study, because it is the biggest OIE corpus to date, containing 6M triples with disambiguated arguments. OPIEC-Linked was constructed by running the OIE system MinIE-SpaTe over the entire English Wikipedia. The links in the text added by Wikipedia authors were kept, which provides golden disambiguation links for the arguments.

OPIEC Filters. The goal of the study is to investigate the limits of aligning OIE triples with KBs. For this reason, we assume both a perfect extractor and perfect alignments between the OIE triples and the KB facts. To reduce the noise from OPIEC-Linked, we followed (Broscheit et al., 2020) and filtered out the triples having the following properties: 1) confidence score is less than 0.3; 2) extraction type is SVOO, SVOC or extractions are made from the *apposition* dependency parse relation. In a preliminary study, we found these triples to be very noisy. For the remainder of the paper, we will refer to this data as OPIEC for simplicity.

Sampling Correctly Extracted OIE Triples for the DSA Study. The DSA implies that for each (correctly extracted) OIE triple which has a KB-hit, the open relation expresses the same information as the KB relation. The goal of the study is to *investigate the limits* of such alignments, which is why we consider only extractions that are correctly extracted. For this reason, we constructed a random sample of 200 OIE triples from the OIE triples having KB-hits, which were labeled for correctness by an expert. To ensure that the information of the triple is complete, the triples which are not self-contained were labeled as "incorrectly extracted". For example, the triple *(Pope Clement VII; "named him inquisitor of"; Modena)* is not self-contained, because it is not clear to which entity "him" refers to. The labeler stopped at the 100th correctly extracted triple. Note that these 100 correctly extracted triples are also self-contained.

Study Design for *Is-a relation* OIE triples. The study for *Is-a relation* triples is similar with the one done on *All relations*. We sampled 100 correctly extracted triples from OPIEC-Typed (i.e. the subset of OPIEC containing triples of the form *(subj, "be"; obj)*). For each correctly extracted OPIEC-Typed triple, we matched the subject link with all the DBpedia entries for types. As a result, we have an OIE triple *(subj, "be"; obj)* and on the KB side we have (subj; type; T). The sampling and labeling logic is the same as the one explained in the previous paragraph.

A.2 DSA Study: KB Data and Methodology

Reference KB. For the alignments, it is very important that the KB contains the same information as the text corpus from which the OIE data was constructed (i.e. that both the OIE triples and the reference KB were automatically constructed from the same domain). This ensures that the information in the KB and the information content in the OIE triples is the same. In such settings, the OIE arguments have the same ID links as the KB entities, which makes the study comparable. For these reasons, we chose DBpedia (Auer et al., 2007) as a reference KB, because it is a well-established KB constructed from Wikipedia (the same resource from which OPIEC is constructed), and because it is the largest KB to date which is automatically constructed from Wikipedia. Prior work for aligning OIE triples with KB facts also exploited the combination of Wikipedia and DBpedia (Wu and Weld, 2010; Dutta et al., 2013, 2015; Yu et al., 2017; Gashteovski et al., 2019).

DBpedia-filtered. For our study, it is essential that both of the KB triple arguments are disambiguated. Therefore, from DBpedia, we filtered out any triples containing literals, abstracts, dates, etc. Many relations in DBpedia are extracted with generic infobox extraction. These KB relations tend to be noisier—sometimes even ambiguous—and they often lack important information describing the precise semantics of the KB relation (Bizer et al., 2009) (e.g. domain/range types or descriptions are often missing). For these reasons, we filtered out these KB triples as well. We retained only the triples that were extracted with mapping-based infobox extraction (i.e. with namespace `http://dbpedia.org/ontology`), because of their higher extraction quality and higher level of details they provide. This way, it is much clearer to an expert labeler to assess the alignments.

CLUSTERDATASPLIT: Exploring Challenging Clustering-Based Data Splits for Model Performance Evaluation

Hanna Wecker[1,2]   **Annemarie Friedrich**[2]   **Heike Adel**[2]

[1]Ludwig-Maximilians-University, Munich, Germany
[2]Bosch Center for Artificial Intelligence, Renningen, Germany
[1]`hanna.wecker@gmx.de`   [2]`firstname.lastname@de.bosch.com`

Abstract

This paper adds to the ongoing discussion in the natural language processing community on how to choose a good development set. Motivated by the real-life necessity of applying machine learning models to different data distributions, we propose a clustering-based data splitting algorithm. It creates development (or test) sets which are lexically different from the training data while ensuring similar label distributions. Hence, we are able to create challenging cross-validation evaluation setups while abstracting away from performance differences resulting from label distribution shifts between training and test data. In addition, we present a Python-based tool for analyzing and visualizing data split characteristics and model performance. We illustrate the workings and results of our approach using a sentiment analysis and a patent classification task.

1 Introduction

In natural language processing (NLP), the standard approach for tuning and selecting machine learning models is by means of using a held-out development set. However, recent work has pointed out that evaluation scores on a development set are often not indicative of the model performance on an unseen test set (Reimers and Gurevych, 2018; Zhou et al., 2020). In addition, it is an open research question how to choose a good development set. While Gorman and Bedrick (2019) suggest to use random splits instead of a given benchmark development set, Søgaard et al. (2020) argue that randomly selecting a development set is not the best option either. This currently ongoing discussion in the NLP community highlights the need for more extensive research on model development using a variety of data splits.

In this paper, we directly add to this discussion by proposing a strategy in which models are evaluated in a setup that is challenging given the available dataset. For machine learning models, it is of utmost importance that they are applicable to different data distributions, possibly even coming from different domains. We argue that models should also be tested under data splits reflecting such real-world settings. Therefore, we propose a **clustering-based data splitting approach** that creates data splits where the development or test data differ from the training set. Our clustering algorithm ensures a similar label distribution across the produced cross-validation folds in order to abstract away from challenges due to label distribution shifts.

In addition, we present CLUSTERDATASPLIT, a **suite of Jupyter notebooks** implementing several possibilities for splitting data into training and development sets, or into folds for cross-validation. In addition, our tool provides functionalities for visualizing different data splits and thus may help clarifying their influence on model performance. Furthermore, it offers several ways to inspect the data, such as visualization of dataset key figures, scatter plots, label distributions and sentence length distributions. The tool is publicly available.[1]

In sum, our contributions are as follows: (i) We propose a clustering-based data splitting algorithm that creates a challenging evaluation setup and has the potential to reveal difficulties when the model is applied on data that deviates from the training data (Section 3). (ii) We present CLUSTERDATASPLIT, a tool that allows to split data into training and development sets and provides different visualizations for analyzing the data splits as well as model performance (Section 4). Finally, we demonstrate a worked example of using our data inspection tool as well as results for our clustering-based data splitting methods for two sequence classification

---

[1]`https://github.com/boschresearch/`
`clusterdatasplit_eval4nlp-2020`

Proceedings of the First Workshop on Evaluation and Comparison of NLP Systems (Eval4NLP), pages 155–163,
November 20, 2020. ©2020 Association for Computational Linguistics

tasks, sentiment analysis and patent classification (Section 5).

2 Related Work

In this section, we give an overview of related work on evaluation and data splitting techniques as well as analysis tools in the NLP community.

2.1 Data Splits for Model Evaluation

Gorman and Bedrick (2019) show that model rankings on standard splits (Collins, 2002) can often not be reproduced using randomly generated splits. In a follow-up study, Søgaard et al. (2020) find that evaluation results on random splits are often too optimistic, even for in-domain test samples. In order to make the data splits more challenging, they introduce heuristic splits based on sentence length and adversarial splits based on Wasserstein distance. The clustering-based data split we propose in this paper follows the same idea of creating a challenging evaluation setup. In contrast to the adversarial splits proposed by Søgaard et al. (2020), our splitting strategy controls for label distribution, allowing to abstract away from the effect of different label distributions on the evaluation score (Johnson and Khoshgoftaar, 2019; Buda et al., 2018).

2.2 Challenging Evaluation Sets

Another direction of work aims at tailoring more challenging test sets by either grouping or hand-crafting datasets. These approaches typically require manual work for each dataset. Hendrycks et al. (2020), for instance, introduce a robustness benchmark[2] by assigning similar datasets as out-of-distribution (OOD) test sets. In their experiments, they show that the OOD test setting leads to severe performance drops for many models except transformers. Gardner et al. (2020) create contrast sets[3] for commonly used NLP benchmark datasets by adding hand-crafted data points for each test set example. Another direction of creating challenging evaluation sets comes from the idea of adversarial training (Szegedy et al., 2013; Goodfellow et al., 2015). In the context of NLP, the creation of adversarial examples typically involves task and dataset specific methods and often relies on hand-crafted rules or other forms of human influence. Examples are reading comprehension or question answering datasets with altered questions or documents (Jia and Liang, 2017; Wallace et al., 2019) or machine translation datasets for which typos are introduced (Belinkov and Bisk, 2018). In contrast to all those approaches, our data splitting approach is purely data-driven and creates a challenging evaluation setting within one dataset fully automatically.

2.3 Tools for Analyzing NLP models

Existing NLP model analysis tools are often tailored towards specific tasks or models (e.g., Wang et al., 2019; Zhou et al., 2020). In the remainder of this section, we give examples for model-agnostic tools as they are more related to our tool. Graliński et al. (2019) introduce GEVAL,[4] a tool for identifying features in the test set (e.g., n-grams) which are especially challenging to models. The tool CHECKLIST[5] by Ribeiro et al. (2020) explores different model capabilities, such as robustness, vocabulary or temporal understanding. Furthermore, it supports the creation of test examples via templates. In contrast to those two tools, our tool offers visualizations of a variety of statistically interesting aspects of data splits in order to better understand model behaviours. Wu et al. (2019) provide an interactive tool for error analysis called ERRUDITE.[6] It supports, i.a., automated counterfactual rewriting for testing hypotheses about errors. In contrast to all mentioned tools, our tool implements different data splitting techniques, making it easy to compare model performance when using different data splits.

3 Clustering-based Data Splitting

We here propose a novel algorithm dubbed **Size and Distribution Sensitive K-means (SDS K-means)** which has two important properties relevant to generating challenging clustering-based cross-validation folds. The SDS K-means algorithm produces clusters that (1) each have approximately the same size, i.e., a similar number of data points, and that (2) are controlled for label distribution. In the default case, all clusters have a similar label distribution. By clustering the data points, we ensure that training and development data are different (for now in a lexical sense), hence creating a challenging evaluation setup. The SDS K-means algorithm thereby overcomes the following two

---

[2]https://github.com/camelop/
NLP-Robustness
[3]https://allennlp.org/contrast-sets

[4]https://gonito.net/gitlist/geval.git/
[5]https://github.com/marcotcr/checklist
[6]https://github.com/uwdata/errudite

difficulties: (1) Varying cluster sizes: If clusters had different sizes, performance differences could simply be attributed to varying amounts of training data. (2) Varying label distributions: If clusters had differing label distributions, performance differences could be primarily due to label distribution mismatches between training and test data. Hence, when using SDS K-means generated data folds with similar label distributions per cluster, differences in model performance can be attributed to qualitative rather than quantitative differences between the folds. In the experiments of this paper, we keep the label distribution fixed. If the user wants to deviate from the default case, s/he can also use the SDS K-means algorithm to generate folds with varying label distributions, and thereby also investigate the effects of different label distributions on model performance.

In the following, we describe technical details and the derivation of our algorithm. All algorithms described in this section produce K clusters that are intended to be used in K-fold cross-validation.

3.1 Preprocessing

As a prerequisite for clustering, we transform the text data (sentences or clauses in our case) into vector representations. First, each token is turned into a vector representation using a pre-trained Word2Vec (Mikolov et al., 2013) model. Then, for each input example the word vectors are averaged. The vector representations are centered and scaled, and dimensionality reduction by principal component analysis is performed. The vectors obtained by these preparation steps then serve as input for the K-means based algorithms.

3.2 K-means and Size Sensitive K-means

For the generation of clustering-based data splits, we decided to work with K-means based clustering algorithms because of their low time complexity and high computing efficiency (Xu and Tian, 2015). The standard **K-means** algorithm (Lloyd, 1982) belongs to the group of partitioning clustering algorithms, i.e., the number of clusters to be formed needs to be specified beforehand. It is an expectation maximization algorithm that has the goal of minimizing the cluster-internal variances. As such, it iterates between an *expectation* step in which data points are assigned to clusters, and a *maximization* or *update* step in which cluster centers are re-calculated. The standard K-means algorithm

produces clusters with strongly varying size and label distributions.

The **Same Size K-means** algorithm is a variant of the K-means algorithm that ensures that all clusters are assigned approximately the same number of data points. We implement this algorithm following a tutorial[7] by Schubert and Zimek (2019). During the initial assignment step, points are assigned to the different cluster centers following an order measure, which corresponds to the difference in distance from the point to the closest and the furthest cluster center. This means that points which have the highest absolute difference in distance from closest to furthest cluster center are assigned to their closest cluster center first. Once one of the clusters reaches its maximum size, the order measure is re-calculated and points are again sorted before continuing the assignment process. In the following, the algorithm iterates between a maximization step in which cluster centers are re-calculated and an update step that differs from standard K-means as follows. During the update step, data points can swap assigned clusters in a 1-on-1 fashion if the swap is associated with a decrease of the overall cluster-internal variances. While this algorithm ensures that cross-validation folds will be of equal size, the label distribution within the clusters may vary and hence result in favoring models that are misled by an unrealistic label distribution in the training or development data.

3.3 Size and Distribution Sensitive K-means Algorithm (SDS K-means)

As a remedy for the above mentioned problems, we propose an extension, the **SDS K-means** algorithm. Like the Same Size K-means algorithm, it consists of an initial assignment and swapping-based update steps. However, in this case, the maximum number of points per cluster are determined separately for each label, corresponding to the desired distribution of labels for each cluster as specified by the user. In the default case, the label distribution per cluster corresponds to the overall label distribution in the training data. The initial assignment and the update steps are conducted separately for each label. This ensures that the label distribution per cluster matches exactly the distribution specified by the user. The pseudo-code of the algorithm is outlined in Figure 1. We initialize the algorithm

---

[7]`https://elki-project.github.io/tutorial/same-size_k_means`

Figure 1 box:

A Initial cluster assignment

1 Initialize cluster centers

2 Sort data points by labels

3 For each label:

   I Order data points by difference between distance to closest and to furthest cluster center that is still "open" for the respective label

   II Assign points in this order to the different clusters, until one of the clusters reaches its maximum size for the respective label, i.e., until we "close" the cluster for the respective label. (Each cluster has a specific maximum size for each label, i.e., the order in which the labels are assigned to the clusters does not change the clustering output.)

   III Iterate over I and II until all points for the respective label are assigned to clusters

B Update cluster assignment

1 Update cluster centers (using all data points belonging to the cluster, irrespective of their labels)

2 Sort data points by label

3 For each label:

   I For each data point, calculate difference between distance to current cluster center and distance to other cluster centers

   II Perform 1-on-1 swapping of points with positive difference at step I

4 Repeat step 1-3 until no swaps happen any more or maximum number of iterations is reached

Figure 1: Pseudo code for **SDS K-means algorithm**.

multiple times and choose the run with lowest average cluster-internal variances as the final partition.

4 CLUSTERDATASPLIT Tool

The tool CLUSTERDATASPLIT consists of three Jupyter Notebooks. Hence, using the tool requires basic Python skills. Communication between the tool and user code for machine learning models is based on .tsv files containing the text data instances and labels. Figure 2 illustrates the workflow and the separation of tasks between the tool and client code. Currently, our tool and algorithm only support sequence classification tasks with a single label per dataset instance. We leave extensions for sequence tagging tasks to future work.

4.1 DATA ANALYSIS

The first notebook provides an introduction to key NLP dataset characteristics, such as label distribution, sentence token length and token frequency. It serves for a first exploration of the data and its key figures before using the data for model training and evaluation.

4.2 CREATING DATA SPLITS

In order to generate clustering-based data splits, this notebook groups the data into a pre-defined number of groups, the so-called data folds. These data folds then serve as input in a cross-validation setting, where they are combined to build the data split in training and development data. To group the data, different K-means based algorithms, which are outlined in detail in Section 3, are available. Moreover, the tool also supports the generation of randomized partitions, which can be combined to form randomized (baseline) data splits.

For generating the data splits, the user has to input the complete training data in a .tsv format and select an algorithm to generate the data folds. In most cases, s/he will want to compare the SDS K-means and randomized splitting. The tool then generates an output file with the data point IDs and the fold ID information per data point. The user then has to input this information into his/her model training setup, using a cross-validation framework in which the model is trained K times, training on K-1 folds and evaluating on the remaining fold in each iteration.

To date, our vector representations of the input texts are mostly based on lexical information (see Section 3.1).[8] For clustering, we use the K-means implementation in the Python scikit-learn package (Pedregosa et al., 2011), and apply the initialization method of Arthur and Vassilvitskii (2007).

4.3 PERFORMANCE ANALYSIS

After the training and evaluation steps based on different data splits are completed, the user can input the predictions obtained on the different evaluation sets into the third notebook using a .tsv format. The notebook calculates performance statistics and analyzes the dependence of results on data split characteristics. For example, the notebook visualizes data split characteristics such as relative size

---

[8]In future versions of the tool, other representations reflecting, e.g., syntactic or contextualized word embedding information, may be included. However, we here opt for a simple lexically-based representation for clustering that does not intend to already capture too many features that may later on be used by the models themselves. If the user of the tool wants to substitute this input embedding method, s/he can easily do so by overwriting the respective Python functions.

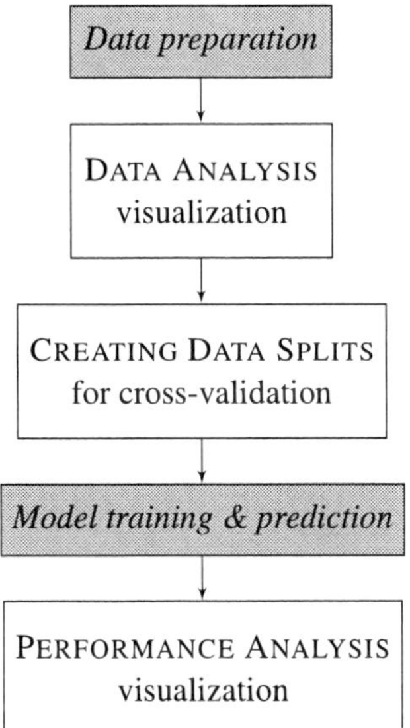

Figure 2: Workflow of the CLUSTERDATASPLIT tool. Grey boxes indicate client code, white boxes indicate functionalities included in Jupyter notebooks.

of the clusters, label distribution for the clusters and the mean sentence length. It also facilitates the comparison of different data splits and the performances obtained on these data splits.

5 Worked Examples

In this section, we give worked examples of using our proposed data splitting method for two sequence classification tasks, the Stanford Sentiment Treebank (SST) binary sentiment analysis task and a patent multi-class classification task.

5.1 Models

As our classifiers, we use simple neural networks for sequence classification based on BERT for SST (Devlin et al., 2019) and SciBERT (Beltagy et al., 2019) for the patent classification task. The latter model was trained on a corpus of scientific publications and is hence closer to the kind of language present in patents. For both models, we feed the CLS token into a linear layer that outputs logits corresponding to the number of classes and apply a softmax activation. For model training, we use a cross-entropy loss. We implement our models using the HuggingFace Transformers library (Wolf et al., 2019). The maximum sequence length of word piece tokens input to the BERT model is 128 and 256 for the two tasks, respectively. We use a batch size of 8, and AdamW (Loshchilov and

Hutter, 2019) with learning rates of $4e^{-6}$ and $4e^{-5}$, respectively. Otherwise, we apply default parameters. We train the models for up to 100 epochs.

5.2 Stanford Sentiment Treebank

We here give an example of using our proposed analysis for a binary sequence classification task.

Dataset. The Stanford Sentiment Treebank (SST) (Socher et al., 2013) is based on movie review excerpts from the website `rottentomatoes.com`. For the task of binary sentiment classification, we use the SST-2 dataset, which is a variant of the original dataset containing only sentences and phrases with the label *positive* or *negative*. The dataset is slightly imbalanced with 44.28% negative and 55.72% positive labels. For our experiments, we use 61,398 sentences and phrases from the training and development part of the SST-2 dataset.

Data splits. We perform the SST classification experiments in two settings, using our SDS K-means based clustered and a randomized cross-validation setting. Figure 3 shows the visualization of the folds/clusters in two dimensions as generated by the CLUSTERDATASPLIT tool.

Performance results. Table 1 provides the results of training and evaluating models on clustering-based and randomized data splits in a cross-validation (CV) setting. The model summarized under the heading "CV-1" was trained on data folds 2-5 and evaluated on data fold 1. Note that the individual CV folds are not comparable between SDS K-means data splits (DS) and randomized DS, as each experimental setting uses different data splits. On average, the models trained and evaluated on the clustering-based data splits have a lower model performance than the models trained on the randomized data splits. Moreover, the standard deviation in model performance scores is higher for the clustering-based data splits than for the randomized data splits. Inspecting the differences between the clustered folds using CLUSTERDATASPLIT revealed that the sentences in the evaluation fold performing worst are on average shorter than the ones in the other folds, often consisting of short phrases that are difficult to classify also for human annotators. This underlines that the formation of training and development data based on the SDS K-means algorithm constitutes a more challenging evaluation environment than the random division of data

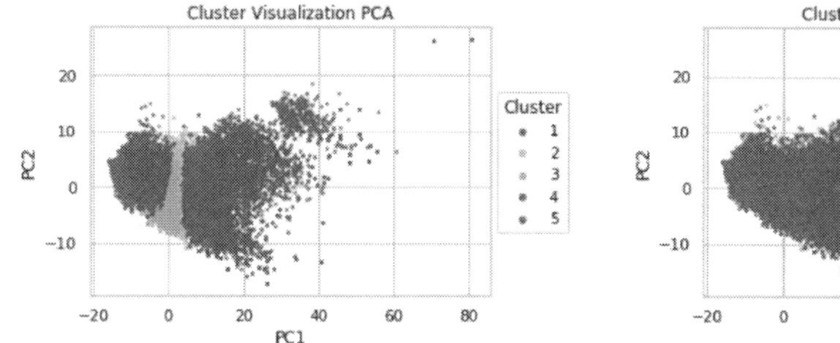

Figure 3: Visualization of data splits for SST dataset: SDS K-means clusters (left) vs. randomized (right).

	CV-1	CV-2	CV-3	CV-4	CV-5	Mean	Std
SDS K-means DS	94.5	89.8	95.2	93.9	92.8	93.2	1.9
Randomized DS	94.8	95.1	95.1	94.7	94.7	94.9	0.2

Table 1: F1 scores for binary sentiment classification on SST data. (Scores for individual folds are **not** comparable.)

into training and development data splits.

5.3 Patent Classification

In this section, we report results for a multi-class classification task, i.e., assigning the correct Cooperative Patent Classification (CPC) code to a patent.

Section	Description
A	Human Necessities
B	Performing Operations, Transporting
C	Chemistry, Metallurgy
D	Textiles, Paper
E	Fixed Constructions
F	Mechanical Engineering, Lighting, Heating, Weapons, Blasting
G	Physics
H	Electrity

Table 2: CPC patent classification scheme.[9]

Dataset. We retrieve a dataset of patents from USPTO[10] and represent each patent by its title and abstract. The latter are rather short, most sequences are shorter than 300 tokens. CPC codes indicate topics or application areas of a patent, and CPC classification is actually a hierarchical multi-label multi-class classification task. For simplicity, as our goal here is to demonstrate how our evaluation methods work for a simple multi-class clas-

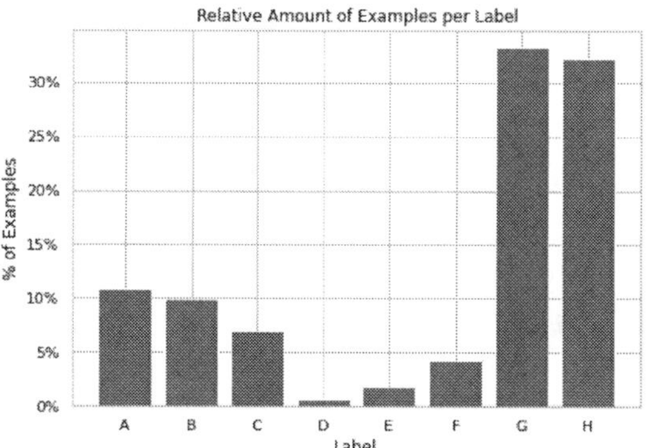

Figure 4: Distribution of labels in patents dataset.

sification task, we filter the dataset, keeping only instances that carry just a single label at the section level (7 labels, A-H, see Table 2). This leaves us with 6,458 instances with a skewed label distribution as shown in Figure 4. Of course, due the availability of machine-readable patents in large quantities, it would be possible to sample a larger training set in order to improve classification accuracy. However, our goal here is not to create an ideal CPC classifier but to highlight the importance of constructing challenging evaluation setups especially in low-resource settings. For reproducibility, we open-source the patents dataset together with our tool.

Performance results. Table 3 shows the results obtained for the various cross-validation folds when assigning documents to folds randomly or

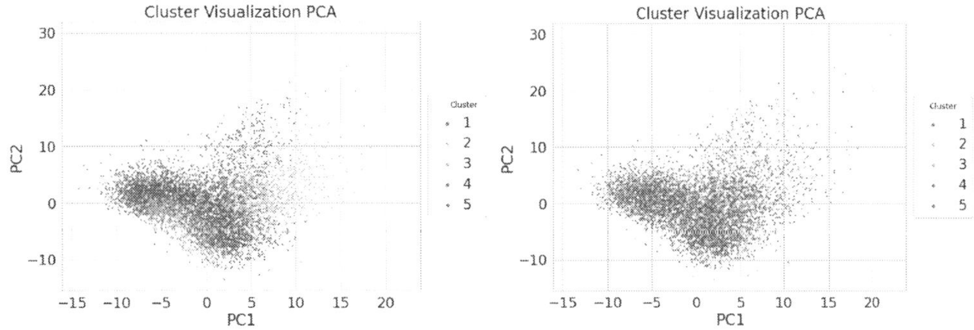

Figure 5: Visualization of data splits for patents dataset: SDS K-means clusters (left) vs. randomized (right).

	CV-1	CV-2	CV-3	CV-4	CV-5	Mean	Std
SDS K-means DS	53.4	57.4	43.3	61.3	51.1	53.3	6.1
Randomized DS	55.1	56.6	56.7	58.2	52.4	55.8	2.0

Table 3: Macro-average F1 scores for multi-class classification on patents dataset. (Scores for individual folds are **not** comparable.)

when using our clustering-based data splits. Macro-avg. F1 is computed as the average over per-class F1s.

For the patent classification task, differences in performance obtained in the SDS K-means evaluation setup differ even more strongly from the randomized cross-validation setup than in the case of the sentiment analysis task. Mean accuracy across the tasks is estimated as 55.8 in the randomized setting, but only as 53.3 in the SDS K-means setting. Again, as in the sentiment analysis task, the standard deviation is much higher when using clustered data folds. Two folds are notable, one exhibiting a much lower F1 and one having a much higher F1 score than the average. There are no sentence length differences in this case. Figure 5 shows that fold 3 concentrates in one region of the plot, while fold 4 has a much higher within-cluster variance. However, this does not yet explain why fold 3 instances are harder to classify, as for instance cluster 1 is also very concentrated in one region and achieves around average results. This finding hints at the fact that while our approach is able to generate challenging and diverse evaluation setups, further research is necessary to develop a systematic understanding of the observed performance differences in the produced clustering-based cross-validation setup. A very likely reason for the result in this case, as we are comparing macro-average F1, is low performance on the rare classes in the folds which possibly do not contain many "good" examples of these classes in the training folds.

6 Conclusion and Outlook

In this paper, we have introduced the concept of clustering-based data splits for model evaluation of sequence classification tasks. We have outlined the steps necessary to generate clustering-based data splits and described different K-means based algorithms for the creation of clustering-based data splits. Our newly proposed SDS K-means algorithm is able to generate clusters with equal (or controllable) size and label distribution. These properties make the algorithm perfectly suited for generating clustering-based data splits for challenging cross-validation experiments. Our worked examples show that model evaluation on clustering-based data splits generated by the SDS K-means algorithm is more challenging than model evaluation on randomly selected data splits.

The experiments conducted in this paper present a first step in exploring clustering-based data splits. Directions for **future research** involve the steps necessary to generate the clustering-based data splits, further exploration of the data splits and additional use cases. With regard to the generation of clustering-based data splits, different text vector representations or clustering algorithms, like for example density-based approaches, could be explored. Experiments with different text vector representations and clustering algorithms could shed some light on the impact of different cluster structures on the evaluation setup. Moreover, it would be interesting to study why clustering-based data splits seem to have a stronger effect on some datasets than on others. Søgaard et al. (2020) introduce an experiment setting to compare the predictive performance of model evaluation on different data splits with regard to test sets coming from the same domain as the training data. Applying our clustering-based data splits in this experiment setting thus could deliver important information about the predictive quality of model performance scores obtained on clustering-based data splits.

Currently, our method works only for classification tasks and clustering is performed mainly based on lexical information. Hence, another interesting direction for future work is extending our ideas to data splitting for sequence tagging tasks, and to integrate other types of information such as syntactic features.

Acknowledgments

We thank Christian Heumann for his insightful comments regarding this work. We also thank the members of the NLP and Semantic Reasoning Group at the Bosch Center for Artificial Intelligence for their support and fruitful discussions on the ideas presented in this paper.

References

David Arthur and Sergei Vassilvitskii. 2007. K-Means++: The advantages of careful seeding. In *Proceedings of the Eighteenth Annual ACM-SIAM Symposium on Discrete Algorithms*, pages 1027–1035, New Orleans, Louisiana. Society for Industrial and Applied Mathematics.

Yonatan Belinkov and Yonatan Bisk. 2018. Synthetic and natural noise both break neural machine translation. In *International Conference on Learning Representations*, Vancouver, Canada.

Iz Beltagy, Kyle Lo, and Arman Cohan. 2019. SciBERT: A pretrained language model for scientific text. In *Proceedings of the 2019 Conference on Empirical Methods in Natural Language Processing and the 9th International Joint Conference on Natural Language Processing (EMNLP-IJCNLP)*, pages 3615–3620, Hong Kong, China. Association for Computational Linguistics.

Mateusz Buda, Atsuto Maki, and Maciej A Mazurowski. 2018. A systematic study of the class imbalance problem in convolutional neural networks. *Neural Networks*, 106:249–259.

Michael Collins. 2002. Discriminative training methods for hidden Markov models: Theory and experiments with perceptron algorithms. In *Proceedings of the 2002 Conference on Empirical Methods in Natural Language Processing (EMNLP 2002)*, pages 1–8. Association for Computational Linguistics.

Jacob Devlin, Ming-Wei Chang, Kenton Lee, and Kristina Toutanova. 2019. BERT: Pre-training of deep bidirectional transformers for language understanding. In *Proceedings of the 2019 Conference of the North American Chapter of the Association for Computational Linguistics: Human Language Technologies, Volume 1 (Long and Short Papers)*, pages 4171–4186, Minneapolis, Minnesota. Association for Computational Linguistics.

Matt Gardner, Yoav Artzi, Victoria Basmova, Jonathan Berant, Ben Bogin, Sihao Chen, Pradeep Dasigi, Dheeru Dua, Yanai Elazar, Ananth Gottumukkala, Nitish Gupta, Hanna Hajishirzi, Gabriel Ilharco, Daniel Khashabi, Kevin Lin, Jiangming Liu, Nelson F. Liu, Phoebe Mulcaire, Qiang Ning, Sameer Singh, Noah A. Smith, Sanjay Subramanian, Reut Tsarfaty, Eric Wallace, Ally Zhang, and Ben Zhou. 2020. Evaluating NLP models via contrast sets. *Computing Research Repository*, arXiv:2004.02709. Version 1.

Ian J Goodfellow, Jonathon Shlens, and Christian Szegedy. 2015. Explaining and harnessing adversarial examples. In *International Conference on Learning Representations*, San Diego, California.

Kyle Gorman and Steven Bedrick. 2019. We need to talk about standard splits. In *Proceedings of the 57th Annual Meeting of the Association for Computational Linguistics*, pages 2786–2791, Florence, Italy. Association for Computational Linguistics.

Filip Graliński, Anna Wróblewska, Tomasz Stanisławek, Kamil Grabowski, and Tomasz Górecki. 2019. GEval: Tool for debugging NLP datasets and models. In *Proceedings of the 2019 ACL Workshop BlackboxNLP: Analyzing and Interpreting Neural Networks for NLP*, pages 254–262, Florence, Italy. Association for Computational Linguistics.

Dan Hendrycks, Xiaoyuan Liu, Eric Wallace, Adam Dziedzic, Rishabh Krishnan, and Dawn Song. 2020. Pretrained transformers improve out-of-distribution robustness. In *Proceedings of the 58th Annual Meeting of the Association for Computational Linguistics*, pages 2744–2751, Online. Association for Computational Linguistics.

Robin Jia and Percy Liang. 2017. Adversarial examples for evaluating reading comprehension systems. In *Proceedings of the 2017 Conference on Empirical Methods in Natural Language Processing*, pages 2021–2031, Copenhagen, Denmark. Association for Computational Linguistics.

Justin M Johnson and Taghi M Khoshgoftaar. 2019. Survey on deep learning with class imbalance. *Journal of Big Data*, 6(1):27.

Stuart Lloyd. 1982. Least squares quantization in PCM. *IEEE transactions on information theory*, 28(2):129–137.

Ilya Loshchilov and Frank Hutter. 2019. Decoupled weight decay regularization. In *7th International Conference on Learning Representations, ICLR 2019, New Orleans, LA, USA, May 6-9, 2019*. OpenReview.net.

Tomas Mikolov, Ilya Sutskever, Kai Chen, Greg S Corrado, and Jeff Dean. 2013. Distributed representations of words and phrases and their compositionality. In *Advances in Neural Information Processing Systems*, pages 3111–3119, Lake Tahoe, Nevada.

F. Pedregosa, G. Varoquaux, A. Gramfort, V. Michel, B. Thirion, O. Grisel, M. Blondel, P. Prettenhofer, R. Weiss, V. Dubourg, J. Vanderplas, A. Passos, D. Cournapeau, M. Brucher, M. Perrot, and E. Duchesnay. 2011. Scikit-learn: Machine learning in Python. *Journal of Machine Learning Research*, 12:2825–2830.

Nils Reimers and Iryna Gurevych. 2018. Why comparing single performance scores does not allow to draw conclusions about machine learning approaches. *Computing Research Repository*, arXiv:1803.09578. Version 1.

Marco Tulio Ribeiro, Tongshuang Wu, Carlos Guestrin, and Sameer Singh. 2020. Beyond accuracy: Behavioral testing of NLP models with CheckList. In *Proceedings of the 58th Annual Meeting of the Association for Computational Linguistics*, pages 4902–4912, Online. Association for Computational Linguistics.

Erich Schubert and Arthur Zimek. 2019. ELKI: A large open-source library for data analysis–ELKI release 0.7.5 "Heidelberg". *Computing Research Repository*, arXiv:1902.03616. Version 1.

Richard Socher, Alex Perelygin, Jean Wu, Jason Chuang, Christopher D. Manning, Andrew Ng, and Christopher Potts. 2013. Recursive deep models for semantic compositionality over a sentiment treebank. In *Proceedings of the 2013 Conference on Empirical Methods in Natural Language Processing*, pages 1631–1642, Seattle, Washington. Association for Computational Linguistics.

Anders Søgaard, Sebastian Ebert, Joost Bastings, and Katja Filippova. 2020. We need to talk about random splits. *Computing Research Repository*, arXiv:2005.00636. Version 1.

Christian Szegedy, Wojciech Zaremba, Ilya Sutskever, Joan Bruna, Dumitru Erhan, Ian J Goodfellow, and Rob Fergus. 2013. Intriguing properties of neural networks. In *International Conference on Learning Representations*, Banff, Canada.

Eric Wallace, Pedro Rodriguez, Shi Feng, Ikuya Yamada, and Jordan Boyd-Graber. 2019. Trick me if you can: Human-in-the-loop generation of adversarial examples for question answering. *Transactions of the Association for Computational Linguistics*, 7:387–401.

Changhan Wang, Anirudh Jain, Danlu Chen, and Jiatao Gu. 2019. VizSeq: a visual analysis toolkit for text generation tasks. In *Proceedings of the 2019 Conference on Empirical Methods in Natural Language Processing and the 9th International Joint Conference on Natural Language Processing (EMNLP-IJCNLP): System Demonstrations*, pages 253–258, Hong Kong, China. Association for Computational Linguistics.

Thomas Wolf, Lysandre Debut, Victor Sanh, Julien Chaumond, Clement Delangue, Anthony Moi, Pierric Cistac, Tim Rault, R'emi Louf, Morgan Funtowicz, and Jamie Brew. 2019. HuggingFace's transformers: State-of-the-art natural language processing. *Computing Research Repository*, arXiv:1910.03771. Version 5.

Tongshuang Wu, Marco Tulio Ribeiro, Jeffrey Heer, and Daniel Weld. 2019. Errudite: Scalable, reproducible, and testable error analysis. In *Proceedings of the 57th Annual Meeting of the Association for Computational Linguistics*, pages 747–763, Florence, Italy. Association for Computational Linguistics.

Dongkuan Xu and Yingjie Tian. 2015. A Comprehensive Survey of Clustering Algorithms. *Annals of Data Science*, 2(2):165–193.

Xiang Zhou, Yixin Nie, Hao Tan, and Mohit Bansal. 2020. The curse of performance instability in analysis datasets: Consequences, source, and suggestions. *Computing Research Repository*, arXiv:2004.13606. Version 1.

Best Practices for Crowd-based Evaluation of German Summarization: Comparing Crowd, Expert, and Automatic Evaluation

Neslihan Iskender, Tim Polzehl, Sebastian Möller
Technische Universität Berlin, Quality and Usability Lab
{neslihan.iskender, tim.polzehl, sebastian.moeller}@tu-berlin.de

Abstract

One of the main challenges in the development of summarization tools is summarization quality evaluation. On the one hand, the human assessment of summarization quality conducted by linguistic experts is slow, expensive, and still not a standardized procedure. On the other hand, the automatic assessment metrics are reported not to correlate high enough with human quality ratings. As a solution, we propose crowdsourcing as a fast, scalable, and cost-effective alternative to expert evaluations to assess the intrinsic and extrinsic quality of summarization by comparing crowd ratings with expert ratings and automatic metrics such as ROUGE, BLEU, or BertScore on a German summarization data set. Our results provide a basis for best practices for crowd-based summarization evaluation regarding major influential factors such as the best annotation aggregation method, the influence of readability and reading effort on summarization evaluation, and the optimal number of crowd workers to achieve comparable results to experts, especially when determining factors such as overall quality, grammaticality, referential clarity, focus, structure & coherence, summary usefulness, and summary informativeness.

1 Introduction

Even though there has been an enormous increase in automatic summarization research, human evaluation of summarization is still an understudied aspect. One the one hand, there is no standard procedure for conducting human evaluation, which is leading to a high degree of variation and different results (Van Der Lee et al., 2019); on the other hand, human evaluation is usually carried out in a traditional laboratory environment by linguistic experts, which is costly and time-consuming to run and prone to subjective biases (Celikyilmaz et al., 2020). Therefore, automatic evaluation metrics such as BLEU and ROUGE have been used as

substitutes for human evaluation (Papineni et al., 2002; Lin, 2004). However, they require expert summaries as references to be calculated and are often reported not to correlate with human evaluations regarding the readability, grammaticality, and content-related factors (Novikova et al., 2017).

In the other NLP domains, crowdsourcing has been proposed as an alternative to overcome these challenges, showing that crowd workers' aggregated responses could produce quality approaching those produced by experts (Snow et al., 2008; Callison-Burch, 2009; Nowak and Rüger, 2010). In the summarization evaluation, very few researchers have investigated crowdsourcing as an alternative, eventually concluding that the chosen crowd-based evaluation methods are not reliable enough to produce consistent scores (Gillick and Liu, 2010; Fabbri et al., 2020). However, the authors did not apply any pre-qualification test, did not provide information about the number of crowd workers, did not apply annotation aggregation methods, or did not analyze the effect of reading effort and readability of source texts caused by the text's structural, and formal composure. Additionally, they used the TAC and CNN/Daily Mail data set derived from high-quality English texts. So, there is a research gap regarding the best practices for crowd-based evaluation of summarization, especially for languages other than English and noisy internet data.

We address this gap in the following ways: 1) We use a German summarization data set derived from an online question-answering forum; 2) We apply pre-qualification tests and set a threshold for minimum task completion duration in crowdsourcing; 3) We collect intrinsic and extrinsic quality ratings from 24 different crowd workers per summary in order to analyze consistency; 4) We use different annotation aggregation methods on crowdsourced data; 5) We analyze the effect of annotation aggregation methods, reading effort, and the number

164

Proceedings of the First Workshop on Evaluation and Comparison of NLP Systems (Eval4NLP), pages 164–175,
November 20, 2020. ©2020 Association for Computational Linguistics

of crowd workers per item on robustness, comparing results from a) expert assessment; b) crowd assessment; c) state of the art automatic assessment metrics. Especially, languages other than English can benefit from our results, since they lack easy-to-use automatic evaluation metrics in the form of simplified toolkits, and a well-executed evaluation can accelerate the research on automatic summarization (Fabbri et al., 2020).

2 Related Work

2.1 Automatic Summarization Evaluation

The automatic evaluation of summarization can be categorized into two categories: untrained automatic metrics, which do not require machine learning but are based on string overlap, or content overlap between machine-generated and expert generated summaries (ground-truth), and machine-learned metrics that are based on machine-learned models (Celikyilmaz et al., 2020).

2.1.1 Untrained Automatic Metrics

The most common untrained automatic metrics for summarization evaluation are BLEU, METEOR, and ROUGE, which rely on counting n-grams and calculating Precision, Recall, and F-measure by comparing one or several system summaries to reference summaries generated by experts (Papineni et al., 2002; Denkowski and Lavie, 2014; Lin, 2004). As Gao et al. (2019) stated, ROUGE is the most popular method to assess the summarization quality, and at least one of the ROUGE variant is used in 87% of papers on summarization in ACL conferences between 2013 and 2018. In recent years, many variations on ROUGE and other measures have been introduced in the literature (Zhou et al., 2006; Ng and Abrecht, 2015; Ganesan, 2018). However, they have been criticized because of the wide range of correlations being weak to strong with human assessment reported in the summarization literature and for being not suitable for capturing important quality aspects (Reiter and Belz, 2009; Graham, 2015; Novikova et al., 2017; Peyrard and Eckle-Kohler, 2017). Therefore, more and more researchers refrain from using automatic metrics as a primary evaluation method (Reiter, 2018). Still, Van Der Lee et al. (2019) report that 80% of the empirical papers presented at the ACL track on NLG or at the INLG conference in 2018 using automatic metrics due to the lack of alternatives and the fast and cost-effective nature.

2.1.2 Trained Automatic Metrics

Over the last few years, NLP researchers proposed new machine-learned automatic metrics trained using BERT contextual embeddings such as BertScore, BLEURT, and BLANC to evaluate the natural language generation (NLG) quality, which can also be applied to summarization evaluation (Devlin et al., 2019; Zhang et al., 2019; Sellam et al., 2020; Vasilyev et al., 2020). BertScore and BLEURT still require expert generated summaries as ground-truth and computes the similarity of two summaries as a sum of cosine similarities between their tokens' embeddings. Zhang et al. (2019) reported that BertScore correlates better than the other state of the art metrics in the domain of machine translation and image captioning tasks, Sellam et al. (2020) showing that BLEURT correlates better than BertScore with human judgments on the WMT17 Metrics Shared Task. Unlike these metrics, the BLANC score is designed not to require any reference summaries aiming for fully human-free summary quality estimation (Vasilyev et al., 2020). BLANC was shown to correlate as good as ROUGE on CNN/DailyMail data set.

2.2 Human Evaluation

Human evaluation can be conducted as pair comparison (compared to expert summaries) or using absolute scales without having a reference. One of the common human evaluation methods using pair comparison is the PYRAMID method (Nenkova and Passonneau, 2004). In the PYRAMID method, sentences in summaries are split into Summary Content Units for both system and reference summaries and compared with each other based on content. So, it measures only the summaries' relative quality and does not give a sense of the summary's absolute quality. In this paper, we focus on absolute quality measurement in which the generated summaries are demonstrated to the evaluators one at a time, and they judge summary quality individually by rating the quality along a Likert or sliding scale. Therefore, we do not use the PYRAMID method in our human evaluation and collect human ratings on two categories: intrinsic (linguistic) and extrinsic (content) evaluation (Jones and Galliers, 1995; Steinberger and Ježek, 2012).

2.2.1 Intrinsic (Linguistic) Evaluation

In intrinsic evaluation, domain experts are usually asked to evaluate the quality of the given summary, either as overall quality or along some specific dimension without reading the source document (Celikyilmaz et al., 2020). To determine the intrinsic quality of summarization, the following five text readability (linguistic quality) scores are most commonly used: grammaticality, non-redundancy, referential clarity, focus, and structure & coherence. In the section 3, we determine these scores based on the definitions in Dang (2005).

2.2.2 Extrinsic (Content) Evaluation

In extrinsic evaluation, domain experts evaluate a system's performance on the task for which it was designed, so the evaluation of summary quality is accomplished based on the source document (Lloret et al., 2018). The most common extrinsic quality measures are: 1) "Summary usefulness" - also called content responsiveness - which determines the summary's usefulness concerning how useful the extracted summary is to satisfy the given goal; 2) "Source text usefulness" - also called relevance assessment - which examines how useful the source document is to satisfy the given goal; 3) "Summary informativeness" measuring how much information from the source document is preserved in the extracted summary (Mani, 2001; Conroy and Dang, 2008; Shapira et al., 2019).

2.3 Crowdsourcing for Summarization Evaluation

Crowdsourcing has been used as a fast and cost-effective alternative to traditional subjective evaluation with experts in summarization evaluation; however, it has not been explored as thoroughly as other NLG tasks, such as evaluating machine translation (Lloret et al., 2018). In the few papers where crowdsourcing has been used for summarization evaluation, the quality of crowdsourced data has been repeatedly questioned because of the crowd worker's inaccuracy and the complexity of summarization evaluation.

For example, Gillick and Liu (2010) found that the ratings from non-expert crowd workers do not correlate the expert ratings on the TAC summarization data set, which contains 100-word summaries of a set of 10 newswire articles about a particular topic. A similar conclusion was reached by Lloret et al. (2013), who created a corpus for abstractive image summarization with five crowd workers per item. However, besides the fact that results were obtained from other domains than the presented telecommunication domain in this work, in both works, the authors did not apply any pre-

qualification test or did not provide information about crowdsourcing task details, which can also cause a rather large influencing effect. Following, Gao et al. (2018); Falke et al. (2017); Fan et al. (2018) have used crowdsourcing as the source of human evaluation to rate their automatic summarization systems. Nevertheless, they did not question the robustness of crowdsourcing for this task and compared the crowd with expert data. Also, we have shown that crowdsourcing achieves almost the same results as the laboratory studies using 7-9 crowd workers, but we did not compare the crowd with experts (Iskender et al., 2020). Fabbri et al. (2020) compared the crowd with expert evaluation on CNN/Daily Mail data set using only five crowd workers per summary. They also found that crowd and expert ratings do not correlate and emphasized the need for protocols for improving the human evaluation of summarization.

To improve the quality of crowdsourcing, researchers have developed several methods such as *filtering* and *aggregation* (Kairam and Heer, 2016). When filtering crowd workers, the first approach focuses on the pre-qualification tasks designed based on the task characteristics (Mitra et al., 2015). While aggregating crowd judgments, the majority vote is the most common technique (Chatterjee et al., 2019). Much more complex annotation aggregation methods such as probabilistic models of annotation, accounting item level effects, or clustering methods have been introduced in the recent years (Passonneau and Carpenter, 2014; Whitehill et al., 2009; Luther et al., 2015).

To provide the best practices for crowd-based summarization evaluation, we apply pre-qualification and focus on the following aggregation methods in this paper: 1) MOS: Mean Opinion Score (MOS) takes the mean of all judgments for a given item and is one of the most popular metrics for subjective quality evaluation (Streijl et al., 2016; Chatterjee et al., 2019), 2) Majority Vote: In Majority Vote, the answer with the highest votes is selected as the final aggregated value, and it is the most popular method in subjective quality evaluation with crowdsourcing (Hovy et al., 2013; Hung et al., 2013), 3) Crowdtruth: It represents the crowdsourcing system in its three main components – input media units, workers, and annotations. It is designed to capture inter-annotator disagreement in crowdsourcing and aims to collect gold standard data for training and evaluation of cognitive computing systems using crowdsourcing (Dumitrache et al., 2018a). Dumitrache et al. (2018b) have shown that the Crowdtruth performs better than the majority vote in different domains, 4) <u>MACE</u>: Multi-Annotator Competence Estimation (MACE) is a probabilistic model that computes competence estimates of the individual annotators and the most likely answer to each item (Hovy et al., 2013). Paun et al. (2018) have shown that MACE performs better than the other annotation aggregation methods in evaluations against the gold standard. This model is possibly most widely applied to linguistic data (Plank et al., 2014; Sabou et al., 2014; Habernal and Gurevych, 2016).

3 Experiments

3.1 Data Set

In our experiments, we used the same German summary data set with 50 summaries as described in Iskender et al. (2020). The corpus contains queries with an average word count of 7.78, the shortest one with four words, and the longest with 17 words; posts from a customer forum of Deutsche Telekom with an average word count of 555, the shortest one with 155 words, and the longest with 1005 words; and corresponding query-based extractive summaries with an average word count of 63.32, the shortest one with 24 words, and the longest one with 147 words.

3.2 Crowdsourcing Study

We collected crowd annotations using Crowdee[1] Platform. Crowd workers were only allowed to perform the summary evaluation task after passing two qualification tests in the following order: 1) German language proficiency test provided by the Crowdee platform with a score of 0.9 and above (scale [0, 1]), 2) Summarization evaluation test containing deliberately designed bad and good examples of summaries to be recognized by the crowd. Here, a maximum of 20 points could be reached by crowd workers, and we kept crowd workers exceeding 12 points. Besides, according to our expert pre-testing, we set 90 seconds as a threshold for the minimum task completion duration and eliminated all the crowd answers under this threshold.

In the main task, a brief explanation of the summary creation process was shown first with an example of a query, forum posts, and a summary to provide background information. After reading all instructions, crowd workers evaluated nine quality factors of a single summary using a 5 point scale with the labels *very good, good, moderate, bad, very bad* in the following order: 1) overall quality, 2) grammaticality, 3) non-redundancy, 4) referential clarity, 5) focus, 6) structure & coherence, 7) summary usefulness, 8) post usefulness and 9) summary informativeness. In the first six questions, the corresponding forum posts and the query were not shown to the crowd workers (intrinsic quality); in question 7, we showed the original query; in questions 8 and 9, the original query and the corresponding forum posts. In total, 24 repetitions per item for each of these nine questions were collected, resulting in 10,800 labels (50 summaries x 9 questions x 24 repetitions). Compensation was carefully calculated to ensure the minimum wage of € 9.35 per hour in Germany. Overall, 46 crowd workers (19f, 27m, $M_{age} = 43$) completed the individual sets of tasks within 20 days where they spent 249,884 seconds, ca. 69.4 hours at total.

3.3 Expert Evaluation

We used a similar approach to the Delphi method to obtain a consensus among experts in an iterative procedure (Linstone et al., 1975; Sanchan et al., 2017). In the first evaluation round, two experts, who are Masters students in linguistics, evaluated separately the same summarization data set using the same task design as crowd workers by using Crowdee Platform to avoid any user interface biases. After the first evaluation round, the inter-rater agreement calculated by Cohen's κ showed that the experts often diverted in their assessment. In order to reach an acceptable inter-rater agreement score, physical follow-up meetings with experts were arranged. In these meetings, experts discussed causes and backgrounds of their ratings for each item they disagreed, simultaneously creating a more detailed definition and evaluation criteria catalog for each score for future experiments. After the meeting, acceptable inter-rater agreement scores were achieved (see Section 4). In total, 900 ratings (50 Summary x 9 questions x 2 experts) were collected.

3.4 Automatic Evaluation

We calculated the BLEU and ROUGE scores using the sumeval library[2] for German, BertScore[3], and

---

BLEURT[4] scores using bert-base-german-cased configuration. All of these four metrics require gold standard summaries, which were created by the two linguistic experts. The gold standard summaries have an average word count of 58.18, the shortest one with 14 words, and the longest with 112 words. In addition, we calculated the human-free summary quality estimation metric BLANC[5] using bert-base-german-cased configuration. The reason for selecting these five metrics is that they either are the baseline of automatic summarization evaluation metrics (BLEU and ROUGE) or the latest AI-based metrics (BertScore, BLEURT, BLANC) which have not been applied to a German summarization data set.

4 Results

Results are presented for the scores overall quality (OQ), the five intrinsic quality scores (including grammaticality (GR), non-redundancy (NR), referential clarity (RC), focus (FO), structure & coherence (SC)) and the three extrinsic quality scores (summary usefulness (SU), post usefulness (PU) and summary informativeness (SI)). We will refer to these labels by their abbreviations in this section. For our human-based evaluation, we analyzed 10,800 ratings from the crowdsourcing study and 900 ratings from the expert evaluation. For automatic evaluation, we analyzed the BLEU, ROUGE-1, ROUGE-2, ROUGE-L, BertScore (we use F-scores for these metrics), BLEURT by taking the mean of scores calculated using two expert summaries and the BLANC scores resulting in 350 scores (50 summaries x 7 automatic metrics).

4.1 Comparing Crowd with Expert

Before comparing expert ratings with the crowd, we calculated Cohen's κ and Krippendorff's α scores to measure the inter-rater agreement between two experts and the raw agreement scores as recommended in Van Der Lee et al. (2019) (see Table 1). Looking at the raw agreement, we see that experts gave the same ratings at least 70 % of the data for all nine measures after the second evaluation round. Further, Cohen's κ scores show that there is substantial (0.6-0.8] or almost perfect agreement (0.80-1.0] between experts for all measures except for NR, PU, and SI being weak (0.40-0.59)

Measure	Raw Agr. in %	κ	α
OQ	82	0.637	0.820
GR	78	0.626	0.815
NR	70	0.520	0.796
RC	88	0.819	0.907
FO	80	0.685	0.777
SC	82	0.743	0.893
SU	76	0.635	0.835
PU	70	0.469	0.630
SI	76	0.565	0.764

Table 1: Raw agreement in %, Cohen's κ and Krippendorff's α of expert ratings

(Landis and Koch, 1977).

Also, we calculated Krippendorff's α, which is technically a measure of evaluator disagreement rather than agreement and the most common of the measures in the set NLG papers surveyed in Amidei et al. (2019). The Krippendorff's α scores for all the other measures are good [0.8-1.0] except for PO and SI measures, which are tentative [0.67-0.8) and PU measure, which should be discarded because it is 0.04 lower than the threshold 0.67 Krippendorff (1980). Because of the minimal difference of 0.04, we decided to still use the PU measure in our further analysis for interpretation. With these results, we achieved a better agreement level than the average expert agreement of summarization evaluation reported in other papers Van Der Lee et al. (2019).

We use the mean of expert ratings for all quality measures as our ground-truth for our further analysis. To test the normality of expert ratings, we carried out Anderson-Darling tests showing that the measures OQ, NR, FO, and SI were not normally distributed ($p < 0.05$). Therefore, we apply non-parametric statistics in the following sections.

4.1.1 Annotation Aggregation Methods

To investigate the effect of the annotation aggregation methods on the correlation coefficients between the crowd and expert ratings, we compared MOS with the baseline Majority Vote and two weighted-rank metrics CrowdTruth and MACE using crowdtruth-core[6] and MACE[7] libraries. Table 2 shows the Spearman's ρ correlation coefficients between crowd and experts by using these four

---

[4] https://github.com/google-research/bleurt

[5] https://github.com/PrimerAI/blanc

[6] https://github.com/CrowdTruth/CrowdTruth-core

[7] https://github.com/dirkhovy/MACE

Measure	MOS	Maj. Vote	Crowdtruth	MACE
OQ	**.730**	.624	.702	.654
GR	.706	.696	**.721**	.633
NR	**.581**	.523	.553	.490
RC	**.741**	.619	.726	.647
FO	**.656**	.516	.636	.516
SC	.828	.690	**.834**	.748
SU	**.688**	.60	.677	.561
PU	**.464**	NS	.435	NS
SI	**.619**	.482	.609	.523

$p < 0.05$ for all correlations
NS: Not Significant

Table 2: Spearman's ρ correlation coefficients between crowd and expert ratings for all measures by the aggregation methods MOS, Majority Vote, Crowdtruth and MACE

aggregation methods, and the bold coefficients correspond to row maxima.

For all measures, Majority Vote and MACE performed worse than MOS and Crowdtruth. For measures OQ, NR, RC, FO, SU, PU, and SI, MOS performed better than the Crowdtruth, and for GR and SC, Crowdtruth performed better than MOS by all correlation coefficients. To determine if these differences are statistically significant, we applied Zou's confidence intervals test for dependent and overlapping variables and found out that the differences between correlation coefficients were not statistically significant for all nine measures (Zou, 2007). Based on this correlation analysis, we recommend using MOS as the aggregation method for crowd-based summarization evaluation since aggregation using MOS delivers the most comparable aggregates compared to experts and easy to apply.

Analyzing the Spearman's ρ correlation coefficients between the crowd and expert ratings by MOS, we see that all correlation coefficients were statistically significant, ranging from moderate (NR, PU) to strong (OQ, GR, RC, FO, SU, SI) and very strong (SC), where SC had the highest correlation coefficient of 0.828 and PU the lowest correlation coefficient of 0.464. This result suggests that crowdsourcing can be used instead of experts when determining the structure & coherence of a summarization. For determining OQ, GR, RC, FO, SU, and SI, crowdsourcing can be preferred since the overall correlation coefficients are strong, but the results should be interpreted with some degree of caution. However, when evaluating the non-redundancy and post usefulness, experts

should be used for more robust results.

To investigate the differences between the crowd and expert judgments, we conducted the Mann-Whitney U test for each pair of nine quality scores. We observed no significant difference between the median ratings of OQ, SC, SU, and SI measures. This result suggests that crowdsourcing can be used instead of experts when determining these four measures without significant deviation in absolute score rating value. Please note that the ratings' distributions allow for significant equality in estimated mean values (here as the median) even on levels where correlations did not show very strong but only strong magnitudes.

However, there were statistically significant difference between GR_{Crowd} ($M = 3.667$) and GR_{Expert} ($M = 4.0$), NR_{Crowd} ($M = 3.865$) and NR_{Expert} ($M = 4.0$), RC_{Crowd} ($M = 3.794$) and RC_{Expert} ($M = 4.0$), FO_{Crowd} ($M = 4.048$) and FO_{Expert} ($M = 4.250$), as well as PU_{Crowd} ($M = 3.856$) and PU_{Expert} ($M = 4.0$), showing that the crowd workers rated these factors statistically lower than the experts. This observation might be explained by the fact that the nature of extractive summarization and inherent text quality losses - compared to naturally composed text flow - are more familiar to experts than to non-experts, so they can distinguish between the unnaturalness and the linguistic quality in more robust ways.

4.1.2 Effect of Reading Effort

In this section, we analyzed the seven measures which achieve a correlation coefficient above 0.6 with experts: OQ, GR, RC, FO, SC, SU, and SI. Because the text's structural and formal composure, among many other factors, can cause difficulty in summarization evaluation, we analyzed the quality assessment performance of crowd workers regarding two distinct factors: a) readability of the text; b) reading effort in terms of overall stimuli length by dividing our data into six groups.

As our first reading effort criteria, we used the automated readability index (ARI), a readability test designed to assess a text's understandability, where a low ARI score indicates higher readability of a text (Feng et al., 2010). We split the packaged data into two groups by the median ARI scores of source texts (ARI-Low, ARI-High) calculated using textstat[8] library. Because the amount of information to be read and understood by any crowd

---

[8] https://github.com/shivam5992/textstat

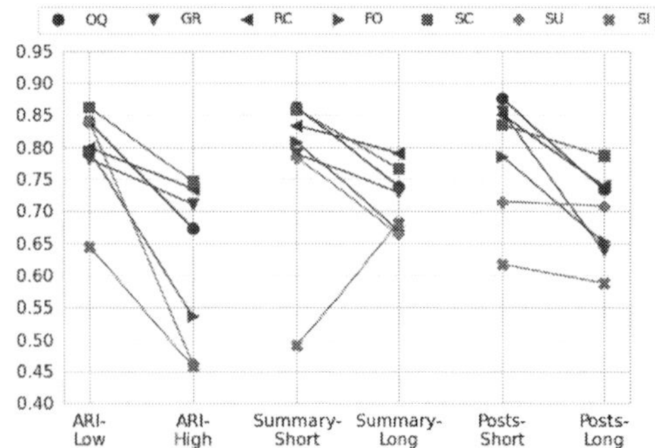

Figure 1: Spearman's ρ correlation coefficients between crowd and expert ratings for six groups

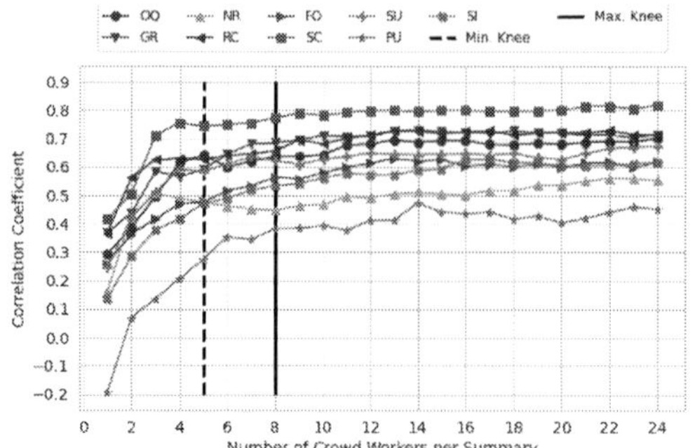

Figure 2: Spearman's ρ correlation coefficients between crowd and expert ratings by the number of crowd workers

participant may cause degrading concentration and motivation levels when the reading effort gets too long, we also split the data by the median of the word count of the summaries ($M = 56$) (Summary-Short, Summary-Long), and by the median of the forum posts ($M = 516$) (Posts-Short, Posts-Long).

Figure 1 displays all the correlation coefficients for the six groups. Here, we recognized that there was a certain pattern for all group pairs where correlation coefficients between the crowd and expert ratings were in groups "ARI-Low", "Summary-Short", and "Posts-Short" higher than the correlation coefficients in groups "ARI-High", "Summary-Long", and "Posts-Long" except for SI. The reason for the opposite trend of SI in groups divided by the summary length might be that the long summaries naturally contain more information, so it is easier for crowd workers to identify the summary informativeness. Other than this opposite trend of SI, we can derive the intuitive assumption that text understandability and reading effort have a noticeable effect on crowd judgments' robustness. Crowd workers may be used instead of experts for the evaluation of rather short summaries derived from documents with high readability.

4.1.3 Optimal Crowd Worker Number

To find out the optimal number of required crowd workers assessments per item, we plot the change of correlation coefficients between the crowd and expert ratings for all nine measures, where the x-axis shows the number of crowd workers per item in measured order, and the y-axis displays the Spearman ρ correlation coefficients between the crowd and expert ratings in Figure 2.

Looking at Figure 2, three or fewer crowd workers as annotators are not sufficient, and a study with

a low number of crowd workers would not deliver a qualitative result since the correlation coefficient increase by increasing the number of crowd workers. However, this increase ends a saturation point between the number of repetitions and the resulting correlation coefficient. In order to determine the accurate optimal number of repetitions, we applied the method described in our paper Iskender et al. (2020), where multiple randomized runs are simulated in order to determine a "knee point" robustly, after which any additional repetitions no longer cause an adequate increase of overall correlation coefficients between the crowd and expert ratings. Our findings are directly in line with our findings in Iskender et al. (2020), where we applied this method to compare the crowd rating with laboratory ratings and stated that 7-9 crowd workers are the optimal number to achieve almost the same results as laboratory results in general.

We found that the knee point is 5 for RC; 7 for OQ, GR, NR, FO, SC, SU, and SI; 8 for PU. This result shows that generally, after collecting data from 5-8 different crowd workers depending on the measure, collecting one more additional crowd judgment was no longer worth the increase in correlation coefficient between the crowd and expert.

4.2 Human vs. Automatic Evaluation

As explained in section 2.1, we calculated BLEU ($\bar{x} = 0.294$), F1-Scores of ROUGE-1 ($\bar{x} = 0.459$), ROUGE-2 ($\bar{x} = 0.345$), ROUGE-L ($\bar{x} = 0.380$), and BertScore ($\bar{x} = 0.371$) as well as BLANC ($\bar{x} = 0.281$) and BLEURT ($\bar{x} = -0.492$) scores for our data set using the summaries from two experts as our gold standard.

While analyzing the Spearman's correlation co-

Measure	OQ	RC	FO	SU	SI
ROUGE-1	0.351	NS	0.323	0.395	0.420
ROUGE-2	NS	NS	NS	0.304	0.326
ROUGE-L	NS	NS	NS	0.284	0.315
BertScore	0.333	0.302	0.322	0.390	0.397

$p < 0.05$ for all correlations
NS: Not significant

Table 3: Spearman's ρ correlation coefficients between ROUGE scores, BertScore, and crowd ratings

Measure	OQ	GR	RC	SI
ROUGE-1	0.315	0.365	NS	0.377
BertScore	0.04	0.320	0.318	NS

$p < 0.05$ for all correlations
NS: Not significant

Table 4: Spearman's ρ correlation coefficients between ROUGE scores, BertScore, and expert ratings

efficients between the automatic scores and the crowd ratings, we observed that only ROUGE and BertScore scores correlated with OQ, RC, FO, SU, and SI of the crowd judgments (see Table 3). Looking at the correlation coefficients between expert ratings and automatic metrics (see Table 4), we also found that there was a significant correlation between only ROUGE and BertScore scores and OQ, GR, RC, and SI of expert ratings. Generally, we observed that overall correlations were of weak level, looking at the magnitude of any significant correlation found. Even though we used most recent metrics other than ROUGE trained on BERT, such as BertScore (Van Der Lee et al., 2019), our findings verify that automatic metrics do not correlate with linguistic quality metrics in the summarization domain.

Although Papineni et al. (2002); Lin (2004); Zhang et al. (2019) reported high correlations with humans on the content-related quality assessment in the corresponding original papers, we showed that these metrics correlate poorly with any human rating, from crowd or expert, verifying the findings of Van Der Lee et al. (2019) for our data set. The reason for this difference is that the BLEU score is developed for measuring machine translation quality and tested on a translation data set. BertScore is also not evaluated using a summarization data set in the original corresponding paper. Only, ROUGE metric is tested on summarization data sets. However, in the human evaluation part of the original paper, the evaluators assigned content coverage scores to a candidate summary compared to a manual summary, which is very similar to the way of working of ROUGE calculating the n-gram match of a candidate summary in comparison to a manual summary. In our human evaluation, we did not apply pair comparison, and the ratings were given on an absolute scale, which might be the reason for the low correlation coefficients between

automatic metrics and human ratings in our study.

We also calculated BLEURT and BLANC scores, but we treat them as preliminary results since we did not apply any special pre-training to these metrics. We found that BLEURT does not correlate with any of the crowd and expert ratings significantly. Similarly, BLANC does not correlate with any of the crowd rating except for NR ($\rho = -0.342$), and surprisingly it correlates significantly and negatively with expert ratings for NR ($\rho = -0.473$) , RC ($\rho = -0.308$), and SC ($\rho = -0.347$). We can not explain the reasons for the negative correlation and speculate that this might be due to not applying pre-training.

5 Conclusion and Future Work

In this paper, we provide a basis for best practices for crowd-based summarization evaluation by comparing different annotation aggregation methods, analyzing the effect of reading effort and readability, and approaching an estimate of an optimal number of required crowd workers per item in order to as closely as possible resemble experts' assessment quality through crowdsourcing.

When determining structure & coherence, we suggest that crowdsourcing can be used as a direct substitute for experts proven by the very strong correlation coefficient. For determining overall quality, grammaticality, referential clarity, focus, summary usefulness, and summary informativeness, crowdsourcing can be preferred as the overall correlation still results strong, but the results should be interpreted carefully. However, when evaluating non-redundancy and post usefulness, experts should be used for more robust results, as correlations result moderate only.

Our experiments further recommend following best-practices when using crowdsourcing instead of experts: 1) In general 5-8 crowd workers should annotate a given summary, 2) MOS should be used as an aggregation method to achieve optimally comparable results to experts, 3) Crowdsourcing may be used at best when readability of the source and reading effort of the task is of rather low and straightforward nature. We also confirm the findings of Dumitrache et al. (2018b) that Crowdtruth performs better than the MACE. Further, we confirm that the automatic evaluation metrics BLEU, ROUGE, and BertScore can not be used to evaluate the linguistic quality, and we show that automatic evaluation metrics correlate poorly with any content-related absolute human rating, from crowd or expert, verifying the findings of Van Der Lee et al. (2019) for our domain. Therefore, crowdsourcing should generally be the preferred evaluation method over automated scores in the summarization evaluation.

Since the vast majority of research on summarization bases on the TAC or CNN/Dailymail data sets, there is a lack of works from other languages or domains. We address this gap by using a German forum summarization data set derived from an online forum in the telecommunication domain. Contrary to the findings of Gillick and Liu (2010) and Fabbri et al. (2020), we achieve significant correlations between the crowd and expert ratings ranging from moderate to very strong magnitude, as well as no significant difference in absolute mean rating in between the crowd and expert assessment for overall quality, structure & coherence, summary usefulness, and summary informativeness. Other scales show a slight but still significant bias towards lower ratings of about less than 0.3pt absolute. These are important findings in the development of NLG tools for summarization. In particular, summarization tools developed for languages other than English for which it is harder to conduct expert evaluations and find easy-to-use automatic metrics could benefit highly from our findings.

However, this study has some limitations since we conduct our analysis using only a single data set derived from an online forum in the telecommunication domain. The level of domain knowledge of crowd workers and experts about the telecommunication service might play a role when determining content-related quality measures such as post usefulness. So, the effect of the domain knowledge should be investigated in detail in future work. Another shortcoming of this paper is that our summarization data set is derived from noisy internet data, and the summary length does not differ much. As shown in section 4.1.2, the readability of the source document and varying lengths of summaries might affect the results; therefore, the same analysis should be conducted on one more data set. Additionally, our data set was monolingual, so exploring the language-based effects will also be part of future work.

Further, this study is that we did not investigate the effect of the crowdsourcing task design and learning effect on the correlation coefficient between the crowd and expert ratings. Questions regarding the limitation to the number of assignments taken on by an evaluator (both for crowd and expert) and evaluators' behavior (becoming more lenient or strict over time) should also be analyzed in future work. Also, we did not use the pairwise comparison in our task design and only focused on absolute quality rating. For that reason, investigating the pairwise comparison using crowdsourcing and its comparison to absolute rating should be considered as an essential aspect of the crowdsourcing task design in future work.

Despite the limitations of our study, this paper is the first paper in the summarization evaluation literature that provides evidence for clear support for using crowdsourcing to evaluate summarization quality and adds to a growing corpus of research on the summarization evaluation.

References

Jacopo Amidei, Paul Piwek, and Alistair Willis. 2019. Agreement is overrated: A plea for correlation to assess human evaluation reliability. In *Proceedings of the 12th International Conference on Natural Language Generation*, pages 344–354.

Chris Callison-Burch. 2009. Fast, cheap, and creative: evaluating translation quality using amazon's mechanical turk. In *Proceedings of the 2009 Conference on Empirical Methods in Natural Language Processing: Volume 1-Volume 1*, pages 286–295. Association for Computational Linguistics.

Asli Celikyilmaz, Elizabeth Clark, and Jianfeng Gao. 2020. Evaluation of text generation: A survey. *arXiv preprint arXiv:2006.14799*.

Sujoy Chatterjee, Anirban Mukhopadhyay, and Malay Bhattacharyya. 2019. A review of judgment analysis algorithms for crowdsourced opinions. *IEEE Transactions on Knowledge and Data Engineering*.

John M Conroy and Hoa Trang Dang. 2008. Mind the gap: Dangers of divorcing evaluations of summary content from linguistic quality. In *Proceedings of the 22nd International Conference on Computational Linguistics-Volume 1*, pages 145–152. Association for Computational Linguistics.

Hoa Trang Dang. 2005. Overview of duc 2005. In *Proceedings of the document understanding conference*, volume 2005, pages 1–12.

Michael Denkowski and Alon Lavie. 2014. Meteor universal: Language specific translation evaluation for any target language. In *Proceedings of the ninth workshop on statistical machine translation*, pages 376–380.

Jacob Devlin, Ming-Wei Chang, Kenton Lee, and Kristina Toutanova. 2019. Bert: Pre-training of deep bidirectional transformers for language understanding. In *Proceedings of the 2019 Conference of the North American Chapter of the Association for Computational Linguistics: Human Language Technologies, Volume 1 (Long and Short Papers)*, pages 4171–4186.

Anca Dumitrache, Oana Inel, Lora Aroyo, Benjamin Timmermans, and Chris Welty. 2018a. Crowdtruth 2.0: Quality metrics for crowdsourcing with disagreement. In *1st Workshop on Subjectivity, Ambiguity and Disagreement in Crowdsourcing, and Short Paper 1st Workshop on Disentangling the Relation Between Crowdsourcing and Bias Management, SAD+ CrowdBias 2018*, pages 11–18. CEUR-WS.

Anca Dumitrache, Oana Inel, Benjamin Timmermans, Carlos Ortiz, Robert-Jan Sips, Lora Aroyo, and Chris Welty. 2018b. Empirical methodology for crowdsourcing ground truth. *Semantic Web*.

Alexander R Fabbri, Wojciech Kryściński, Bryan McCann, Caiming Xiong, Richard Socher, and Dragomir Radev. 2020. Summeval: Re-evaluating summarization evaluation. *arXiv preprint arXiv:2007.12626.*

Tobias Falke, Christian M Meyer, and Iryna Gurevych. 2017. Concept-map-based multi-document summarization using concept coreference resolution and global importance optimization. In *Proceedings of the Eighth International Joint Conference on Natural Language Processing (Volume 1: Long Papers)*, pages 801–811.

Angela Fan, David Grangier, and Michael Auli. 2018. Controllable abstractive summarization. In *Proceedings of the 2nd Workshop on Neural Machine Translation and Generation*, pages 45–54.

Lijun Feng, Martin Jansche, Matt Huenerfauth, and Noémie Elhadad. 2010. A comparison of features for automatic readability assessment. In *Coling 2010: Posters*, pages 276–284.

Kavita Ganesan. 2018. Rouge 2.0: Updated and improved measures for evaluation of summarization tasks. *arXiv preprint arXiv:1803.01937.*

Yang Gao, Christian M Meyer, and Iryna Gurevych. 2018. April: Interactively learning to summarise by combining active preference learning and reinforcement learning. In *EMNLP*.

Yanjun Gao, Chen Sun, and Rebecca J Passonneau. 2019. Automated pyramid summarization evaluation. In *Proceedings of the 23rd Conference on Computational Natural Language Learning (CoNLL)*, pages 404–418.

Dan Gillick and Yang Liu. 2010. Non-expert evaluation of summarization systems is risky. In *Proceedings of the NAACL HLT 2010 Workshop on Creating Speech and Language Data with Amazon's Mechanical Turk*, pages 148–151. Association for Computational Linguistics.

Yvette Graham. 2015. Re-evaluating automatic summarization with bleu and 192 shades of rouge. In *Proceedings of the 2015 conference on empirical methods in natural language processing*, pages 128–137.

Ivan Habernal and Iryna Gurevych. 2016. What makes a convincing argument? empirical analysis and detecting attributes of convincingness in web argumentation. In *Proceedings of the 2016 Conference on Empirical Methods in Natural Language Processing*, pages 1214–1223.

Dirk Hovy, Taylor Berg-Kirkpatrick, Ashish Vaswani, and Eduard Hovy. 2013. Learning whom to trust with mace. In *Proceedings of the 2013 Conference of the North American Chapter of the Association for Computational Linguistics: Human Language Technologies*, pages 1120–1130.

Nguyen Quoc Viet Hung, Nguyen Thanh Tam, Lam Ngoc Tran, and Karl Aberer. 2013. An evaluation of aggregation techniques in crowdsourcing. In *International Conference on Web Information Systems Engineering*, pages 1–15. Springer.

Neslihan Iskender, Tim Polzehl, and Sebastian Möller. 2020. Towards a reliable and robust methodology for crowd-based subjective quality assessment of query-based extractive text summarization. In *Proceedings of The 12th Language Resources and Evaluation Conference*, pages 245–253.

Karen Sparck Jones and Julia R Galliers. 1995. *Evaluating natural language processing systems: An analysis and review*, volume 1083. Springer Science & Business Media.

Sanjay Kairam and Jeffrey Heer. 2016. Parting crowds: Characterizing divergent interpretations in crowdsourced annotation tasks. In *Proceedings of the 19th ACM Conference on Computer-Supported Cooperative Work & Social Computing*, pages 1637–1648. ACM.

Klaus Krippendorff. 1980. Content analysis: An introduction to its methodology.

J Richard Landis and Gary G Koch. 1977. The measurement of observer agreement for categorical data. *biometrics*, pages 159–174.

Chin-Yew Lin. 2004. Rouge: A package for automatic evaluation of summaries. *Text Summarization Branches Out*.

Harold A Linstone, Murray Turoff, et al. 1975. *The delphi method*. Addison-Wesley Reading, MA.

Elena Lloret, Laura Plaza, and Ahmet Aker. 2013. Analyzing the capabilities of crowdsourcing services for text summarization. *Language resources and evaluation*, 47(2):337–369.

Elena Lloret, Laura Plaza, and Ahmet Aker. 2018. The challenging task of summary evaluation: an overview. *Language Resources and Evaluation*, 52(1):101–148.

Kurt Luther, Jari-Lee Tolentino, Wei Wu, Amy Pavel, Brian P Bailey, Maneesh Agrawala, Björn Hartmann, and Steven P Dow. 2015. Structuring, aggregating, and evaluating crowdsourced design critique. In *Proceedings of the 18th ACM Conference on Computer Supported Cooperative Work & Social Computing*, pages 473–485. ACM.

Inderjeet Mani. 2001. Recent developments in text summarization. In *Proceedings of the tenth international conference on Information and knowledge management*, pages 529–531. ACM.

Tanushree Mitra, Clayton J Hutto, and Eric Gilbert. 2015. Comparing person-and process-centric strategies for obtaining quality data on amazon mechanical turk. In *Proceedings of the 33rd Annual ACM Conference on Human Factors in Computing Systems*, pages 1345–1354. ACM.

Ani Nenkova and Rebecca J Passonneau. 2004. Evaluating content selection in summarization: The pyramid method. In *Proceedings of the human language technology conference of the north american chapter of the association for computational linguistics: Hlt-naacl 2004*, pages 145–152.

Jun Ping Ng and Viktoria Abrecht. 2015. Better summarization evaluation with word embeddings for rouge. In *Proceedings of the 2015 Conference on Empirical Methods in Natural Language Processing*, pages 1925–1930.

Jekaterina Novikova, Ondřej Dušek, Amanda Cercas Curry, and Verena Rieser. 2017. Why we need new evaluation metrics for nlg. In *Proceedings of the 2017 Conference on Empirical Methods in Natural Language Processing*, pages 2241–2252.

Stefanie Nowak and Stefan Rüger. 2010. How reliable are annotations via crowdsourcing: a study about inter-annotator agreement for multi-label image annotation. In *Proceedings of the international conference on Multimedia information retrieval*, pages 557–566. ACM.

Kishore Papineni, Salim Roukos, Todd Ward, and Wei-Jing Zhu. 2002. Bleu: a method for automatic evaluation of machine translation. In *Proceedings of the 40th annual meeting of the Association for Computational Linguistics*, pages 311–318.

Rebecca J Passonneau and Bob Carpenter. 2014. The benefits of a model of annotation. *Transactions of the Association for Computational Linguistics*, 2:311–326.

Silviu Paun, Bob Carpenter, Jon Chamberlain, Dirk Hovy, Udo Kruschwitz, and Massimo Poesio. 2018. Comparing bayesian models of annotation. *Transactions of the Association for Computational Linguistics*, 6:571–585.

Maxime Peyrard and Judith Eckle-Kohler. 2017. Supervised learning of automatic pyramid for optimization-based multi-document summarization. In *Proceedings of the 55th Annual Meeting of the Association for Computational Linguistics (Volume 1: Long Papers)*, pages 1084–1094.

Barbara Plank, Dirk Hovy, Ryan McDonald, and Anders Søgaard. 2014. Adapting taggers to twitter with not-so-distant supervision. In *Proceedings of COLING 2014, the 25th International Conference on Computational Linguistics: Technical Papers*, pages 1783–1792.

Ehud Reiter. 2018. A structured review of the validity of bleu. *Computational Linguistics*, 44(3):393–401.

Ehud Reiter and Anja Belz. 2009. An investigation into the validity of some metrics for automatically evaluating natural language generation systems. *Computational Linguistics*, 35(4):529–558.

Marta Sabou, Kalina Bontcheva, Leon Derczynski, and Arno Scharl. 2014. Corpus annotation through crowdsourcing: Towards best practice guidelines. In *LREC*, pages 859–866.

Nattapong Sanchan, Ahmet Aker, and Kalina Bontcheva. 2017. Gold standard online debates summaries and first experiments towards automatic summarization of online debate data. In *International Conference on Computational Linguistics and Intelligent Text Processing*, pages 495–505. Springer.

Thibault Sellam, Dipanjan Das, and Ankur P Parikh. 2020. Bleurt: Learning robust metrics for text generation. *arXiv preprint arXiv:2004.04696*.

Ori Shapira, David Gabay, Yang Gao, Hadar Ronen, Ramakanth Pasunuru, Mohit Bansal, Yael Amsterdamer, and Ido Dagan. 2019. Crowdsourcing lightweight pyramids for manual summary evaluation. In *Proceedings of the 2019 Conference of the North American Chapter of the Association for Computational Linguistics: Human Language Technologies, Volume 1 (Long and Short Papers)*, pages 682–687.

Rion Snow, Brendan O'Connor, Daniel Jurafsky, and Andrew Y Ng. 2008. Cheap and fast—but is it good?: evaluating non-expert annotations for natural language tasks. In *Proceedings of the conference on empirical methods in natural language processing*, pages 254–263. Association for Computational Linguistics.

Josef Steinberger and Karel Ježek. 2012. Evaluation measures for text summarization. *Computing and Informatics*, 28(2):251–275.

Robert C Streijl, Stefan Winkler, and David S Hands. 2016. Mean opinion score (mos) revisited: methods and applications, limitations and alternatives. *Multimedia Systems*, 22(2):213–227.

Chris Van Der Lee, Albert Gatt, Emiel Van Miltenburg, Sander Wubben, and Emiel Krahmer. 2019. Best practices for the human evaluation of automatically generated text. In *Proceedings of the 12th International Conference on Natural Language Generation*, pages 355–368.

Oleg Vasilyev, Vedant Dharnidharka, and John Bohannon. 2020. Fill in the blanc: Human-free quality estimation of document summaries. *arXiv preprint arXiv:2002.09836*.

Jacob Whitehill, Ting-fan Wu, Jacob Bergsma, Javier R Movellan, and Paul L Ruvolo. 2009. Whose vote should count more: Optimal integration of labels from labelers of unknown expertise. In *Advances in neural information processing systems*, pages 2035–2043.

Tianyi Zhang, Varsha Kishore, Felix Wu, Kilian Q Weinberger, and Yoav Artzi. 2019. Bertscore: Evaluating text generation with bert. In *International Conference on Learning Representations*.

Liang Zhou, Chin-Yew Lin, Dragos Stefan Munteanu, and Eduard Hovy. 2006. Paraeval: Using paraphrases to evaluate summaries automatically. In *Proceedings of the main conference on Human Language Technology Conference of the North American Chapter of the Association of Computational Linguistics*, pages 447–454. Association for Computational Linguistics.

Guang Yong Zou. 2007. Toward using confidence intervals to compare correlations. *Psychological methods*, 12(4):399.

Evaluating Word Embeddings on Low-Resource Languages

Nathan Stringham
Pomona College
Claremont, CA, USA
nes02014@mymail.pomona.edu

Mike Izbicki
Claremont McKenna College
Claremont, CA, USA
mike@izbicki.me

Abstract

The analogy task introduced by Mikolov et al.
(2013) has become the standard metric for tuning the hyperparameters of word embedding
models. In this paper, however, we argue
that the analogy task is unsuitable for low-
resource languages for two reasons: (1) it requires that word embeddings be trained on
large amounts of text, and (2) analogies may
not be well-defined in some low-resource settings. We solve these problems by introducing
the `OddOneOut` and `Topk` tasks, which are
specifically designed for model selection in the
low-resource setting. We use these metrics to
successfully tune hyperparameters for a low-
resource emoji embedding task and word embeddings on 16 extinct languages. The largest
of these languages (Ancient Hebrew) has a 41
million token dataset, and the smallest (Old
Gujarati) has only a 1813 token dataset.

1 Introduction

Imagine you're given the task of training a text classification model for Middle English. This form of
English was spoken in the Middle Ages from 1066-
1500 CE. It is significantly different from modern
English (Chamonikolasová, 2014), and only a handful of historians speak this language today.

A natural first step would be to train word embeddings. So you use the Classical Language ToolKit
(CLTK) (Johnson, 2014) to download the largest
corpus of known Middle English documents (only
7 million tokens, 0.3 million unique tokens), and
Gensim (Řehůřek and Sojka, 2010) to train the
embeddings. To evaluate the embeddings, you follow the current standard practice established by
Mikolov et al. (2013) of using an analogy test set.
Of course, you can't use Mikolov et al. (2013)'s
test set—it is in Modern English, and Middle English is not Modern English. But you also can't
even use translations of their test set—many of the

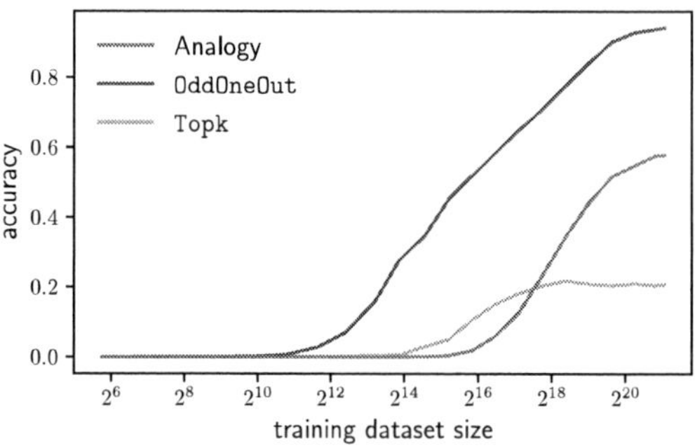

Figure 1: The standard analogy task (Mikolov et al.,
2013) fails to measure the quality of word embeddings
trained on small datasets, but our novel `OddOneOut`
and `Topk` tasks succeed in this regime.

analogy concepts simply didn't exist in the Middle
Ages. For example, the analogy

London is to England as Paris is to France

can be translated perfectly fine into Middle English,
but the concept of nations and capitals didn't exist
in the Middle Ages, so the analogy is not semantically meaningful. To create a meaningful analogy
test set, you hire a historian fluent in Middle English, and with considerable effort and research she
creates custom analogies that make sense in Middle
Age England.

With this analogy test set in hand, you train
dozens of models with varying hyperparameters.
Unfortunately, all these models get 0 accuracy on
your test set. You simply don't have enough data
to get good results on the analogy task. As Figure
1 shows, the analogy task requires a large training
dataset before it begins getting non-zero results
(Details provided in Section 3.1 below). But that
does not mean that you cannot train word embeddings on Middle English.

In this paper, we introduce the `OddOneOut` and
`Topk` tasks for evaluating word vectors on low-

Proceedings of the First Workshop on Evaluation and Comparison of NLP Systems (Eval4NLP), pages 176–186,
November 20, 2020. ©2020 Association for Computational Linguistics

resource languages, successfully train word embeddings for 16 extinct languages (including Middle English), and perform a low-resource emoji embedding task. To get a sense of scale, the original word2vec paper trained English word embeddings on a dataset with 6 billion tokens (Mikolov et al., 2013) with subsequent work improving performance by training on datasets as large as 630 billion tokens (Grave et al., 2018). In this paper, the largest dataset we consider has 41 million tokens, and the smallest only 1813 tokens. We argue that different evaluation techniques are needed for datasets like ours that are more than 1000 times smaller. Figure 1 shows that the `OddOneOut` and `Topk` tasks are better suited than the analogy task to measure improvement in embedding quality with datasets like these.

1.1 Related Work

Other work in the low-resource regime has focused on developing new training methods rather than evaluation methods. Specifically, the goal has been to reduce the sample complexity of word embedding models by adding new regularizations (Adams et al., 2017; Jiang et al., 2018; Gupta et al., 2019; Jungmaier et al., 2020). A common thread of this work is the difficulty of evaluation. Unfortunately, each of these works evaluate their method only in a simulated low-resource environment using Modern English text and not on any actual low-resource languages. They do this specifically because no evaluation metrics were available that were suitable for their low-resource target languages. More theoretical work has also shown that these simulated low-resource design methodologies give biased hyperparameter estimates which systematically overestimate model performance (Kann et al., 2019). This highlights the need for new evaluation methods like ours, which are suitable for the low-resource regime.

From an evaluation standpoint analogies are not the only metric available to tune the hyperparameters of low-resource embedding models. Other work has focused on similarity tasks, establishing evaluation benchmarks based on human annotation of English language word pairs (Finkelstein et al., 2001; Radinsky et al., 2011; Bruni et al., 2012). Compared to the analogy task, these methods are more sensitive to low-resource experimental design, however, they suffer from the high overhead costs associated with manually generating test datasets.

In contrast, our tasks leverage the Wikidata knowledge base to automate the process of creating custom test sets while still maintaining sensitivity to low-resource settings.

High-resource languages also directly benefit from our methods in two ways. First, we help automate evaluation on many languages. Grave et al. (2018) trained FastText embeddings on 157 languages using data from the Common Crawl project. But they were only able to explicitly evaluate 10 of these language models using the analogy task due to the expense required in developing appropriate test sets. A major advantage of our `OddOneOut` and `Topk` methods is that test sets can be generated for them automatically in any of Wikidata's 581 supported languages (including extinct languages like Middle English).

Second, many applications of word embeddings investigate low-resource subsets of high-resource languages. There is growing body of digital humanities work where English language text is subdivided into smaller corpora based on time periods (e.g. Kulkarni et al., 2015; Hamilton et al., 2016b,a; Dubossarsky et al., 2017; Szymanski, 2017; Chen et al., 2017; Liang et al., 2018; Tang, 2018; Kutuzov et al., 2018; Kozlowski et al., 2019) or different political ideologies Azarbonyad et al. (2017). Word embeddings are then trained on these smaller corpora, and differences in the resulting embeddings are used to track changes in word usage. Our evaluation methods can be used to improve the ability to evaluate this work as well.

1.2 Contributions

Our contributions can be summarized with the following three points.

1. We introduce the first word embedding evaluation tasks designed specifically for the low-resource setting, `OddOneOut` and `Topk`. Code for computing these metrics is released as an open source Python library.[1]

2. We introduce a method for automatically generating test datasets for the `OddOneOut` and `Topk` tasks in the 581 languages supported by the Wikidata project.

3. We perform the largest existing multilingual evaluation on low-resource languages using 16 extinct languages from the Classical

---

[1] `https://github.com/n8stringham/gensim-evaluations`

Language ToolKit (CLTK) (Johnson, 2014). Specifically, we provide word embeddings for 16 of the 18 languages with corpora in the CLTK library (Johnson, 2014) and introduce the Language Comparison Task (LCT) to investigate which topics are included in these classical language corpora.

The remainder of the paper is organized as follows. Section 2 formally defines the `Topk` and `OddOneOut` tasks. Section 3 empirically demonstrates that these tasks are better than the analogy task in low-resource settings. We use a synthetic English language experimental design common in previous work, and demonstrate the versatility of our evaluation metrics by applying them to an emoji embedding task for which the analogy task is not even well defined. Section 4 computes word embeddings for 16 extinct languages and introduces our technique to automatically generate test sets for the `OddOneOut`, `Topk`, and LCT tasks using Wikidata. We also provide a semantic analysis of the topics covered in each of the 16 language corpora. Section 5 concludes by discussing how extensions to this work could serve communities working with low-resource languages.

2   Evaluation Methods

The `OddOneOut` and `Topk` tasks are simple and widely applicable. Both tasks require a test set consisting of a list of categories, where each category contains a list of words belonging to that category. Figure 4 shows some example categories generated through a fully automated process (described in Section 4.1). The `Topk` task measures a model's ability to identify words that are related to each category, and conversely the `OddOneOut` task measures a model's ability to identify words that are unrelated to each category,

Formally, assume that there are m categories, that each category has n words[2], that there are v total words in the vocabulary, and that the words are embedded into $\mathbb{R}^d$. The method of generating the embedding (e.g. word2vec, GloVe, fastText) does not matter. Let $c_{i,j}$ be the jth word in category i, and let $C_i = \{c_{i,1}, c_{i,2}, ..., c_{i,n}\}$ be the ith category.

2.1   The `Topk` method

Let $\mathrm{Sim}(k, w)$ return the k most similar words in the vocabulary to w. We use the cosine distance in all our experiments, but any distance metric can be used. Next, define the `Topk` score for class i to be

$$\mathrm{Topk}(k, i) = \frac{1}{n} \sum_{j=1}^{n} \frac{1}{k} \sum_{x \in \mathrm{Sim}(k, c_{i,j})} \mathbb{1}[x \in C_i] \quad (1)$$

and the `Topk` score for the entire evaluation set to be

$$\mathrm{Topk}(k) = \frac{1}{m} \sum_{i=1}^{m} \mathrm{Topk}(k, i). \quad (2)$$

The runtime of Sim is $O(dvk)$.[3] So the runtime of $\mathrm{Topk}(k, i)$ is $O(dnk^2v)$ and the runtime of $\mathrm{Topk}(k)$ is $O(dnmk^2v)$. Typically k is small (we recommend $k = 3$ in our experiments), and so the runtime is linear in all of the interesting parameters. In particular, it is linear in both the size of our vocabulary, the number of categories in the test set, and the size of the categories.

2.2   The `OddOneOut` method

Define the `OddOneOut` score of a set S with k words with respect to a word $w \notin S$ as

$$\mathrm{OddOneOut}(S, w) = \mathbb{1}[w = \hat{w}], \quad (3)$$

where

$$\hat{w} = \arg\min_{x \in S \cup \{w\}} \frac{x \cdot \mu}{\|x\|\|\mu\|} \quad (4)$$

$$\text{and} \quad \mu = \frac{1}{k+1}\left(w + \sum_{i=1}^{k} s_i\right). \quad (5)$$

We define the kth order `OddOneOut` score of a category i to be

$$\mathrm{OddOneOut}(k, i) = \frac{1}{|P|} \sum_{(S,w) \in P} \mathrm{OddOneOut}(S, w) \quad (6)$$

where

$$P = \{(S, w) : S \text{ is a combination of } k \text{ words}$$
$$\text{from } C_i, \text{ and } w \in V - C_i\}. \quad (7)$$

In Equation (7) above, the total number of values that S can take is $\binom{n}{k} = O(n^k)$, and the total number of values that w can take is $O(v)$, so

---

[2]In practice, the number of words per category can vary for each category, however for notational simplicity we assume that each category has the same number of words.

[3]We use Gensim's implementation of Sim, which uses the naive loop strategy for computing the nearest neighbor. Data structures like the kd-tree or cover tree could potentially be used to speed up this search, but we did not find such data structures necessary.

$|P| = O(n^k v)$. Finally, we define the k-th order `OddOneOut` score of the entire evaluation set to be

$$\text{OddOneOut}(k) = \frac{1}{m} \sum_{i=1}^{m} \text{OddOneOut}(k, i). \tag{8}$$

The runtime of $\text{OddOneOut}(S, w)$ is $O(dk)$. So the runtime of $\text{OddOneOut}(k, i)$ is $O(dkn^k v)$ and the runtime of $\text{OddOneOut}(k)$ is $O(dkmn^k v)$. This exponential dependence on k is very bad. In practice, we used $k = 3$ in all of our experiments, but even this small value required prohibitively long run times.

To solve this problem, we use a sampling strategy. Let $\tilde{P}$ denote the set of p samples without replacement from the set P. Then we rewrite Equation 6 as

$$\text{OddOneOut}(k, i) = \frac{1}{p} \sum_{(S, w) \in \tilde{P}} \text{OddOneOut}(S, w) \tag{9}$$

With this definition, the runtime of $\text{OddOneOut}(k)$ is $O(dkmpv)$, which is linear in all the parameters of interest. In our experiments, we found $p = 1000$ to give sufficiently accurate results without taking too much computation.

3 Experiments

We demonstrate the usefulness of our evaluation metrics with two experiments. First, we show that the `OddOneOut` and `Topk` metrics are better measures of word embedding quality than the analogy metric in the low-resource regime using simulated English data. Second, we show that the `OddOneOut` and `Topk` metrics are useful for model selection in an emoji embedding task where the analogy task is not well defined. This experiment also demonstrates that the `OddOneOut` and `Topk` metrics correlate with downstream task performance.

3.1 English Experiments

This experiment measures the performance of the `OddOneOut`, `Topk`, and analogy metrics as a function of dataset size.

For training data, we use a 2017 dump of the English-language Wikipedia that contains 2 billion total tokens and 2 million unique tokens. The dataset is freely distributed with the popular Gen-Sim library (Řehůřek and Sojka, 2010) for training

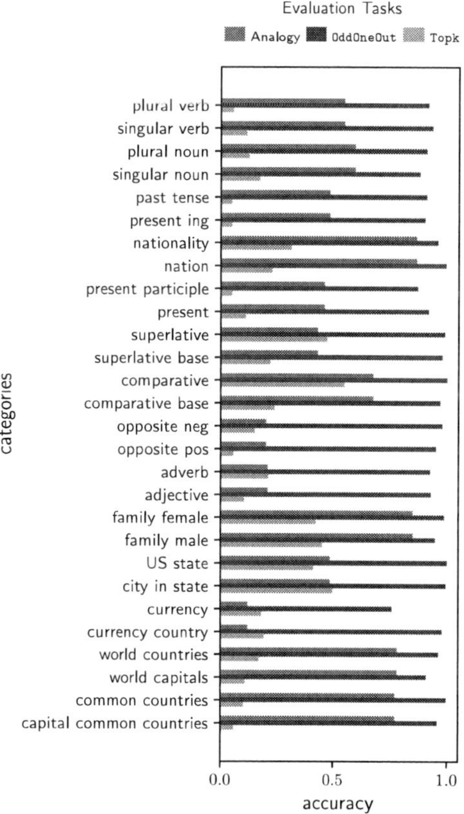

Figure 2: Breakdown of model performance by category. There does not appear to be any correlation between the performance of the three tasks, indicating that each task is measuring a different aspect of linguistic knowledge.

word embeddings, and it is therefore widely used. State-of-the-art embeddings are trained on significantly larger datasets—for example, datasets based on the common crawl contain hundreds of billions of tokens even for non-English languages (Buck et al., 2014; Grave et al., 2018)—but since our emphasis is on the low-resource setting, this 2 billion token dataset is sufficient.

Using the Wikipedia dataset, we generate a series of synthetic low-resource datasets of varying size. First, we sort the articles in the Wikipedia dataset randomly.[4] Then, each dataset i contains the first 2^i tokens in the randomly ordered Wikipedia dump.

---

[4]This sorting is required for our low-resource datasets to be representative of English language text. Without this random sorting step, most of our datasets would be based only on articles that begin with the letter A, and therefore would not contain a representative sample of English words.

179

On each of these low-resource datasets, we train
a word2vec skipgram model with GenSim's default
hyperparameters[5], which are known to work well
in many contexts. Importantly, we do not tune these
hyperparameters for each low-resource dataset. Instead, we use the same hyperparameters because
our goal is to isolate the effects of dataset size on
the three evaluation metrics.

For the analogy task, we use the standard Google
Analogy test set introduced by (Mikolov et al.,
2013). This test set contains 14 sets of analogies, and each analogy set contains 2 categories
that are being compared. We generate test sets for
the OddOneOut and Topk tasks from all 28 categories in the Google test set. For example, the
countries-capitals analogy set has analogies like

London is to England as Paris is to France

In order to convert this analogy to work with
OddOneOut and Topk test sets we use the set of
all capitals and the set of all countries as separate
categories. Applying this same method on each
analogy pair in the original Google Analogy test
set results in an evaluation dataset that is compatible with the OddOneOut and Topk tasks. Note
that this dataset conversion, results in explicitly
losing information about how these categories relate to each other. While the analogy task tests
a model's knowledge of the relationship between
categories, the OddOneOut and Topk tasks will
only test a model's knowledge about each category individually. Since these tasks are testing
less knowledge, it makes since that they will get
improved performance on smaller data sets. This
intuition is confirmed in the results shown in Figure 1. The accuracy broken down by category for
our model trained on the full dataset is shown in
Figure 2. How a category performs on one task
does not seem correlated to how a model performs
on other tasks, which indicates that all three tasks
are in fact measuring different aspects of linguistic knowledge (and not just representing the same
knowledge scaled differently).

3.2 Emoji Experiments

This second experiment demonstrates the versatility of our methods by applying them to the domain
of emoji embeddings. We show that our generic
Topk and OddOneOut metrics perform as well

---

[5]Embedding dimension 100, number of epochs 1, learning
rate 0.025, window size is 5, min count is 5.

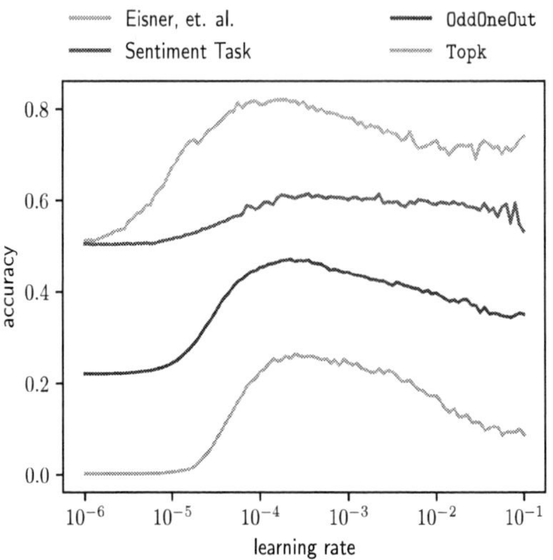

Figure 3: The performance of the generic OddOneOut
and Topk tasks mirrors the performance of Eisner
et al. (2016)'s emoji-specific model selection task as
the learning rate varies. All three tasks provide can be
used to estimate the optimal learning rate for the downstream sentiment classification task.

as a custom designed emoji evaluation metric. That
is, we don't sacrifice performance by choosing
our easy-to-use and widely applicable metrics over
harder-to-use domain-specific metrics.

Emoji embeddings are an important topic of
study because they are used to improve the performance of sentiment analysis systems (e.g. Eisner
et al., 2016; Felbo et al., 2017; Barbieri et al., 2017;
Ai et al., 2017; Wijeratne et al., 2017; Al-Halah
et al., 2019). Unfortunately, the standard analogy
task is not suitable for evaluating the quality of
emoji embeddings for two reasons. First, emoji embeddings are inherently low-resource—only 3000
unique emojis exist in the Unicode standard—and
thus evaluation techniques specifically designed
for the low-resource setting will be more effective.
Second, the semantics of most emojis do not allow
them to be used in any analogy task. In particular,
the original emoji2vec paper (Eisner et al., 2016)
identifies only 6 semantically meaningful emoji
analogies.

In order to tune their emoji embeddings, Eisner
et al. (2016) therefore do not use the analogy task,
and instead introduce an ad-hoc "emoji-description
classification" metric that required the creation of a
test set with manually labeled emotion-description
pairs. Due to the expense of manually creating this
test set, only 1661 of the 3000 Unicode emojis are

included.[6] The `Topk` and `OddOneOut` metrics improve on the "emoji-description classification" metric because they are able to evaluate the quality of all emojis and require no manual test set creation. For our test set categories, we use the categories that the Unicode standard provides for each emoji.[7]

To test the performance of the three metrics, we use them to tune the hyperparameters of an emoji2vec model. To ensure the fairest comparison possible, we use the original emoji2vec code for training and model selection, changing only the function call to the metric used. In particular, this means we are only embedding and evaluating on the subset of 1661 emojis supported by the "emoji-description classification" custom metric. The code allows tuning of the model's learning rate, dimension, epochs, and three other hyperparameters unique to Eisner et al. (2016)'s custom metric. We found that the learning rate was the only hyperparameter to have a significant impact. Figure 3 shows how it affects performance on the three evaluation metrics and a downstream sentiment analysis task. All metrics show optimal performance with a learning rate of approximately 8×10^{-4}, which also results in the best performance on the downstream task. This indicates that our `Topk` and `OddOneOut` metrics generate the same models as the specialized "emoji-description classification" metric, but our metrics have the advantage of being simpler, more widely applicable, and easier to generate test data for.

Note that it is incorrect to conclude that the Eisner et al. (2016) method is better than the `OddOneOut` and `Topk` values because it achieves higher accuracy rates in Figure 3. When evaluating a model selection metric, the important point to consider is the location where the metric is maximized, and not the maximum value itself. The location is used to determine the optimal hyperparameter, and all three metrics have maximal performance at the same location.

4 Multilingual Content Analysis

In this section we perform the first highly multilingual analysis of word embeddings for low-resource languages. We analyze 18 languages provided by the Classical Language ToolKit (CLTK) library

Human Biblical Figures: *Abednego, Abraham, Azor, Chedorlaomer, Christ, Goliath, Hilkiah, Lo-Ammi, Matthew the Apostle, Peter, Sheba, Uz, Yael, Zerubbabel*

Buddhism: *Adharma, Buddha, Bhagavan, Bindu, Guru, Impermanence, Karma, Meditation, Mu, Mudra, Nirvana, Nondualism, Reincarnation, Sutra, Vipassanā*

Hinduism: *Adharma, Ashvadamedha, Brahmin, Bhagavan, Guru, Hindu Prayer Beads, Karma, Mahātmā, Mudra, Nirvana, Reincarnation, Rishi, Samadhi, Sutra*

Figure 4: A sample of 3 categories and their respective terms from our test set that we automatically extracted from Wikidata. Only the English translations are shown.

(Johnson, 2014).[8] Each is "extinct" in the sense that no new native text will ever be generated in these languages. That is not to say that CLTK is necessarily comprehensive in its coverage, nor that it's impossible that new data sources in these languages will be discovered. Rather, we claim that data representing them in their historical context (and consequently the theoretical amount of information we are able to extract) is capped. It's true that some classical languages are studied and used in modern times; however, this is almost always motivated by the need to extract meaning from historical corpora, not to add to them. For these reasons, the prospect of improving models on extinct languages through additional data collection seems unlikely. Instead, we must develop better techniques for the low-resource setting.

Among our datasets, the largest is Ancient Hebrew, with 41 million tokens, and the smallest is Old Gujarati with only 1813 tokens. Our techniques successfully let us choose hyperparameters for 16 of the 18 languages under consideration, including the tiny Old Gujarati model.

First we describe a procedure for automatically generating test set data for the `OddOneOut` and `Topk` tasks using Wikidata. Then, we describe our model training and selection procedure for each language. Finally, we perform the LCT task and an interlanguage analysis of the corpora's content.

---

[6] New emojis have been added to the Unicode standard since the publication of Eisner et al. (2016), but these emojis have not been added to the test set.

[7] For the full list of categories, see `https://unicode.org/Public/emoji/13.0/emoji-test.txt`

[8] Specifically, we analyzed all languages for which CLTK provides both a training corpus and a tokenization function, as these are the minimum requirements needed for training word embeddings.

Corpus			Hyperparameters [*]							Metrics		
Language	Total Tokens	Uniq. Tok.	Model	Type	Dim	WS	LR	MC	Lem	OddOneOut	Topk	Avg
Helenic												
Anc. Greek	37 868 209	1 877 574	w2v	cbow	40	9	0.1	4	False	0.1900	0.0178	0.0327
Italic												
Latin	17 777 429	470 790	w2v	cbow	50	10	0.1	7	False	0.1527	0.0645	0.0908
Old French	68 741	8 343	fast	sg	250	6	0.1	8	False	0.0001	0.0109	0.0003
Germanic												
Mid. English	7 048 144	314 527	fast	sg	90	5	0.1	7	False	0.0239	0.0012	0.0024
Mid. High German	2 090 954	60 674	fast	cbow	15	6	0.1	3	False	0.0005	0.0029	0.0010
Old English	104 011	33 018	fast	cbow	425	3	0.1	3	True	0.0000	0.0005	0.0002
Old Norse	458 377	59 186	w2v	cbow	60	10	0.1	3	False	0.0569	0.0093	0.0161
Old Swedish	1 297 740	116 374	fast	sg	50	8	0.1	5	False	0.0031	0.0001	0.0004
Indic												
Bengali	5 539	2 323	fast	cbow	15	3	0.1	4	False	0.0000	0.0065	0.0002
Gujarati	1 813	1 140	fast	sg	80	3	0.1	5	False	0.0000	0.0292	0.0002
Hindi	587 655	55 483	fast	cbow	45	4	0.1	8	False	0.0175	0.0038	0.0064
Malayalam	9 235	5 405	-	-	-	-	-	-	-	-	-	-
Marathi	797 926	96 778	w2v	sg	400	4	0.1	6	False	0.0214	0.0065	0.0101
Punjabi	1 024 075	31 343	fast	sg	50	8	0.1	5	False	0.0000	0.0001	0.0001
Sanskrit	4 042 204	896 480	w2v	sg	35	9	0.1	10	False	0.1391	0.0093	0.0175
Telugu	537 673	276 330	w2v	cbow	60	10	0.1	3	False	0.0042	0.0000	0.0002
Semitic												
Classical Arabic	81 306	20 493	-	-	-	-	-	-	-	-	-	-
Hebrew	41 378 460	893 512	fast	sg	30	4	0.1	3	False	0.0646	0.0056	0.0104

(∗) w2v = word2vec, fast = fastText, sg = skipgram, Dim = Dimension, WS = Window Size, LR = Learning Rate, MC = Min Count, Lem = Lemmatization

Table 1: The optimal hyperparameters selected for training a model on each corpus, and their corresponding evaluation metrics. (Avg denotes the harmonic mean of OddOneOut and Topk.) We successfully trained models on 16 of the 18 languages provided by the CLTK library (everything except Malayalam and Classical Arabic). Previously, word embeddings had only been trained on Ancient Greek and Latin.

4.1 Test Set Generation with Wikidata

One of the most difficult and time consuming steps of evaluating word embeddings on a new language is generating a high quality test set in that language. We now present the first fully automatic way to generate these test sets. Our method uses Wikidata[9], which is the knowledge base that powers Wikipedia and contains millions of items and their semantic relationships. Wikidata supports 581 languages, and our test set generation method works for all of them. This method does not work for generating analogy test sets, but only works for generating the category test sets needed for our OddOneOut and Topk tasks. We implement this process using the Wikidata Query Service and SPARQL in our open source Python library, making it easy to generate arbitrary test sets.

The idea is straightforward. Some items in Wikidata actually represent categories, and other items can be an "instance of" or "facet of" these categories. For example, item Q9181 (the Biblical patriarch "Abraham") is an instance of item Q20643955 (the category of "Human Biblical Figures"). We can then generate a category of "Human Biblical Figures" by gathering all the items that are an instance of this category, and extract-

ing the translation of these items in our chosen language(s).

There are two minor complications to the process above. First, the item may not have a translation into all languages. Item Q3276278 (the minor Hebrew prophet Hilkiah), for example, does not have a translation into any of the languages we are studying except for Hebrew. We replace all of these words with a special out-of-vocabulary token. During the evaluation tasks, the models will be guaranteed to miss any test case involving these words. This will cause the model's performance to decrease, but it will not cause the optimal set of hyperparameters to change because the model's performance will decrease uniformly for all hyperparameters. This is acceptable because our primary goal with the OddOneOut and Topk metrics is model selection.

Second, the item may have a multi-word translation. Item Q43600 is translated into English as "Mathew the Apostle" which is guaranteed to be out of vocabulary because our embeddings are only for individual words and not phrases. We handle this case simply by treating phrases the same way we would treat any other out of vocabulary word for these models. For a word2vec model, these phrases are commonly replaced by a single out of vocabulary token, but fastText models incorpo-

[9] https://wikidata.org

rate sub-word information and are therefore able to generate reasonable vectors that are good representations of these phrases. We therefore expect fastText models to perform better on datasets with many multi-word translations.

Given the relative ease with which categories of similar items can be generated from Wikidata, it's natural to wonder why our method could not be adapted to extract analogies instead. In some cases, it is possible however the task requires more effort and is difficult to generalize. For example, we could generate items that follow the state-capital analogy with a query that first returns all instances of US states and then finds all items that are related to those instances through the "capital" property `P36`. However, if we consider another popular analogy relationship such as singular-plural we run into trouble. Since there is no Wikidata property relating singular nouns to their plural forms, it's not clear how to generate a test set for this analogy relationship. Even if the lack of appropriate Wikidata properties could be overcome by developing more complicated queries, it's unlikely that these would generalize to other analogy relationships. Compared to `OddOneOut` and `Topk`, extracting test sets for the analogy task is much less automatic.

Using the method described above, we evaluate on a broad set of 18 categories which includes the semantic categories from the Google Analogy set along with others such as Fruit, Sports, Ancient Cities. Given the historical nature of many of the languages we are studying, we also choose three Wikidata categories dealing with religion `Q20643955` (Human Biblical Figures), `Q748` (Buddhism), and `Q9089` (Hinduism), for a subsequent qualitative evaluation of corpus content using the LCT. Table 4 shows representative examples from these religious categories. Since they are large, with between 100-400 items each, we do not reproduce them here.

4.2 Model Selection

There are 7 hyperparameters for our language models, and we use the random search method (Bergstra and Bengio, 2012) to tune these hyperparameters. Random search is simple to implement, computationally efficient, easy to parallelize, and avoids the curse of dimensionality inherent to grid search and Bayesian optimization methods. Table 2 defines the hyperparameters and the range of values sampled for each. All hyperparameters are argu-

Hyperparameter	Sampled Range
Model	word2vec, fastText
Type	skipgram, CBOW
Dimension	5, 10, 15, 20, 25, 30, 35, 40, 45, 50, 60, 70, 80, 90, 100, 125, 150, 175, 200, 225, 250, 275, 300, 325, 350, 375, 400, 425, 450, 475, 500
Window Size	3, 4, 5, 6, 7, 8, 9, 10, 11
Learning Rate	$10^{-3}, 10^{-2}, 10^{-1}$
Min Count	3, 4, 5, 6, 7, 8, 9, 10, 11
Lemmatization	True, False

Table 2: The set of values sampled from for each hyperparameter during our random search hyperparameter optimization.

ments to GenSim's model training functions with the exception of lemmatization. This boolean argument indicates whether we used CLTK's built-in lemmatization tools to preprocess the datasets before training with GenSim. In theory, lemmatization can improve sample efficiency by giving words with the same stem the same word embedding. The results in Table 2, however, show that this was not the case in practice, and this indicates that the lemmatization models built-in to CLTK likely have very high error rates.

To ensure a fair comparison, we randomly sample 100 sets of hyperparameter combinations.[10] We then train each language on these same sets of hyperparameters. The best results are reported in Table 1. The optimal set of hyperparameters is different for each language, which underscores the importance of proper model tuning in the low-resource regime. In particular, we note that there is no pattern regarding whether the word2vec model is better than the fastText model, or whether the CBOW type is better than the skipgram type.

In previous work, Al-Rfou et al. (2013) trained word2vec embeddings on 100 different languages using Wikipedia as the training data and Grave et al. (2018) extended this work by training FastText embeddings on 157 languages using data from the Common Crawl project. In both cases, the researchers tuned the model's hyperparameters on

---

[10] We found that 100 combinations was sufficient to give good results without being too computationally burdensome.

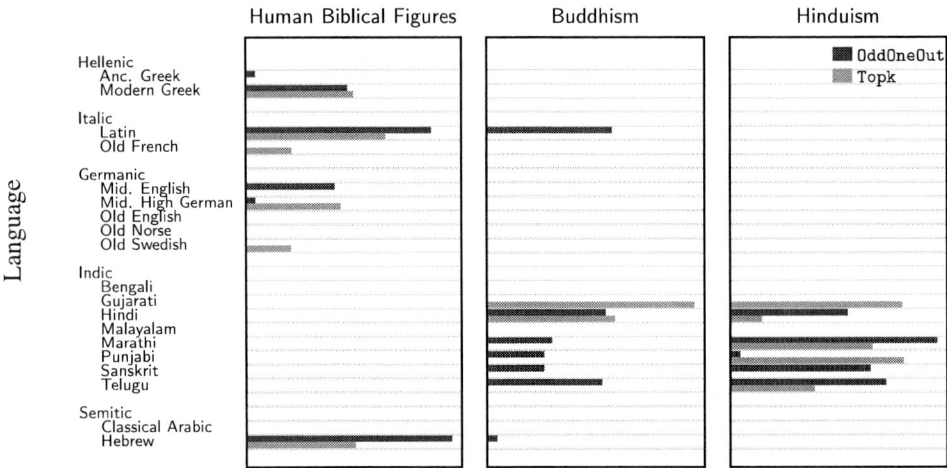

Figure 5: A qualitative investigation of religious topics across the different language models. For the most part, results match our intuition regarding which topics are relevant to each language.

only a single language (due to the difficulty of adapting an analogy test set to so many different languages), and then applied the same set of hyperparameters to all languages. Our results here suggest that performance could be improved if each model's hyperparameters were tuned individually, and our Wikidata technique would make this a realistic option.

4.3 Language Comparison

We now breakdown the performance of each of our language models on the three religious categories shown in Figure 4. The goal is to better understand which topics are discussed in each of the ancient languages. Figure 5 shows the results. There are three interesting results in this visualization.

1. As expected, the European and Semitic languages perform best on the Human Biblical Figures category, while the Indic languages perform best on the Buddhism and Hinduism categories. More surprisingly, all of the "old" European languages have smaller accuracies on the Human Biblical Figures category. We speculate that discussion of Christian topics was predominantly carried out in the church's official language of Latin, which might explain this shortcoming.

2. Most Indic languages perform well on both Buddhism and Hinduism partly because these categories share 36 words in Wikidata. We

suspect different categories are needed to extract the subtleties between these languages.

3. Latin, and to a lesser extent Hebrew, were the only non-Indic languages to perform well on the Buddhism category. Investigation revealed that the Latin model had success almost exclusively on comparisons containing more generic words like *meditatio* and *orsa*.

5 Conclusion

In this paper we introduce the first word vector evaluation methods designed specifically for the low-resource domain, OddOneOut and Topk, along with a method for automatically producing test sets in Wikidata's 581 supported languages. We believe Wikidata is an underutilized resource in the NLP evaluation community, and in particular, that its massively multilingual support can be used to better serve under resourced languages.

References

Oliver Adams, Adam Makarucha, Graham Neubig, Steven Bird, and Trevor Cohn. 2017. Cross-lingual word embeddings for low-resource language modeling. In *Proceedings of the 15th Conference of the European Chapter of the Association for Computational Linguistics: Volume 1, Long Papers*, pages 937–947, Valencia, Spain. Association for Computational Linguistics.

Wei Ai, Xuan Lu, Xuanzhe Liu, Ning Wang, Gang Huang, and Qiaozhu Mei. 2017. Untangling emoji popularity through semantic embeddings. In *Eleventh International AAAI Conference on Web and Social Media*.

Ziad Al-Halah, Andrew Aitken, Wenzhe Shi, and Jose Caballero. 2019. Smile, be happy:) emoji embedding for visual sentiment analysis. In *Proceedings of the IEEE International Conference on Computer Vision Workshops*, pages 0–0.

Rami Al-Rfou, Bryan Perozzi, and Steven Skiena. 2013. Polyglot: Distributed word representations for multilingual nlp. *arXiv preprint arXiv:1307.1662*.

Hosein Azarbonyad, Mostafa Dehghani, Kaspar Beelen, Alexandra Arkut, Maarten Marx, and Jaap Kamps. 2017. Words are malleable: Computing semantic shifts in political and media discourse. In *Proceedings of the 2017 ACM on Conference on Information and Knowledge Management*, pages 1509–1518.

Francesco Barbieri, Miguel Ballesteros, and Horacio Saggion. 2017. Are emojis predictable? *arXiv preprint arXiv:1702.07285*.

James Bergstra and Yoshua Bengio. 2012. Random search for hyper-parameter optimization. *The Journal of Machine Learning Research*, 13(1):281–305.

Elia Bruni, Gemma Boleda, Marco Baroni, and Nam-Khanh Tran. 2012. Distributional semantics in technicolor. In *Proceedings of the 50th Annual Meeting of the Association for Computational Linguistics (Volume 1: Long Papers)*, pages 136–145.

Christian Buck, Kenneth Heafield, and Bas Van Ooyen. 2014. N-gram counts and language models from the common crawl. In *LREC*, volume 2, page 4. Citeseer.

Jana Chamonikolasová. 2014. Middle english. *A concise history of English*, pages 46–61.

Baitong Chen, Satoshi Tsutsui, Ying Ding, and Feicheng Ma. 2017. Understanding the topic evolution in a scientific domain: An exploratory study for the field of information retrieval. *Journal of Informetrics*, 11(4):1175–1189.

Haim Dubossarsky, Daphna Weinshall, and Eitan Grossman. 2017. Outta control: Laws of semantic change and inherent biases in word representation models. In *Proceedings of the 2017 conference on empirical methods in natural language processing*, pages 1136–1145.

Ben Eisner, Tim Rocktäschel, Isabelle Augenstein, Matko Bošnjak, and Sebastian Riedel. 2016. emoji2vec: Learning emoji representations from their description. *arXiv preprint arXiv:1609.08359*.

Bjarke Felbo, Alan Mislove, Anders Søgaard, Iyad Rahwan, and Sune Lehmann. 2017. Using millions of emoji occurrences to learn any-domain representations for detecting sentiment, emotion and sarcasm. *arXiv preprint arXiv:1708.00524*.

Lev Finkelstein, Evgeniy Gabrilovich, Yossi Matias, Ehud Rivlin, Zach Solan, Gadi Wolfman, and Eytan Ruppin. 2001. Placing search in context: The concept revisited. In *Proceedings of the 10th international conference on World Wide Web*, pages 406–414.

Edouard Grave, Piotr Bojanowski, Prakhar Gupta, Armand Joulin, and Tomas Mikolov. 2018. Learning word vectors for 157 languages. *arXiv preprint arXiv:1802.06893*.

Vishwani Gupta, Sven Giesselbach, Stefan Rüping, and Christian Bauckhage. 2019. Improving word embeddings using kernel PCA. In *Proceedings of the 4th Workshop on Representation Learning for NLP (RepL4NLP-2019)*, pages 200–208, Florence, Italy. Association for Computational Linguistics.

William L Hamilton, Jure Leskovec, and Dan Jurafsky. 2016a. Cultural shift or linguistic drift? comparing two computational measures of semantic change. In *Proceedings of the Conference on Empirical Methods in Natural Language Processing. Conference on Empirical Methods in Natural Language Processing*, volume 2016, page 2116. NIH Public Access.

William L Hamilton, Jure Leskovec, and Dan Jurafsky. 2016b. Diachronic word embeddings reveal statistical laws of semantic change. *arXiv preprint arXiv:1605.09096*.

Chao Jiang, Hsiang-Fu Yu, Cho-Jui Hsieh, and Kai-Wei Chang. 2018. Learningword embeddings for low-resource languages by pu learning. *arXiv preprint arXiv:1805.03366*.

Kyle P. Johnson. 2014. CLTK: The Classical Language Toolkit. https://github.com/cltk/cltk.

Jakob Jungmaier, Nora Kassner, and Benjamin Roth. 2020. Dirichlet-smoothed word embeddings for low-resource settings. In *Proceedings of The 12th Language Resources and Evaluation Conference*, pages 3560–3565, Marseille, France. European Language Resources Association.

Katharina Kann, Kyunghyun Cho, and Samuel R. Bowman. 2019. Towards realistic practices in low-resource natural language processing: The development set. In *Proceedings of the 2019 Conference on Empirical Methods in Natural Language Processing and the 9th International Joint Conference on Natural Language Processing (EMNLP-IJCNLP)*, pages 3342–3349, Hong Kong, China. Association for Computational Linguistics.

Austin C Kozlowski, Matt Taddy, and James A Evans. 2019. The geometry of culture: Analyzing the meanings of class through word embeddings. *American Sociological Review*, 84(5):905–949.

Vivek Kulkarni, Rami Al-Rfou, Bryan Perozzi, and Steven Skiena. 2015. Statistically significant detection of linguistic change. In *Proceedings of the 24th International Conference on World Wide Web*, pages 625–635.

Andrey Kutuzov, Lilja Øvrelid, Terrence Szymanski, and Erik Velldal. 2018. Diachronic word embeddings and semantic shifts: a survey. *arXiv preprint arXiv:1806.03537*.

Shangsong Liang, Xiangliang Zhang, Zhaochun Ren, and Evangelos Kanoulas. 2018. Dynamic embeddings for user profiling in twitter. In *Proceedings of the 24th ACM SIGKDD International Conference on Knowledge Discovery & Data Mining*, pages 1764–1773.

Tomas Mikolov, Kai Chen, Greg Corrado, and Jeffrey Dean. 2013. Efficient estimation of word representations in vector space. *arXiv preprint arXiv:1301.3781*.

Kira Radinsky, Eugene Agichtein, Evgeniy Gabrilovich, and Shaul Markovitch. 2011. A word at a time: computing word relatedness using temporal semantic analysis. In *Proceedings of the 20th international conference on World wide web*, pages 337–346.

Radim Řehůřek and Petr Sojka. 2010. Software Framework for Topic Modelling with Large Corpora. In *Proceedings of the LREC 2010 Workshop on New Challenges for NLP Frameworks*, pages 45–50, Valletta, Malta. ELRA. `http://is.muni.cz/publication/884893/en`.

Terrence Szymanski. 2017. Temporal word analogies: Identifying lexical replacement with diachronic word embeddings. In *Proceedings of the 55th annual meeting of the association for computational linguistics (volume 2: short papers)*, pages 448–453.

Xuri Tang. 2018. A state-of-the-art of semantic change computation. *arXiv preprint arXiv:1801.09872*.

Sanjaya Wijeratne, Lakshika Balasuriya, Amit Sheth, and Derek Doran. 2017. A semantics-based measure of emoji similarity. In *Proceedings of the International Conference on Web Intelligence*, pages 646–653.

Association for Computational Linguistics
209 N. Eighth Street
Stroudsburg, Pennsylvania 18360

ISBN 978-1-7138-1985-1